About the A

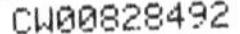

Adam Daly was born in 1954, and has spent most of his life in London, attending Westminster School and doing degrees in Philosophy and Social Sciences. He has worked in a number of jobs, originally in sales, and more recently as a London Tour Guide. He has produced seven works of fiction and one work of non-fiction along with numerous essays, short stories, poetry, and prose-poetry. He was one of sixteen authors to win The World Fantasy Prize in 2004, for his contribution to a short story Anthology called *Strange Tales*. And he had an excerpt from his prose-poem, ‘Eye of the Abyss’, published in *The London Magazine* in 2005. He has always drawn his inspiration from the Bohemian *demi-monde* in and around Hampstead during the 1970s; subsequently, his main interest has been in neglected and forgotten writers of singular talent and outlook, who for various complex reasons have failed to make their mark, or have deliberately shunned the literary/cultural establishment.

Also by Adam Daly:

Novels:

The Outcast's Burden. Matador, 2002.
The Minotaurs of Terror. Matador, 2007.

Short Story:

'The Self-Eater',
in Rosalie Parker (ed) *Strange Tales*. Tartarus Press, 2003.

The Outsider-Writer:

Volume 1:

Colin Wilson, Albert Camus, 'Walking' John Stewart, John Cowper Powys, Fernando Pessoa, Carlo Emilio Gadda

by

Adam Daly

[Colin Wilson Studies #20/1]

Paupers' Press

Published by:
Paupers' Press,
37 Quayside Close,
Turney's Quay,
Nottingham NG2 3BP
England.

I.S.B.N. vol. 1: 9780956866301 (Paperback)
vol. 2: 9780956866318 (Paperback)

I.S.S.N. 0959-180-X (Colin Wilson Studies #20/1 & 20/2)
Series edited by Colin Stanley

Limited edition of 100 copies

Publisher's Note:

The views expressed by Adam Daly in this book are not necessarily those of the publisher.

For our complete catalogue of books, write to the above address or e-mail us at: **books@pauperspress.com**
Visit our website at:
http://www.pauperspress.com

Contents

Acknowledgments
Preface by Adam Daly....**i**
Foreword by Paul Newman....**v**

Introduction....**1**
Chapter One:
The Problematics of Placement....**7**
Chapter Two:
Revising the Groundwork: Stewart, Camus and Wilson....**31**
Chapter Three:
Glimpses of a Future for Outsider-Writers....**99**
Chapter Four:
A Brief Miscellany of More Obscure, Mainly Female Outsider-Writers....**141**
Chapter Five:
The Evolution of the Ichthyosaurus-Ego into the Cosmic Celt....**164**
Chapter Six:
Fernando Pessoa: Hidden in the Heteronyms, the Man Who Never Was....**242**
Chapter Seven:
Gadda the Untranslatable: the Forbidden Genius Scowling in Society's Shade....**307**

Acknowledgements:

The publishers gratefully acknowledge the assistance of the following in the compilation of this book:

Paul Newman

The Powys Society
www.powys-society.org/

Penguin Books Ltd.

Peter Owen Publishers

The Edinburgh Journal of Gadda Studies
www.gadda.ed.ac.uk

Dedication:

In Memory of
Gabriel Duffy

Preface

Having spent many years researching the works and lives of people I've regarded as Outsider-Writers, producing a long series of essays in the process, around two years ago I thought I had enough material for a book—and a pretty substantial book at that. And though one part of me has a Borgesian horror of long or big books, another part of me might just be a latent sucker for the Accolades invited by the production of at least one doorstopper! And so I decided to put my fiction on one side and concentrate on my first, full-length non-fiction work. And this book is the result. On one level it is akin to a declaration of war, because I have for a long time now thought of myself as being on a kind of very unreligious mission on behalf of Outsider-Writers. I have certainly always seen myself as one, and I've never accepted that we must be relegated to the dustbin of literary history, purely by virtue of being Outsiders. Whilst we may not wish to either compromise with, or even assimilate ourselves into mainstream literary culture—or established society for that matter—we can and in my view should assert our claim to be worthy of attention, as serious authors, critics, thinkers, and visionaries; and I should add: revolutionaries also. For this book is very much a polemical manifesto, attacking the dominant culture and having a political as well as a literary and philosophical dimension to it. And Outsiders are extremely well-placed to dissect the ills of contemporary life and civilization, and to propose alternative Ways of Being filtered through the whole prism of their works. And this objective is central to my concerns in the book, even though I also address many other aspects of what it is, and what it means, for a writer to be in the predicament of an Outsider.

In the last century, Colin Wilson was chiefly instrumental in this country in bringing attention to the existence of Outsiders as such, and the importance of recognizing the special qualities they possessed. And I've been willing to draw upon his example and legacy in developing my own ideas about Outsider-Writers, as it's high time he was brought in from the critical cold again, and given his due as the major figure in what may be called The English Existentialist tradition. And I've devoted a section to him in the book, along with other seminal figures like Albert Camus, and the obscure, but extraordinary 'Walking' John Stewart. Unfortunately, I omitted to look at the work of the most blindingly obvious thinker in this whole tradition—who was literally staring me in the face!—namely, Jean Jacques Rousseau. This solitary wanderer, and Great Anarch of the lonely Soul, was a true precursor of the modern Outsider—a troubled Beacon of a new Enlightenment, the lessons of which have been largely forgotten today. His Totalitarian Social Contract may be forgiven him, when we recall all his impassioned invective against the 'argument from Authority', in its most pernicious Religious and Political clothing. For all his quirks and foibles, this 'much-abused man' in the words of that other Giant among Outsiders, John Cowper Powys—who I most certainly have not overlooked in this book!—could serve as the veritable Patron Saint, albeit a pretty sacrilegious one, of Outsiders. But I must thank my old friend, Paul Newman, the first man to publish me against all odds, for rectifying my omission and elucidating the salient points in Rousseau's contributions to the field, in his very generous introduction. And I must also of course thank Colin Stanley for being quite possibly the only publisher on the planet who would take on 'the most unpublishable author in Britain', as one editor once described me! Though I think he meant it as a compliment—at any rate, I've always chosen to construe it as such. But the fact that Colin Stanley is the leading expert on Colin Wilson's work must have automatically pre-disposed him in favour of the subject-matter, if not viewpoint, of this book.

I refer to this book as though it were only one book. But in fact it is two books, because Colin Stanley decided that the spine might disintegrate in readers' hands if the 700 plus page monster were produced singly in his delicate trademark paperback format! So—a second volume awaits all you spell-bound devourers of this first volume, to be published hopefully before the end of this year. So it only remains for me to wish you Bon Voyage in the 'Black Barge', as Lawrence Durrell put it in a little-read missive to an aunt, rounding off his peerless description of the liquefied landscape of Hades! Though as with Blake, there are Heavens here too.

Adam Daly

Foreword

☸

A 'Great Tradition' for Outcasts

☸

Paul Newman

Adam Daly flared up on my personal horizon around the time of the collapse of the twin towers, a post-millennial apparition who emerged after the filth and concrete pall had cleared, exposing a brighter, harsher prospect. The nations of the west had been rinsed by tragedy and the world was a more vexed, cathartic habitat. Ironically, a book of mine had just come out: *A History of Terror: Fear and Dread down the Ages* (the most dreaded thing about it being its price: £20), and I was editing a small magazine called *Abraxas*, featuring regular articles and reviews by Colin Wilson, who kindly cooperated and supported the project, as well as poems, short stories, literary essays and philosophical articles by new and established authors. It had as its by-line 'incorporating the Colin Wilson Newsletter', because I liked Colin's broad literary sweep and thought the topics he explored – crime, sexuality, the occult, literature, philosophy and ideas – bound to stimulate discussion and controversy. Colin Stanley, founder of Paupers' Press, offered instant, unfaltering support, supplying a list of his subscribers and allowing me to share and promote his diverting range of critical studies, as well as titles from the Borgo Press of California.

What was I doing bringing out such a periodical? Well, there are many who live fulfilled, happy lives, with loving wives proffering cups of tea and fond embraces – not to mention their Bambi-like children clustering around their knees – as opposed to those holed up in garrets with mounds of interminable, unreadable submissions from a shambling, fanatical sub-species of hominid who toil at assembling sentences rather than a sensible table or dog kennel. The latter are picked out by the ravenous, nearly-published glints in their eyes and the listless ashes of rejection slips littering their souls. Although I had published titles to my discredit, essentially I was a reject, so I decided to rebuke my failure by setting myself up as the judge of the work of others. Hence I took a perch at the apex of a tiny, obscure dunghill, set among the clay-tips of St Austell's china clay district, and started crowing for submissions. I was one-eyed King in the Kingdom of the Blind, a realm of exile and aggrieved pride, a minor circle of Dante's Hell, in which I *had* to live, for no other place would have me.

My co-editor, Lee Cooper, designed the layout as well as writing reviews and admirable articles, notably on Arthur Miller, Douglas Adams and Ben Elton. Positively speaking, the venture did attract contributors from the world of books and journalism.[*] One afternoon the postman knocked and I went

---

[*] Among others, Gary Lachman, founder member of rock group Blondie & author of *New York Rocker* & occult titles; Roger Morris, prize-winning novelist; Bill Hopkins, late Angry Young Man & author of *The Leap*; D.M. Thomas, poet & author of *The White Hotel*; Kenneth G. Steven, Scottish poet; Gabriel Duffy, late Irish memoirist & media critic; Laura Del Rivo, author of *The Furnished Room*, *Animals* & *Queen Kong*; Nicolas Tredell, critic, books on CW & B.S. Johnson; Phil Clarke, reader, critic & short story writer; Ted Brown, musician, CW scholar & bibliographer; Maurice Bassett, author, E-book publisher & authority on CW & Abraham Maslow; Steve Taylor, broadcaster, self-help guru & author of *The Fall*; Mark Valentine, author, publisher & editor of *Wormwood*; Vaughan Robertson, maverick Maori academic & author of *Wilson As Mystic*; Matthew Kerr,

down to receive an immense ring-bound book from Adam Daly, packed with short stories that were non-generic in that they often merged into essays, prose poems, reflections. I glanced through some and realised that all in their slightly hectoring way were of an acceptable standard. Daly's voice had a commanding, projective tone, ringing yet ironical, soaring to lyrical peaks then descending into off-the-wall diatribes that wittily deployed zany, entertaining metaphors and shock adjectives like 'unshrinking'. His sentences drew their loads swiftly and effortlessly. At times, language was applied thick as paint, supplying a strong, sculptural quality, and he had a good ear for orchestrating a cadence. The essays and vignettes flourished arresting titles like 'Coffinement', 'The Print Psychopath', 'The Censor's Ordeal', and jousted neatly with their themes. Some were mildly defiant, defending arrogance as a virtue deriving from arrogate, to "pronounce on subjects by virtue of their superior intellect and erudition."

Scottish artist & lecturer; Patricia Tyrrell, author of *The Reckoning* & *Grandmother Wolf*; John Gower, writer of disquieting short stories; Beryl Bainbridge, novelist; Antoni Diller, lecturer in Artificial Intelligence & author of *Stuart Holroyd: years of anger and beyond*; Anthony Harrison-Barbet, late professor of philosophy; Mathew Coniam, feature writer; A.R. Lamb, poet & author of *Divers* & *Secession*; Lee Cooper, playwright, ecological pioneer & director of DGR Books; David Power, critic, musicologist & author of *David Lindsay's Vision*; Tony Shaw, academic & biographer of Lionel Britton; Derrek Hines, poet & founder of Cargo Press; Derek Fanning, Irish poet, mountaineer & journalist; Bruce Charlton, psychologist; Joseph Felser, academic & spiritual visionary, author of *The Way back to Paradise*; Pamela Smith-Rawnsley, poet & short story writer; Raymond Tallis, physician, philosopher & novelist; John Thorkild Ellison, surreal poet; D.F. Lewis, short story writer, critic & potentate of the strange; Mark Thomas, critic & poet; Colin Stanley, poet, CW bibliographer & author of *First Novel*.

Others were poetically searching, like the note on 'Fin de Siècle Man': "It was made real [decadence] by acts of imagination whose lustre hung in high atmospheric pools like a densely dispersed purple cloud. There were vast riches and visionary depths in those luminously lugubrious pools – as well as all the velvety affectations and Arcadian artifices." What galvanized me were the sketches that conjured bizarre, ethereal manifestations in an astonishingly vivid way, fleshing out goblin lineaments and ghostly cartilage until the full-bodied spectre arose from the page. The prose showed a precision and wit akin to that of Nabokov when he evoked the red reflector disc on the rear mudguard of a bicycle as "an anal ruby". In particular, in 'The Man with Half a Head', there was an unforgettable description:

> Today a man with half a head passed me in a fleeting space. I only half saw him in the half-light in a half-instant, hurrying through some deserted courtyard off an alleyway leading to a minor road parallel to a major road, in this city of London where I have always lived. I am certain he wasn't a ghost. He looked altogether too purposive and strangely substantial – in spite of the grey velocity of his shadow and the viper's nest of spirits tailing him like a comet streaming from his neck. Everything about him was grey – like a carboniferous spectre. As I approached the courtyard, my head was turned briefly by his apparition in transit – flying from the rectum of one alley into the mouth of another. The back of his head had shelved away like the incline of a quarried hill, or the sliced plane of a steel shaft. He was manifestly human in profile, albeit vaguely grotesque like an etiolated version of Grendel. He was not present long enough for me to discover if I either possessed or required the courage of Beowulf. He had a cloudy indistinctness, on the verge of melting into the textures, contours and consistencies of the cosmos shaping his space.

Foreword

> He was completely soundless, yet indicative of density and friction – the candle of a stricken consciousness burning his body down to a grisly, ashen form.

Soon I realised that everything he had written deserved to be between hard covers, but my job was to fairly represent a cross-section of subscribers to *Abraxas*. So, as I was unable to opt for epic inclusiveness, I put together an article about him featuring extracts from his shorter pieces in hope of spreading his name, and after that came many more interesting essays and reflections from him, on writers like Lionel Britton, Lord Rochester, and the poet, Richard Savage.

Unfortunately, despite a captivating style, Adam Daly had been consistently rejected by publishers. Admittedly some of his stuff was as potent and threatening as a large, dark donation from a torturous bowel movement. Other times it gestured imposingly, like a Gothic folly designed by Beckford, or else it hid itself amid chants, sigils and talismans, coiling into catacombs and deep, occult recesses. And then there were rhetorical rushes and verbal surges that accumulated a fair amount of froth. But basically, here was a talented, dedicated writer, whose prose was far superior to the average lucid tap-water, being consistently and unfairly turned down. But I could see the problem. The manuscripts were often densely textured – hence not always *that* easy to read – with a content that was erudite in its range of reference. The publishers were simply not prepared to take the risk. But fortunately this was happening at a time when a technological revolution was rendering printing easier, cheaper and more flexible than it had ever been. So today several of Adam's titles have appeared and are on sale, including, happily, this present work.

Foreword

To fill in the background detail, Adam Daly, critic, essayist and novelist of the Postwar, Neo-Gothic Renaissance, was born in London in 1954 and attended London Polytechnics, gaining degrees in Philosophy and the Social Sciences. Graduating was followed by lay-abouting and working in Sales and as a London Guide. Many of these early experiences fed into his first novel *The Nameless Revolutionary* (1300 pages) about a man who single-handedly takes on modern civilization and goes on the rampage throughout Europe and the rest of the world, returning to Hampstead in dialectical mode at the end. Although Daly's creative ventures evoke the spectacular excesses of his literary idols, he prefers to eschew the thrilling depredations and addictions of his heroes. Like Yeats, he might admire the heavy drinkers and drug-takers, but is far too sensible to emulate them. His excesses are of the intellect, and may be sampled in his outstanding debut novel on the Beowulf theme, *The Outcast's Burden* (2003).

Other works include *The Resurrection Men,* exploring the idea "that the past and present are controlled from the future, the end of science being time-technology or the mechanics of re-directing time as the means of manipulating life and death, the implications for human destiny and identity being my principal concern within the context of a dystopian nightmare scenario in which the dead are resurrected and become indistinguishable from the living." Also, *Eye of the Abyss*, a marathon prose-poem "exploring the nuances and resonances of Nietzsche's saying about the Abyss staring back at those who stare into it."

Daly has aimed to incorporate as much diverse material as he can in his books: "I am continually groping – and sometimes striding – across numerous territories to arrive at a statement which might never in the very nature of my projects ultimately become clear. I have no religious or moral or political axes to grind and much of what I write is literally off the top of my head. I believe in seizing the moment, creativity dictating craft."

The Outsider-Writer is his major critical study to date. It calls attention to the fact that, for every artist who fits into a niche, a dozen are consigned to the Alcatrazes and Badlands where dwell the Wolf-Man, Cyclops, Clubfoot Ghoul, Loathsome Leopard and Grendel's Mama. With vigour, compassion and irony, Daly presents a troupe of great literary artists who also happen to be hashish dreamers, defiant recluses, mazed mystics, destructivists, suicidalists and occultists – decoding bulletins from their pits of despair and pinnacles of ecstasy. Here, among others, are Fernando Pessoa, poet of a thousand faces; Gerard de Nerval, promenading with a lobster on a lead; John Cowper Powys, watering his barren lusts and malices; and 'Walking Stewart', celebrated eccentric of Georgian London, who strode across the major continents and authored strange titles like 'Roll of a Tennis Ball Through the Moral World'; plus distinct female talents like Jean Rhys, Dorothy Richardson, Lucy Swan, Ann Quin and Sylvia Plath. This adds up to an enchanting, alternative canon for every university shelf, a 'Great Tradition' for outcasts.

Lest this require qualification, first it should be pointed out that the title harks back to Colin Wilson's *The Outsider* (1956), a book that ruffled controversy on account of its polymath erudition. Critics asked: how did a young, working-class man manage to read so many important European works of literature? Wilson's book comprised a study of a group of artists, dreamers and mystics who nurtured a profound sense of non-belonging, of not feeling at home among people and social conventions. It incorporated penetrating appraisals of relatively exotic texts like the *Diary of Vaslav Nijinsky*, Van Gogh's letters and George Fox's *Journal*. In addition, it helped bring to the fore major European artists like Henri Barbusse and Herman Hesse, whose works were subsequently re-printed and re-translated. The condition it diagnosed was claimed to be the sickness at the heart of 20th Century civilisation – as though asking questions about man's place in the world was an ailment. Properly speaking, *The Outsider* was an Existential enquiry into 'reality' and 'meaning', arguing a state of aloneness was a useful position from which to explore the gap between oneself and the world. What was demanded was an effort to 'break through' or a leap of faith. And then Wilson considered mystics like William Blake, Ramakrishna and Gurdjieff, hinting the Outsider might prove essential for the redemption of society: "The individual begins that long effort as an Outsider; he may finish it as a saint."

Possibly, as Daly reflects, he is launching his book at a time not ideal for Outsiders. Inserted in Colin Wilson's original study is a slightly caustic aside on the semi-zombified state of the average citizen back in the mid–1950s, suggesting that, were lines from T.S. Eliot's *The Hollow Men* set up in large letters on a placard in London ("We are the Hollow Men/The Stuffed Men/Headpieces filled with straw"), the average city man would stare at it blearily, registering nothing. Possibly today, with so many texting or encoiled by headphones, the reaction might be blanker. Consumer economies do not require those who read deeply or harbour idiosyncratic agendas of their own as they fall outside their target market. They prefer a conditioned response from a population who will continue to buy surplus goods and keep the economy on track.

Foreword

The recent riots in London confirm there are many who are disgruntled with their lot. But they probably do not constitute Outsiders in the intellectually questing sense, but Insiders who are aggrieved at being unable to attain the possessions and trappings of status that come so naturally to celebrities and the wealthy. They feel left out of the Big Party that theoretically is whooping it up elsewhere. But even so, each one of them must vaguely feel at times the melancholy pressure haunting Colin Wilson's first book, touching on the meaning or meaninglessness of things. Can life be said to have a purpose that an individual should pursue? And was it in place before men and women evolved? The question is confined by the assumption implicit in the phrasing. It requires a straight answer rather than an analysis of the physics that gave rise to the Big Bang and lesser cosmic perturbations. What meaning can be attributed to seemingly random, pre-human events? Far easier to answer: what does the universe mean to me? So Wilson replies, using the limited if inevitable vocabulary of human striving, arguing that we are here to broaden and intensify consciousness and raise life to a higher level.

This hunt for meaning pervaded Wilson's literary explorations. He postulated the idea of 'Existential Criticism', rating a novel by the attitude it adopted to "being here" in a philosophical sense. A writer should attempt to beat a path through the world as he finds it and should be judged for the depth of his thought as well as the convincingness with which he notates the tumultuous surface of existence. This was a high bar indeed, but it was also seen as highly subjective, tending to overrate dry, lofty narratives like H.G. Wells's *The World of William Clissold,* to the detriment of finely wrought black comedies like *Decline and Fall* by Evelyn Waugh. Jane Austen was dismissed for writing girls' wish-fulfilment stories, and

Graham Greene for being devoutly pessimistic. Even so, Wilson's approach was bracing and mindful of 'Being' in the Heideggerian sense, drawing attention to a host of problematical and fascinating neglected authors.

Though populated by misfits and dropouts, Adam Daly's outlook in *The Outsider-Writer* is dramatically different from Wilson's. Less hubris is evident, and he has a tendency to delight in scribes who exult in ideological breakage, narcotic hazes and denunciatory frenzy. He is not trying to save the world or privilege a type, but salvage a selection of forgotten or often-overlooked literary geniuses and, since every project involves a line of demarcation, he uses the term 'Outsider-Writer', testing their temperatures of aloofness and exclusion – from vague dottiness to severe psychosis and clinical insanity. But still the stubborn question persists: what does 'Outsider' denote exactly? How does one know when to apply it? For at some point in their lives, almost every writer was a rebel or black sheep, from Geoffrey Chaucer to Ted Hughes. That distinguished Bostonian of the English literary establishment, T.S. Eliot, upheld tradition and became a member of the Church of England, yet dressed like a bank clerk, explaining as he was so much a bohemian inside, he preferred to at least *outwardly* conform. And what of the Bronte sisters, Charlotte, Anne and Emily in particular – could any three girls have ever felt more bitterly isolated and put-upon? And yet today their reputations are iron-cast, their works shelved amid titles of canonical significance; their plotting and characterisation studied for exams, and their lives biographically extended and annotated. And what of the wondrously gifted, cruelly smitten, ploughboy poet, John Clare, who broke out of his asylum in Epping one morning and walked 80 miles back to his beloved Helpston with the intention of proposing to his already-dead sweetheart? With his admiration for Byron and rage at the establishment, surely Clare could not be classed as conformist in any way, and yet his place in the Pantheon is secure.

So, in view of the broad international reputation of certain of the selected writers – Fernando Pessoa, for instance – it would be misleading to cast Adam Daly as a lone upholder of neglected powers. Though that certainly *does* apply so far as the novelist Lionel Britton and the philosopher John Stewart are concerned. Is Daly's selection of scribes less likely to receive approval than a more conventional group? It hardly matters because, relatively speaking, the academic standing of novelists and poets hardly matters. Traditional meritocracies have been absorbed in a massive swamp of democratization. With the entire domain falling under the umbrella of World Literature, embracing film, folk art, journalism and oral tradition, national hierarchies and touchstones of achievement are less honoured and officially saluted than was formerly so. The big, English-speaking pyramid with Shakespeare at the apex has flattened out. Today everything and everyone is relatively interesting and worthy of study, however irritatingly various, not excluding novelist-madmen or poet-incendiaries.

Writers like Henry Miller and Jean Genet, formerly classed as beyond the pale, are applauded for their candour, vehemence and literary skill; and Kafka himself acknowledged Robert Walser as an influence. John Cowper Powys's admirers place him alongside Hardy, and Albert Camus has a status on par with Sartre. Gadda's best work has been equated with that of Joyce and Céline, and Alfred Jarry, though not *that* popular in Britain, is renowned as an innovator and prankster. If there's no clear strategy of exclusion, there is a mild educational problem wrapping around the idea of a rounded, well-balanced, university course retaining a humanitarian, civilizing aspect and eschewing violent extremes of articulation. If devisers of such a curriculum include a handful of firebrands – like Henry Miller, say, or Blaise Cendrars – they are likely to be counterbalanced by the steadier flames of, say, Henry James or E.M. Forster. For becoming a qualified expert on literature does not imply a great deal of erudition or encompass a massive swathe of learning. You are not required to know *that* much to gain your gown and sceptre, only a selection of representative works. That's why there's a need for omnivorous readers and exciting critics like Daly to re-light lost lamps.

Another more serious drawback is that teachers of literature may become conservative – far less likely to venture into unknown territory. Students at a college where I was employed in the 1960s bothered their young English teacher, asking whether he had read the latest books by Richard Brautigan, Ken Kesey and Kurt Vonnegut, but he replied that, since leaving university, he had ceased reading novels, apart from those on the A-Level curriculum. Today the problem is far greater; fields of study proliferate on all sides. Novels and poetry collections tumble out along with film, television and stage productions. What with the vast expansion of IT studies, there are more specialized literary and language courses than ever, and yet less and less broad, contextual background knowledge in the minds of individuals.

Thus, reflecting an eclectic range, *The Outsider-Writer* is a spur to anyone who wishes to expand his literary horizon. It has at last appeared in a limited first edition, thanks to the courage and tenacity of Colin Stanley, head of Paupers' Press, a small publishing house which has issued major works by Laura del Rivo, Colin Wilson and Nicolas Tredell, as well as landmark critical studies of Jeanette Winterson, Ian McEwan, E. H. Visiak and numerous others.

Thankfully, Daly's work is an accessible read with a refreshing dearth of jargon. It does not pretend criticism is a science of breaking down a story into particles or cells that can be analysed like a germ culture. There are no attempts to chop up paragraphs in a pseudo-anatomical way; no clumping 'constructions' or syntactical mist. Neither does he reel out claptrap of a psychological sort, telling us, say, John Cowper Powys was a stereotypical, self-mythologizing son of a crushing patriarch, from whom he drew his sadism, while his doting, meek-mannered mother conferred on him an onanistic bent, thwarting his sexual maturity and securing his literary genius. Instead he treats his subjects as if they are Outsiders, standalone originals, unique outcomes of specific backgrounds and states of affairs, explaining why they are important and deserve to be taken seriously. He hones in on their techniques and stylistic strengths and submits a précis of what they are saying. Perceptively, he strikes up lines of likeness and communication between odd-assorted pairs like Powys and John Stewart, imagining the latter crossing paths with William Blake in 18th Century London, two extraordinary visionaries sharing common space yet each incubating his own unique psychic hatchery.

While his choice of writers is occasionally startling and often amusing, the archetypal outcast, Jean Jacques Rousseau, is omitted, presumably because he is already embedded in European culture, a cornerstone and exemplum, a towering symbolic presence. Rousseau is a pleasure to read simply because he extends comfort and sympathy to the reader as he goes wheedling, persuading and vagabonding through France, Germany and Switzerland, staying at inns, introducing himself to high-born ladies, constantly flattering and begging a commendation or introduction. He is refreshingly grateful for small mercies, like meeting two attractive girls while riding a horse or enjoying a free night at a comfortable inn from a large-souled landlord. Though slandered as overly sensitive or touchy, this is not the person we encounter in *Confessions* (1781). Adrift in the fractured, edgy political landscape of the 18th Century, Rousseau comes over as a perpetual student, an absorbed onlooker, immersed in his diverting amours, music, literature and the rites of privilege and patronage that compound his social strategy. He nurtures a bedrock belief in those who are honest, preoccupied and unaffected. Many caricature him as a vain, deceitful, egoist who treated his children deplorably. Such flaws are regrettable, but Rousseau was a man with a mission, who strove to agitate the intellectual horizon, to rattle the chains of oppression, write startling novels, compose songs and successful operas as well as penetrating works of political philosophy. Granted that, he was never going to be *that* bland or easily compromised, for it required a self-centred zeal – a stubby, upfront forcefulness – to achieve the breakthroughs he wanted. Those who publish their most shaming thoughts and deeds will tend be branded as pariahs, and Rousseau's *Confessions* caused shock and uproar because candour and openness *are* offensive to those who prefer not to indulge.

However, another intrepid tourist, less significant than Rousseau, is thankfully included, and that is John Stewart (1749-1822) the philosopher who, after serving as a writer in the East India Company, walked all the way back to England through India, Persia, Ethiopia, Turkey and Lapland, proving himself fluent in eight languages on his return. He later made walking tours in Europe and America and became renowned in

Georgian London for appearing in the streets in full Armenian costume and inhaling the mild, sweet breath of cows in St James's Park. With Spinoza as his inspiration, he evolved a philosophy that he judged a fine, proud, lofty system, essential to the survival of the human species, maintaining "the body emits half a pound of matter every half an hour from its mode". Hence, what with all this ceaseless bartering of atoms and exhalations between people and creatures – for animals are part of the process too – no man should feel superior or privileged. Everything is actively mingling, giving off and receiving. So highly did he prize his insights that he wanted copies of his works to be buried in sites all over the world, their locations only known to an elect few, so that certain evil Kings, who would connive to destroy them, should be foiled. He also wanted their titles carved on a massive rock in the Atlantic: thus passing ships would get the message. And he urged his literary confidant, Thomas de Quincey, to implement these measures. He also invited Thomas to translate his works into Latin, so that folk might have recourse to his brilliance in the event of English ceasing to be spoken. He devised a universal calendar from their appearance, hinting that the history of the world began with them. If this sounds crazy, it is because I am projecting the stereotypical, eccentric view of 'Walking Stewart'. But Adam Daly, who penetrated the vaults of British Library and went through the delicate, precious manuscripts, especially the long poem *The Harp of Apollo*, offers us the first in-depth assessment of a thinker who – if not as exalted as his self-estimate – emerges as an apostle of 'inner revolution', anarchic, holistic and far in advance of his time.

If Rousseau, high priest of self-abasement, is honoured in this work by oversight and Walking Stewart by full inclusion, "the overrated, sick adolescent who wrote *The Songs of Maldoror*" – to quote Martin Seymour-Smith – deserves some prefatory notice for his enduring contribution to the literature of horror and revolt.

To students of black books and literary by-ways, *Maldoror* is a fascinating, pseudonymous work attributed to 'Le Comte de Lautréamont'. The author's real name was Isidore Ducasse (1846-1870), and he was a young Frenchman whose family had set up business in South America. In 1867, Isidore was sent to Paris to board first at the Imperial Lycée in Tarbes and then at the academy at Pau. Proficient at mathematics, drawing and Latin verse, he was reported to be a pale, withdrawn boy, long-haired and aloof, whose literary agenda was made manifest in a stylistically orchidaceous novel that became a *succès de scandale* through its portrayal of perversions and partialities. Featuring a cast of gravediggers, hermaphrodites, pederasts and angels, this 'roman noir' was ignored on original appearance, later being singled out as a textbook for the Surrealists, tirelessly praised for its ferocity and putrescent playfulness.

Ducasse was an inconstant narrator, a shape-shifter, varying from a superior, mockingly orotund tone to something swifter and more urgent. Several monologues in *Maldoror* recall Aesop, as when the reader is made privy to the meditations of the brother of a leech or the voyeurism of a high-minded, slightly prudish walking-stick who has been forced to observe his young master's lechery and viciousness. Showing a masterly control of tone, he underlies his soliloquies with a disquieting layer of irony. Both grimly melancholic and oddly flippant, a curious stylistic quirk of his is to upstage the savage and visceral with the tedious and trivial. Midway through a description of the ghastly violation of a naked man, who is being lynched by two women, he digresses to clarify a minor point of grammar, a hair-splitting nuance, wrapping atrocity in folds of circuitous pedantry, thus demonstrating an exemplary sense of warped priority.

In view of the overall nihilism of *Maldoror*, a reader may be surprised to learn that Ducasse hoped for a civil reception. On hearing that the printer was quailing at the thought of being involved in so twisted and sulphurous a text, he wrote to his publisher Verboeckhoven, assuring him. "I have written of evil," he emphasised, "as Mickiewicz, Byron, Milton, Southey, A. de Musset, Baudelaire, etc., have all done. Naturally I have exaggerated the pitch along the lines of that sublime literature which sings of despair only to cast down the reader and make him desire the good as the remedy."

This is unintentionally comic, trying to persuade his backer that his paean of blasphemous contempt is a work of piety by dint of omission. In other words: "My book is so profoundly vile that the reader has no escape save into higher thoughts – for he cannot possibly envisage lower ones!" And yet, behind the smokescreen of diabolical swagger, lurked a modest, middle-class ambition to become known as a man of letters. Considering a good deal of *Maldoror* is abloom with cancerous growths, leaking pustules and anus-eating crabs, one might assume young Ducasse wished his audience to respond by fainting, vomiting or at least passing out. But no, like any other aspiring, literary hopeful, he craved his groat of praise.

Despite the ferocity of its sentiments, *Maldoror* stands for little more than an insurrection of the spirit. Ducasse does not seek to tear the world apart. The edifices he strives to shatter and scorch are metaphysical in character. He is not driving home a dystopian vision like *1984* or disseminating a pernicious ideology like *Mein Kamf.* His revolt is of the imagination and not the body politic. Interestingly, at the high school in Paris where he studied, Ducasse was known by his fellow pupils as “a good fellow”. I like to imagine him smiling sheepishly at this: Le Comte de Lautréamont, a Bob Cherry of blasphemy and relished revulsion.

It is chastening to realize so many disturbed and disturbing works were resorted to as ‘entertainments’ or ‘pillow books’ in the same way that the spectrally elegant, wittily obscene drawings of Aubrey Beardsley became the choice pieces of rich collectors. Hence subversive texts may not so much rock the world as generate a flutter of furtive enjoyment among the literati. For devout radicals, the arts tend to prove less than adequate. A friend of mine was passionate about promoting political drama, namely Theatre of Poverty and Theatre of Revolution. Visiting rural communities in South America, he founded small groups who would devise and enact scenarios involving revolts of the people against tyrannical bureaucracies and governments. He recalled his dismay when his cast, who had wholeheartedly enjoyed acting their parts, asked whether they were now ready to start the revolution proper. He felt at a loss when he had to inform them that his campaign was frozen at the conceptual level, and the real thing lay beyond his remit.

Possibly the theatrical rebel of the 20th century, who also made an idol of Ducasse, was Alfred Jarry, who strove to *èpater les bourgeois* and suck the starch from their façades. Rejecting metaphysics, he founded the school of ‘Pataphysics’ that privileged the rule of the ‘exception’, denying the validity of any generalisation. Each incident was *unique* rather than an example of a *type*. Fascinated by the terminology and prim, cog-like engagement of scientific prose, Jarry managed to skilfully pastiche it, mixing it in with fictional twists and elopements and charges of surreal desire. Of course, in kinetic terms, apparatus and delicate instruments will break down if subject to violation, but language, being fluidic, will accommodate the impossible. Jarry's pataphysical dialectics were initially less persuasive than his skill at making people gape and prick up their ears. By the latter, he was able to instil a new approach to drama and literature, opening a hitherto unexplored domain of mirth, doubt and anxiety.

In his little house beside the Seine, he lived simply for his art, fishing for food, using a bicycle to get about, a revolver to protect his diminutive person and absinthe for relaxation. In the wake of Freud, whose psychological theories pervaded the literary and visual arts of the 20th Century, he grasped that sexuality was a major fault-line in the personality that deserved a fuller treatmcnt. You could even employ coitus to give birth to an idea.

Alfred Jarry's theatrical breakthrough was the naïve and colourful *Ubu Roi* (1896), about a monstrous bullying king who devotes his life to the pursuance of injustice and cruelty. A grim, fantastical farce, blending elements from cinema, ballet and pantomime, it provoked riot and scandal on its first night. Catulle Mendès applauded its satirical zest in portraying "the eternal imbecility of man, his eternal lubricity, his eternal gluttony, the baseness of instinct raised to the statue of tyranny; of the coyness, the virtue, the patriotism, and the ideals of the people who have dined so well." W. B. Yeats was less intoxicated, noting the players "are supposed to be dolls, toys, marionettes, and they are all hopping like wooden frogs, and I can see for myself that the chief personage, who is some kind of King, carries for a sceptre a brush of the kind that we use to clean the closet." Following the subtle colourations and exquisite patterns of the Symbolists, he speculated as to the new era the play symbolised. "After us, the Savage God."

Foreword

Ubu Roi was as paining as it was entertaining, creating a world without values – a world that might be destroyed at no emotional cost. Some Absurdists – like the Futurists – saw war and discord as necessary breakage, constructive destruction, a stance that degraded into a glib, slick fatalism, almost a nostalgia, as in Ionesco's *The Killer Without Reason* (1958). Usually nostalgia is associated with friends and fond memories, downing goblets of wine or barrels of beer in a pleasant, thatched construction beside a blazing fire. But some like to dwell on warm memories of comradeship shared in battles long ago. J. G. Ballard's preference might be the departure lounge at Heathrow or a patch of wasteland beside the crashed skeleton of an RAF Hurricane. Another well-developed tendency is deriving comfort from scary or apocalyptic entertainment, the latest end-of-the-world scenario or God's vengeance movie. Interestingly, detonations and destructions that take place elsewhere may convey a delusive assurance, deflecting personal dread. By dying our dooms, others secure our mortal leasehold.

When Alfred Jarry died in 1907, the poet Blaise Cendrars was only twenty-four and poised between literary and commercial ventures. Of mixed Swiss and Scottish descent, he became a forceful literary presence in the Paris of 1920s, a great traveller, adventurer and exaggerator of the incredible events he lived through, including loss of an arm while fighting in the French Foreign Legion during the First World War. He favoured chaotic, shuttling scenarios, being entranced by the poetic voyages of Gerard de Nerval. He was at a loss to distil a lucid philosophy from the hectic, bizarre exploits in which he involved himself. "There is no truth," he wrote in *Easter in New York*, "other than life shaking its ass's ears. Wait for it, lie in ambush for it, kill it!" His picaresque narratives are not especially moderated by commonsense and restraint, but part of him was deeply sympathetic. *Antarctic Fugue* (1927) introduces his millionaire anti-hero Dan Yack – an audacious creation if ever there was. Amoral, cynically exuberant and generous to the point of irresponsibility, Yack is wastefully destructive of acquisitions and relationships. He enjoys generating disaster and mayhem because it is kinetically exhilarating. In a Dionysian or Darwinian sense, Yack is as life-affirming as a stampede of mastodons. Though replete with tragic, brutal incidents, the ultimate effect is not tragic, simply because the rampageous spectacle carries one along. Ultimately it is not values that matter to Cendrars so much as energy, complexity and persistence of the life force. And yet his anti-hero is left at the end deflated by a sense of alienation and ennui that is derived from an ancient, intractable *déjà vu*. By contrast, the follow-up novel, *The Confessions of Dan Yack*, chronicling an obsessional love affair, sexual hang-ups and film-making, is wounded, tender and nostalgic.

It is notable that several of Daly's star performers are Decadents or possess an affinity with Decadence. This is revealing. Decadents owe more than most to the beguilement of the symbol that hoards a charge designed to infiltrate at a subconscious level. Decadents are often styled as surrounded by artefacts that stand in for the world. Famously they are shown affecting a preference for gaslight rather than direct sunlight, a laboratory perfume to the scent of fresh-cut grass, a painted landscape on a drawing-room wall rather than being amid the buzz and blare of nature. Insofar as this is not affectation, it is revealing of character, especially as several of these writers were fascinated by occultism. Indeed, it would be accurate to style them as practitioners. Fernando Pessoa drew up horoscopes, translated dreams and helped Aleister Crowley fake his suicide in Portugal. Jean Lorrain was a friend of Huysmans, a connoisseur of weird rites, sexual and narcotic; to quote Philippe Julian "truly, at the *fin de siècle*, Sodom's ambassador to Paris" – but he did, however, ardently love his mother. John Cowper Powys saw himself as a potentially dangerous natural magician and projected his *doppelganger* to the writer, Theodore Dreiser. Sylvia Plath had recourse to the Ouija board and ritually cursed those whom she identified as her betrayers and ill-wishers.

Moreover, practical attainments aside, occultists take the realm of symbols a stage *further* than the Decadents, believing mastery of the *physical world* may be obtained by use of sigils, colours and talismans, manipulating invisible relationships and coordinating astrological correspondences. Desires may be honed and sharpened to specific ends. Allowing such notions govern their relationship to what they see and touch, and that for them an object can be vitalized by a spiritual charge, it is scarcely to be wondered that these writers dramatize the frustrations of their inner selves. These frustrations arise out of the attempt to reduce existence to formulae. Occultists are privileged in that they can walk across a carpet patterned so as to resemble a map of the world rather than undertake the long, irksome journey. Predictably, all this subconscious effort-taking may generate a sense of profound disengagement with ordinary things.

Hence, either by way of an obsessive esotericism or an urge to simply burrow deeper, we find frustration in Daly's authors, surfacing in manifold shades and projections: frustration of sexual repression and obsessive mentalization, as in Powys's epics; frustration in discovering an excess of adventure cannot ease the troubled soul, as in Cendrars; frustration at being ordained to be a snail-like recluse, never quite touching life, but always contemplating it, as in Pessoa; frustration at the vacuously assertive, endlessly reducible 'I' and the probably worse implications of effacing it, as in Gadda; frustration at the deadpan drollness of existence and the lack of essence, as in Camus. This frustration – this ostensible failure of life to deliver – is the very steam arising from a profound revolt, and there is anger there as well as a sense of impotence. The cry is that of the Existentialist who believes that, should some missing part of the pattern be filled, life might be rendered mysteriously complete – alas, another illusion.

Naturally there may be a reward for excelling at the occult arts: to become a God or imbibe a drop of divinity. Among the more disquieting coronets likely to descend are gibbering insanity and paranoid delusion. Fernando Pessoa drank himself into states of misery, psychosis and ultimately death. Jean Lorrain died in Paris, June 30, 1906, his fifty-year-old body raddled by alcohol, drugs and debauchery. John Cowper Powys wallowed in mania and obsession disorders, actually writing a self-help book that recommended leaps of consciousness so psychically unfeasible that they were likely to bring on rather than dispel the fretful humours of which he complained.

Preternaturally aware, Sylvia Plath canalised her disintegration into stabby, extraordinary poems, redolent with animistic slapstick and darting irony. Adopting the voice of a clinical autocrat, she slides into the personae of a mirror, analyzing the woeful appearance of her reflection. The whole of nature, the moon, trees, frogs, birds and insects, conspire to mock her plight – little malicious, cartoon beings snickering at the madwoman. For her part, she is good-humoured, sophisticated and at home amid the blue surgical gowns, skulls, bones and Gothic din. Frantic to the point of flippancy, she gibes at her yellowy, starved features and swelling hysteria. By dint of a luminous despair that feigns madness, she is able to distil language into a pure, controlled scream that is also lyrically ravishing as when the red-mouthed poppies, on seeing her, voice their alarm:

> O my God, what am I
> That these late mouths should cry open
> In a forest of frost, in a dawn of cornflowers.
> (*Poppies in October* by Sylvia Plath)

Plath's suicide by gassing herself was as tragic and startling as that of Ann Quin, another icily controlled yet vividly perverse female novelist, who deliberately swam out to sea in Brighton in 1973 and never came back. Her celebrated novel of Oedipal vengeance and fatal attraction, *Berg* (1964), revived the slightly chill, inimical atmosphere of the resort's seamier side, previously highlighted in Graham Greene's *Brighton Rock* (1938) and Patrick Hamilton's *West Pier* (1951). A similar female in the shadows is Laura Del Rivo, whose debut novel *The Furnished Room* (1961) has just been reprinted. At its heart is a cold, pointless murder plot, redeemed by the prowling rage and troubled thoughts of the protagonist, Joe Beckett, who exists in an ice-grey half-light of stunted affections and sympathies. It is as if he hopes that killing an innocent woman will force him awake.

Finally, Robert Walser was also besieged by demons – although he never dabbled in the dark arts. After the First World War, he took a position in Bern in the national archives, but within months had been dismissed and was suffering from insomnia, voices in the head, nightmares and panics. He tried suicide, but failed to put together "a proper noose." Curiously his best-known long short story is called *The Walk*, detailing a complicated bucolic ramble in a euphoric, rippling style that is disquieting too – a journey sadly echoed by his own last stroll, when his body was recovered from a snowy field on Christmas Day, 1956, near the town of Herisau in Switzerland. Apparently he had escaped from the mental hospital that had been his home and froze to death.

This was a tragic end to a warm, delicate and dextrous talent. But frustration is liable to take on colourful, complex projections, arising as it does from a tension set up by expectancy as opposed to what is delivered, and the latter is often more interesting. Hence many of the works Daly deals with have a negativity that is thrilling in the way that T. S. Eliot's *The Waste Land* is an exciting poem. It is the sound of healthy breakage preparing the way for new structures. Not surprisingly, the satirical diatribes in Walser, Britton and Stewart Home are often riveting. Readers like their fictional equivalents to be insulted and harangued in a non-specific, generic way. It is a minor pleasure of literature, seeing one's failings spikily dramatised.

The problem has always been making revolt new, avoiding cliché and conditioned response. Teeth-baring and slashing satire may harden into reflex. The only escape is through discovering or creating fresh enemies, boundaries and obstacles. In what has been called his most effective fiction, *Blood Rites of the Bourgeoisie*, the engagingly innovative, Proletarian writer, Stewart Home, imagines an 'Abstract Literature Manifesto' equivalent to a key of G major, resembling "deep space; black with flashes of darker blackness..." It is so unimaginably obscene that it cannot be penetrated, and he evokes its imploding inertia amid the grandiose expiry of words:

Foreword

> "An exhausted sun compacted into itself. The slow but painless death of literature…Syllables should be moved around the page like clouds passing across the moon. Dense thickets of rhetoric must grow inexorably into an impenetrable jungle of words that overrun any and all attempts to extract a coherent meaning from them."

Shadowy and lyrical, the language has a tang reminiscent of being "in love with easeful death", a Neo-Romantic, cosmic shutdown scenario as found in Byron, Nerval and Beddoes. Just as the moth is unable to attain the star of its desire, simply because it stands for a mysterious longing and not a measurable satisfaction, the writer cannot find an equivalency. Maybe, historically speaking, there's little one can do save wait for some new ideological affront or psychic violation to replenish and extend the vocabulary of protest.

Presently there is a vogue for anti-novels employing pulp themes and comic-book techniques. An example that appealed to Daly was *The Adventures of Little Lou* by Lucy Swan, dealing with the tainted spawn of tall, spare, sinister leading man, Doctor Mengele, who maintains a shaky constitution by downing Bloody Marys livened with lashings of human blood and a dash of Worcester. His children – as befitting the spawn of the Holocaust – drag their way through a drear, eidetic metropolis, drug-glazed and unwinsome. Little Lou swears proficiently, has an S & M fetish as well as heroin addiction, but is able to resist the skeletal charms of Mengele. "This isn't porn for weirdos," the blurb assures us, "it's a satirical exploration of a society bereft of morality, of ethical values, of sensitivities and emotions, that unfortunately never quite manages to convince." Though challenging, intelligent and caustic, *Little Lou* is not satire so much as an antinomian spree among the clichés accruing from the commercial absorption by the media of Nazi death camps and eugenic experiments. It demonstrates the de-sensitization of atrocity, a sci-fi *danse macabre*.

Whatever their differences, Daly finds in these authors a bold, buccaneering tendency to clear away the literary rubble of previous generations and say things not previously said. "In a new country shooting is necessary," Auden wrote, and these writers come out barrels blazing, making the task of salvaging and recovery more difficult. But then, as Daly puts it, they were neither looking for nor expecting easy victories:

> They were all revolutionaries, blazing their own almost inimitable trails, in Ethers so headily heightened and toxically rarefied, that few others even spotted them, let alone shared in the same atmosphere. And yet they remained unshakably fixated on the destruction of all that had preceded them and the creation of new worlds that were so radically different, they could barely even be acknowledged to exist in any of the traditions to which these writers were so vehemently hostile. And so a conspiracy of silence has formed in the stale and crusty upper echelons of the literary mainstream establishment, against all these lethally dangerous marginalized invaders of the centralized citadels of so-called high culture, to protect fashionably moribund and meretricious writers from swift fates delivered at the hands of masterful literary assassins.

It is impossible to be comprehensive in a book of this kind, but my choice for an Outsider Writer would be Wolfgang Borchert, who died at the age of 26 in Basle, Switzerland, in 1947, after fighting with Hitler's army in Russia during the Second World War and being imprisoned by the Nazis for "plain speaking in private letters". Borchert's drama *The Man*

Foreword

Outside, presented on West German radio in 1947, was a bitter, existential rant, a dream play about God, war, suicide, despair and rejection. God appears as a poor, lost old man whose children have deserted him. As Stephen Spender noted, Borchert was the perfect victim of our times, forced to fight for a cause he hated, to confront horror, death, disease and degradation and finally to die young of a hepatitis infection that he had contracted as a soldier.

Borchert has been called an 'expressionist', signifying a direct, throbbing, emotional response, the inspiration flowing quickly from brain to hand rather than a prolonged, laborious 'perfecting' of an original draft. Indeed, reading his shorter pieces, there is a sense of being among shards and fleeting instances. His vignettes are akin to blazing embers snatched from civilisation's wreckage, especially as in 1943 his birthplace Hamburg was bombed during the RAF's 'Operation Gommorah'. "We came out into a thundering, blazing hell," recalled a witness. "The streets were burning, the trees were burning and…burning horses out of the Hertz hauling business ran past us..."

Likewise Borchert's writing deploys an apocalyptic backdrop, a shattered landscape of ruin and privation. Yet the protest is leavened by a delight in small mercies, the yellow blaze of a dandelion or a lone fragment of affection, like the shred of pink vest from a girlfriend that a soldier keeps as a talisman. The railing tone might prove monotonous, were it not for the catchy, colloquial rhythms that endow his characters with a troubled, anxious vitality. His brief, collected works resemble a cry in the night – akin to a stricken deer. Though the tragedy is over, the terrible belling will hang in the air, echoing amid the iceberg indifference.

Foreword

His short story *Radi* lasts three pages yet its impact is profound. A soldier in Germany is visited by the ghost of a comrade who died on the Eastern Front. He knows Radi from his broad, weak face, small, frightened eyes and few blond tufts of beard. "Don't laugh at me," Radi pleads, adding that he is unhappy and cannot rest. He finds the idea of being dead oddly unsettling. He fears the dark alders near his body and the cold, strange-smelling, black soil of Russia. To impress the point, Radi takes his friend to the place where he died, pointing out his white skeleton and brown-green helmet. This foreign soil is 'repulsive' to smell, he complains, but his comrade reassures him that it's perfectly good, pure, blameless earth. Not convinced, Radi tries to smell it again. Gradually his horror dwindles as he draws it in and gets used to its coolness and lightness. Very delicately his comrade leaves him to resolve his plight, tiptoeing back to Germany and stepping barefoot over the ground and breathing it in. "It smells good, Radi, I whispered. It smells like red earth. You can rest in peace."

The foregoing preamble amounts to little more than jottings around an idiosyncratic, stimulating selection of writers who, in order to pursue their calling, were prepared to threaten their livelihood, healthy and sanity. Several literally sacrificed themselves for their pen, and our ability to read and appreciate them is vastly aided by this authoritative and pioneering critical work by Adam Daly that I hope will nurture a whole generation of new readers and lovers of literature. I know that I felt humbled the moment I began to read it. I know I have learned a great deal from it and will continue to do so as I follow up his leads and enquiries.

Introduction

The term 'outsider writer' might well be one that I myself invented—and few people know who I am, so I remain unacknowledged as such!—as I can't recall ever coming across it in the work of any other author. But if so, I claim no great credit for it, as it was a very simple and obvious step to take from the pre-eminent examples of Albert Camus and Colin Wilson, who coined the terms *L'Etranger* and *The Outsider*, as the titles for two books that soon became canonical in their respective fields. But Camus used the term to describe a man who had no discernible talent, certainly not a literary one, but who was mysteriously or inexplicably cut off from the rest of humanity, and therefore from the very source of his own feelings. Whereas Wilson used the term in a much wider philosophical sense to denote people of diverse talents and genius who felt totally out of step with both the Everyday and the Zeitgeist, and so gave voice to singular grievances they suffered in truly pioneering work. Whilst of course the term 'outsider artist' is familiar, referring to artists who work outside the Mainstream and are often completely unknown to it throughout their lives, who are usually self-taught and cultivate nostrums utterly at odds with those of fashionable schools of thought.

But I can see no reason why writers—nor for that matter musicians and philosophers—shouldn't have the prefix 'outsider' attached to their occupations or callings every bit as much as artists. But for some reason it hasn't caught on as an alternative label with writers in the way that it has with artists.

And I intend to start the process of rectifying this omission in the course of this study. My main contentions will be, firstly, that the phenomenon of 'outsider-writing' has existed for a very long time in many different cultures; secondly, that though it has certain quite special features it is as legitimate a cultural practice as mainstream and canonical writing; and thirdly, it has at times, not least in recent times, proved in some instances equal if not superior in its merits to the best that mainstream and canonical writing have produced. These are all questionable claims, especially the third one, and I shall need by way of a Prolegomenon to prepare the groundwork by disposing of numerous deeply entrenched myths and fallacies that have bedevilled writers of this often precociously gifted yet perniciously accursed ilk. These range from the belief that such writers are mad or brain-damaged, via the belief that they are amateur, mediocre and bad, to the belief that they are criminal and sociopathic; and that therefore their work can at best be regarded as being of very doubtful value, and at worst dismissed as totally worthless and irrelevant to literature.

I guess I had better come clean at this point, and admit that I consider myself to be in some senses an outsider-writer. And whilst I don't regard all outsider-writing to be of equal value—any more than insider-writing, if one can put it that way!—I do consider it by and large to comprise a formidable body of work that provides a counter-blast to the conformist pieties of the Mainstream, and a veritable Paradigm on its own terms. So although I shall seek to observe the most rigorous scholastic scruples, I shall make no bones about my triumphantly subjective championing of outsider-writing in a study that aims in no capacity to be yet another tedious, dry-as-dust, post-graduate Thesis meant for the myopic eyes only of a gang of decomposing peers, followed by terminal consignment to the great Gargantuan piles of Semiological slush! Academic conventions nowadays have become little more than petrified degradations of once-serious scholarly procedures, especially in the Arts and Humanities, and I refuse to be hide-bound by any of them in asserting my own native right to examine with as much authority as anybody a subject I know as intimately as my bone-marrow. The Doctoral Industry is like a vast, pointless, unread mound of rotting whale-blubber, going phonily proxy for the grey eminence of a Pantheon of noble papyrus! Most Ph.D students, frankly, would be better off digging up their back-gardens—if they have back-gardens—and so anybody imagining this study is going to be the latest addition to that Necropolis of ink-soiled sewage-paper had better stop here, or they might well be in grave danger of suffering a fatal apoplexy at a later stage!

Instead, I shall be writing in a vein not unfamiliar to the seditious pamphleteers of early Eighteenth Century England, savaging at my whim and taking no prisoners, being a shamelessly sardonic and even Solipsistic satiric denouncer of all that has ever stood in the way of the full emancipation of the True Individual Voice. So as such, I shall not be writing from the point of view of any established tradition. For my overriding concern is to elucidate the most elusive and untameable aspects of the Outsider's predicament and vocation, which in my understanding necessitates a total distancing from all accepted rules, standards and values of writing. The outsider-writer is privileged, in the sense that he is not constrained in any wise by the social and cultural preconceptions of what constitutes writing. He might well be a by-product of osmosis, and therefore to that extent never completely original. But he has a head-start on insider-traditionalists, in so far as the freedom of the wilderness breathes through his veins and thereby seeps into his words. I can discern this spirit in the work of writers almost immediately, as it singles them out in terms of voice, vision, style, theme and thrust, from the vast mass of writers, who however accomplished technically, have a tendency to converge in their central preoccupations, nostrums or broad outlook. They may write very well, but they rarely if ever innovate, or emerge seemingly from nowhere like elemental forces of nature.

Even the all-time Greats of Canonical Literature: Aeschylus, Dante, Shakespeare, Milton, Goethe, Tolstoy, etc. cannot be indisputably claimed by the advocates and Guardians of 'The Canon'—as if in their most elevated and inspiring 'moments of creation' they were wholly and solely inside the traditions that otherwise moulded them. In the silent solitude of their incubating genius, they were in the profoundest and most essential modality or echelon of their Being, outside of everything which stood in those moments in a relation of otherness to them. They were all intimately familiar with the mainspring-sources of what may be termed outsider-writing in its broadest sense—even if they chose and came to be known as Exemplars, within the fields of literature that they excelled at. And so I acknowledge from the very outset that it is hard, if not impossible, to draw clear-cut distinctions between insider- and outsider-writers. The areas of overlap between them provide the shifting boundaries of any study of this kind. Yet I hold it to be strongly axiomatic that outsider-writers cannot all simply be lumped together in one obvious category, then relegated to the realm of curiosities who in no way engage with 'the problems of the writer', as T. S. Eliot once absurdly remarked of William Blake. On the contrary, they all fall into a bewildering basket-load—no

Bedlamite pun intended!—of categories, or even none at all. They display the widest range of talents, engaging with and disengaging from 'the problems of the writer' at many different levels—some of whom, people of T. S. Eliot's ilk would have serious difficulty either recognizing or comprehending.

The plan of this study, if it can be called such—since I'm inclined to see it as more of a gathering stream, with deviating and returning tributaries—will commence with an examination of the principle definitions of the term 'outsider writer' and the possibly irresoluble difficulties associated with them. Then I shall give an outline of my own philosophical thinking on the subject, followed by more detailed examinations of the works, both fictional and non-fictional, of various writers and thinkers considered as Outsiders, including a few very obscure ones who I regard as scandalously neglected. Then I will compare and contrast the more or less salient features of their works with those of the works of some well-known mainstream counterparts. And finally, I shall attempt to draw the numerous threads of the central running argument—if it runs that far, without shooting off in showers and trickles!—together with a personal summary of what I take to be the truest conclusions of all. I shall cite sources for references or quotes where I think it helpful or instructive. But I won't be providing a doorstopper of an index or bibliography, or endless cyber-scrolls of fetishistic footnotes, which I must admit to finding a pretty tiresome distraction at best, and at worst a masochistic monument to pompous pedantry! If I ever allowed myself to get intestinally bogged down in the labyrinthine bowels of exegetical annotation, not only would I never get to say what I want to say, but I should end up being mummified in the minutiae of a senile idiotic shitload—and I'm quite happy to leave all that to academic drones! As such, this study will be studiously anti-academic, in I would hope the best mould of quirkily iconoclastic, yet intransigently cerebral, counter-cultural Tractarianism.

Chapter One:

The Problematics of Placement

The very existence of Outsiders—amongst whom outsider writers are a rather special variant—is in itself profoundly problematical, as it clearly demonstrates that the ideal model or paradigm of an organic, harmonious, holistic human society has fundamentally failed. Whether this is because such a vision of human potentiality is in essence a flawed one, or because we have not measured up to our full stature as the cooperative species we are supposed to be or become, is a fascinating conundrum. There are many very complex and maybe intractable reasons for, or causes of, this sorry predicament. And sorry it is too. For however bold and defiant some Outsiders are, there can be no denying the pain that invariably dogs their embattled sojourn through life. Wilde may have been joking when he once declared his genius to an American Customs official. But underlying the witty bravura was an almost Kafkaesque burden of consciousness of the absurdity of not only that gesture along with many others, but also the blessing of a unique gift segueing into a curse in the face of officious incomprehension. A less well-known anecdote about Wilde relates how on one occasion he hid from one of his admirers on a train, because he could not for the life of him think of another witticism to top the previous witticism he had uttered, in a long line of witticisms that he had in a sense sentenced himself to endlessly enacting, through his stringent cultivation of a Persona that for all its dazzling magnificence was in the end cripplingly artificial.

Wilde might not strike some readers as an obvious case of an Outsider, except maybe as far as his sexuality was concerned, at a time when people paid a penalty for daring to speak its name. But he in fact provides me with an excellent entrée into my subject. For in spite of his brilliant classical education at Oxford, and his subsequent success as a playwright and socialite, he was quite obviously in ways that actually had little or nothing to do with his sexuality *per se*, estranged from many of the people he moved amongst and after a fashion fawned on and offered a sop to in all his ironically coded light comedies. Whilst a professed socialist, with the interests of the simple, common working man at heart, he also cultivated an incredibly rarefied decadent aesthetic that manifested in a thorough-going, almost systematic, high cynical a-moralism, directed at absolutely anybody from any social class or background who he regarded as failing to measure up to his exquisitely exacting standards of refinement. And yet he would not think any less of himself for consorting with rent-boys in sordid purlieux, than he would for wasting his creative talents holding court at the tables of Society Hostesses with *Reader's Digest* intellects. What I am suggesting here is that he was terrifyingly hollow at the core, even though he had a peerless capacity for masquerading as a man of infinite parts. He genuinely did not know who he was, or where he was in relation to his fellow-humans, at not just a social level, but a profound psycho-existential one too. And so he employed all his remarkable gifts to become a consummate social performer, concealing and disguising the anguish of his interior isolation. And whilst in that state, he was very much one type among many of what I define as an Outsider.

Problematics of Placement

But the fact that there are so many types of Outsider and of course 'type' is not itself an apposite term to denote anyone so quirkily and idiosyncratically singular, separate and individual, but it shall have to serve for now—presents the first major problem of definition, and placement as I wish to call it, if only in a purely discursive context. It suggests that Outsiders emerge on a very broad spectrum along with just about everybody else, in which case they may not have any special defining characteristics which separate them altogether from insiders. They may overlap with insiders in all sorts of different ways, insiders themselves having outsider-aspects, moments and phases, etc. So what then am I talking about here? It may be said by some that we're all Outsiders nowadays, in which case there's little or nothing to distinguish them. Alternatively, it may be said that we're all insiders, whether we like it or not, since there's no escape for any of us from the all-encompassing reach of our media-saturated society! Yet if as John Donne said, 'No man is an island, entire of itself', then some at least of those deemed to be Outsiders in one sense or another may test this axiom to the limit, if not represent special cases and exceptions. But of course an Outsider doesn't necessarily have to be a literal wolf-man or—lady-wolf-person!—to qualify as an Outsider. Even today, in our increasingly polymorphously perverse global culture, it may very well be possible, indeed is possible I would say, for various individuals to stand out from the broad mass by virtue of certain radical peculiarities of expression and cultivation that may or may not be publicly acclaimed as such. And if these peculiarities prompt the sustained, or even periodic or occasional creation of written work, then we can in these cases speak of outsider-writers, as distinct from outsider-artists and so forth.

However, the peculiarities that interest me the most are not invariably, if at all, those that are still commonly associated with Outsiders or outsider-writers. And so in order to make a case for the outsider-writer as a unique kind of talent or genius, I will need to some extent to debunk other, conflicting notions of what it is precisely that makes outsider-writers—and Outsiders in general—so different, and above all, so interesting. The first commonplace—or stereotype—is that most if not all of these people must in some sense be mad. Or they would not be so out of step with society. Moreover, it is obvious from even the most cursory examination of their work that this is so. This is by far and away the easiest charge to refute, though there are of course some cases of Outsiders with psychiatric histories. But I'd say the majority of them have never been diagnosed with any mental illness, or disorders of any other kind. This is not the place to launch into a full-blown critique of psychiatry, which has been done by many other people over the last half century or so—most notably Laing, Cooper and Szasz; somewhat forgotten figures nowadays, although their contributions still remain very crucial in my own opinion—but suffice to say, it is without question as much a socio-political mechanism as it is a medical-therapeutic one. And though genetics and neuro-science have made huge advances in their explanatory power since the heady days of the anti-psychiatry movement, they too can be used as tools of institutional suppression in the wrong hands. And at the root of every psychiatric diagnosis are not genetic or neurological flaws, but behavioural maladjustments to social norms that are always open to question, even if psychiatrists and their ilk prefer not to question them at all. So such diagnoses are riddled from the very outset with subjective and sometimes ideological value-judgements, which make the classification of anybody as mad in some measure unsafe. And historically, any society with an iniquitous vertical power- and authority-structure, or hierarchy, has had a vested interest in keeping deviants of every kind in their place. Hence the 'science' of madness has proved extremely useful to them.

Just because somebody is deemed to be 'mad' by somebody else—which happens all the time in every social stratum, whether levelled by those with letters before or after their names or none—is never in itself a sufficient criterion to dismiss either them or what they do. And when the concept of madness is critically unpacked, even if it can never be entirely explained away, it is invariably found to be strictly relative to some more or less arbitrary and far from infallible set of normative standards or rules which purport to define sanity. No psychiatrist would have dared to question George Bush's sanity in pursuing his catastrophic gung-ho so-called 'war on terror'. Yet the poor sod who had the temerity to hurl a shoe at him—which sadly missed its target!—at a conference, was I'm sure subjected to every psychiatric evaluation in the book! This is not to say that madness is not in some sense a genuine phenomenon. But in view of the very serious consequences that ensue for anybody deemed to be mad, in whatever context, it is vitally important for all of us to be acutely conscious of the highly shifty criteria people employ when they make that judgement about others. There are many kinds of madness, as there are sanity no doubt, and not all of them should be viewed in a pejorative light. To take two very famous examples from history: Blake and Van Gogh were both considered, and still are by many people, to have been mad in a very real sense of the word—even though few would deny today that they were both in no small measure geniuses also. The relationship between madness and genius is a well-trodden territory, but it is of especial relevance to any discussion of Outsiders. And in my opinion the two states can coexist in such persons, if not altogether happily. Blake saw angels everywhere, even in trees and clouds, and believed he was taught painting by a 'man' who he depicted as more like an alien than a human. And Van Gogh might well have been literally driven mad by tinnitus, a condition then unknown—hence the severed ear. Though it is even possible that Gauguin cut off his ear with a sword in a fight—the jury's still out. But tinnitus has certainly driven some people to suicide.

Both of these figures suffered alienation in their periodic bouts of visionary insanity, which militated against their achieving recognition and success in their lifetimes. But they persevered against seemingly overwhelming odds, driven by Demons of despair and Angels of delight. Yet their compulsion to create was not merely an obsessional craving, but a disciplined dedication to a profound and truly inspired calling. Their posthumous reputations could scarcely be so assured if this were not the case. And it may seem paradoxical that such famous and justly canonical figures were in any sense Outsiders. But given their comparative isolation, obscurity and neglect, along with their unrelenting state of embattlement both within themselves and against the society in which they lived, they must I think be considered such. And the strangeness of their work also qualifies them for this epithet. But the fact that their work is also great—or some of it certainly is—complicates the whole notion of an Outsider, especially an Outsider who is undeniably mad, if only in the most obvious sense of occasionally or regularly losing their grip on rationality. And much the same could be said of Salvador Dali too, who systematically willed his madness in the pursuit of surreal logic. The man was a monster, fetishizing money to a disgusting degree. And his relentlessly tyrannical, narcissistic, mythomaniacal, reality-twisting antics would have driven any half-sane person to violent distraction within minutes. Yet he was without question one of the greatest artists of the twentieth century, and no mean writer and thinker either, as his paranoical-critical method testifies. He even had a serious, and informed, interest in science and mathematics. Although filthily famous, and certifiable but for the impregnable fortifications of his wealth, status, and army of admirers, he produced a whole string of works that were second only to the best of Picasso. And in his moments of creation, his genius and his madness were one. He then stood quite outside the world that he so cynically manufactured and manipulated in his puerile, masturbatory displays—a truly complex case!

So whilst in some cases I would readily concede that madness definitely hinders, if not ruins, creative, imaginative, and intellectual output, there are other cases in which it mysteriously enhances the spirit, if not the quality, of the work produced under its spell. Although perhaps this is only true when the persons concerned are in manic moods, which could in fact be ritually induced by any follower of Dali's approach, so are therefore far from being purely chaotic, uncontrolled inner states. But if they are in depressive moods, then it would be much more difficult for them to produce sustained and coherent work of any real merit. That much I accept. But a driven state is very different from a depressive state. And much of the work that Outsiders produce is dictated by their inner need to create, not by a desire for fame, money or success—or even recognition necessarily. They have a truly remarkable resilience in conditions where they often receive little or no feedback from others, and an uncanny resolve to keep on going when it gives them no advantage, which would deter or finish any less determined, or else more calculating, persons. They may appear mad for continuing with their work in obscurity and oblivion. But the alternatives would, in most cases, be much worse: institutionalization and suicide. Their work becomes a reason for Being, a charm against the Horror Vacui. These persons interest me especially, because their madness is like some poisonous gift from which they manage to extract the rarest gold through sheer courage and self-transformation alone. These are the truest Outsiders of all in my opinion, so I will be devoting more space to a few individual examples of them in later chapters.

If nowadays madness is regarded with rather more suspicion than fascination, that is probably because there is so much more of it about than there was, and many of us are petrified of being sucked irresistibly into its almost ubiquitous vortical tides. But Outsiders have far more of a struggle in contending with this than anyone else. And whereas it may be important for us to know whether or not Outsiders are in at least some sense mad in evaluating their work, we should still approach their work and them with a willingness to be struck, or even awed, and not with preconceived bias waiting on its own confirmation. I often wonder whether Beethoven was mad, and if so in what sublime sense, when he wrote in a notebook he kept while he was composing his final works, *Missa Solemnis*, The Ninth Symphony, and the String Quartets—compositions almost without compare, in the history of music—'Only I exist.' The simplicity of the statement, mantra-like in his mind, is staggering. And yet when one reflects on it, it is the purest expression of solipsism imaginable. The outside world and others were an encumbrance that he had to regard as illusory, in order not to be deflected for a moment from the enormity of his undertakings.

And of course his celebrated deafness served to cut him off doubly from others, not only frustrating and exasperating him in his inability to hear his own notes, but radically isolating him also in a tremendously brave, yet resoundingly lonely, vocation. His statement on the face of it was obviously false. Though it was also true in the sense that he could imagine or envision himself at the centre of a created world in which nobody else had, or could have, a place. And in as much as he was single-handedly carrying music into regions which it had never entered before, his solipsistic vision was truly coming into its own. The Outsider had to be mad to free his genius.

I think I've said enough to show that madness does not automatically disqualify an Outsider from being a serious creative person, and can even in some cases be a *sine qua non* of certain kinds of exceptional output. However, there have been odd cases of brain-damaged people trying to portray their inner turmoil either pictorially or in words, or both. And in practically each case it has to be admitted their efforts failed to cohere creatively, and are therefore of more clinical curiosity-value than anything else. But one can still see in this kind of work evidence of a desperate inner struggle towards coherence, which is often profoundly moving and sometimes even inspired. Although I know of no brain-damaged writers who have managed to finish an entire book, unless one cites Robert Walser as an example, a schizophrenic who produced a six hundred page manuscript, which he wrote using only pencils in a progressively miniaturized and illegible hand. This came to be known as *The Micrograms*. And it has only fairly recently been translated from German into English. Whether Walser *was* brain-damaged is a moot point, as some psychiatrists claim there might well be a degree of brain-damage in extreme cases of schizophrenia—and Walser did spend the last twenty three years of his life in an Asylum. There's no evidence he suffered brain-damage as a result of an injury or accident, but faulty genetics combined with a lifetime of intolerable psycho-spiritual stresses can perhaps alter the chemistry of the brain in a totally irreversible manner. Although the capacity of the brain to heal itself by generating new circuitries is a well-established fact. But this might only be possible when the stress-burdens are reduced or relieved. And in Walser's case, the stress-burdens intensified as he grew older. So it is quite probable his brain suffered a degree of damage, which necessitated his incarceration. He had previously been a very gifted and highly prolific, and at times successful, if singularly odd, writer. In fact, it would not be an exaggeration to describe him as a Kafka before Kafka—for unlike Kafka, Walser did achieve some recognition in his lifetime, and Kafka was an early admirer of his work. But I shall say more about him in a later chapter.

There have been some brain-damaged outsider-artists however, who did succeed in completing paintings after a fashion, some of whom were in the habit of scribbling across their canvases in a manner not unlike Walser's pencil writing. Joseph Radler and Adolf Wolffli were two of the most interesting examples of this phenomenon—both of them spending much of their lives in secure institutions. Radler had epilepsy and temporal lobe damage as well as schizophrenia, whilst Wolffli suffered periodic manic fits and rages and made several assaults on children. Yet both men developed highly elaborate internal systems of meaning, represented in coded form in their art. They gradually acquired a disciplined and focused application, which enabled them to produce a whole series of works, that may have been odd, and even superficially deranged in content, yet revealed a formal balance of composition and a signifying, if symbolically private, point of view. Radler painted scenes from his Asylum, with cryptic captions scrawled over caricatured human figures in *tableau vivant* settings, and imaginary paradises populated by strange birds. In fact, birds were the common theme for both figures, as Wolffli painted pictures in which birds semi-mutated into humans, women especially, and angels. There were suggestions of metempsychosis, the sense that mankind evolved from birds originally, coupled with the desire to fly away from confinement, to be freed in a transcendent realm. Wolffli did pictures on single sheets, 'bread paintings' for money he never earned, and also scribbled a two thousand page unending memoir. In both men a strong self-organizing motif was at work, providing continual streams of imagery and words, and a compulsive urge to translate these into more or less well-ordered representations. It was as though their damaged brains were striving to heal themselves by means of channelling the work. And I'd like to think that some measure of contentment was thereby afforded them, even if they could never of course be successfully rehabilitated into society.

A more nebulous factor in assessing Outsiders is so-called sociopathy, which overlaps with psychopathy, but doesn't necessarily render a person completely, or even partially, incapable of functioning in society, and of course doing creative work of some kind. Sociopaths have been defined as people who are incapable of empathy, and who lack a moral sense. They are quite likely therefore to be inclined towards anti-social behaviour—and not just in the PC New Labour sense of the term!—and also criminality. The life-prisoner Charles Bronson—no relation of the late actor!—is considered the most dangerous man in Britain, even though ironically he hasn't ever killed anyone. But the security measures adopted by staff in dealing with him are not unlike those used with the fictional Hannibal Lecter! He knows he is never likely to be released from prison—and he was only sent to prison in the first place for a botched robbery, but reacted so violently to incarceration that he has become pathologically institutionalised as a result—and so he has discovered a therapeutic release from his own hell through very pure, if primitive forms of outsider art and writing. He has had little or no formal education, and is entirely self-taught in his art and writing. But he has managed to tap into a rawly potent source of wounded anger, and even a curious, earthy humour, in his psyche, which govern his modes of self-expression. Thus, a highly dangerous individual, deemed to be bestialised beyond help, has gradually reconnected with a deeply touching humanity.

It's highly doubtful whether the same could be said of Ian Brady, the infamous moors murderer, an extremely intelligent, self-cultivated man, who nonetheless delighted in enacting the very worst imaginable Sadean excesses in an attempt to not just extend, but smash, the boundaries of human decency and Taboo. He has never expressed any remorse that I know of, and has even made a frequent point of complaining about his treatment at the hands of robotic functionaries, brain-washed by a totally inhumane system! But if he has redeemed himself at all, it is in the sphere of writing, where his immensely powerful, individualistic, outsider-voice is instantly apparent. He has not compromised his warped vision one jot, but as a stylist, a critic and a philosopher after a fashion, he has perhaps gone some small way towards justifying his execrable existence on this planet. He pushed sociopathy and psycho-pathy combined into regions where psychiatric categories break down altogether, and only the classical invocations of monsters truly come close to conveying and capturing the hideous essence of his conceit. That said, there have probably been many people throughout history, including the famous, who have occasionally fantasized along not dissimilar lines, or else felt sudden, inexplicable impulses to destroy others, and yet have had neither the courage in a sense, nor the inner license, to act accordingly. However humanly and morally abominable Brady's actions were, there was also a grotesque kind of imaginative sublimity in what he did, which writers such as Dostoyevsky and Sade—who he'd already read at fifteen; 'absolutely brilliant', as Lord Longford remarked after his first meeting with him!—would undeniably have recognized and understood, if not exactly unequivocally admired. Brady is one of very few individuals in the twentieth century to have advanced, in one direction at least, our conception of what is psychologically and amorally possible for humanity. And as such, his example will assuredly be studied for a long time to come. He is also a true Outsider in Colin Wilson's sense—so much so in fact that Wilson even decided to correspond with him and encouraged him to write his book *The Gates of Janus*, though Brady later rebuffed him!

Yet another kind of Outsider, complicating the issue of definition still further, is the untrained person or amateur, discovering or otherwise developing some gift or nervous tick as cynics might call it, and going on to produce a body of work that defies classification—if not belief, in some cases. People who fall into this slippery marginal category are not necessarily in any way ill or handicapped or damaged, let alone institution-alised. Yet a good many of them have somewhat troubled relationships with mainstream life, shall we say, and don't take up art or writing or whatever it may be in quite the same vein as a genial suburbanite trying their hand at a spot of weekend water-colouring! In fact, the people that I have particularly in mind here are engaged in a kind of war against the world, which becomes a solitary, single-minded, all-consuming mission, to transform reality itself, as well as produce an enduring legacy of their own. Not everyone in this category is quite so infernally bloody-minded, of course. But those who fascinate me the most certainly are! I can swiftly dispatch the lazy assumption that uneducated amateurs are invariably inferior to educated professionals, just by citing a few famous counter-examples: Shakespeare, Blake, Keats, Dickens, Shaw and Orwell. Why have I cited these indisputably great household names? Because none of them attended university, and they were all self-taught writers. Most may not have been Outsiders, or certainly not in any straightforward sense as such, though all of them stood in a somewhat angular, if not oblique, relation to the literary establishment—including Shakespeare and Dickens. Marlowe and Jonson were very dismissive of Shakespeare's talent, perhaps partly from envy, and Thackeray was similarly dismissive of Dickens at first. They were all quite uneasy with professionalism too, Blake and Keats especially. Shaw and Orwell too had very challenging radical agendas in their work, and they both attempted to help, unsuccessfully, an obscure English writer called Lionel Britton, who for me embodies the very archetype of the outsider-writer at his best or greatest. He became known to editors everywhere as 'the man who would not be cut'—as he threatened to 'cut their throats' if editors dared to cut a word of his manuscripts! Leaving school at fourteen and then building his own 'universe' of knowledge, he went on to produce a massive body of truly extraordinary work that is today all but forgotten. So I shall be resurrecting his memory in a later chapter. And are any writers trained as such to write? I know nowadays there are a lot of so-called 'creative writing' courses, but my own opinion of them is quite frankly unprintable even in a hard-hitting tract-cum-treatise of this sort! Yet before their advent some writers might have gone to university and read English or whatnot. But after that they didn't undergo training in the way that artists or designers do. They learnt their trade unassisted, by trial and error, maybe supplementing their income with journalism and the like. But in this general sense, all writers could be described as amateurs. And bearing in mind that an amateur by definition, is somebody who loves what they do as distinct from somebody who gets paid for what they do, why does the word have such a pejorative connotation, smacking nearly always of incompetence, when amateurs strongly eschew the mercenary? It could be argued in this sense, that amateurs are the true writers—even if their techniques are in some measure unpolished. Often they exhibit a creative power that eclipses their rough and ready craft, and sustains them in the creation of the most singular works of fiction ever conceived. John Cowper Powys was a great literary oddball if ever there was one, churning out a long series of doorstoppers that didn't really slot into any canon, tradition, or school of writing in existence. And yet they all stood out on their own, especially *Porius* and *Wolf Solent*, like cosmic cathedrals shimmering in magic splendour, unique, uncategorizable and truly spectacular. He had few equals, even among the twentieth century Greats. And he too was very largely an autodidact, with a deep-forged Bardic vision all his own. He had a robustness, pugnacity and energy in him, burnishing a belief that he could 'bowl out Hegel', as he once declared. And bowl out that muddle-headed Germanic windbag he did! He deserves a chapter to himself alright!

Problematics of Placement

Another giant of twentieth century literature, Fernando Pessoa, may seem to be an odd choice of outsider-writer, given how famous he is—not only in Portugal, but also in other European countries. Yet in England he is less well-known, and for me it is the highly complex and superlatively strange spiritual psychology of the man, as well as the ultra-rarefied exquisiteness of his writing, that qualified him as an Outsider. There was something intensely singular and ultimately great in his overarching Project of synthesizing all the faculties in a map of the mind, which he superimposed on base reality. His master-work, *The Book of Disquiet*, was conceived and written in nocturnal isolation, and on his death he left behind him a record-number of compositions in a trunk, which have only quite recently been fully annotated. He invented a large number of Heteronyms, fictional alter-egos that acquired the identity of doubles or multiples of himself, and took it in turns to write much of his work. They were in some respects like astral entities, which he conjured in occult rituals as substitutes for himself, filling the voids in his own Being. He was weirder than Kafka even, and a better stylist, with a rich stock of imagery, a wide range of allusions, very profound visionary ideas, and phenomenal reserves of erudition. He wrote English almost as fluently as he did Portuguese, and as well as founding two new doctrines was the first person in his country to publicize the theories of Einstein. As such, he drew on many sources as disparate as the classics, mythology, mathematics, science, history, the occult and all the arts, like a polymath in hiding, who only got a few articles published in his lifetime, and hasn't been widely appreciated since his death, even though his name is renowned in his country and elsewhere. The fact is, he and his work are far too forbidding ever to be truly understood in the popular domain. But he assuredly has pride of place in a study of this kind, as I intend to show.

Carlo Emilio Gadda was a not dissimilar figure in Italy, immensely learned and supercilious, a brilliant scientist, mathematician and engineer—who designed a power-station for the Vatican of all things, and was hailed as a national hero in Italy! But he was a tortuously complex, embittered man, who despised his fellow-countrymen, and took refuge in an ivory-tower of his own making, founded on all manner of esoteric studies in Metaphysics and the Corpus Hermeticum, etc. producing a number of exceedingly difficult works of fiction and philosophy, which the reading public considered 'grotesque' and many scholars regarded as 'untranslatable'. But fortunately, many of his works have now been translated into English, and present a fascinating challenge of interpretation. I was struck by a photograph of him as a young man, sitting bolt upright on a chair in a Bohemian Salon, surrounded by art-objects and palm-trees, dressed like a severe Dandy, and facially resembling Salvador Dali. Only his expression was even madder and fiercer and more assuredly Olympian than Dali's, one of the most petrifying and supremely arrogant stares I have ever seen a human being affect. I was absolutely mesmerized and made it my business to find out more about him, writing an essay later on. But I've discovered some fresh material since then, which is more than sufficient to confirm him as a genuine outsider-writer, fully in spite of his fame. So I'll be devoting a chapter to him too.

Blaise Cendrars was yet another example of a writer who was profoundly out-of-step with modern civilization, and yet had his finger on the very pulse of his time. Immensely gifted and quirkily erudite, he produced a large body of very singular work in many fields—fiction, memoirs, journalism, scholarship, film, art, and polemics. He travelled all over the world; trained in the French Foreign Legion, lost an arm in the First World War; befriended everyone of note in the Arts, Bohemia, high and low society; was a drinker and a smoker, a fighter and a womaniser; a lover of Jazz, seedy dives, fast cars, flying, and the sea. He observed every facet of life in practically every country, and evoked its mysteries without ever being judgemental. He wrote like an angel and a devil all at once, eschewing the merely conventional and celebrated, the bourgeois and the philistine, carving out an extraordinary niche for himself, straddling the divide between the margin and the mainstream. But above all he never lost the eagle eye of the Outsider, usually preferring the company of unknown outcasts to that of the respectable and the well-to-do. His life was a testament to Humphrey Bogart's saying 'Life is for the Living'. And yet the man himself retained a core of solitude and mystery, utterly eclipsing the shallow gesturism of a Hemingway. He was at least the equal of Céline, if not greater, but is less well-remembered even, being less rabidly prejudiced, though more exhilaratingly dangerous. So I'll certainly be granting this charmed mythomane his own chapter!

Other writers too numerous to mention here fall into the broad category of self-taught Outsiders, cultivating their voices and pursuing their visions to the very last, and refusing to compromise their integrity or their stand on life, literature and everything. But here I am really just sketching the outlines of the territory. Having dealt with the ignorant prejudices and rigid dogmas affecting Outsiders, which play such a large part in exacerbating the problems they have in placing themselves within society and culture, I am now in a better position to attempt to define more clearly what it means for a writer in particular to be an Outsider, and what it is about this predicament and vocation that especially concerns me in this study. A writer must first and foremost be conscious in a very powerful and definite kind of way, usually from an early age onwards, of being singular and out of step with the world about him, of 'listening to a different drummer' as the American composer Charles Ives once said of himself. This may not be such a rare experience, since quite a lot of people report it nowadays. But each individual will presumably experience it differently. And those amongst them who then go on to create arresting work, that challenges or resists mainstream orthodoxy, are well on their way to becoming fully-fledged *bona fide* outsider-writers. A certain uniqueness of style and viewpoint, combining with a quirky idiosyncrasy and robust resoluteness mark out a talented outsider-writer from a merely fanciful eccentric or fickle dreamer or self-deluded pretender. There is a disciplined desire from which brilliant perseverance is forged. The source of this dedicated genius resides in an elusive strand of inspiration, connecting the margins to the mainstream and balancing intellect with imagination.

Freud's artist, who 'finds a way back to reality' is a conundrum, for if reality changes in his rendering of it he will return to something very different from what he started with—assuming he returns at all! The Outsider's aim is not to ultimately accept reality as it is, but to transfigure it through the power of his imagination, to carry it with him in an altered aspect. So he doesn't resign to reality, nor exactly abandon it either. Reality is a burden, a bug-bear, a great obstacle with only a few redeeming features, a mountain-wall against which to bash one's head with more injury than illumination, an indisposable curse inside a deceitful blessing—pressed upon one by dull pragmatists and bossy therapists alike. If Marx's

Utopia could never be realized, then Outsiders are still at the forefront trying to dream it into Being. The Bourgeois insistence on facing up to reality must end where the work of the creative imagination begins. And who knows where that might lead us, and where it ends, if anywhere? One of the great themes, if not THE great theme of outsider-writing is precisely the sheer, intractable nature of existence itself, which is both an Existentialist problematic and an Essentialist one too. What I mean by this is that while the brute fact of what exists or what is may appear to set the limit or boundary to what we can experience and be directly conscious of, we can still in truth imagine or conceive of infinities and eternities that open up the textures of Being in the sense of conveying or even conjuring essences. We may penetrate towards the suppositional core of existence, or else fly away from it into imaginary ethers which give us the profoundest bearings of our spiritual homes. Outsiders are drawn to these dense and difficult regions of palpable phantasmagoria most of all, for their Phenomenological grounding in the wildernesses of the Human makes them long the most acutely for the Ontological assurances of a pivotal domain they can think of as Home. Isolation has to be the main defining characteristic of all outsider-writers in my view, even though they may not all be total recluses. But they must have at the very least an inner isolation that in some quite radical sense cuts them off from others, even when they are at their closest proximity to them. From Autism to Auteurism is a truly problematical step! Though in a clinical sense the people I have in mind here, are not necessarily suffering from Autism or Asperger's Syndrome, but may have very deliberately withdrawn themselves from the world or have some innate sense of their own special separateness. Nietzsche's 'artifice of self-preservation' is more pertinent here than Freud's famous defense-mechanisms, relating as it does to the withholding of something rare and precious in a 'Higher Man's' secret inner chamber as it were, that it is not timely or right to reveal, or which the world is not yet ready to receive. True works of art burn softly along a slow fuse, threading together the fabrics in the Thebaid of an intimate, yet finely distancing communion. Rarely if ever are they suddenly dashed off the tops of people's heads, like casual outpourings of momentous whimsy or crapulous effusions of marsh-mallow-minded, would-be Mozarts of Literature. Although I suppose it can never be entirely ruled out that some ingénue will occasionally appear from nowhere and just dump a work of genius on an editor's desk—but it doesn't happen every day of the week! And most outsider-writers in my estimation have a very keen awareness of the importance of self-disciplined attentiveness to both the detail and the overall plan or purpose of their projects.

Watchfulness is then the watch-word of Outsiders who might be looking in so to speak, but who do not necessarily wish to join the human party. They seek instead to find their Homes at the interface of solitude and spectacle—objectifying their visions of otherness while prizing their subjective privacy from it. This may be a damaging and a dangerous form of alienation, but it can also vouchsafe a quality of the purest authenticity in those upon whom it is visited. It is a crucial part of that Faustian Pact intangibly signed up to by every outsider-writer who feels called upon to monitor and record everything of import and purport that happens to and around them—including, of course, the innermost agitations of their consciousness in its sealed off rooms of unregistered broodings. The reward is the fruit of the labour itself. And the punishment is a silenced severance from the Muses of their own minds. This is a dark and destructive domain that only the strongest Outsiders can dwell in for very long. But the work they weave from its all-entangling web is the sternest gold in Creation. Dispassion is here carried to the utmost heights of cold magnificence. Only an almighty barbaric bastard can withstand the tortures of such self-eviscerating ordeals. And some of them—the Sades and the Bradys!—are well up for it. Others descend into the pit—the Nervals and the Poes—and never recover. A laughing magnanimity is required for triumph.

An emphatic eccentricity, wedded to bloody-minded defiance and an indefatigable energy of output, spares outsider-writers for their most exacting projects. Contrariety is the spice of their lives, as it muscles them through their thankless, self-imposed Sisyphean tasks, fuelling all their diatribes and digressions with the positive force of a negative animus. Being *contra mundum* defines them more than any hankered after Heaven of reuniting with others, in bonds from which they were born—broken. And it is actually a close cousin in feeling to the joyful exhilaration of wild musings and meditations, cosmic hymns and red glimpses of passing perfections, that punctuate and counter-point the darker strains of their work. Being an Outsider is not only about pain and suffering and misery, but it is also about proud aloofness and the notion of a justified superiority, and having a personal conduit to the well-springs of ecstatic creativity unmuddied by mass sentiment. There is something almost heroic and Messianic about it, as if it's a special sort of spiritual status mysteriously conferred upon certain individuals with gifts of Christ or Anti-Christ proportions, enabling them to achieve truly great things. The element of fantasy in this conceit is potent. But it is not in all cases misconceived—the subsequent work proves this. Thus fantasy is as powerful an engine of great literature as thought, if not a greater one.

And all Outsiders are in some measure drawn to great fantasies of human potentiality, which purport to transcend, supersede or transform prevailing Reality, and create if not a better world for Mankind, certainly one that is at the very least more interesting for truly imaginative persons to inhabit. That of course is an extremely difficult goal to attain, and many Outsiders fail in their attempts to do so. But some succeed quite awesomely, and to just make the attempt in itself is arguably the finest motive one can have for writing, even if it isn't confined to Outsiders. But to behold Mankind in the round as it were, one really has to step outside the familiar orbit of consciousness and embrace a more majestic perspective. And this comes more readily to those who feel themselves to be inwardly detached from people's common concerns, and automatically attuned to loftier spiritual and intellectual issues—as Outsiders usually do. That does not mean they will necessarily or invariably go further than their 'insider' counterparts, in finding the solutions to the problems which face Mankind. But in many instances they will articulate greater visions and philosophical frameworks within which those solutions should be found. The Sociologist Emil Durkheim was said to have had an advantage over other Sociologists in respect of his most crucial insight into how human society worked, because he was a diagnosed schizophrenic. Therefore he was curiously inured to the shared assumptions of others, and proved able to view their thought-processes and correlated behaviours from an 'alien' perspective. And his illness did not in fact damage his remarkable analytical and synthesizing capabilities.

In the next chapter, I intend to develop these ideas further—not just in terms of my own thinking, but also by examining contributions from three major thinkers, namely, Walking John Stewart, Albert Camus, and Colin Wilson. These three thinkers inaugurated a new field or branch of Studies, which has perhaps not been properly acknowledged since, as few people have taken up the baton they have striven to pass on. This was partly due to dismissal and rejection, especially of Stewart and Wilson, mainly on ignorant or prejudicial grounds, as I shall argue. Otherwise, their achievements were not sufficiently understood, and bequeathed a set of Problematics that later thinkers—Wilson is still very much alive of course, and cerebrally kicking!—have perhaps had insuperable difficulties in resolving or advancing. And so the subject remains in something of a quandary—if not a morass—at present. But I shall therefore make a serious stab at rescuing it, and try to suggest some fruitful lines along which it can be pursued in future—even if my only real qualification for this task is that I myself have always felt that I belonged amongst Outsiders!

☸

Chapter Two:

Revising the Groundwork: Stewart, Camus and Wilson

If we take as our starting-point for the study of outsider-writers, the tenet that any such writer must be singled out as someone special in terms of a capacity for both eccentricity and genius, then we are sticking our necks out just about as far as we can in the contentious, if noble cause of valorizing human freaks. But I am no stranger to neck-sticking, and I intend in the forthcoming pages to extend the said appendage further than I have perhaps ever done before—even at the risk of losing my head! Yet Danton lost his head fighting in the cause of a truly libertarian, as opposed to an authoritarian, revolution. And cocooned in the clinical safety of a metaphor, I am willing to go the self-sacrificial distance in the defense of a justly outraged tribe of Titans. Outsider-writers could easily be dismissed if their work is merely odd, and lacks substance, seriousness and profundity. I acknowledge this fully, seeing no good reason to publicize works by obscure, neglected or forgotten writers, who justly deserve to be left to rest in oblivion forever. There are reasons why some writers are widely rejected or never gain recognition in the first place—the main one being quite simply that their work is too bad for them to merit acknowledgement! But this judgement could of course apply equally to writers, who by temperament and inclination would be insiders, if their reputations were ever established. So this cuts both ways, and on grounds that are never wholly objective. Even Time itself is not always the best court of appeal, as Dr. Johnson believed, since there are some writers who would never be discovered and acclaimed in a million years, if it were not for the almost crazily obsessive sleuthing efforts of a comparatively small number of rarefied enthusiasts, who make it their business—if not their life's work!—to exhume the literary corpses of the Great Abandoned Ones.

My case for resurrecting these figures can only be strengthened by the talents or even genius they can be shown to have possessed. And this is in fact one of the best reasons, aside from space, for my being highly selective in my choice of examples. I can remember being told once that recent research had revealed that during the *Fin-de-Siecle* period—the Decadent 1890s—there were no less than three thousand poets of the acanthus-adorned aesthete-variety in England alone! My only honest response to this arcane piece of information was that it may very well have been true, but only about a dozen of them would be worth reading! Whilst I am sure there is a small army of dandified symbolist anoraks hot on the trail of the missing three thousand as I write, I can assure the reader that for all my compulsive fascination for outsider-writers I will not be joining their far from martial ranks any time soon! The moment I sniff poetasters and florid pseuds their trails go cold for me. I am on the perpetual look-out for the real heavy-weights among the mighty weirdos of literature. And it is these, and these alone, that I shall be examining in this study. What perpetually connives at the 're-forgotten' stigma of these writers, in Iain Sinclair's telling phrase, is the imaginative myopia of the masses counter-pointing the utterly intransigent extremity of the writers' concerns and preoccupations. I can't imagine Sade's *120 Days of Sodom* ever filling the '3 for the price of 2' tables in Waterstone's! And there is I think an instructive, if a slightly pernicious, logic in this fact, as one just has to accept that people have their limitations—even if true outsider-writers often write for 'Everyman', rather than for an exclusive clique. Yet as 'poor' old Blake discovered when he exhibited 16 paintings, including his lost work 'The Ancient Britons', in his brother's shop: Everyman was Noman!

But there might still be ways of bridging the blind divide between the margins and the mainstream through increasingly ingenious uses of the communicative media that can indeed link us all. And so I won't altogether abandon hope that great oddities in the Literary Canon may one day reach a much wider and still discerning readership than they have hitherto enjoyed. And to make outsider-writers interesting and appealing to those people who would otherwise almost certainly pass them by or pointedly shun them—without of course in any way watering down their 'difficult' attributes—one has to emphasize the universal scope of their work as well as their striking individuality. It may be supposed that writers achieve Universality by addressing big general themes in a highly abstract manner *a la* Tolstoy. And certainly this is one way of doing just that—and Tolstoy was perhaps equally an insider- and an outsider-writer, and great in both domains. But Universality is also achieved by an insistent immersion in the Particular, which becomes gradually magnified, like a microcosmic reflection of the macrocosm. And outsider-writers are especially attuned to this whole approach to writing, because as individuals they feel themselves to be so cut off from the Collective. They are therefore steeped in both themselves and their immediate worlds, which in their works can go proxy for the larger world or universe that contains them. The nature of their calling will in itself provide the keys that unlock 'the doors of perception' onto other realities.

Stewart, Camus, Wilson

The auto-compulsion of outsider-writers, already alluded to, appears to dictate the agendas that they follow, often quite irrespective of any outside influences such as significant others, education, culture, money, environment, and wider society. There may be complex accidents of birth and early upbringing which play an important part in moulding these people as outsiders. But the patterns of acculturation that they are later exposed to, which ought to some degree to militate against their further distantiation from the human norms, clearly fail to do this in respect of their unassimilably unique characteristics. At a critical point they not only become conscious of their anomalous exceptionality, but also decidedly bent in favour of cultivating it to extremes, in full defiance of all the restrictive forces arraigned against them. So their lives, and their inner worlds, then become battlegrounds on which they fight endlessly to preserve the pristine essence of their vocations from burial beneath the dull cement of conventional sensibilities. And if this sounds a tad precious in a post-modern world, there is nothing remotely precious about the arduous struggles which then ensue inside the heads, hearts and souls of these wondrous wretches, as they stake their creative territories in the barren outlands of Civilization. The famous picture of Thomas Chatterton, lying dead in a Holborn garret, brings this home more powerfully than almost any image I know—even though it is suffused with the tragic romanticism of genius in despair, that was shortly to become one of the silliest cults in history! But Chatterton's loss at seventeen was at least as injurious to the legacies of the Literary Canon as Keats's loss at twenty five. And one wonders how many more Chattertons there might be out there today, suicidally suspiring in the cold economic winds of this heartless, uncomprehending, insufferably stupid excuse for a Christian country?! There may not be the same levels of absolute poverty as in the past, but there certainly are comparable, if not even greater, levels of human alienation.

Outsider-writers are in a sense the angelic voices of alienation, reminding us all in their works of just how poignantly and unbearably tenuous our shared humanity is. They offer us an ultimate load-bearing litmus test of our human compassion and understanding. If Christ could touch a leper, should we not read an outsider-writer? And the comparison is not so far-fetched, when you consider just how utterly cast out from the annals and chronicles of Time so many of these figures are: ‘Walking’ John Stewart was regarded by Thomas de Quincey as the most remarkable man of his time. Yet not only did he fail to get his extraordinary writings published, he was also so petrified of being persecuted by kings and ‘tyrants’ he insisted on having his pamphlets buried by anybody who came into possession of them! It’s unsurprising then that he was so quickly forgotten after his death. And I would say that only a handful of people today have the slightest familiarity with his works. So if ever there was a literary leper, it was poor old Stewart! Not that he mooched about like some ghostly misanthrope. Far from it! He was a man of colossal conviction, who strode across the world—literally, as his sobriquet suggests!—and took it on, like a fearless madman on a mission. But it did him little good in the end, for like a comet blazing then burning out he left few visible traces on Earth of the ether that he soared in. And yet the few remnants of his works held by the British Library today outline in some detail and depth what might have been the first truly philosophical foundation and framework for what later writers and thinkers like Camus and Wilson developed into a fully-fledged Creed.

Stewart, Camus, Wilson

Outsider-Visionaries are of course as old as the hills—declaiming bards and peripatetic mystics and prophet-seers of antiquity being as far removed from the social ranks as wilderness-wolves in many instances. Authors were often nameless, producing sagas and epics, verses and songs, that later became the sacred and profane texts of entire civilizations, embedding all their Creation-myths, religious world-views and heroic adventure-tales. *The Epic of Gilgamesh* is the greatest—along with the Nordic and Icelandic sagas. Ezekiel and St. Simeon Stylites were formidable spirits and wrath-fuming desert-dwellers. Heraclitus and Diogenes were pioneering Outsiders, like Socrates and Christ. Cato, Catullus, Spartacus, and Catilene the Indigent, were violently opposed to, and estranged from, the Imperial Hierarchy of Rome, and fought isolated wars of words and weapons, to the very last. *Beowulf*, and *The Mabinogion*, were written by unknown Luminaries, embattled against the reigning orders. Pariah-figures like Francois Villon, the poet, thief and murderer; Boccacchio, the soul of debauchery; Gilles de Rais, the child-sacrificer; Francois Rabelais, the carnal Grotesque; Aphra Behn, the lone woman of proud Genius stuck in the pig-sty of Patriarchalism; Abiezer Coppe, the ranting prophet; Rochester, the Dramaturge-rake; and Savage, the Grub Street gad-fly; filled the gaps up to the Ages of Dissent and Revolution—when Chatterton, Blake and Stewart made their self-ushering entrees onto the world-stage, in a struggle of Transfiguration; likewise Ossian, the legendary Gaelic warrior-poet, and Foscolo, the melancholic meditator on tombs, corpses, and deathless dreams.

Stewart made a clean sweep of all this hidden history, declaring the received wisdom of centuries peddled through the gigantic sausage-machine of formal education as worthless as a turd-pile of superstitious dogmas. He resolved to unlearn everything he'd been taught to fashion his philosophy anew. And this involved learning directly from observation, experience and exertion, as well as from reading books. He had no time for useless facts and theories, which in no way advanced Human Civilization practically or intellectually. Instead, he applied his uniquely penetrating mind to the moral and spiritual elevation of the species, using himself as the first experimental test-case for a new leap in consciousness, thought and Being. There was nothing of Negativeness in the man, which fore-shadowed Wilson's concept of Positive Consciousness, whereby people can develop innate faculties which enable them to overcome the self-destroying tendency inherent in both negative psycho-pathology and what might be termed the negative ideologies of movements like Existent-ialism, Fascism, Totalitarianism, Nihilism and Apocalypticism. Stewart, for all his radical eccentricity, was a tremendously powerful force of nature, who at no point capitulated to apathy, lassitude or dispiritedness. The more he was ridiculed or shunned as a lunatic at liberty and large, the more he resolved to hit back at his scoffers and accusers and champion his untimely, yet far-sighted cause. And he never let up in this capacity, even in old age. And at a time when people were incarcerated in asylums, prisons and workhouses on the slightest pretexts, he demonstrated fantastic courage in his persistent refusal to abide by any of the prevailing social conventions and mores; and also enjoyed enormous good fortune in managing to avoid arrest or detention, if not suspicion. In fact, he was so far ahead of his time in his thinking, that he would have been quite at home as a towering anti-guru figure in the counter-cultural movement that so captivated the West in the 1960s!

Stewart, Camus, Wilson

For Stewart, there was bound to be a sea-change in human consciousness if individuals took it upon themselves to think for themselves for the very first time in history. Before the Enlightenment—toward which he felt ambivalent as he abhorred mass political uprisings of the French sort, leading to tyranny of licentiousness—it was customary for individuals to defer to the Church or other authorities in their judgements about a whole range of matters. But the part of the Enlightenment that he extolled and actively promoted on his own terms, concerned the emancipation of the Individual from essentially Feudal power and authority structures, anticipating 'the mastery of life and destiny' that Marx was to adumbrate well over half a century later. But he distrusted Collectivist movements, which by his reckoning substituted what we would now think of as totalitarian regimes for the oligarchic and autocratic regimes of the dynasties that sought to perpetuate absolute monarchy and other forms of despotism, before the ideas of the Enlightenment took hold of the popular imagination. If there was to be a revolution, it had to occur in the heart, soul and head of each and every individual, as a necessary condition of its translation from theory into practice. And whilst Stewart was far from endorsing the new Bourgeois ideology which gained ground in the wake of the French Revolution, he was first and foremost committed to changing Mankind from within, and only secondarily with the social and political changes following on from this, which were in any case in the hands of individuals themselves. He may have had something of the self-righteous mania of an Old Testament Prophet. But being essentially a free spirit he did not seek to dictate to others how they should live, but to provide such a scintillating example of autonomous advancement in his own case, that they were duly inspired to develop a corresponding capacity within themselves, only differing in expression.

The paradox at the heart of Stewart's whole philosophy was, that for all his concern about spirituality, evolution and emancipation, he remained a kind of Materialist, or Atomist of organic motions, and in a curious sense also a Conservative, *vis-à-vis* the conduct and regulation of human affairs. He had an almost mystical, intuitive sense of the omnipresence of cosmic energies, which drove material life—including species like ourselves—to a realization of its potentialities in an endless Continuum, in which everything emerged, lived and died, and re-emerged. Nothing in the Whole could be annihilated. Yet he repudiated Religion, Metaphysics, Mythology and the Occult as one great tissue of nonsense! God was a tyrant, projected into Being by Man's craven stupidity. He rejected all forms of Theocratic power and authority, believing the universe, nature and life to be eternal—without beginning or end, and therefore without a First Cause. Irrational superstition, dictatorial design, and pig-ignorance had all been responsible for enslaving Mankind within systems of false belief and ritual practice. Men could only become Gods over their own minds when they liberated themselves from all these systems and recognized that they were part of an all-encompassing Whole. This was in no way supernatural, but a fusion of the natural and the human in which men were special, in terms of their ability to impute authority to themselves by virtue of their unique self-reflexivity of consciousness.

Animals had consciousness, but not self-consciousness. Only humans had this faculty, giving them a privileged position within the overall scheme of things. Yet any talk of hierarchies was anathema to Stewart. Humans were the stewards of the Earth, and as such responsible to it and all its other life-forms. And although they were possessed of superior attributes, especially mind and spirit, these were essentially by-products, or Epiphenomena, of material life—on the same spectrum and partaking of the same Substance. So it was therefore possible for humans to communicate, or to 'exchange energies' with other life-forms, sharing a generous celebration of the joys of life—the Teleological end or purpose of which was purely to sustain it for its own sake, in the gift of self-conscious Higher Beings, who ascribe meaning, significance and value to both existence and experience. In this context only did it make sense to foster and cultivate a Holistic Mythos, replacing Organized Religion, deracinated Hermeticism, and segregated Science. As for Laws, they should not be handed down from on high, in a Theocratic or Jurisprudential manner, but be socially contracted for the mutual practical benefit of everyone. In this sense, he was willing to curb his otherwise irrepressible anarchic largesse in the interests of securing a balanced and stable social harmony, which would then facilitate cultural, spiritual and moral growth in the Human Family. The irony is he himself was so humanly detached, being stoically solitary—albeit a spell-bindingly uplifting, convivial Sage, whenever he encountered fellow-humans on his travels, or engaged them in lofty discourse at social gatherings.

Perhaps only an Outsider could have developed the kind of radical philosophical system and method that Stewart did in late eighteenth and early nineteenth century Britain. Godwin, Wollstonecraft, Shelley, Byron and Hazlitt developed highly radical ideas of their own, and had elements of the Outsider in their make-up. But none of them were as cut off from the mainstream society of their time as Stewart was, and they all succeeded in establishing their names and reputations, both through their work and through the highly public manner in which they led their lives. With the possible exception of Hazlitt, they were all far better connected socially and culturally than was Stewart in the strict, class-bound, English social system. Stewart left Harrow at just fourteen—and left England for India not long afterwards. And although he was after a fashion gregarious and sociable, his marked idiosyncrasies, founded less on the shock-tactics of Byron than on the prophetic presence of a Blake-like visionary Seer, did him no favours whatever in polite society! Yet his estranged position in society afforded him a privileged vantage-point from which to examine its failings and limitations, with the ruthlessly dispassionate critical eye and inspired animus of a transcendent perfectionist. And no mere insider would ever have matched him in this endeavour, for his perseverance in it was truly awesome and unearthly, indeed almost superhuman.

He even looked extraordinary. The one faint surviving drawing of him I have seen on the Frontispiece of one of his small rogue press pamphlets, shows a large proud face with a prominent nose and all-seeing eyes, surmounting a wide, robust physical frame. His hair was long, and he wore exotic travellers' clothes when in London, and smoked foreign pipes. He walked everywhere, eschewing horse-drawn modes of transport. Whenever he encountered animals he would commune with them, exchanging breath with cows for instance. If he had been a hippie, he'd have led the Kathmandu Trail personally—and on foot of course! He may have taken Opium on his travels, though if so, he didn't seem to suffer debilitating, still less addictive effects. He would frequent taverns and coffee-houses, where he would mesmerize strangers and then declaim to them for hours in a loud voice like an ancient mariner on all subjects under the sun, and above it no doubt. He also frequented Brothels, as a substitute for living with a female partner, who would have distracted him from his personal mission on Earth. Likewise children would have been a distraction, and in a sense his writings became his children. His living was precarious it must be said, although he managed to survive by teaching and going on lecture-tours in America—like Oscar Wilde after him! But he was owed a lot of money by an employer in India—amazingly, he had risen up the ranks of the army over there!—which he eventually got. And so then his life was comfortable and secure, and he was able to open a Salon in his Apartments, where absolutely anybody was welcomed. When he wasn't orating to assembled galleries of scholars, thinkers, writers, bohemians, prophets, madmen and vagrants, he'd play Handel to them on an organ, like a deranged Franz Liszt or John Taverner in flowing robes, much to the annoyance of his neighbours no doubt, who probably felt he should have been confined in—if he hadn't escaped from!—a certain notorious institution near Moorfields! But miraculously, he avoided this fate.

De Quincey found him overwhelming at times, full of the impassioned rectitude of the autodidact, and yet spell-bindingly brilliant at the same time. Wordsworth met him in Paris in the wake of the Revolution, and was so struck by him there is some suggestion that Stewart might have been the mysterious Double referred to by Wordsworth in *The Prelude*. It is as if Stewart's spectre was haunting Wordsworth during his walks in the Lake District and the West Country, imploring him to personify the spirit of nature as an eternally recurrent force, sufficient unto itself and manifesting in all the transient forms of beauty, mystery and terror, that surrounded him in the remote regions of the landscape. The textual evidence for this may be tenuous, but prophets were said to possess the power to make their voices sound in people's heads long after they had fallen silent, and Stewart's hypnotic intensity was widely attested to. If it is true however, then Stewart can be said in a sense to have provided some, if not much, of the inspiration for one of the very greatest poems in the English language, which isn't bad for an otherwise almost totally forgotten figure! And in fact he was no mean poet himself, in addition to being a self-styled philosopher-king and Lord of the Earth in a Post-Enlightenment World of the purest and headiest kinds of freedom. *The Harp of Apollo* is today entirely unread, I think it's safe to say. Though anyone taking the trouble to read it at The British Library could readily think it worthy of any of the more celebrated Romantics of his day. It's difficult to know quite what to compare it with, as Stewart's voice was so distinctive it contrasted very clearly and sharply with that of Keats, which was more dreamy and lyrical; or Byron, which was more loftily patrician; or Shelley, which was more stridently radical; or Coleridge, which was more religiously mystical; or even Blake, which was more mythically Pagan. Stewart uncannily combined a ruthless application of Occam's Razor with a cosmic generosity of Spirit, manifesting in a visionary overflow of the Human into the realms of the Non-Human—or what I would call a Great Hymning in the Choir of the Faithless.

He never lost sight of the fact that Apollo, like any other god, and God himself, was no more than an Anthropomorphic device. And yet as he turned it on its head, he also invoked something else, something New, which adumbrated a Sphere of the Faculties that was neither scientific nor religious—nor merely symbolic. And this was truly Revolutionary. Sophiometry may be a good word to designate such a Sphere, derived from Stewart's own method of acquiring moral and spiritual wisdom—the Sophiometer. Instinctive Spinozism is another apposite expression for describing Stewart's whole manner of engaging with the world, in the sense of his seeing and grasping the Continuum between Mankind and Nature that makes a Transcendent God superfluous. Whilst matter is mobilized by energy, the twin-modality in the one Substance of life. This isn't Pantheism or Pandeism, since no God or gods are involved. But it is a kind of Essentialism, like the breath of life or even the Holy Spirit, recast as a sort of Gnostic glue binding every part of the Whole together. Yet ultimately, the one Substance or Essence is material. So in Spinozistic terms, Stewart was a materialistic Monist for whom the life of the universe was energistic rather than spiritual. He anticipated Vitalism—which was later rejected by Darwin. But perhaps Einstein's matter-energy equation could be said to have come to Stewart's aid in a sense, over-riding the older Vitalism-Mechanism dispute in Biology. Mechanistic Determinism is too reductionist and simplistic as a model for the whole of life, and Stewart had an intuitive understanding of this over a century before Einstein *et al* smashed the clockwork universe.

Organisms were far more complex than mechanisms, being vibrationally attuned to one another, even across evolutionary gaps. They emerged and developed in accordance with musical principles first and foremost, that could be understood philosophically, poetically, and even energistically, as well as mathematically and scientifically. Stewart revived the Atomist Philosophy of the Ancient Greeks, especially Democritus, but with a new twist: the atomic clusters, of which organisms and things in general were composed, were life-forms in themselves, possessed of a corresponding consciousness that undeveloped humans were not attuned to. And these clusters might not have a finite end, which suggests that Stewart intuited the infinitesimal minutiae of the sub-atomic realms, like a prophesier of Quantum Physics! Consciousness was built into the very integuments of the whole Fabric of Creation itself—orchestrating the Continuum of Life that runs through Nature. This was a startlingly radical and original idea, which few philosophers even nowadays would be at all keen to entertain. The idea that a stone e.g. may be conscious, invites ridicule in Academic Philosophy circles. Yet it may not be quite as absurdly far-fetched as the smug guardians of logic-chopping conceptual correctness automatically tend to assume. If we cannot yet explain how we humans have come by what we generally take to be our shared gift of consciousness, by a converse token how can we explain that something we regard as inanimate comes by its inanimateness in the first place? The fact is, we just do not know what consciousness is; in which case if it exists at all we can't say what exactly its parameters are, in terms of where it is present or absent in the hierarchy of entities comprising all that there is. The atoms which make up a stone may well have a conscious life of their own that we are not directly privy to in our own habitual modes of consciousness.

Yet there may equally be some way of adjusting our own consciousness to that of entities we somewhat arbitrarily take to be totally inferior to us in the overall scheme of things. Is a stone inferior to us, simply because it cannot communicate its nature to us in some way we comprehend? Is it not just different to us, and yet self-sufficient in its apparently limited complexity of structure? Perhaps we should envy a stone, for not being more like it in terms of an existential satisfaction with our being simply what we are. Instead, we are profoundly existentially dissatisfied with our failure to become what we more or less continuously strive to be! It may even be to a stone's existential advantage that it is in a sense more satisfiedly self-complete than we are in its resolute stoneness! Readers may think I'm just being facetious here. But in all seriousness I'm not, for it may not matter one jot that a stone doesn't appear to do calculus or compose symphonies, etc. when it's all too busily engaged in being just a stone rather than something else, inhabiting a separateness of its own that requires no hierarchical comparison with any other. This is a very slippery, elusive way of thinking, to try and get our human heads around. But short of our ontologically merging with a stone, it may be the best means of developing a proper cosmic modesty in our relationships with things that share in the entire scope of existence with us. We don't have to expect a stone to converse with us in the best English or whatnot to undertake a thought-experiment in which we try to correct our routine habit of missing out on how a stone aggregates its position in the plurality of phenomena. Such an experiment may very well test to the limit our capacity for mental penetration, and yet at the same time not be a *prima facie* absurd approach to such a seemingly incomprehensible and incommensurable cousin in contiguity. And it's only a short step up The Great Chain of Being from a stone to a cow—Stewart's favourite animal! Cows are often caricatured by us sapient snobs as inveterately stupid and useless creatures—fit only for cud-chewing, fly-swatting, and stewing in their own pastoral stink, not to mention providing us all with a handy, if shameless, at any rate from a vegetarian standpoint, source of food! But they also display a kind of effortless insouciance, a serene magnificence in being so contentedly embedded in their own sublimely fulfilled form of life, an almost Buddhic enlightened indifference to effort and purpose that can only derive from a consciousness of being complete, of their not needing to be anything more than everything they already are, that ought to fill us with awe rather than prompt us to derision. And I am certain it was this quality in cows that Stewart responded to, impelling him to engage with the creatures in a kind of energistic Communion whenever he encountered them. And he was of course totally unafraid of other people thinking him eccentric or mad on these occasions. Far from being totally inferior to humans on the basis of their simpler anatomies, cows had one advantage over us in view of their almost spiritual composure in the face of natural fate—which was something we could learn and benefit from if only we could live in a more integrated way within the natural world.

Existentialists and Phenomenologists have in the main regarded humans as being in the world, but not of it. Stewart would certainly have agreed with the first part of this statement—and who would not?—but not with the second part. Humans might be more advanced than animals in terms of language and thought. But our whole consciousness was on the same spectrum as that of animals—and that of the entire organic material universe. So we had no right to regard ourselves as special or privileged or unique. We were the latest outcome of the continuous process of cosmic evolution—no more, and no less. And of course we may not be the final outcome, if the pioneers of artificial biology and intelligence are correct in their prediction that living synthetic machines will one day supersede the human race. Stewart might have baulked at this notion—living as he did in the very earliest stages of the Industrial Revolution, which he had scant regard for it seems. But that human beings could evolve further in some direction at least, preferably a moral and spiritual one, vouchsafed by the self-stirred enhancement of consciousness and thought, he had no doubt. This may beg the question as to how exactly consciousness could meaningfully be said to be raised, as the hippies would put it! But it isn't necessarily a matter of applying one separate part of the mind to another part and exerting a measurable influence. It's more like a kind of willed and willing immersion of the mental faculties in the stream of consciousness as a whole. Raised consciousness equates to a penetration of Being, a heightened, sharpened sense of the hidden essence of phenomena.

In the above sense, Stewart was a precursor of the Phenomenologists, in stressing the positive as opposed to the negative aspects of Existence, or the fulsome and sensuous reality of nature grounding the exercise of our more abstract cognition. The mind was a truly Holistic entity for him, in tandem with the greater Totality of Being. And the study of phenomena had a purpose that transcended science and common sense, philosophically weaving the disparate parts of the natural and human worlds into an organismic unity. And the Self—or the Subject—played a very important role in this whole process for Stewart. He reckoned we all assembled our Selves like universal pictures, creating and combining elements from the psychic soup of our Being and corralling them into the conscious shapes we then carried with us through the world—like experiential muscles we exercised increasingly at will, along the interstices of the Not-Conscious and the Not-Self. Whether we were at source *tabulae rasae* or lattice networks of innate categories intrigued him far less than the actions we performed with the swirling, semi-unpossessed matter of Self in the motion of our minds. We had to conceive the purpose for all this activity, which may or may not cohere or correspond with some inbuilt Teleological end. We had to think to some purpose—and in so doing pull our Selves up by our, to use a modern term, Synergizing bootstraps. Whether the Self was discovered or created was less important than how one engaged with, or utilized it, in pursuing the goals and ideals of one's philosophy of life.

Very few philosophers—even Socrates—have lived in quite the way or to the extent that Stewart did. This might not always matter of course, at any rate in a purely technical sense, as one could be an intellectual genius and scarcely ever venture out of one's hovel! But if Stewart's Experientialist Philosophy is truly well-founded, as I believe, then the whole manner in which he actually lived is of crucial relevance and importance to it. Time and Space for him were not the boxed dominions summed up in Benjamin Franklin's pithy Mantra for nascent mercantile capitalism: Time is money. Stewart insisted on being a free agent unshackled from social convention and economic constraint, by virtue of literally 'walking the world' on his own without so much as a horse for company, somehow surviving on the material generosity of those he encountered who were no doubt struck by his complementary spiritual generosity. This in a sense made him a kind of pauper-prophet, only with one difference: he was not seeking to found a religion, but to end all religions! If he sought disciples at all, it was only by way of passionate encouragement to find their own way to an enlightened clarity of vision and purpose. The Collective was only a vehicle for the Individual as such, and just so long as individuals proved themselves capable of civilized conduct, they could be entrusted with total freedom of thought and action, ungoverned by oppressive political systems. And once this emancipation was enjoined, whole new worlds of life-altering experience and visionary imagination were opened up to them. As such, Stewart was an intensely unorthodox Apostle of the Enlightenment.

He stood completely at odds with a society in revolutionary transition, a true Outsider in his spirit and outlook, who militated equally against the tyranny of Rule and the tyranny of Revolt, by embodying the Exemplar of the illuminated Individual, the 'man of nature' in a world that turned its back on nature by extolling stale custom or new-fangled, half-baked nonsensicalities. The new Type of Human Society in the Stewart mould, should be small, simple, organic, harmonious, based on agriculture, arts and crafts, barter and co-operation. Self-governing regional Assemblies should run communities, devolving powers and minimizing laws. When people's economic needs are met, then all their social, cultural, creative, intellectual, moral and spiritual desires and aims should be pursued and cultivated without let or hindrance. No Powers should mediate in these processes, as individuals should decide for themselves how to progress without needing to compete against each other by way of one-upmanship or to live out their lives in some framework of externally enforced collaboration. He was an early example of a libertarian anarchist, albeit possessed of a great zeal for an individual-cum-collective improvement and elevation. And Anarchism has always been a perfect philosophy for an Outsider, with its emphasis on self-sufficiency and voluntary mutual aid. It has never been as chaotic or confused as its opponents maintain, being concerned with the practicalities of ordering social life in such a way as to maximise individual autonomy, which assuredly must be the most desirable aim of humanity on its own behalf. It doesn't have to be violent, and it could be feasible if it were ever allowed to be tried, and enough people were willing to make a concerted effort to that end.

Prince Kropotkin was perhaps the model-Anarchist: peaceable, rational and benevolent. Utopias would be achieved if people were prepared to go the extra distance in terms of actively and continuously committing themselves to the realization of essentially practical ideals. Though this certainly demands a very great deal of people, it doesn't fundamentally contradict the tendencies inherent in human nature, but rather insists on their being pushed beyond comfortable norms in order to establish that which is in the highest and best interests of each and all of us. And the status-quo is always the result of our lazily and self-satisfiedly settling for a very imperfect approximation of that goal, which we can confuse with brute, unchangeable reality. Exploitation and oppression become standard practices in societies that are to some extent rigidly stratified and less preoccupied with individual freedom than with state-security. Socio-economic classes may or may not develop conspiratorially. But each generation is born into a pre-existing trap that requires collective loosening of the boundaries, to emancipate individual members. And this goes far beyond so-called social mobility, which is a professional concept only. What is at issue is self-determination, which should take place at a far more fundamental level than that of bourgeois possessive individualism, in which 'having one's little acre' defines the extent of one's individual freedom. Each of us should determine the very nature of our relationship to the land, property, occupation, society and others, before we can consider ourselves in any truly meaningful sense free.

Outsiders may not be able to change the conditions of life in the ways they envision, given the enormous repugnant forces arraigned against them. But they are in some senses uniquely well-placed to exert their integral influence on people with an absolute directness, like ingénues who miss the point of the conversation going on around them because their attention is fixed on another far more penetrating point, that they will not conceal because they lack all guile. Stewart was such an Outsider, who not only saw that the Emperor had no clothes, but also and above all that in a truly open society there would be no Emperor in the first place, naked or otherwise. In his inimitable, officially unacknowledged way, he sounded the clarion-call for a revolution in human consciousness, and as such laid the foundation for an entire philosophical system, that would lie pretty well dormant in many parts of the world before being developed further by Stewart's spiritual successors, as it were. Albert Camus was one of these figures. And in his work for the first time the word 'Outsider' entered the language as a philosophical category of referent. *L'Etranger* is of course famous to generations of English schoolboys—and girls too no doubt!—as an A-Level set text, which I myself remember studying at school. Though I don't know if it's still studied today. I'd rather doubt it, for at the risk of outrageous arrogance on my part, it seems to me young people scarcely read anything nowadays, apart from the odd *Wikipedia* print-out—which does not of course stop them being showered with piles of straight A's like meaningless confetti or sweets from a charlatan-conjuror! But this is not the place to launch into a full-scale attack on mal-education.

Not that I intend here to rehash an earnest adolescent essay with good marks in mind, but to enlarge on the themes of the famous novel with a view to situating Camus within a wider and larger body of thinking about the potential or otherwise of detachment, in the mind and spirit of what since Marx and Sartre may be called Alienated Man. As well as *The Outsider*, Camus wrote *The Rebel*, a philosophical exposition and defence of the various different strategies and ideologies adopted by the estranged and embattled throughout history. But the Anti-Hero of *The Outsider* is not strictly speaking a rebel, because he is way too passive and remote in his inner desolation to even attempt any sort of struggle against his own predicament, let alone the condition of wider society. He is a quietly malign enigma, going through the motions of life without really feeling anything for anybody, yet doing nothing to draw others' attention to himself. He is an absence, an emptiness that haunts and subtly disturbs all those he comes into contact with. He is obviously a pathological case psychologically, but Camus hints at the deeper Existential mainsprings of his pathology, and thereby elevates the book beyond the plane of mere psychoanalysis, suggesting that an otherwise ordinary person can be truly freakish in the extreme. Rather than attempting to explain his motives, in terms of some reductionistic and simplistic over-arching theory, Camus shows through his depiction of the character the ineffably mysterious and maybe ultimately inexplicable depths of incommunicable turmoil in a spiritually totally unanchored member of the human race. And this phenomenon had never really been essayed before in Fiction, or certainly not in the same manner.

Meursault, the infamous anti-hero of the novel, felt nothing at his mother's funeral, viewing it as an inevitable coda to a meaningless life, that affected him no more than the death of anybody else—or even an insect, blood-ties notwithstanding. There was no place for feelings of pathos, when everything that everyone else held dear was as transient as blown fluff on gusts of wind. He didn't hate or even dislike his mother. She had done all she could to help him and inspire his affection. But he still couldn't summon from within himself even the seed of a solid and enduring feeling for another Being, who was so distant and eternally out of reach, they might just as well not exist at all. It was as if Existence conspired to separate each individual from all others in an absolute vacuum of Being, an illusion of connexion that was negated by isolation. This ontological rupture could not be healed or even combated, and so there was simply no point or purpose in feeling, or rather affecting, to feel anything—especially for others. Although Meursault did not try to concretize his fragmentary philosophy in writing, being the narrator of his own tale, he wrestled constantly with ideas drawn from disparate sources, and so qualified as a kind of intellectual Outsider. But he really dissipated his intellect in endless morbid self-interrogations which ultimately led him nowhere. The great anomaly of his existence was that he was at one critical moment suddenly impelled to commit a murder. This action so contradicted the inherent passivity of his entire animus that it seemed completely absurd. And indeed that was precisely what it was, an *acte gratuite*, that didn't even succeed in galvanizing him out of his lifelessness. On the contrary, it only landed him in terminal trouble, on the inevitable path towards execution.

The fact that the murder was also committed out of revenge still didn't alter the utter senselessness of it, within the overall pattern of his otherwise inert if obscurely troubled life. He was in part a creature of the turmoil of his era, a philosophically eviscerated fall-guy for the fathomless foundations of the Zeitgeist. Doubtless we would have to say nowadays that he was not 'wired up' neurologically like other—or most other—people, being constitutionally cut off from the roots of human empathy and compassion. Camus gave this interpretation no real consideration, if only because it wasn't yet on the map scientifically, and went against the grain of anti-Deterministic philosophical schools of thought, such as Existentialism. The background to the murder involves Arab-French mutual distrust in Algiers: a French friend of Meursault suspects his Arab girlfriend of infidelity and Meursault agrees to compose a break-up letter on his behalf. Later on, they encounter the girl's brother and an Arab friend on a beach, a fight ensues, and Meursault's friend Raymond is stabbed. Meursault takes a pistol from Raymond, to prevent him from retaliating. He returns to the beach alone, where he spots the Arab, then simply shoots him dead five times. He later explains this not in terms of his personal loyalty to his friend, but rather the effect of the heat on his senses. It was just an impulsive act, that needed no justification in the overall scheme of things. It was like an attempt to energize himself out of his ennui, which still failed. However, he was not so sensorily inert that no woman could ever excite his passion, since he was sexually involved with a girl at the time of the murder. He seemed to see his only salvation in the love of a stranger transcending the embrace of the mother-figure, which was cruelly denied him in the tragically senseless turn of events that overtook him. Yet he had no expectation of this love being requited or fulfilled in a meaningful manner, as there is no meaning in life, and so such an expectation would be futile. It was no more nor less than a random infatuation that may or may not have grown or lasted—it didn't matter either way. He took refuge in the Absurdist Philosophy that provided him with no real comfort or solace, but allowed and enabled him to articulate the endless evaporating nullity of everything, so he could derive some succour at least from his superior insight into the inveterate misery of existence.

So what kind of Outsider exactly is Meursault? And why should we take him seriously as one among a number of fictional prototypes challenging our way of thinking about the human condition within more orthodox traditions? He is principally a philosophical creation by Camus with autobiographical elements, since Camus' background was French-Algerian and working-class, and he felt alienated from both the ethnic Arab and colonial French communities during his adolescence. But he was precociously intelligent, able to articulate his own estrangement in psychological-cum-philosophical as well as nationalistic-cum-racial terms. He was also physically tough, needing to release his energies on the Football field instead of on the streets with knives and guns, which he did, thereby avoiding serious trouble with the Law. So Meursault is like a version of Camus, an alter-ego, who fails to resolve his existential crisis through work and friendship and writing, and as a result of a terrible accident falls prey to a fate that might well have befallen Camus himself, if his life at some point had suddenly lurched onto a criminally destructive trajectory. But his intelligence and thirst for education and the company of European Intelligentsia saved him from such a fate. And in an authorial capacity he was able to put thoughts into the mind of Meursault as narrator which Meursault on his own might not have been capable of even entertaining. Yet this slight incongruity doesn't detract to any serious degree from the power and authenticity of the unfolding tragedy in the story. If there was something essentially arbitrary in the contingency of the murder committed by Meursault, there is something repugnantly inexorable in the corresponding, counteracting contingency of his execution. And all the philosophizing in the world could not save him from his cruel, yet authorized fate. Of course, on the face of it there is nothing especially remarkable about a man being executed for a murder that he could very easily not have committed, in a country where life may not be held dear, but punishment is its own rationale.

Meursault was less an Outsider from choice and cultivation than from his own constitutional make-up and circumstance. He was an Outsider of the perplexed and tragic type, who can make no sense of anything or anybody, and probably therefore was doomed in a sense to be precipitated at some critical point onto a destructive, and self-destructive, course with a pointlessly terrible end, after failing to fulfil whatever talent and promise he had. But above all, he failed to connect in any deep, true or lasting way with anybody else, including his own mother, his girlfriend, and his best male friend—even himself, never mind any notional God. And he could not articulate his thoughts so well that like Camus the author, he could succeed in writing books. And Camus' Autobiographical identification with Meursault probably ended not only at the point of death, be it murder or execution, but also at the point of intimacy, be it sex or friendship or love. For I think we can safely assume that Camus himself was not a pathologically dehumanised person in the way that his creation, Meursault, undoubtedly was. It is unlikely that he could have written the novel, with its necessary authorial detachment and putative objectivity, if he had been. But he was sufficiently imaginatively aware of such possible propensities within himself to be able to summon them vicariously in fleshing out the inner demons that plagued Meursault, and which may have plagued him had he been less homeostatically balanced, or less plain fortunate in the way in which his life and career played out. Camus had a capacity for Passion, which Meursault was not truly capable of. And Camus' Passion made him a kind of Romantic Existentialist, which to my mind was a curious contradiction-in-terms, or veritable paradox, since Existent-ialism was really a dead-end philosophy, whereas Romanticism strove to transcend and supersede the seemingly intractable limits, boundaries and surdness of Existence. Unless Existence can be charged with the energies of life itself, then it reduces everything to the gravitational graveyard of extinct matter, the nucleus of negation itself. And though there may be no rationale, or greater rationale, for passion or positiveness, it is an option that any non-pathological person would surely choose and prefer, if only for the sheer hell of doing so.

Meursault is interesting and important in Literature, because he is a classic test-case of what it is for a person to fail totally at the human level: to be so inwardly detached from human feelings and responses as to be in a sense non-human, or even anti-human. As such, he provides the acid-test of compassion, and a case-study in negation, the negation of all that most humans strive for. He embodies Anathema for normal humanity, and yet for all that he repels he also fascinates. It is difficult for many people to even believe or imagine that such a person can actually exist. But Camus' creation—like Wilson's after him—triggered readers' 'Inner Outsider' so to speak, and they all jumped on the Alienated bandwagon, discovering or inventing similarities between themselves and what Camus and Wilson were able to articulate and analyze so presciently in their work. Though they were only really drawn to a character like Meursault because of their romanticized image of the man as a privileged Pariah-figure with a superior insight into the human condition. His pain, in its truer aspect, was not in all honesty so attractive to them, or not if they had the misfortune to suffer it themselves. And his fate was certainly not attractive to them, unless they were masochistic to the point of martyrdom. And Meursault's masochism was so deep that his response to police interrogation after the killing was one of near-total self-incrimination, at least in so far as it was pre-meditated. Though there is tragic irony in the fact that at times his consciousness becomes so transient that he is not aware of any motive, good or bad, that he may have had—revenge, for a start!—or of any impulse to care about this one way or the other. His indifference to the news of his mother's death, combined with his paradoxically illogical or ingenuously truthful insistence on the heat being the main causal factor behind his action, seal his fate on the guillotine as surely as that of an Aristocrat brought before the Revolutionary Tribunal in the Reign of Terror—with nothing to declare but his status! His philosophy doesn't help him here any more than obscene gestures or violent assaults. But he is truly past caring at this point, and we have to ask ourselves if there is anything for us to admire in him that might justify the absurd cult that he or rather Camus engendered through his example, intentionally or otherwise.

I have to say at this juncture that Meursault is not a favourite Outsider of mine, because he fundamentally wastes his life in stupid speculations, idiotic actions, and shameless exculpations. His philosophy is essentially a rather shallow prop to conceal and disguise his emptiness, and his twisted sub-human monstrosity. He borrows ideas from many sources, like an obsessive magpie, without really digesting them, nor testing them in anything other than a randomly capricious, casually nihilistic, manner. He is only interesting in so far as he is a grotesque freak, but one who for the most part, until the killing, is too passive and meek to even draw attention to himself. He would be more interesting if he'd killed many people and had then defied Justice with his own ingenious defense. But he had neither the courage, nor probably the wits, to do that. Instead he merely resigned himself to destiny with a shrug and a sigh. He is more a pathetic than a bathetic figure, like a low-lying demon in Camus' unconscious, which Camus had to wrestle with and banish in the exorcism of the novel. And so he, Camus, could then go on to achieve greater things, having earned this right through his self-deliverance from the fanciful weaknesses and morbid sensitivities of youth. And his own philosophy developed thereafter in a far more fruitful fashion than had been promised by the twin dead-ends of the meaningless and the gratuitous. Whilst recognizing that the foundations of value and purpose in human life are in a sense arbitrary, shifting, subjective and relative; in choosing positive rather than negative values, and then committing himself to them, he was giving himself the chance at least of achieving more, and indeed much more, than he otherwise would. And in the process, he would be adding to, rather than subtracting from, the sum-total of human knowledge, understanding and progress. It might always be possible to question the point of such an outlook, as the Meursault in Camus did, but it's just as possible to question the point of questioning the point of that, or anything else—and so on *ad infinitum*. So this sort of tail-swallowing scepticism is actually no more philosophically privileged than staking our claim to any Existential territory so to speak, with a bold, adventurous assertion.

So Meursault is in this context, a stepping-stone—if a significant one—to larger destinations on the map and journey of a true Outsider. He is the troubled talent who fails to record his dilemmas, and falls by the wayside of cruel contingency. Camus on the other hand, is the far stronger, more stable and resolute other half of Meursault, who eclipses his own alter-ego creation and then goes on to shine in the French intellectual and cultural elites, befriending Sartre, and winning the Nobel Prize for Literature—excelling *L'Etranger* with *La Peste*, and *The Rebel*. It is also questionable in what sense Camus himself could be called an Outsider. He was socially well-integrated, attractive to women, and entirely sane. He may have had as profound an understanding of the plight and mentality of Outsiders as anybody, but this was acquired more from a capacity for objective distancing and analytical penetration than from his empathetic identification. In a word, he was simply too 'normal' a human being to be regarded as an Outsider, certainly in a psychological sense, and his work, undeniably great in parts, justly belongs to the 'insider' mainstream canonical tradition more than to the 'outsider' field, as does Sartre's. But the ideas he developed after *L'Etranger* have to my mind, a far profounder relevance to the theme of what may be termed the 'successful' as opposed to the 'failed' Outsider. Meursault was certainly a 'failed' Outsider, but the historical, prototype 'Rebel' figures later examined by Camus were anything but. Even if they failed to achieve their overriding aims in reality—and by no means all of them did—each one of them strove ceaselessly to be, in Baudelaire's words, 'a Saint by one's own standards.' But one could, in some cases, substitute the word 'Sinner' for 'Saint'—or for that matter, Genius, or Creator, or Hero, or Seer, or even Pariah, as Outsiders are rarely Saints, and Baudelaire was maybe being perversely paradoxical in his own case. But what a Saint has in common with an Outsider is an almost fanatical preparedness to be extreme, or to do extreme things, in order to enlarge Man's capacity for Transcendence, whether in a religious sense or in some other sense of the word altogether.

Camus' Rebels were people from many walks of life—Philosophy, Literature, Art, Politics, etc.—who were waging wars of ideas and ideals and passions inside their own heads against the world. They despised authority and power in all their forms, and were warriors not in the military sense, but the poetic and revolutionary senses. They fought for the triumph of the Individual over Hierarchy, and even the Collective where it subordinated rather than emancipated the Individual. They were marked out by an almost innate singularity and contrariety, which they became conscious of at a very young age, and which propelled them into conflict with the entire status-quo that was arraigned against them: the ossified detritus of history and tradition propping up the controlling classes above the more or less cowed heads of the vast mass of humanity. This paradigm can shift periodically in different societies, but it remains essentially the same everywhere: a great piggish pecking-order of those who strive to lord it over everyone else, instead of properly refusing power to pave the way for a truly free and open society, in which every individual is fundamentally equal. And Rebels living in different times and different societies have found themselves confronted by all the Hydra-headed manifestations of this Molochian Form or Nietzschean 'monster' of the Corporate State, and have fought very similar battles, albeit with different intellectual and physical weapons, to try and overhaul this Hypertrophic Behemoth, and then substitute a more or less practical Utopia of their own—with pretty mixed results! Cobbett's word for the Establishment, famously, was 'The Thing', a powerfully evocative, albeit strikingly simple epithet for the bewilderingly complex, and seemingly overwhelming, machinery of human suppression and alienation, replete with associations of a horrible, unnatural entity, looming over the heads of humanity. For Marx, this phenomenon corresponded to the outward form of men's unrestrained desire to exploit and oppress each other through the formation of socio-economic classes. And Camus' Rebels were, from their earliest experience, affronted by the total injustice, and sheer unnecessity, of such a structure assuming a central predominance in the conduct of human affairs.

Camus draws a distinction in *The Rebel* between rebels and revolutionaries, suggesting that rebels are like the Romantics of radical movements, utopian idealists whose practical efforts usually, if not invariably, evaporate away in small-scale riots and uprisings, that lack organization and a specific purpose. They are the libertarian anarchists as opposed to the authoritarian socialists, who end up like Lenin's 'useful idiots' or 'Leftists with infantile disorders'. However, Camus sought to extract everything of positive value in their often brilliant visions of human possibility, and then ally this with more pragmatic progressive movements. The revolutionaries may have been more successful in their opposition historically. But once they have acquired power, in nearly every case they have been corrupted by it and betrayed their original ideals. So what purported to be a great communistic emancipation of mankind just became a vile totalitarian tyranny over it. Enemies of Radicalism would say that this was always inevitable, due to the ineradicable complexity of human nature and behaviour, and that top-down hierarchies are the unavoidable by-products of our socio-biological programming as a species. Therefore, if any attempt is made to 'correct' the errors of a revolution in a re-run, this smacks of a wilful, also wicked, blindness to the fundamental facts and laws of life, and a totally immoral regard for the human sacrifice incurred in the process. Against this, Radicals have said that the sum-total of carnage and suffering in human history, under all the hierarchical regimes of antiquity, feudalism, asian despotism and capitalism, not to mention tribalism and theocracy, has completely dwarved that occurring during revolutions, which have always been motivated by a profound desire to create an enduring peace in human society, underpinning the progress and prosperity in which all can share.

Camus' resolution of this dilemma involved placing a special emphasis on the role of the Individual in collective society, counterbalancing the power of the State, through the exercise of freedom and autonomy, and Humanist Ethics. Egalitarianism is not incompatible with Difference, and the organic unity and harmony of large, complex societies such as ours isn't necessarily threatened or ruined by excellence. This is a seemingly impossible circle to square, but Camus thought that the balance of forces playing out their combinations and permutations through history definitely favoured or tipped towards benevolent rather than malign outcomes for at least the vast majority of mankind. This might seem to be contradicted by the accumulated weight of evidences drawn from different periods in different societies. But the rewards of Time eventually endorse more of an optimistic than a pessimistic philosophical outlook. And the very persistence of Life itself in all its rich and insatiable diversity surely testifies to this naturally assumed belief. For Camus, Man is not 'a useless passion' in Sartre's cynical dead-end phrase, but a persevering and ultimately prevailing life-form or creature, driven to point the Existential scales at hope and away from despair. Perhaps there is an in-built Telos that commands such a deep and fundamental attitude in all of us—partly found in Evolution itself, and also in the superior mechanisms of the brain and the inner directives of consciousness. The fact that all of us, or very nearly all of us, cling to life with every last fibre of our Being when confronted by death, might be adduced as the most telling evidence there is of our inherent bias in valuing positive states of Being over negative ones.

Camus' Rebels were therefore, first and foremost, inspired by creative acts, which may or may not involve destructive elements as well. Sweeping away the dead wood of a rotten social system is a creative act, because it releases the potential for advancement that is blocked by our imprisonment in an outmoded way of life. So a violent response to it stems from a healthy impulse towards self-enlargement. Although our politics lacks this crucial dimension if it is not also an Art. Thus revolutions call for the kind of spontaneous and imaginative ingenuity that takes authority or the powers-that-be by surprise. But this almost invariably involves crossing the boundary between civil disobedience and criminality, for laws are primarily made to protect those very institutions and practices that revolutionaries aim to overhaul and supersede. So at a critical point a clash of forces becomes inevitable. And Rebels might lack the disciplined organization of revolutionaries, but they can provide the spark of insurrection that revolutionaries feed on to power their strategies to victory. So there was a crucial Dialectic between them for Camus. However, Rebels can also be creative in realms outside politics, like in art or writing or thought—or even sex. And the striking originality of their creative outputs in these realms is characteristic of the genius of Outsiders. Camus admired unreservedly these types of Outsider, who seek to recreate the world anew and in their own image. But he also preferred to see Diderot's 'thousand flowers bloom', so as to prevent the solipsistic equivalent of a fascist autarky, which might literally result from just one man's vision being imposed on the world. Hitler and Stalin were such autarkists—if at opposite ends of the ideological spectrum. Yet they were arch-enemies of Rebel-Outsiders, crushing anarchy in all its forms, even though both men were lone mavericks with profoundly unorthodox visions and methods. If they had not been so ruthlessly successful in eradicating deviation, they might have become no more—and no less—than artists, writers and even philosophers of a sort. But cynics may say that Hitler could only have become a half-competent house-painter, and Stalin a dreary minute-keeper! Yet this would have saved tens of millions of lives.

Camus concentrated primarily on political, philosophical and literary Rebels, who attempted, vainly or otherwise, to change the course of history or create new paradigms of human thought. But there have also been Rebel-scientists, mathematicians, engineers, technologists, inventors, and entrepreneurs, who have very broadly fitted into the Outsider-categories too. Rebelliousness has not been solely the preserve of those with an Arts bent shall we say, nor Outsiderdom neither. There have been many people of a highly eccentric and intransigent character, whose gifts have been very much science-based. Often it's supposed that such people must be totally sanguine in their temperament and attitude, being so governed by the Dictates of Reason in their work. But nothing could be further from the truth. Scientists, being as human as anyone else, can be utterly irrational and violently obsessive and world-hating, even in their dogged belief in the sanctity of Reason itself. Nietzsche reminded us that Reason is only a tool, not an ideal or the sure guide from above in everything we think, say and do. And it is quite possible to have an irrational conception of the nature, functions and limits—or limitlessness, as the case may be—of Reason, in being some sort of Rationalist. In fact, it might actually be far more rational, or reasonable at any rate, to be an irrationalist rather than a rationalist, at least in certain contexts or universes of discourse. In affairs of the heart or in the realms of the

Unconscious, this is undeniably true. And if the tenets of chaos-theory are valid, then the universe is not ordered in such a way as to be neatly predictable and controllable or coherently patterned in accordance with purely rational/logical laws and principles. And the cleverest scientists, and mathematicians and philosophers, have always known, or had an inkling, of this fundamental truth. So it isn't perhaps pure rationality that marks out the superior scientists, but instead a far more elusive capacity for highly unusual, often counter-intuitive and non-commonsensical modes of thinking, which people of a Rebel-Outsider bent often tend to excel at.

Newton, for all his pioneering efforts in physics, astronomy, cosmology and optics, as well as mathematics and geometry, also retained a strong belief in and compulsive fascination with astrology, alchemy, magic, numerology and the esoteric symbolism of the Bible, which he reckoned was ultimately more important than his scientific work, as he never once doubted the existence of a Supreme God who ordered the hidden clockwork machinery of the cosmos. On several occasions he had mental breakdowns as a result of his obsessive delvings into the Arcana of these ancient disciplines, which other men of the Enlightenment like Bacon, Locke and Hooke, regarded as mere superstitious nonsense of a lower category than Religion. Yet are we to say now, even with the benefit of several centuries' hindsight, that the greatest genius of his time with the possible exception of Leibnitz, who developed a weird metaphysical system of his own, was wrong about all these matters, and the lesser lights of that time were right? I am not certain we even know quite how to answer this question yet, and might never be able to do so conclusively. But of one thing I am certain: Newton was a pre-eminent Outsider in his cast of mind and his austerely solitary way of life and habits. He was also a Rebel in the sense of revolutionizing science and philosophy, and along with Leibnitz created the Infinitesimal Calculus—which is part of the bedrock of mathematics today. And if he had been a poet, he would have written in a vein as dark as Dante, belonging as he did to the mysterious 'School of Night', which Marlowe and many other grey, or not so grey, eminences did before him. This very secret, shadowy Brotherhood comprised people drawn to the dark arts—not only of govn't, espionage and intelligence, but of esoteric influence or manipulation as well. Such societies always draw Outsiders, who are also on the Inside.

Madness is not the preserve of artistic Outsider-Rebels either. For Cantor, the inventor of the Transfinite Calculus, went mad through the proliferation of his Alephs, and the death of his son; Godel briefly went mad, trying to solve the Continuum Hypothesis; Klammerer, another maths wizard, took his own life; John Nash is a schizophrenic; Charles Babbage, the father of computers and inventor of the Analytical Difference Engine or Calculating Machine, was a maverick supremo constantly raving against idiot-bureaucrats and politicians and academics and businessmen: 'Confound them! I am a philosopher!' And the list goes on, crackpot scientists being as familiar to us as mad poets, and exemplified of course in the fictional Frankenstein. And they could certainly be added to the ranks of Camus' Rebel-Outsiders, for whom Existence is an obstacle to be confronted rather than denied, while Life is to be embraced in all its contradictoriness of challenge and enticement. But suicide is the great sticking-point, and Divide. Camus' most enigmatic statement of all was that 'Suicide is the fundamental problem of philosophy.' I never quite understood what he meant by this when I was a student, but my take on it now would be that it addresses the whole issue of choice: the freedom to live or die—'to be or not to be, that is the question.'—and the courage to face up to Reality, of which, in T.S. Eliot's famous words, 'Humankind cannot bear too much.' It is only secondarily, if at all, about people's rights to commit suicide, in view of its being traditionally considered a sin. Camus detached the issue from the grip of religious morality, proclaiming the refusal of suicide to be a triumph of the human spirit over the abysmal terror of the Existential Void. Suicide is a cop-out in other words, a failure to get a grip on ourselves, even though we should not be denied the freedom to commit it, nor be condemned to eternal damnation for doing so. But we are all prey to some degree of weakness.

The truly strong Outsider-Rebels may be tempted by the thought of suicide, whether in an abstract or a deeper personal way, and even semi-driven to it in some cases. But they find some reserve of inner conviction that pulls them back from the brink of oblivion. And oblivion, like the sleep of Nepenthe, is intoxicatingly attractive to those people who know all too well the anguish of ontological separation from others, and even from themselves, the nausea of the rudderless Ship of Self on the bleak ocean of evanescent insubstantiality. It is the final plunging release from the dreary perpetuity of existential pain. But those who also know their own special human and creative worth shall find a means of resisting this fatal choice. And what therefore does not kill them—to paraphrase Nietzsche—will make them stronger than they already are. There is a feeling in such people that they must spare themselves for a great work, and also that nothing outside of themselves—especially corrupt social systems, and even a heartless existence—is worth their own sacrifice. They know inwardly, whether from unique insight or sheer bloody-minded arrogance, that they are worth more than that, that they have an importance in the overall scheme of things that necessitates their survival in aid of their productivity, even if their social peers do not recognize them in this light at all. So they soldier on, against globally not to say cosmically overwhelming odds, and most succeed in making a statement through their subsequent work that serves as a rationale and justification for Being, on a planet that always feels alien to them, and among a race with whom they never feel true fellowship. Yet they are human, and perhaps more deeply so than others, since they are furthest out on the limb of exposed nerves, but return to tell the tale.

Camus' Rebels are perhaps the 'usual suspects': Sade, Baudelaire, Rimbaud, Lautréamont, Nietzsche, Nechayev, Bakhunin, etc. Each in his own way lent a new twist at the very least, to the licentious motif that runs through the history of rebelliousness in human affairs. Camus isn't blind to the childishness in their antinomian rants against everything and everyone they deemed to be standing in the way of the fullest possible expression of their higher egoism. But he acknowledged the sheer honesty of their challenges to the hypocrisy and idiocy of their times. These bad boys were courageous extremists lighting beacons in the darkest places for all of us to see, even if they also burnt the evidence as it were in their relentless Apocalyptic manias. Camus recognized their creative power and critical penetration, but in so far as their work has had an impact on mankind and society he cautioned against the excess of violent anarchic revolt that they may have inspired. Instead, he recommended a doctrine of 'the Limit', which need not apply to written work in literature or philosophy, but should apply to life, the conduct of affairs, and the sphere of real relationships, where no man can be coerced by another man's vision and a measure of collective respect for individual freedom of thought and action must be endorsed. There may be a case for certain kinds of extremism, which result in enlarging men's capacity for self-realization over and above the tepid strictures of moderation. But the right of the extremists to spread their license in the real world, still extends only as far as the notional boundaries between public and private space. Thus the brilliant fanaticism of the imagination can never segue into the suffocating tyranny of a palpable distopian nightmare. If this is refused by some, then their right to refuse it in their own lives, however small-minded they may or may not be, must still be respected by society.

Camus was thus a liberal humanist in his ethics, while aesthetically and philosophically he was highly receptive to the often egregious emanations from the wilder shores of literature and politics. Though not exactly a classic case of an outsider-writer and -philosopher himself, he was a seminal figure in the Canon of authors and thinkers who attempted to describe and explain, if not justify, in great depth and detail, the innermost mysteries of some of Mankind's more alienated members, alongside fictional counterparts. And in this vein he stepped aside from the orthodox confines of Marxism, Freudianism and Existentialism to develop a kind of neo-Romanticist Phenomenology of the Outsider, albeit in a proto-Classicist language, and with his eyes wide open and unblinking in the face of the sternest Stoical conundra. The Myth of Sisyphus has always resonated most profoundly with me. And Camus made it his own myth in the work of that title, imploring us to imagine Sisyphus happy in his eternal cycle of repetitive labours—senseless yet inexorable, noble through his contending with despair. This Titan punished by Zeus for defying his majesty, was sent to Tartarus, lower even than Hades, where the worst ordeals awaited its victims. Prometheus was another one, who was perhaps even bolder in his offence. But he was sentenced to a more passive, if perpetually painful fate. Sisyphus symbolizes all men who grind away at some endeavour—whether great or otherwise—without having any assurance of its eventual completion, nor of its meaning or purpose or acknowledgement by others. And yet they cannot honourably abandon their endeavours, and often persevere through the greatest suffering.

Sisyphus had punishment inflicted upon him. But it is in truth hard to distinguish between the visited torment of this archetypal ancient anti-hero—or paragon of almighty masochism!—and the self-imposed labours of Outsiders, not least writers, who work away throughout their lives in twilight wildernesses, with no assurance of success, fame and fortune, should they even want these things. Yet they suffer almost equally after a fashion, and chain themselves to the treadmills of their excruciating, if outstanding vocations till death do them part, from desperate dedication and the sheer lack of anything better to do with their often wretched and miserable lives. But if they also possess real talent or genius even, then something of enduring value will shine out of the works that their dark, shadow-obscured lives are to a point sacrificed in order to achieve. Sisyphus was thus a granite-hard source of inspiration, as well as a warning to the curious and an emblem of the grim despair of eternal torture, whether self-inflicted or other-imposed. I know of no better image for the troubled yet persevering human beast of burden that is the Outsider in general, or the Outsider-Writer in particular, the subject of this book. And it is a fitting stage-post from which to leave Camus in his seminal perpetuity as a great modern torch-bearer for the alienated and 'wretched of the earth', in Frantz Fanon's famous phrase. And that torch, taken unknowingly from Stewart across the ether of time, even if other more well-known figures intervened with their uplifting sweeps, from Dostoyevsky to Kafka, Stirner to Sorel, was then handed on or taken up more wittingly by the great excommunicated pariah of English Letters and Thought himself; namely, Colin Wilson. And so it is to his *oeuvre* that I now turn.

Wilson is perhaps the most unjustly maligned British writer and thinker of the last half century or so. His name is of course forever associated with his early work, *The Outsider*—which was by far and away the most successful book he ever wrote. Though it was the start of a series that has since become known as 'The Outsider-Cycle', and it contains the main body of his thought on the whole subject of Outsiders: what it is to be one, their relationship to society, and their radically singular and often exceptional attainments. He has since revisited the theme in his later works, as well as tackling other matters as diverse as Existentialism and Phenomenology, the Occult, life-failure, psychopathic murderers, the Paranormal, Maslovian Psychology, Whitehead's Organicist Philosophy, Postmodern Theories, Science Fiction, Horror, Fantasy, and cultural criticism. He has been accused in his time of everything: from naivety and arrogance, to wrong-headedeness and pretentiousness—and even perversity. And although I certainly shan't pretend here that I agree with everything he's ever written like some slavering disciple—and to his credit, he's never sought disciples as such, seeking rather to encourage in his readers the independence of mind he himself epitomizes to a very marked degree—and that he's somehow elevated himself above all criticism; in view of the monumentally ignorant and biased bad press he's received over the last half-century or so, I think it only fair that somebody somewhere should make the case for redressing the balance of judgement with regard to his uncomfortably probing and challenging rebuke to our intellectual and spiritual complacency as a race. In fact, it would not be an exaggeration to say that he is the forgotten man of our time, as his name is rarely mentioned if at all in the press and learned journals, except for purposes of denunciation.

Other writers of his generation, like Amis, Osborne, Pinter, Ballard, Burroughs, and their younger successors, like Moorcock, Iain Sinclair, Peter Ackroyd, and Will Self, are often cited as the pioneers of literary, political, anti-establishment and counter-cultural trends from the 1950s until today, while his name is often absent from the lists. And yet, at his best, he is head and shoulders above most of his contemporaries and more recent figures, if not as a stylist or even a writer of fiction, which has not perhaps been his strongest suit, then as a thinker and a prolific outpourer of works—close on 180 books to date—on all manner of subjects, rendering him close to a contemporary polymath. But he is first and foremost a kind of English Seer, very much in the lineage of Blake and Stewart and Coleridge—and in a way that is not remotely fashionable or popular nowadays. Thus nobody can accuse him of being a phoney New Age celebrity, because he takes his stand right at the other end of the missionary spectrum, being uncompromisingly demanding and difficult—the very reverse of superficial. Yet he is perceived as being a jack of all trades and a master of none, falling between the innumerable stools of philosophy and literature and politics and cultural studies, etc. without having distinguished himself exceptionally in any one field. Clearly this has been his perennial bug-bear, even though as I shall argue, it has been a very unjust load for him to carry, as the whole nature of his Project has been to defy the rigid classifications of writer and philosopher, etc. and to work out an alternative framework for human civilization and evolution, in which outsiders like himself can feel far more at home, if not assume a privileged position. For Wilson, fiction or literature has always been more than merely itself, so to say; meaning that if it isn't a vehicle for the promulgation of an author's philosophy of life, and in a way that advances human understanding and realization, then it fails in much of its purpose as a serious creative and intellectual endeavour.

This may be a transcendentally tough requirement of fiction, well and truly sorting out the heavyweights from the rest, but it still sets a high and useful standard for writers to aim for. We needn't be too bothered about the lowest common denominators among the scribbling herds of ghosted celebrities, but can without a shred of guilt focus here on the little oases of quality shining out from the murky bogs of sedimented pap that purport to go proxy for any semblance of a literary culture nowadays. Writers can of course entertain, without being shallow. But if they are merely reflecting back at readers what they already know of themselves without even trying at the very least to shed fresh light on some aspect or other of their predicament or mentality, still less point the way towards some positive transformation of their lives and destinies, then one may be entitled to question the worth of their enterprises. Much non-fiction is educational and cultural after a fashion, but a lot of fiction is frankly just trivial and pointless. Perhaps a bonfire of the books—vanities!—would not be such a barbarically philistine gesture as is generally supposed. On the contrary, it might well make it all the easier for the good books to rise, as it were, from the ashes of the bad! The Nazis were of course the last people in history to do this, prompting Freud to remark that mankind had made some progress as in the middle ages they would have burnt him! Although dying in 1939, he was never to learn of the horrors of the Holocaust. But if the Wilsonians of this world had their way, then I venture to suggest that all those books spared the flames would be among the very best ever written.

And this vein of intellectual and spiritual elitism poses a truly great challenge. If it smacks of a certain high-minded and maybe slightly provincial puritanism, advocating the purification by fire of the culture of crap, there is nevertheless a bracing honesty and strength of purpose about this that must appeal not only to the most self-assured intellectuals, but also to the rather less self-assured, and yet still seriously aspiring people who thirst after the well-springs of authentic wisdom and understanding beneath the poisoned veneer of deeply inauthentic conceits. These people are more likely to lose their way in being burdened by the dross of civilization, and generally fobbed off with the droppings of third-rate patronage. Instead, they crave absorption in the very best that civilization has to offer. In which case, they can do worse than throw their televisions out of the window, switch off their computers *en masse*, clear their shelves of excess pulp, and settle down to read a man like Colin Wilson. Even if he has his flaws and blind-spots, pet hobby-horses and repetitive tropes, he has managed at some point or other to speak to the true heart and mind of those individuals who feel troubled, obscurely or otherwise, by the dilemmas and conundra of the day, and in some way out of step and tune with Society and the Zeitgeist. This is his great strength, allied with his unyielding 'optimism' and long war against 'negativity', and provides a good entrée into his work—not least with regard to Outsiders. Of course, his detractors choose to regard his strength as a weakness, in the sense that they see an analogy between his sweeping dismissal of the literature and philosophy of dark depression and despair—from Goethe's *The Sorrows of Young Werther*, through the collected writings of Schopenhauer, to Beckett's *End-Game*—and the gleaming, cheesy, cosmetic materialism of Transatlantic consumer capitalism, with its glowing displays of the cult of positive attitude and self-esteem, endlessly gratifying the arbitrary urges and senseless addictions of the 'Me, Me, Me' generations.

But this caricature of Wilson's positive philosophy is as misconstrued as the Establishment's pillorying of him as a charlatan, poseur and fraud. He is as keenly aware of the obscene absurdities of sugary sentiments and simulated joys as his most morbidly Misanthropist adversaries. He has fully taken the measure of Keats's 'negative capability', and plumbed the infernal Abysms of Dante and Dostoyevsky, delineating the most pointed pessimist Dialectic along the axis of his own conviction. Wilson's Positiveness is not a diluted, Persil-cleaned simulacrum of Swedenborg's white-light kingdom, or a DIY-synthesis of Samuel Smiles's self-help with Muscular Christianity. Still less is it a Chakra-empowering engine of New Age health fads, meditation manuals and apple-cheeked, saccharine smile therapies. It's far more akin to the power of Imagination and Vision in Blake, or the will to self-transformation in Nietzsche—saying Yea rather than Nay to life at the cosmic crossroads of Being and Non-Being. Wilson is in truth a Vitalist *après la lettre*, championing the free choice of self-affirmation on the cusp of self-negation, which is a crisis-point, or even a crisis-line, in our lives, which we are all confronted by at some level of self-awareness. Not everyone experiences such crises in as intense and powerful a way as the Wilsons—or Outsiders—of this world. But nobody possessed of a thinking brain and a feeling heart, however conditioned they may be to ignore them through the blandishments of consumerism, can be totally unaware of the whole issue of what they are doing on this earth and what meaning or purpose or value their lives may, or indeed should, have. And if they allow themselves to be struck by these and other questions, and to ponder them awhile, then they are entering a territory of their Being where our streamlined Society does not wish them to go.

They are in a sense entering Wilson's territory, even if they never think of themselves as Outsiders as such—though some undoubtedly will. They are detaching themselves from the transient flow of largely or increasingly artificial stimuli which comprise the near sum-total of the immediacies of our experience, to be technical for a moment. Their motives for doing this may be multiple and complex in psychological or philosophical senses. Or they may be quite simple: to do with money and material things, jobs and relationships, family and environment, etc. They are discontent with their situation and wish to change it, though they aren't quite sure how. So they need to step back from their immediate position and take a wide view of it in its totality to see where they have gone wrong and how they might improve it. Yet the constant treadmill of diurnal existence makes this very difficult for them, and it requires a highly concentrated effort of will and mind to step off the mechanical wheel of productive, or not so productive, life, so they can examine themselves and their lives in a fresh light. But this is the necessary beginning of wisdom, if Socrates' famous saying 'the unexamined life is not worth living' can serve as a valid axiom—which by and large it can do. Some people appear quite content leading lives of bovine stupor, unquestioningly following orders, pursuing ordinary pleasures, not being bothered by boredom and the empty passage of time, slotting harmlessly into the dumb strata of society without ever wishing to leave their marks on anything. And maybe they shouldn't be 'forced to be free'. Though in so far as they act as an inertial break on others in the same strata trying to emancipate themselves from their stifling confines, then the dead weight of their mass predicament actually becomes a problem for society.

And far more people feel trapped in the industrial/ bureaucratic machinery of society, leading Thoreau's 'lives of quiet desperation'—fretting continuously about the unwanted burdens placed upon them and their conviction that they are failures, who at the end of their lives will feel that they have 'nothing to show for it.' These people are usually the more hopeful cases of Wilson's 'life-failure', because they are actually more likely to stumble upon a Wilsonian rescue package, thrown to them like a life-line perhaps, or serendipitously discovered in a lull during their dulled progress through the replicating time-tables of their stagnant routines, than the contented bovines above, or less charitably, Socrates' 'satisfied pigs'. And then options will begin to open up for them, if only in terms of the gradual deepening of their interior lives, which they may not necessarily be able to translate into successful working practices or even fulfilled lifelong pastimes. But merely thinking about one's philosophy of life is better than just bumping along on the bottom of society like a great bruised bundle of inconsequential slights. At least one is giving oneself more of a prospect of getting a grip on one's destiny at some more or less sudden, critical juncture on the Causeway of human casualties, that stretches out ahead for so many millions of people. And although one may not be another Nietzsche or Kierkegaard in the offing, one may come to take up one's place in the family of Beings for whom philosophical enquiry and self-advancement are not at all removed from the central business of living. This should not in fact make one an Outsider, for we should all be engaged in such activity. But as things stand, the majority of people who do this are likely to be Outsiders, in the sense that they have to detach themselves to some extent from the significant others or familiars around them: in the family-home, school, college, the work-place, club—or even Pub!—to be able to focus on matters other than the quotidian, without distraction or disturbance for any appreciable length of time each day.

All this philosophizing in the corner as it were, need not be as furtive or as narcissistic as may be thought, and can certainly be done to some purpose not only within a private context, but also a public one. If Wilson has been accused of a-politicism and even ivory-tower aestheticism, as well as flaky mysticism and lurid obsessiveness, he has never been afraid of putting himself about in the public domain, both to promote his own ideas and challenge those ideas he fundamentally disagrees with. He has not been drawn to the Marxist tradition, it is true—as I have—but he should not be too heavily criticized for that. He has always repudiated any links with the political Right on the grounds that he is not governed in his thinking by political ideology as such. But as an independent free thinker, he draws his principal inspiration from philosophers, like Plato, Nietzsche, Husserl, and Whitehead; and from writers, like Shakespeare, Goethe, Blake, Dostoyevsky, Mann, Musil and Powys; from religious mystics, like Swedenborg, Steiner and Rasputin; and from assorted oddballs, like Gurdjieff and Aleister Crowley. And this is not to say that he has no concern for social change, and sees no connections between philosophy and practice. But he insists that the individual has to do all this necessary work for himself—a lot of it in his head—before he is able to apply it in his life or seek to persuade others of its profundity and importance. Wilson understands just how dreadful, and desperately limiting of the individual's expressive freedoms, so many aspects of reality are. But rather than advocate some form of universal, dogma-dictated barricade action, or conversely, aetherial opiated escapism, he invites individuals to take their own intellectual and spiritual responsibility for their lives and fates, as the necessary condition of any desirable, evolutionary, collective change.

This places Wilson nearly in the Anarchist camp, although he might baulk at the label, freighted as it is with so much convoluted baggage as to be almost completely meaningless nowadays. But if, as he insists, he is neither on the political Left nor Right, affirms the vital and central importance of the Individual and independence or autonomy of mind, believes in creating a new Religion not founded on authoritarian organization or hierarchy, and entertains the wildest and wackiest ideas of all manner of Outsiders with a scrupulously fair and open, if sceptically rigorous, mind, what then does all this make him if not some sort, and a very elevated sort, of Anarchist? In this context the label ceases to matter, as it is the explicit philosophical content that gives the whole concept its meaning. He might want to draw the line at throwing bombs and wearing circled A stickers, and might not readily embrace the Teepee commune variants of Anarcho-Syndicalism. But he would I think concur with the likes of Chomsky—a similar figure in some regards—who has said that his Anarchism entails extremism, in the sense that he is always prepared to stick his neck out in favour of bold assertions that may upset the balance of the Moderatist mean. In other words, only unadventurous thinkers fear to deviate from moderation towards extreme positions—which don't of course necessarily involve any of the Heinz 57 varieties of crackpot fanatical religious fundamentalism, since these could not be further removed from what Chomsky, and Wilson, are promulgating. Wilson's Anarchism is one of order, purpose, meaning and value, in which the chaos and unruliness of life is redirected by conscious, rational and intelligent means to other, purportedly higher, ends. And I see no real contradiction or conflict of reason in this, as anarchy has never meant absence of order but absence of rule, which is something quite different, a state of natural order in social harmony.

Wilson's fascination with killers, and nihilists like Nechayev, suggests a degree of thwarted violent romanticism in his make-up, even though I'm quite sure he would never succumb to the sort of depraved and twisted tendencies that he analyses with such profound, and empathetic, penetration. He is after all a happy, settled, family man, who has said that he likes people too much to wish them any serious harm—and has even described himself as 'a cheerful, jolly kind of bloke,' rather than 'the dour, screwed up existentialist' that his detractors believe him to be. And yet, his fascination for all the forms of human deviancy indicates an internal split in his psyche, which obviously he has always managed sufficiently adeptly to maintain his equilibrium. And he certainly belongs to the school of thought which maintains that we are all on the same broad spectrum of normality and abnormality. Only some of us are far more able than others to operate our inner censor in such small matters as rape, torture, bestiality, murder and mass-genocide! But people who are not able to prevent the flood-gates of ravenous psycho-pathology from bursting are suffering from terrible afflictions which actually deserve our sympathy, and certainly our understanding, even if the horrendous actions they commit cannot possibly be condoned by anybody possessed of a shred of conscience and civilization. De Quincey devoted a long essay, 'Murder considered as a Fine Art', to investigating the notorious case of John Williams, the Ratcliffe Highway murderer, in which he didn't so much convey sympathy for Williams's afflictions as literally revel in the perceived Olympian grandeur of a man who could jettison the whole moribund apparatus of human morality, and butcher seven innocent simpletons to death in the most brutally horrific manner imaginable. Wilson investigated this case in his works on criminals—Iain Sinclair has dwelt on it as well; even P.D. James co-wrote a book on the subject, *The Maul and the Pear Tree*—and it does, I maintain, provide a real test of his capacity to engage with the most monstrous manifestations of the outsider-gene running through the entire gamut of deviancy from the Divine to the Diabolic. Especially as Williams saw himself as a superior aesthete.

The most terrible, and possibly sublime, Outsiders are the men—or women—who commit appalling acts and then glory in them without seeking any kind of redemption or justifying their existence in terms of what they produce, i.e. works of art, literature or philosophy. Murder IS their art—and their only art at that. Williams cultivated a refined contempt for the lower orders amongst whom he moved, but gave no expression to his superior aesthetic by way of any records he left behind. It was the splattered blood from the bludgeoned bodies of his carefully chosen victims that was the sole, and pure, testament to his diabolically deranged, if hideously heroic, calling. As such, he was at the very outermost edge of the spectrum of Wilsonian Outsiderdom. And to crown his achievements, he committed suicide in prison before he could be hanged—even if he was subsequently dismembered and buried near the site of the killings. So he escaped Justice, and the judgement of human society, from which he always felt himself to be utterly, and unutterably, excluded. Such cases provide the truest acid test of the universality of the 'Good Society' that Wilson's alternative Religion or Utopia of emancipated Outsiders really endorses, through the development and spread of positive consciousness. Williams and his ilk sought a separated Kingdom of unashamed Evil, a lofty Inferno of Satanic indulgence, going unpunished or at least conquering the pain of banishment. Quite how this monstrous mentality may be incorporated into the essentially optimistic Brave New Heaven of Wilsonian Evolutionary endeavours is hard to say. But Wilson shouldn't be criticized too harshly for maybe failing to square this impossibly difficult circle.

More productive and less pathologically disturbed Outsiders in the Wilsonian mould however possessed to a greater than average degree what Wilson called 'Faculty X'. This denotes a presumed inner capacity, that transcends the five familiar senses and ordinary powers of consciousness, thought and Reason. More specifically, it's a means of knowing the reality of other times and places. This is not supposed to involve directly the use or cultivation of so-called ESP, telepathy, pre-cognition, and paranormal activity in general. But I don't see how else one acquires such knowledge directly—as opposed to indirectly through inference—without falling back on some such method. But before I myself fall prey to the just resistable magnetic pull of the great Wilson-bashing bandwagon, let me say at once that if Wilson has from time to time betrayed himself ever so slightly into absurdity over these and other related matters, this has stemmed in part from his insistence on open-mindedly testing every hypothesis to destruction; and also in part on the need to sing for his supper by way of pleasing the *hoi polloi*. And most writers have done the latter, at some stage in their careers! But if he has produced a few turkeys in his time, it would be a travesty of truth for us to judge, let alone condemn, his entire output on that basis alone. And I reckon that Faculty X is not as prima facie absurd a postulate as some may claim. And it may be so multi-faceted and -layered that it could be involved in anything ranging from prophetic daydreaming to sudden surges of pioneering creativity in a great work of literature, art, philosophy, or in any other field of endeavour. The fact that we only understand, and utilize, approximately ten percent of the potential of our brains, alone signifies that some such faculty, or faculties, may very well lurk in the as yet undiscovered recesses of what, as far as we know, is the most complex single organism in the whole universe.

Although it may not only be the brain that plays a crucial part in governing the modes of consciousness associated with such faculties, since the jury is still out on whether or not consciousness in some shape or form might survive brain-death. If—as I have suggested in my account of Stewart's philosophy—consciousness is far more widespread amongst life-forms and even conceivably inert or inorganic matter, than materialists and rationalists are willing to concede, then it goes without saying that the brain is not the *sine qua non* of consciousness. Consciousness is out there in the world, and not just in us and in other life-forms. And as such, it is truly the last frontier of human knowledge, because scientists are coming far closer to cracking the codes of matter than ever before, whilst consciousness and mind are not at all understood. Although some scientists duck the issue by simply denying that they exist, because they know they cannot account for them yet in any other way. Maybe they will be conclusively proven one day to be material mechanisms or epiphenomena of matter, even if it's impossible to imagine how at present. The old Wittgensteinian chestnut *vis-à-vis* the non-commutability of physicalistic and mentalistic language still remains unresolved, as far as I can see. So scientists cannot really know what they mean when they say that the mind, e.g. is the brain. All they're really saying is that the brain is the brain, which is a tautology. Or else they're contradicting themselves. And yet even if they do prove to be right, they will surely still have to acknowledge that mind is an energy and force in matter, an agency that gives motion to matter. And so, the relationship between mind and matter will still remain a complex one, even if it becomes better understood. And the 'miracle' of consciousness—especially the wilder shores encompassed by Faculty X—will become the last outpost in the battle for the subjective freedom of Outsiders against the objective, or quasi-objective, manipulations of scientists, technologists and society's programmatic brain-washers. And Wilson is a tireless champion of this anti-deterministic freedom.

It isn't a question of being opposed to science and technology, still less an intelligent ordering of society, but of holding onto some notion and sense, even if it proved to be illusory or mythical, of an Individual's choice of belonging, in a social structure that deems him to be no more nor less than a means to a purely mechanistic end. So even if it could be proved that none of us are truly free, it would still be vitally important to cling on to the belief at least that we can exercise responsibility for our life-choices. Otherwise we shall all literally become the robotic puppets of Technocrats with a far from politically and ethically neutral agenda for social progress. And perhaps the best defense we all have against this tendency is to adopt what might be regarded as a particular variant of Faculty X, namely, the bird's-eye viewpoint of the Holist that Wilson contrasts with the tunnel-visioned perspective of the narrow specialist, or the Individual fixated on the small details that bog him down, rather than the larger picture that liberates him. Our lives are so streamlined, and over-burdened by innumerable stresses, we are all inclined to lose sight of the greater possibilities of self-emancipation. We've become increasingly imprisoned in the fragmented and self-fragmenting routines of work, relationships and leisure. And all of this has made us especially vulnerable to the deeper social conditioning of our behaviour, attitudes, and outlook. If freedom means anything nowadays, and it has always meant everything, or the basis of everything, to Outsiders in particular, then it involves consciously resisting all those external and internalized influences which militate against the cultivated will of our self-determination. This sidesteps the old freedom versus determinism dispute by asserting not that we all have absolute control over every signal in our brains and bodies, but instead that we can acquire relative control in quite practical ways over our responses to unwelcome pressures from the alien methods of doing things, which threaten to Bureaucratize our Being.

Wilson is drawn above all else to the Superman-type of Outsider, who is able not only to detach himself from the common herd and look dispassionately upon it, but also to elevate himself—at any rate mentally—above the predicament of the broad mass of mankind. In this capacity he strives to set an example without seeking disciples as such. And whilst he is concerned about the collective evolution of humanity, his first priority is with himself; and only secondarily does he wish to entice, never coerce, others into following if not his example, then examples of their own. This comes perilously near to Fascism at various points, or certainly a kind of elitism that is considered unfashionable, unappealing and even criminally repugnant, in most right-on, left-wing-liberal consensus, ideological groupings. But I really shouldn't need to revisit the argument here, that our dear old moustachioed friend of Germanic descent with a celebrated gripe against Christianity, who anticipated a corny Hollywood Film, was well and truly travestied by a small bunch of illiterate gangsters who muscled their way to power decades after his death. Yet Wilson's debt to Nietzsche with respect to the doctrine of the Higher Man—and to Shaw, who developed it further in *Man and Superman*—is well-known. And the emphasis is clearly on the Individual cleansing his consciousness of all the rotting Augean dregs of moribund doctrines in order to fashion himself anew, without so much as a nod in the direction of anti-semitism and the corporate state. If the slur of racism and extreme reactionary politics persists, it may have a little to do with Wilson's association with a figure like Bill Hopkins—the author of *The Divine and The Decay*, scandalous in its day, yet forgotten since—who unashamedly, and it should be said, courageously, embraced right-wing doctrines at a time when it was becoming positively heretical to do so. And yet the argument from association is no argument at all.

Even Marx is often coupled with Nietzsche, which on the face of it is perhaps puzzling, given the sharp points of divergence between their world-views. But people often forget that Marx came out of just the same heady nexus of German philosophy and literature and politics as Nietzsche did only a little later on in the nineteenth century, his first love being poetry. In fact, when he was young he described himself as a Romantic, steeped as he was in Goethe, Schiller, Heine and Holderlin. In philosophy he was of course immersed in Hegel. And in politics he was even a kind of anarchist, preoccupied with the total emancipation of the Individual from the tyranny of the State. In his early work on alienation, he laid bare his true philosophy, declaring that money was the alienated essence of Man. This held the key to the development of a libertarian anarcho-socialist society more positively than the purely negative critique and analysis of Capitalism in his later work. And although Nietzsche sometimes praised hierarchical societies on the ancient model, and the men of virtue in Plato's Republic, there was not a lot else that separated him from Marx in the wide sweep of their respective writings. Both men reviled religion and morality. Both men despised states and championed individual autonomy. And both men sought to inspire revolutions in the mind, spirit and consciousness, as well as the material world. Marx was not opposed to spiritual values. On the contrary, he upheld them, but in a converse relation to religious ideals. And though consciousness and ideology were by-products of material conditions, the recognition of 'false consciousness' was the essential requirement for developing true consciousness. So Marx, like Nietzsche, was far closer in his general thinking to Wilson than Wilson himself would admit perhaps. And if one removes the wrong predictions and occasional dogma of ideological correctness from Marx's overall philosophy, it can still provide a quite sound pragmatic foundation and framework for the mundane working out of some of Wilson's more metaphysically inclined ideas.

But of course, in a world where as the cliché goes, 'We are all Capitalists now,' it is exceedingly unlikely that the Marxist experiment will ever be seriously attempted again, especially as Marxism was so roundly corrupted and betrayed by figures like Lenin, Stalin and Mao. If Marx could say late in his own lifetime that he was no longer a Marxist, how much more emphatically would he have reiterated that if he could have come back to life to witness the horrors of the Gulag? He would have been drawn more to developments in phenomenology and existentialism I think, than to the increasingly stale and sterile comrade-confessing auto-critiques of the neo-Marxist theoreticians, not to mention the deconstructionists and post-modernists, who Wilson also condemns. So to those critics of Wilson who say that the economic, social and political counterparts to his philosophy are missing, I would reply that a simple derivation of libertarian anarchism or socialism from Marx's thought ought to furnish the ground for the kind of post-capitalistic society that would enable the Wilsonian Outsider to find his place in the Human Family—rather than being permanently left out in the cold of the Capitalistic slag-heap and wilderness. I do not know whether Wilson would accept this—perhaps not. But if not, then how could he argue that Capitalism is in any way sympathetic to Outsiders, or indeed a lot of insiders who are still trapped within the System and cannot free up their true humanity in all of the various roles which govern their relationships to others? It's not enough to have a richly fulfilled inner life if it has no impact or bearing on anything outside one's own head. One's survival may still be at stake, and society's pressures cannot be effectively resisted in this manner. And one might even question the genuineness of such cultural and spiritual detachment, if it stems from isolation to begin with.

Stewart, Camus, Wilson

It takes a truly exceptional specimen of humanity to work out a new philosophy of life, and to apply it in practice from a position of pure autodidacticism and social disengagement. There might have been isolated historical examples of this, but the vast majority of people feeling or believing themselves to be Outsiders flounder in their desperate attempts to anchor themselves in a solipsistic ether unsupported by concrete reality and significant others. But Wilson still comes to their rescue with his contention that Outsiders can not only make partial differences to the world as it exists, but in a quantum leap or paradigm-shift can illuminate, and even transfigure, the world as a whole. What makes this possible is not only a fortuitous occupation, literature, art, philosophy, etc. but above all the unity of the Self, impregnable against the porous incursions of the Not-Self, which threaten to engulf the Self so it evaporates away into the inarticulate mulch of history and culture. Husserl's Transcendental Ego holds the fort of this Everyday Self, objectifying itself in the realms of thought and action. Derrida's disintegrated droppings cannot unmoor the embedded plumb of our psyches. Kierkegaard's 'Incognito' Subjects escaped from the suffocating clutches and confines of Hegel's all-encompassing Dialectical Synthesis. Schopenhauer's blind, pessimistic agency of Will receives a leonine blast of fresh air above its miasmas of misanthropy. And Wilson still holds out against the crashing tides of relativistic chaos and confusion that threaten to suck us all into the Almighty oceanic vortex of the crumbling, collapsing Zeitgeist. And good on him for doing so. Even if one might still argue that he is, sadly, philosophically mistaken. There is no proof that I know of, that the Transcendental Ego exists, and the problematic goes all the way back to Kant, who failed to deduce the transcendental categories. And thinkers like Husserl ultimately ran aground with essentially the same difficulty.

But it would still be nice to think that there may be a Transcendental Ego, or what I would call an Integrating Self, which gathers up all the detritus of our subjective impressions to corral them into a working unity. Yet try hard as I may, I cannot for the life of me see how this can be done. Even if as Chomsky and Piaget have shown, there must be innate ideas in some sense or other, we still cannot say exactly what, or indeed where, they are. We still cannot witness or capture them in our heads. All we can do is try to pierce the surface of our streams of consciousness, to reveal an underlying structure. And yet all we see is a morass of evanescence. Our ideas of ourselves are maybe less fleeting than our impressions, but they're just like mole-hills of the mind purporting to be mud-banks that can withstand constant flooding by the sheer dead weight of transience. We're more like continuously redrawn designs of ourselves rather than completed products built to last. And so Derrida's Sceptical Relativism, which is not original, but just a dwarf's derivation from a giant's insight, is unfortunately all too true. And yet, as Wilson well understands, we do not have to capitulate to the monumental forces that deprive us of our individual autonomy, and in the particular variant of special relevance to this study, deprive authors of their authorship. It is still incumbent on each and every one of us to make sense of all that threatens to undermine sense in the external culture, and to thereby rescue some sliver of the Self from the drowning wreckage of Semiological signs. Derrida *et al* would be more admirable in my view if they were out-and-out Philosophical Nihilists, rather than tepid Sceptical Relativists. But Derrida for one, distanced himself from such an extreme position, thereby denying us a clear opportunity to shoot him down from a countervailing extreme position of our own. Derrida gives Outsiders no real comfort, with the jungle of his jargon spreading the spilt mess of the corpse of Epistemology into discursive spaces that are no spaces. If all is relation, identity is nothing. So definiteness dissolves into indefiniteness. And no statement survives its own subversion, including this one.

Vaughan Robertson's splendidly named 'Doctrine of Ultimate Pointlessness' is doubtless true, but also then falls victim to its own statement that no statement can ever be made about anything whatever to which we cannot reply 'So what?' Indeed. So it follows that the statement that there is no statement that cannot be followed by the question 'So what?' can itself be followed by the question 'So what?', and so on *ad infinitum*. And this leaves us—precisely where? Nowhere. And nowhere can be a fascinating non-place to not-be in. But it also poses a bloody frustrating Conundrum, for we feel, think, say and do all sorts of things, on the very opposite assumption that we are somewhere in the overall scheme of things and have a sense at least of our purposes in going on as we do. So even if this fact is bottomlessly contingent on other contingencies, we might as well start at some point to affirm something or other, however pointlessly! And in making this arbitrary but essential gesture, we create something of value and significance in an otherwise valueless and insignificant world. There is in us a fundamental existential need to do this, even if logically we can still carry on picking holes in ourselves and our animi till the proverbial, non-existent kingdom comes—in the form of an hallucinated mirage! We are illusions made real in the very act of mental projection and introjection. We build on these shaky foundations the most fantastic castles in the air of our speculations and imaginings. And we need not banish them to the lairs of our self-underminings, the autotrophy of annihilation. We can run with them in the Hermetic wind of our creations, sailing into the horizons of Hermeneutics, blissfully unconcerned with the Hubris of our inherent insubstantiality, and the forever postponed Nemesis of Death.

And so where does this leave Wilson? It leaves him standing proudly on his crag above the slipping tides of our crumbled civilization, a Prospero of our time insisting on his vision outlasting the dud reality of the world. His crag might not be the Rock of Ages, yet it is a thoroughly earned Olympian height from which to view the lower Parnassian slopes on which the bovine cadres of humanity are assembled. But instead of micturating on these specimens—although he might well have been sorely tempted to at times!—he offers them a helping hand through the dynamics of a new Anthroposophy. Being and more fully becoming a true Outsider is a path to human salvation in a sense, albeit not a specifically moral or religious sense. It helps to safeguard and further the wisdom of ages, and suggests a new and radically different paradigm of Being and social engagement, where the Individual is more fully in control of his life and destiny, and maps out the territory on which he negotiates the world. Outsiders might not always be towering figures in their own lifetimes, but posthumously they can acquire unassailable places in the Canon, Blake and Van Gogh being obvious examples. Not that they should live for posterity—or posteriority as one might say!—for they want the confirmation of their Being that acknowledgement or recognition of their abilities and achievements brings while they are alive to appreciate it, and not when they're dead or else in some Limbo or Afterlife where they're unable to communicate to the living. But in so far as the world is blind or resistant to their attempts to gain its attention, such a fate may still befall them. However, the urge and the skill to get their messages or signals out into the world will tend to elicit the feedback that helps them in building up their public profiles. And even if this goes against the grain of their essential solitude, it may in many cases enlarge their scope and enrich their creative outputs.

The real importance of Wilson's legacy lies in his unrelenting insistence that we can all cultivate the independence of mind needed to furnish our own philosophies of life, and then act upon them in the various different ways in which each one of us actually lives. His claim to be the greatest writer of the twentieth—and no doubt the twenty first!—century, may be exaggerated. But as a thinker and Seer of a sort, who refuses to conform to the dictates and conventions of established orthodoxies—in particular academic authorities—he has set an example that very few others during the last half century or so have equalled, let alone excelled. He has held out hope for Individuals that they still matter and count in the machinery of collectivist power and influence that threatens to utterly overwhelm us. Even if we have to become Outsiders in some sense to achieve a relative degree and kind of autonomy, Wilson has shown in his life and work that this is not only attainable, but doesn't necessarily involve great sacrifices of an undesirable kind. We don't have to become Trappist monks or total recluses—Wilson's a contented family man living in the beautiful wilderness of Cornwall—nor risk our sanity in off-the-wall experimentation. We can keep an even keel, whilst ploughing our own furrows with unyielding determination and focus. We should experience all that we can throughout our lives, and absorb it for our own development—be it from books, from travel, from discourse, from sex, from intimacy, from spiritual endeavour, from open-mindedness and a general receptiveness to elevated influences. We may make small compromises in matters of work, etc. but we should not make big compromises *vis-à-vis* integrity, adventurousness, devotion to a calling, and the advancement of mankind. We should draw a Sartrean circle of consciousness around us to fortify ourselves against the negative intrusions of materialism, media, and politics. Yet we should also extend an olive branch of solidarity to others willing to do likewise, to establish common ground in difference. This is Wilson's ideal type of Outsider.

To be a Wilsonian Outsider is not simply to be in a predicament, but to be engaged, not to say immersed, in a great undertaking, which may even go against the grain of one's more instinctive inclinations. One may not feel oneself to be so radically out of step with society and the human race that one automatically considers oneself to be one of nature's Outsiders. Life's proverbial misfits are perhaps more often than not sadly unfulfilled, due to the unremitting burdens of their inherent pathological afflictions. But one may be relatively well-adjusted socially and psychologically, and yet still be acutely aware of a sterile void at the heart of human affairs nowadays, which necessitates a certain distancing to perform the great work of mind and spirit that might one day inform a widespread healing of the wasteful and stunting disease of human conflict bred of ignorant incomprehension. And this, in a nutshell, is Wilson's challenge to us all. He is not in the end doctrinaire or dogmatic, still less an off-the-shelf Guru or Prophet, a mere Groupies' Icon. He is rather a highly singular illuminator of the pathways we can pursue, a facilitator of willing adventurers who does not lay down the Law as such, but shows one example—and a very exceptional one—of how we can emancipate ourselves from the hypnotic tyranny of Society's insider-mechanisms and become in the process True

Individualists. And to do this we must constantly exercise our faculties, and not just intellectual ones either, to keep ourselves strengthened against Gurdjieff's 'Negative Emotions', and Society's crassly superficial currents of taste and fashion, thereby readying ourselves for our serious assaults on the peaks of human thought, creativity, imagination and spiritual enlightenment, the 'peak experience' of Maslow, which might just be the greatest cure for depression and despair there is. Though we have to learn to modulate it too, so as not to inundate ourselves continuously with high energies for which we have no practical or beneficial use. And the self-discipline this requires singles out the strongly accomplished Outsiders from the weakly aspiring ones.

Wilson's philosophy goes a few steps beyond Stewart's and Camus', and it remains to be seen who he will pass the baton onto so to speak. Though, in his ninth decade, I would hope his best work is not done with yet, and his Magnum Opus will materialize before he ascends into the eternal ether. For all that he's been dismissed by people, ranging from analytical philosophers to continental theorists, from liberal leftists to metropolitan gliterati, there are growing numbers of other people—including eminent figures like Roger Scruton, who praises Wilson's independence of mind—who are at last recognizing the rather unique and special position which he occupies in modern intellectual and cultural life. And though I do not intend to strike too reverential a note here, I myself view him as one of a mere handful of writers and thinkers today, who at the very least help us to come to terms with the truly terrible morass of the world as it is today, even if he cannot lead us all through it, and out into an Empyrean Transfiguration of what exists. But we all need to struggle towards that Light, finding and following our own paths with the inspiration that such Luminaries give us. And in the next chapter, I shall be aiming to develop my own ideas and arguments about this, on the strength of the foregoing.

Recommended reading:

'Walking' John Stewart:
The Apocalypse of Nature. London, 1792?
The Sophiometer. London, 1818?

Albert Camus:
L'Etranger. Alfred Knopf, 1946 (Trans. Stuart Gilbert)
The Rebel. Penguin, 1974 (Trans. Anthony Bower)
The Myth of Sisyphus. Hamish Hamilton, 1955 (Trans. Justin O'Brien)

Colin Wilson:
The Outsider. Victor Gollancz, 1956.
Religion and the Rebel. Victor Gollancz, 1957.
The Age of Defeat. Victor Gollancz, 1959.
The Strength to Dream: Literature and the Imagination. Victor Gollancz, 1962.
Origins of the Sexual Impulse. Arthur Barker, 1963.

Adam Daly: 'Walking' John Stewart. *Abraxas Unbound* (vol. 1), 2007, p. 133-43.

Chapter Three:

Glimpses of a Future for Outsider-Writers

By bringing the general philosophical concept of the Outsider back into the more specific frame of reference of the writer, I reckon I might just be able to propel myself up onto the shoulders of the three Giants in the preceding chapter—if only to ape the proverbial dwarf in claiming to see further than they can! For me there is a truly awesome variety of Outsiders in literature, who not only struggle under the burdens of their alienation, but also strike chords—and discords—of superlative strangeness on the edges of Culture, displaying a ferocious, not to say triumphal animosity and bloody-minded intransigence in their vengeful tirades against the obloquy of Mainstream-Mediocrats. Marked idiosyncrasies and eccentricities, extreme anti-social tendencies, positively pathological, even totally inhuman, habits, conceits, and driving obsessions, go with the territory, where these figures lurk and prowl, wounded and snarling, mad with mythomania. Such characteristics trouble a lot of people, who might otherwise be prepared to take a serious interest in them, or at any rate meet them half-way, if not entirely on their own terms. But they don't trouble me in the slightest, perhaps because I'm not without these characteristics myself—but that's another story!—and in fact, they offer me a great deal of amusement, fascination and excitement, in what would otherwise be an extremely gruelling area of research. What many people would regard as defects, even totally disqualifying ones, for me are often the identifying signs of quintessential, unconforming minds, that can never be swayed by the indoctrinating tunes of society's pedestal-squatting peers. So I frankly couldn't care one whit if these people appear unfathomably weird in others' eyes—nor even if their weirdness, or madness, seeps into and permeates their work—just as long as their work still has the inherent power to resonate, disturb, astonish, and exhilarate.

True Outsider-Writers in my view actually *should* appear to others somewhat strange and out of the ordinary, or they're unlikely to have the complex originality of temperament and vision that quite often feeds the production of great work. Although obviously mere eccentricity does not invariably equate with talent, still less genius. But in a fair number of cases it is a concomitant. And I've always been interested in the notion that an eccentric perceives things that a non-eccentric cannot, purely by virtue of being an oddball, with therefore a necessarily oblique view of the world. Of course, there are some eccentrics who have such a skewed view of the world, that they acquire or develop quite false pictures of it, which are in truth more akin to insanity, or even stupidity. But in so far as they have a different picture of the world from many or most people, then they have a relatively unique perspective from which to draw in fashioning a work of fiction. And this may give them a head-start in developing revolutionary paradigms of perception, which in deviating from standard models throw fresh light upon them. The onus of justification may well be on eccentrics to prove in their works that their angular distortions of reality merit being taken seriously as challenges to more entrenched norms—never mind advances upon them. But there is still a favourable supposition to the effect that one has to step outside, or be outside, a general framework of reality, in order to comprehend its limitations more fully, and to point the way to revealing more of its true nature. Eccentrics have always been persecuted softly, or comparatively softly, in societies which can even go so far as to venerate them as 'national treasures'—not least in England!—whilst at the same time the mass of the population remain uncomfortable in their company, so quite often tease, abuse, or shun them. This is typical of the genteel hypocrisy that sentimentalises preferably harmless freaks, yet retains a tribally inhuman separateness and self-protective supercilious-ness.

Such sentimentalism is almost as much of a curse and a blight as shallow cynicism. The celebrated 'English Eccentric' —think Patrick Moore; and David Bellamy; and even Stephen Fry, the Twittering, Tweedy Renaissance Man, all-round Fame-addict and waster of his Wildean genius—is a quite ridiculously quaint feature of our pseudo-tolerantly indulgent socio-cultural customs. In idolizing these figures, we tame them and co-opt them into the cosily conspiratorial club of our small c-conservatism, never allowing anybody to cast a genuine gimlet eye upon the fossilized foibles of a failed nation still dimly nostalgic for fake imperial glory. The best kind of Eccentric in my view, is one who refuses point-blank to be type-cast in the grey aspic of soap-opera gentrification, and quite deliberately and self-cultivatedly, adopts an uncomp-romisingly sharp, austerely sardonic, fearsomely combative stance, with regard to the entire society that has spawned them, or in which they have settled only to stay in essence unassimilable. In other words, they are never about being soppily amicable. They know damned well that there is an awful lot wrong with the far from poetic and mythic State of Denmark, and they're damned if they're ever going to collude in the preposterous fiction that all is rosy in the Garden of

England. God has never been in his Heaven and all is most certainly not well with the world. Life's proverbial bed of roses and bowl of cherries are, tellingly, blood-red images of tantalizing deception. If they seem cold, aloof and caustic, it's because there's nothing around them to engage their sympathies, and a dispassionate contempt is more honest and exacting than any simulated affability. It demands more of everybody, renouncing mediocrity and insisting on elevating the tone of human discourse. The awkward personae of these unaccommodating types of Eccentric threaten complacency and superficiality, the twin-religions of our time, sharpening our sense of the numb-skulled indifference of empty, sterile, contemptible cliques.

Wyndham Lewis, Julian McClaren-Ross, Maurice Richardson and Austin Osman Spare were all notable examples of the above type of eccentric Outsider. Even Bertrand Russell and J. M. Trevelyan could be added to the list. All of them had a stern, forbidding, condor-like, majestic magnanimity in their serenely scathing satires, critiques and commentaries on modern life and its discontents, which brooked no contradiction from pompous bigots defending all manner of orthodoxies and the Status-Quo. They were not in the slightest bit concerned about being liked by anybody, and were always ready to provoke offense and outrage in the interests of exposing painfully bitter truths about the way in which the world was run, or the crass artifice of charlatans and poseurs, which was almost calculated not to endear them to the Establishment or any of the cadres of the sham social hierarchy. Although Russell was plainly revered for his intellect and sagacity, as well as his support for numerous political and ethical causes, he behaved just like a Satyr with ladies, and could strike anyone, apart from Wittgenstein, dead with a single quip—'squash them flat', as he once said about his students. He had a Swiftian turn of phrase, rejected Religions and thought morality was a purely subjective matter. He presided like a merry Magus over the Bloomsburyites, and almost followed his friend, D. H. Lawrence, into the exotic Pagan wilderness. In private, he was intimate yet waspish. And in public, he was severe and lofty. He was never a friendly, cuddly figure in the classic English Eccentric mould. He had too much Gravitas in him for that. The man who said when asked about the state of the world: 'Terrible! Terrible! Terrible!' also placed politicians below pigs in his pecking-order. Yet his impish wit was as irrepressible as his crushing cruelty, as when he opined: 'Mothers-in-law are a particularly intractable part of the Problem of Evil.' In spite of his aristocratic pedigree and erudition, there was something stubbornly *sui generis* about him—a Renaissance Man of the Devil's Party, standing apart from other men to size up the species and summarize it in a sentence: 'People would rather die than think.' Harsh, but true! Russell even befriended Lionel Britton, writing the introduction to Britton's Magnum Opus, *Hunger and Love*, and supporting him in his long-running feud with The Society of Authors—but I'll say more about Britton in volume 2. He was no-one's sycophant when it came to sticking his neck out in favour of a crank—which he even speculated Wittgenstein may have been. He did not automatically respect a fellow-Toff or a Bourgeois Gent any more than a Proletarian, which reflected a suppleness of sympathy cutting across the arbitrarily rigid dividing-lines of the English Class-System. Highly placed people nowadays could still learn a great deal from such an attitude, being so often inverted snobs of the vilest variety, with their snootily facile equations of superiority with money and material taste, rank and status. There's a dreadful new snobbery about today, not based on either heredity, culture or education—which in truth are far preferable, given the choice—but on a sort of Finishing-School code of etiquette, encompassing everything from dress-mode to table-and-telephone-manners, and what J. K. Galbraith once brilliantly lampooned as 'Restaurant-presence'! All this combined with an execrable celebrity-culture makes for a deplorable dog's dinner of a social heap that positively cries out for the Donnishly savage put-downs of someone of Russell's calibre—of whom there are, sadly, few around. But he was living proof at his peak, that an eminent sage could also be an intransigent anti-establishmentarian, and yes, even an Outsider-Philosopher to boot! If he was an Eccentric as well, it was above all else in the sense of his being so far ahead of the centric pack of human plodders, that he stood out from them like a blinding star of white-heat brilliance laced with black shafts of devastating venom. He wrote better than any other twentieth century Philosopher, and might have become the Byron of his Age if he had turned his hand to poetry. But his prose served instead as a peerless paradigm of true clarity and concision, elegance and restrained fire, rendering the genuinely complex seemingly simple, and the merely convoluted or vainly simplistic deservedly ridiculous. He may have been wrong about certain things, even many things, but that is only par for the course with all great philosophers. The point is to be interestingly wrong, when not right. And he was that.

Wyndham Lewis was another awkward Giant of the 'counter-blasting' tendency of his Time. The arch-Vorticist and saturnine chronicler of decadent culture and civilization oozed dyspeptic chagrin and was an Outsider twice removed: an angular aesthete and a foreign alien! Aside from the Slade and

Fitzrovia, he saw nowhere congenial in England to settle and find his home in any sense, political, cultural, or spiritual. Only a few degrees to the Left of the lunatic Divine, Ezra Pound, he had both the tweedy Conservatism of the British Establishment and the Neo-Marxian correctitude of the Literary Lions to contend with. So he was duly banished into his brooding, prolific Lair, where his splendidly maleficent mental machinations slowly poured out into the public domain like spilled jewels from a shipwreck, dazzlingly dangerous and coruscatingly contagious. The self-styled 'Tyro', with his jagged off-centre gaze and murderous Modernist slant and thrust, essayed his own 'degree zero' assaults on contemporary life long before it became the fashion. *The Apes of God* rendered T. S. Eliot speechless, spoofing all before it, from the upper classes, through philosophers and psychologists, to Hemingwayesque blood-cult buffoons, the arsehole acrostics of Joyce, and the Priappist pipe-dreams of Lawrence. *The Human Age* was written by a man who was, in a sense, no longer human—if he ever had been. The tarry *Trilogy of Tarr*, the *Malign Fiesta* and *Monstre Gai*, was an exquisite distillation of poisonous ire aimed at the fatty hearts of a porcine Populus. His *Rude Assignment* was untrumped, an intoxicating tonic for the eponymous victim of *Self Condemned*. Growing blind as Tiresias, he saw more clearly in his own mind's eye, like a drunk Dylan Thomas blotting out the world, only with sharper clinical dissection and less Logorrhoeic lyricism. Forgotten in his own lifetime, he is re-forgotten for posterity. He was not forgiven for his dalliance with the Nazis. Yet in his scope he eclipsed the swinging arc of the pendulum along the static line from Right to Left. Outsiders like Wyndham Lewis will their high exclusion from the human race through a cultivated contempt for mass-ignorance and idiocy; for the crass vulgarity of entertainment, and the false facades of whatever passes for Respectable Society. They may or may not be born with the Outsider-gene so to speak, but with a combination of bitter experience and ruthless intelligence they feel impelled to absent themselves from the mainstream culture, and strike a studied pose of estranged defiance and ultra-refined insouciance. They stand or fall on the Flaubertian conundrum of loathing human folly, whilst cynically learning to live and contend with it—albeit as far as possible on their own stringently acerbic terms. They are in truth the modern and post-modern variegated spawn of Nietzschean Supermen. Austin Osman Spare, the artist and magician, ranted and raved in language that almost excelled Nietzsche in *The Anathema of Zos*. An Outsider from choice more than circumstances, he came to despise the shallow, money-grubbing art-world, turning his back on it with a penuriously Promethean vengeance, producing a unique body of writing, as well as art, thereafter. Maurice Richardson and Julian McClaren-Ross were Soho habitués and Grandees of Bacon's gilded gutter, ultimate *éminences grises* growling in the shade of Society. They could out-talk anyone from the Pariah's Panopticon of the Bohemian bar-stool. These two gadflies and pub-philosophers didn't entirely waste their unbottled Genius in streams of golden urine, as they distilled the juices of their gripes in works of fantastical fiction: *The Exploits of Engelbrecht*, and *Of Love and Hunger*. Though much admired by the likes of Waugh and Greene, and later on Amis, neither man sought the accolades or comforts of high literary society. Resolutely unsycophantic, they settled instead for the ignominious eyries of sleazy oblivion.

G. B. Shaw set an example in *Man and Superman*, rejecting religion yet rescuing ethics from the egotistical quandary by endorsing altruism after a fashion. Though the man who chose vegetarianism on the grounds that animals were his friends, and he didn't eat his friends, and advocated the communitarian principle of shared work, was also the 'chucker out' who sympathized with eugenics early on, and was fooled by Stalin later on, if not by Hitler. The tug-of-war between Left and Right was very strong in him. Just a basic core of non-racist humanitarianism saved him from embracing one or other of the twin-tyrannies of the twentieth century. It did seem ironic to some people that so many Fascists or Nazis liked animals and were vegetarians. But this was only because they didn't like people! It was alright to massacre one's human enemies, but one should never be cruel to dumb animals—that would be bullying! Every tyrant had his redeeming feature, or sentimental kink more like. Shaw's intellect and abhorrence of philistinism saved him from such extremism. But he had an almost Tolstoyan sense of vocation that set him apart from the masses. This made him a nihilistic anti-traditionalist in his thought, yet a sort of People's Seer in his living role and Persona, the great Irish Panjandrum turned self-made Philosopher. He had a strongly Didactic streak in him, not unlike Brecht—although unlike Brecht, he was also humorous, and did not regard his plays as being merely vehicles for the propagation of dogmas. He displayed far more subtlety and complexity concerning the inherent lack of fit between human beings in the round and the abstract theories that writers of the Brechtian School sought to impose on them. However, he never lost hope that human beings would muddle through all their dilemmas, and build something akin to a New Jerusalem.

Other famous contemporaries of Shaw in literature, like Orwell, Greene and Huxley maybe didn't quite measure up to Shaw's stature. Although they developed highly singular visions of the world, and came to occupy deservedly high places in the continuing Canon. They were deeply concerned about humanity, but there was a bitter comedy in their depictions of humanity *in extremis*, which served to undermine slightly the serious warnings they were issuing. The 'slither of ice in the heart' grew into a veritable pick-axe on occasion, suggesting a somewhat sadistic literary sensibility at work. The Outsider-Writer as sadist *par excellence* found echoes in *Brighton Rock* and *Stamboul Train*; and in *Brave New World* and *Keep the Aspidistra Flying*. Patrick Hamilton's *Hangover Square*, Henry Green's *Living*, and William Gerhardie's *Futility* went arguably even further in twisting the tourniquet of torture and torment close to a point of expiring. And these authors were less well-known, and had far more marked Outsider-eccentricities: Hamilton was a stalker and low-life bum; Green a melancholic luminary; and Gerhardie a superstitious recluse. Yet they all possessed in massive abundance the true Spirit of the uprooted Outsider—Gerhardie especially, as he was not English, but settled in England, only to find that he had no home in the world. And so he retreated into a darkened room for the last thirty years of his life. The others were true born Englishmen, who nonetheless felt they were Aliens in their own land, and lived and wrote as if they were burdened by this plight, or stigma even. And yet these burdens were also sources of illumination for them, which they almost needed, in order to justify their existence through their work. Their experience of the lives of the poor and lonely, the miserable and depraved, gave them the muck of a real subject, that they were then able with their odd-ball talents to turn into true gold. This was better than simply succumbing to squalor and sordidness, or merely reflecting it back at itself without transmuting it into something else, something greater, something approaching Art.

All these boldly creative, harshly eccentric, Outsider-Writers, suffered for their art to one degree or another. Yet they didn't however wallow passively or unproductively, still less suicidally, in their suffering, but extracted something of positive value from the negative riches of their personal tragedies. And their triumphs, even if they achieved far more recognition posthumously than during their lifetimes, pointed the way towards new horizons where more recent and contemporary self-aware Outsider-Writers can stake their territorial claims, in defiance of whatever opposes or oppresses them, and in defense of new visions of new orders of Civilization. The Outsider-Writer, far from being a relic and an anachronism, a living ghost forever seeking abandoned wastelands in which to hide from Humanity and slowly waste away into a mirage of nullity, still has a tremendous Project—a whole range of Projects!—to undertake and pursue in the contemporary world, with all its nightmarish scenarios and intractable dilemmas. He is, or certainly can be, an immensely significant and important figure, if not exactly an Icon, which may rather contradict his purposefully distanced status. Yet he can be consulted in much the same sort of way as Sages or Seers were long ago—like Coleridge in his day, the 'Sage of Highgate', for whom the likes of Mill, Carlyle, and Emerson, would often climb that Great Northern Height of London, to sit at his feet and imbibe his unearthly wisdom. So perhaps there might be Coleridges in our day who could, and should, command similar audiences—however possessed of post-modern sophistication and circumspection! Though whether this may be the extent of such a person's influence today, combined with their written output, is an interesting question.

Glimpses of a Future...

It is now a commonplace in studies of Outsider-Artists that the incongruous fame or celebrity that has been somewhat thrust upon them, has not only complicated their already quite complicated enough relationships with society, but also inhibited them, and damaged or distorted their subsequent work. And if, as I maintain, Outsider-Writers come from the same stable so to say psychologically, or a good number of them do, then they may well be affected in the same ways by the various forms of publicity that have come to prevail. So it is to this extent unlikely that they could ever be in high profile positions in society, like politicians, academics, media-personalities, opinion-formers and cultural arbiters, who are totally at ease in the spotlight of the world, and can thereby openly perform the roles and tasks that were once attributed to the 'hidden persuaders'.

Yet the problem with this is that influence, and power, are always far too important for the rest of us simply to leave to the armies of the all-too-willing, smugly scheming moguls and pundits among the 'Commisariat'. These peoples' motives always need to be questioned—not to say condemned—in societies which still encourage what Situationists used to call the 'spectacular' divisions of the 'cadres' which comprise them. We should never rest content in societies that blithely continue to grant power to the few over the many, because in any emancipated society nobody could exercise power in any shape or form over anybody else. The very structure of Power itself is what is fundamentally at fault, and practically nobody in public life is questioning it—if only because they're the beneficiaries of it! And the structure of influence, though more elusive or subtly porous perhaps, operates in a similarly pernicious fashion. And Outsider-Writers are in my opinion, pre-eminently well-placed to articulate, or even orchestrate, the opposition to these most entrenched mechanisms in our society and culture. In this sense, Outsider-Writers can have radical political agendas that complement the more rarefied aesthetics of their speculative, experimental work. And I can see no real contradiction here, even if for some such writers it may be an impossibly difficult and demanding synthesis to attempt. Some Outsider-Writers feel such visceral repugnance at the very thought of a politicised society and culture, let alone the reality of it, that it brings them out in psychosomatic rashes—just as though plagues of locusts were crawling all over their flesh! And I do understand this sentiment—believe me, Dear Reader!!!—as I have actually felt it myself in respect of the more unconscionably invidious and insidious aspects of political, and of course, consumer- and celebrity- so-called Culture! Even the merest notion of publicity has this effect on me sometimes. So I empathize with rabidly a-political writers.

But there are other Outsider-Writers—and I have striven to rival their outlook and practice—who have less trouble or no trouble whatsoever in producing fictions that can be read on so many seemingly contradictory levels, from aesthetics to politics, philosophy to pulp, etc.... that by all conventional criteria they cannot be judged to work. And yet they CAN and DO work—and sometimes triumphantly so! It's a cliché of course, but the rules of fiction are made to be broken. And Outsiders have an almost instinctive or inveterate grasp of both the appeal and the urgency of this imperative. Indeed, there is no need for rules as such to have any bearing at all on the writing of fiction. So one could write as if they don't even exist and do not need to be invented, still less dis-invented. 'There are no rules in Art,' as Goya wrote, and the same principle applies to writing in my view. And to the classic riposte that one needs to know the rules first, before one can earn the right to break them, I have just one riposte of my own—which is no doubt unprintable even in this context. Though I'm sure I can rely on the rich imaginative resources of the readers who have stayed with me so far on this 'Journey Experience', to provide it for me in the un-policed privacy of their own minds—only think of the once-celebrated catch-line of a certain Northern comic!! Seriously though, the flaw in the above-argument—if one call it an argument—is that none of us ever knows the exact status of the supposed 'rules' governing our use of language as we actually engage in writing and speaking and thinking. The 'options' as I would rather call them are always in the making as it were, as we endlessly generate or regenerate the chaotic flux of elements that churn constantly in the reservoirs of our cognition. And so we can never arrive at a stable formulation of what the supposed 'rules' of fiction might actually be.

And the people who usually lay down the Law on these ridiculous, oppressive fabrications of correctness, tend to be those who are the most at risk of being toppled from their sedimented Pedestals—the Grand Old Farts of Letters, who are long past their literary use-by-date, yet who cling on viciously to their wilted laurels like cantankerous clams, dry and desiccated as semen-dust, whilst they strain their wobbly necks to catch sight of the galloping Young Turks in their wake, coming to consign them to a fully deserved oblivion. It is always in these groaning geriatrics' interests to try and shore up what they falsely and ignorantly imagine to be timeless standards—eternal verities!—which the younger generation, and they too were once young though they've conveniently forgotten this, has eroded to an intolerable degree! This hypocritical cant gets repeated—and not only in the literary world of course—by every generation, with slight differences of language, tone and emphasis, but with essentially the same tiresomely tireless message; and one would suppose that by now at least, the piled-up preposterousness of this message would have finally sunk into the degenerating heads of our ageing Peers. But Alas, no! And I fear it shall be ever thus. But if it were not for the contagious influence of this pseudo-venerable nostrum on the purveyors and promoters of fiction—i.e. those abominations, the Publishers, about whom I had better restrain my ire for now!!—Outsider-Writers could blithely ignore the dribbling denunciations of the GOFLs above, and not only them, but the middle-aged mediocrats of the mainstream also, the MAMMs no less! Not that age *per se* is necessarily the issue, as some Outsider-Writers retain the fiery resolution of their youthful Being well into middle- and even old-age. For True Writers, their voices and visions do not age, but remain essentially the same, since maturity does not interest them. They know we all mature like rotten apples, and it is better to hold onto the pulse and quick of youthful vigour and output than to just capitulate to decay, swallowing the myth of senescent wisdom.

We may grow up, but we must all fight against growing old, even if this is a battle we are all doomed in the end to lose. Retaining a childlike wonder and sense of pristine experience is more valuable to a writer, or any creative person, than merely being grown up in judgement. And there is a degree of timelessness and immutability in the defiant young identity of such a person that renders them almost immune to ageing in attitude, even as they age in body. And this is not to be confused with mere childishness or immaturity, as it is an essential pre-requisite of attaining an overview of the continuities of life. But there are few people nowadays involved with mainstream-writing in particular or mainstream-culture in general, who have any clear understanding of the central importance of this outlook, not only for Outsider-Writers, but for what I would insist on calling True Writers. The principle articles of faith amongst the GOFLs and the MAMMs are the stale cycles of maturation following the moribund pattern of linear narrative: a beginning, a middle, and an end. Fiction has to obey the dictates of a pre-Modernist, not to say a pre-Einsteinian, world, where everything happens sequentially, and a proper story is told, *un piece bien fait*, about believable characters in real-life scenarios, depicting the panorama of human life from a single, proto-authoritative, reassuring viewpoint. James Joyce blew this Victorian, Bourgeois, clockwork-fiction out of the water, the echoing ripples of the explosion still spreading to the far shores of our culture today, if largely unheeded by more recent and contemporary authors, who are in the main still trying, and failing, to beat old Dickens at his game. But great as he was in his day—albeit an incurable sentimentalist—Dickens has had his day today. Sometimes I'd happily send all stories back to Homer—where they arguably belong, if not began—but they continue to belch out interminably from the engine-room of the literary psyche in some shape or form. Yet writers should be producing new forms of fiction that our forebears, ignorant of the amazing modern advances in human thought and science too, could barely have imagined to be possible. And in various pockets of sub- and super-culture this has of course been happening. But either it hasn't been sufficiently absorbed into the wider culture, or else it has been but in distorted ways that have deprived it of its essence. And in some instances, experimentation has essayed the worst kinds of pretentiousness; even though in one sense at least pretentiousness is an entirely valid, indeed desirable, kind of conceit, giving full expression to aspirations and ambitions that would otherwise never be pursued in predominantly static cultures. But the stagnant backwaters of post-modernism are best left to percolate in the endlessly recycled rot of their own effluence. It is I think incumbent on writers to seek to advance the very corpus of literature, rotating it in the prism of its four base modes: fiction, non-fiction, meta-fiction, and anti-fiction. And this is the sphere in which great Outsider-Writers can shine most brilliantly, because it comes most naturally to them to proceed from an oblique position, and then to deviate from all the standard conventions of writing.

Although we've had multiple viewpoint, stream of consciousness, the unreliable narrator, sub-text, para-text, the death of the author, fragment, unconcluded narrative, the *avant-garde* and *après-garde*, Bardism, psycho-geography, secret society conspiracy, Grimoires, Socialism-Anarchism-Situationism, Oulipo, Mauvism—plus post-post-modernist phantasmagoric piss-pot trickery; along with pulp, genre, sci-fi, fantasy, occult, horror, hard-core, slip-stream, weird, new weird, abject, trans-gender, fetish, bestiality, metamorphism, Absurd, Cruelty, slander, libel, blasphemy, heresy, banned—and unclassifiable forms of fiction, being produced all over the planet for many decades now; they are still in varying degrees marginalized, and even ghettoised in a whole plethora of sub-cultures, that the literary and cultural mainstream establishment is struggling to keep at arm's length. The power of the Internet, the revolution in self-publishing, and the resurgence of the counter-culture in all its forms, political, social, cultural, etc. may help to tip the balance a little in favour of a greater movement towards the centre from the periphery. But if this happens at all it will take a long time, and it will be fraught with pitfalls and setbacks. Outsiders can't assume that any such solidarity amongst themselves will always hold fast in the various different contexts in which it could emerge more or less spontaneously. This hasn't happened often in politics. And in the cultural sphere, it might be even more transitory and fractious. But there are grounds for hope that Outsiders can come out of the Existential cold as it were, then join forces in a real opposition to everything that conspires against pioneers and pariahs alike.

Taking to the discursive barricades, the stalest literary trope of all is surely Plot, which has not only survived the barrage of assaults from modernism and post-modernism, etc. but it is still positively thriving in a great deal of twenty first century fiction. Why this is so is truly bewildering, when you consider that we are no longer in the Age of the Plot—barring espionage, that is! And I exclude thrillers from this discussion, of course. Politics may resemble a bad game of chess, but Life is not in essence a Plot. There might be plots from time to time, but many, indeed most, people do not experience plots in their lives, whether they wish to or not. Their lives are either too dull or else too chaotic to permit such worked out Scenarios to occur, step-by-step, leading to neat conclusions every time, following the mandatory twist or two. And if Life is not in the main like this, then why should Fiction be? Of course, Fiction does not necessarily have to mirror Life exactly, or even at all; contrary to B. S. Johnson, who maintained that Fiction is a lie, and so writers ought to depict Life and their experience of it without ever making anything up. For whilst I do agree with the wonderful old curmudgeon, I put the opposite construction on it: let fiction *be* a lie, and see whither the lie leads us! However, we do not have to follow the parameters of plotting, in pursuing the headier realms of speculative experimentalism. On the contrary, we can jettison them altogether and play around with the infinite possibilities of fiction, which is arguably the truest, and the best literary/philosophical project that writers can engage with today. And Outsider-Writers are leading the field in these realms.

Character is another outmoded Shibboleth of fiction, crying out be shot down forthwith. Let's leave the George Eliot imitations to the Edwina Curries of the literary world, and put them in the critical equivalent of the Pillory, then hurl Salmonella-infected eggs at their wretched heads! It's a contemptible Bourgeois notion if ever there was one, imprisoning the Individual in the cosy carapace of a formulaic identity and uniform even, as if the essence of a person, any person, could ever be bound up in such a cripplingly finite, and stiffly obnoxious, nutshell. It should not surprise us that such a nostrum held so much sway in the petticoated purlieux of Jane Austen's social scene. But we are under no more obligation now to revisit this charade of caricature than we are to people our fiction with the progeny of Beatrix Potter's risibly sentimental ducks and rabbits et al. Character resembles a snake-skin, that we can and should slough off at will. It's just a phoney costume that we've never wanted to wear, but may be forced to wear by Society, or else in Fiction, unless we have the guts to refuse, and then rip it off—to reveal not so much Naked Emperors, but our more fully complex Selves. And any writers concerned with political, psychological and philosophical issues bordering on the Trans-Human, will be striving to carry Fiction far beyond the confines of Character into Allegorical, Mythical and Archetypal regions, where Individuals cease even to be Personalities, and become Figures or figments of a whole instead.

Narrative does not have to develop along a gradient, building up suspense towards a climax. It may not develop at all, or if so, in stutters of surprise and nuclei of incident, punctuated by threads that multiply and ramify and criss-cross, and never get tied up in the end. Looseness is an essential ingredient of Fiction, as it is of Life and Experience. Chaos lies at the root of everything, and if a hint of coherence can be conjured from the morass, then so be it. But if it isn't, then it need not matter. The challenge of producing a Soup of Language, that conveys and captures something of the gist of Creation itself, the complexities of Cosmic constituents, is maybe beyond our powers in the Isomorphic resonance and reach of our mind-brains, and any other faculties we possess. It is like a blacked out Star, that glows in a Light we do not yet comprehend. To approach it in writing, we have to let go of our traditions, and grope in the dust of linguistic Entropy to spread out new maps of the dangling voids at the edge of our ken. The compendium-map alluded to earlier involves the matrix-grid of base-modes, graphically representing all the possible combinations and permutations, in Fiction, Non-Fiction, Meta-Fiction, and Anti-Fiction. And this for me is perhaps the greatest challenge facing any serious writer, who strives to bring the future into the present, in whatever shape or form. Experiments in writing all fall into one or other, or more than one, of the above categories, while aiming at best to abandon all categories. Only through syntheses that supersede the stasis of contradiction and conflict, can higher orders and new possibilities in writing be achieved or opened up. So I shall try and make clear in the rest of this chapter how exactly I envisage such syntheses.

A good starting-point is the perennial stand-off between the mainstream literary culture and what since the 1960s at least has been called the counter-culture. This set up a vital Dialectical clash between those who had an essentially conservative vision of what it is to be a writer and what writing is for, and those who wanted to revolutionize writing in just about every conceivable sense. It was obviously not the first period in history when literary orthodoxies were challenged and to some extent or another overthrown. But it pitched what was otherwise an age-old tension between order and chaos onto a radically new plane where the paradigm-shifts being threatened struck at the very root of writing-as-practice as distinct from writing-as-theory or writing-as-art and Bourgeois self-indulgence. It wasn't simply a question of launching intransigent or extreme new forms of writing against the thick and impervious Bulwarks of bland, boring, limited, un-adventurous, established forms of writing—in the manner of Futurism, Surrealism, Dadaism, and Lettrism, etc. All those movements may have had their 'moment of necessity' in the far greater Dialectical struggle. But they never achieved much more in total, than a series of systematically side-lined spectacles of ridicule, spinning off critiques and satires like catherine-wheels fizzing out in sequestered spaces, without sparking off irresistible ripples of conflagration in the larger space that mattered most of all. What purported to be mass-movements only ended up as unintended elitist cults or cliques, nihilistic niches on the less than fertile ground of the Lunatic Fringe, as delineated by the dictat of Cultural Power. Some ideas did filter through and became absorbed into the bloodstream of the dominant culture. But they were then neutralized and badly imitated. Tzara smashed his plates, playing with *papier mache*; Malevich blacked his squares; Marinetti went insane with techno-babble; Breton re-plotted Paris in pipe-dreams; Duchamp invited mass-micturition; Beuys smuggled found objects; and Burroughs cut up junkie-trifles, etc....

Glimpses of a Future...

But the Situationists went further, much further. Writing was the weapon that would not only destroy Establishments, but also and above all else, itself. The writer, like the artist, the academic, and the politician, would ultimately resolve himself into the Praxis of the world through the renunciation of his own pseudo-privileged position, *vis-à-vis* the world. Writing would become superfluous at that critical juncture in History when men took full possession of their own lives and destinies, as their dreams were fleshed out in the concrete tissues and textures of Reality itself. Writing then would go beyond itself—into spontaneous speech and unscripted actions, fulfilling the potentialities of our Being in the opened up domains of our own finally reclaimed Society. There wouldn't be a need any longer to chronicle or chart the course of History, and the travails of our experience, because we would not be separated any more as Subjects from the Objects of our desires. We would well and truly be at one with the world, our own world. And so in the process of living in and through this world we would thereby transcend and supersede the essentially alienated Act of Writing, and indeed of creating and producing in any other medium or art-form. Living itself would become our only ongoing work of art, political process and philosophical mode of enquiry and engagement. Even Science would become a function of this Dialectical Synthesis. Every human activity would become collective, even if Individuals would be fully autonomous within the Collectivity as such. This was the most radical theory of Politics and Culture ever developed. And if the Praxis hasn't followed suit, that may be because we all need more time to fully absorb its import.

The Situationists were far more in tune and touch with issues on the ground as it were, than were any of the other trendy, pseudo-intellectual, jargon-infected, academic theoreticians, from Structuralists to Post-Structuralists, Deconstructionists to Post-Deconstructionists, Post-Modernists to Post-Post-Piss-Pot-Modernists, Neo-Marxists to Post-Neo-Marxists, Feminists to Neo-Feminists to Post-Feminists to Neo-Post-Fucker-Feminists, Semiological, semolina pudding, senile idioticists, ist-ists, anti-ists, and every bloody els-ist! This farrago of bloated bilge, emanating from the profoundest pseudo-philosophic posteriors on the fog-obscured Continent, started floating across the Channel more than half a century ago, and has slowly contaminated just about every form of life in Britain, and of course elsewhere, indeed almost every-where, except perhaps the remotest Amazonian tribe, remaining blissfully ignorant of its taxonomic inclusion in the polymorphously perverse iconography of state-of-the-art Cultural Anthropology! The Situationists, to their eternal credit, cut right through all this sophistical institutional shit, and affirmed unequivocally the centrality of anti-academic thinking in a great emancipation of everybody from the false categorizations and specializations of divisive hierarchies. And they also retained a classical clarity of language that had tremendous power, not only poetically but viscerally: 'Mallarme with fire in his belly!', as Vaneigem once put it. They were the True Prometheans of all Revolutions.

But inevitably their ideas were sucked into the culture and then spat out with a sugary coating, as they themselves so presciently forecast. And the cataclysmic change in consciousness that they triggered began to collapse in on itself—along with all the dope-coshed detritus of the counter-culture as a whole, descending into the comatose reactionary backwaters of the status-quo ante in a cryogenic revival of bankrupted conservatism. And since then radical thought and practice have never really recovered, being polarized at an invisible end of a sclerotic pluralistic spectrum. The Marxian Project has been to all intents and purposes abandoned, as single-issue activists battle feebly against increasingly centralist consensus or coalitions, quite unaware of the holistic enormity of their own ideological blindness. And all manner of other issues beset us: environmental, ecological, economic, social, and psychological. The culture cannot cope. And the new counter-culture has only recently emerged. We are in a state of transition, and we might end up falling between the two stools. We have to relearn the lessons of the old counter-culture, in so far as the tools and weapons which it furnished were blunted by the asinine Mantras and soft-brained Rubrics of the Psychedelic movement, frying neural circuitries in lieu of raising consciousness. We must sharpen the political thrust underpinning the cultural exuberance, matching the analysis to the aspiration, applying the first principles to the prevailing conditions. And there is hope in these times of crisis, conflict and chaos, verging on catastrophe, that a return to the radical essentials could develop into a viable force for fundamental change involving all of us.

The Situationist vision of 'generalized self-management' involving 'workers' councils' may have been put on hold in a sense, as we take stock of just how far we still have to go in breaking down the barriers that alienate us from land, property, and free activity, geared to the satisfaction of our needs and wants. Outsider-Writers have crucial parts to play in articulating the flaws in the fabric of society, and envisioning how those flaws might be healed. And if they can draw inspiration from any one of the butts of Situationist invective, it might be found in the work of Deleuze and Guattari, especially with regard to their liberating concept of the Rhizome.

Originally this term had a use only in organic chemistry. But they stole it for an ingeniously roguish purpose, redefining it within the broad framework of so-called 'cultural studies' as a horizontal, plural, open-ended plateau of human expression—opposing both the top-down hierarchies of academic thought on the one hand, and the bottom-up militant movements of revolutionary reversal on the other. These twin-tendencies represent and embody closed systems as opposed to open systems—perhaps even in a Popperian sense, to some extent—of human thought and practice. After a fashion they were saying: anything goes, wherever it comes from and whoever is saying, writing, thinking, feeling or doing it. Obviously there's still some need for a 'truth-test'. But validation can come from within a system, as well as from without. It may or may not be consensual, and can employ many different sorts of criteria.

Once the Rhizome-Genie is let out of the bottle of organic and polemical culture, it spreads fast across the globe like a cluster of Dawkins' Memes, only with a difference. Memes are transmitted programmatically from mind to mind with collectivistic brain-washing agendas. The Rhizome manifests on the ground of all cultures in any shape or form, without dictation, granting autonomous expression to both groupings and individuals. The resulting cultural cornucopias then cross-fertilize, and fructify into further combinations and permutations of human culture. And so it soon gathers an unstoppable momentum of its own, incoherent and chaotic in places, but also self-correcting, and above all else people-created, side-stepping the elitist-popular divide. It negates the dominant culture, while at the same time affirming something different and new. And though primarily a cultural phenomenon, it totally embraces the political, social, personal-interpersonal, and even economic and environmental domains. After all, communities can be self-creating, and self-sustaining, organic entities, as well as cultures or sub-cultures. The Rhizome is infinitely porous, absorbing all ethnicities and geographical areas as well as more abstract cultural formations. It admits no assumption of pre-eminent superiority amongst the diverse forces and voices that emerge within it. If occasionally cacophonous, it can also tend to its own harmoniousness.

To the objection that it may fall prey to the Cultural Relativist trap of the equivalence principle, in which all cultural forms of expression are automatically assumed to be of equal value, it—or its proponents rather—can retort that in a full cultural democracy, this principle should at the very least be tested, if not to destruction, then for good measure. Such judgements of value could still be made, but won't carry the automatic institutional weight that for many centuries Eurocentric Imperialists simply took for granted, by arbitrament governing fiat—'No one good ever came out of the Dark Continents, damn it!...and we've got Leonardo, Michelangelo, etc.: QED or QED!' Having a genuine 'level playing-field' would guard against the more imbecilic bigotries of antediluvian patrician Blimps, and a darn sight more besides. And would it not always be preferable to inhabit the kind of global civilization and culture in which every attitude and opinion and prejudice and outlook, etc. was up for grabs, freely expressed and freely shot down, rather than one where certain of these expressions were authorized, and others not? Welcome to the world of the Rhizome, is I think the best and indeed the only answer to this question. And we have already been welcomed to it without knowing perhaps, not only in the writings of Deleuze and Guattari—and others of their ilk—but also in the cultural and technological developments that have been occurring throughout the world for a long time now.

Glimpses of a Future...

The Internet is the most obvious candidate for the viral spread of the Rhizome. But a few caveats need to be entered here, as we all know how much the Internet is policed by agencies that are utterly hostile to any notion like the Rhizome. In addition, we can become so narcissistically sucked up into the anal entrails of long-distance cyber-communications and the mindless masturbatory indulgences of solo-searches, that we become not only cut off at one remove from the world and others, but also and above all, cut off from our own selves in an empty, sterile, artificially drained and suspended space. There is in the end no substitute for real relationships with real others in a real world, fully in spite of the enormous opportunities, and openings, and labyrinthine byways that we can all explore and exploit for our own ends. And of course for Outsider-Writers, the privacy of the Internet—or its relative privacy—gives them an easy entrée into what may be the only social world they are capable of, or willing to, inhabit. And so the Internet is, as Chomsky said, 'a double-edged sword'. It could be one of the greatest vehicles of personal, social, cultural, and even political, emancipation that the world has ever seen—certainly on a par with the Gutenberg Galaxy. And yet at the same time it could be an almost Molochian trap for the over-curious and the psychologically vulnerable, as well as yet another instrument of Neo-Goebbels-style media-manipulation and mass mind-control. Unless the Internet can be used to connect us with each other in mutually self-empowering ways, that impact on the real world and the obstacles to freedom through a positive transformation, then its uses might be limited to information hunts, entertainments, and trifling exchanges.

More potentially productive Forums than the Internet could be conjoined in public and open spaces, like 1960s

'Happenings' or 'Be-Ins', only without the corny old drawling-voiced Hippie overtones—'Like Man—all us heads together would sheerly rip the sky off! You dig?'—or the earnest commie-comrade correctitude of what the Situationists called 'Marxist Thought-weeks'—'Anyone wearing a blue jacket, or worse still a black shirt, is in need of some serious re-education, Comrade.' But the technology of 'flash-mobbing', if put to very specific uses in a whole variety of contexts, ought to have the potential to galvanize people out of their desensitized sloth, and to re-energize them in unconventional settings for purposes that just might spill across the parameters of Power—at any rate if it were done on a sufficient scale frequently enough. Obviously any such initiatives could be co-ordinated via the Internet, or else mobile phones, but the calculated spontaneity of these gestures and motions, pushing at the boundaries of what is feasible, requires a mentality that is far more outwardly driven than merely inwardly brooding. And Outsiders deserve the option of breaking down all the barriers that separate them from Insiders, whether they choose to exercise this option or not. But if they do not wish to crawl away into holes for forty years, and to come out as Outsiders so to speak, and then wear their Outsiderdom on their sleeves, by voting with the oddballs of their feet in overwhelming displays of imaginative insurrection, they might be amazed at just how much could be achieved. The attempt at the humanization of Hesse's Steppenwolf didn't work out too well for the poor old anti-hero. But it doesn't have to be all that traumatic for an Outsider to join hands in a circle of human fellows to reclaim his birthright.

My own idea for these massive public gatherings, providing points of focus for the radical alternative, anti-mainstream-establishment, counter-culture, would involve regular Symposia in open-air Arenas and Geodesic Domes, bringing together people from many different fields in the arts and sciences, for brain-storming sessions and great Solidarity drives, with no dogmatic or doctrinaire programmes at all, yet unlimited Agendas in the making. These Free Universities for all would, I suppose, be reminiscent of the Dialectics of Liberation Congress, at the Roundhouse in London in the summer of 1967, where people as diverse as Herbert Marcuse, R. D. Laing, Max Ernst, Allen Ginsberg and Stokely Carmichael were present, in an extraordinary exchange of ideas and consciousness-raising initiatives, that dealt with the political foundations of the revolutionary transformation of society, whilst also and above all, addressing the far wider cultural, intellectual and spiritual issues of the time. Also, the whole Project of restoring human beings to themselves, to their own essential nature in the overall socio-historical framework, aside from the purely mechanistic roles and functions they were performing within State-Capitalism and the military-industrial complex, was their principle concern, upon which they reached unanimous agreement. And yet it's difficult to say how much was actually achieved in reality, on the basis of gatherings such as that. Though one shouldn't be negative about the apparent mis-match between theory and praxis in these contexts. Instead, we should constantly be looking for new ways in which to extend and refine their Dialectical inter-relationships in the contemporary world, as the issues that would be addressed are as urgent today as they have ever been—if not more so. And the alienation of Outsiders from insider-milieux goes to the heart of the main issue of necessary and total social change.

Outsider-Writers should be proud to be Outsiders in the sense of being inherently unco-optable by societies and cultures which shun them, and are not in truth worthy of their highest aims. But at the same time, they ought never to rest content with being ghettoised in marginalized backwaters on or beyond the outermost fringes of society. They ought to be proud enough in my view, to want to fight back against these pernicious and unconscionable acts of excommunication, with the intent of smashing the citadels of culture high and low, infiltrating the corridors of cultural if not political power, and re-animating the engines of creative activity throughout the whole of civilization. If this sounds preposterously grand in design, only think of the historical antecedents and precedents: The Storming of the Bastille, the Fall of St. Petersburg, the Long March. These iconic events in history may have led subsequently to disastrously barbaric and corrupted regimes, as already noted. But this did not mean that there was not a profound need, and indeed rationale, for the doubtless unavoidably violent shaking up of the brutally oppressive stasis of the preceding regimes that were overthrown. The counter-argument that the people involved should have waited more patiently for the imminent reforms doesn't really wash in my view, not just because the tendencies to true reform were not in evidence, but also because the people were so desperate, and in many instances literally starving, that they would have been dead if they'd waited much longer. The consequences of their actions may have been unforeseen, and unintended, as is so often the case in history. But the human case for revolution was overwhelming. And I know of no revolution in history that has not involved some measure of violence, not even the so-called Glorious Revolution, which was only a palace-revolution in any event, but still involved a conquest. Violence may be ugly and horrific in its visceral immediacy, but it can also serve as a cleansing force in stale and oppressive tyrannies, and could well be an inalienable element in human nature. Also, all self-serving hierarchies will tend to create laws that make it virtually impossible to undermine or overthrow them. At some critical point in other words, all revolutions involve law-breaking. And law-breaking on a revolutionary scale will lead invariably to violent conflict. So this is a tough Conundrum to resolve.

But Outsider-Writers, ever-mindful of the Situationist injunction, not to say imperative, to strive after the culmination of the Word in its ultimate embrace of the Deed, can in the meantime play their crucial part in trying to evoke the possibilities of revolution, and evolution as well, which is its necessary complement, in ways that never lose sight of the greater glories of Peace, if they can ever be attained. For a condition of peace is what we should all be aiming for in the world, and not the phoney Royal peace but a real peace, stemming from the cessation of the tensions which divide us from each other in all the controlled spaces of society. New forms of culture can break down these artificial and arbitrary divisions at least as well as more purely political movements and mechanisms. Class could well be the last barrier or boundary to break down here, as it continually reasserts itself in different forms and compositions, if only because there aren't any forces in society that are addressing or attacking it at its very roots, which is categorically what needs to be done to finally extirpate it from our lives. And maybe there needs to be something like an Outsider-Class in order to combat the entrenched universality of the phenomenon of class, which is always managing, like water, to find its own level wherever it is. But this new class would need to exist only temporarily, as a sort of all-round capillary action-device, drawing the pus of the entire class-system into itself first of all, and then abolishing, or better still abandoning, itself after that. Mannheim's Intellectual Class, or the Fourth Class as he called it, was intended to put a revolutionary spoke in the wheels of the well-established three-tier class-system—upper, middle and lower—by encouraging Intellectuals from all socio-economic class backgrounds to step to one side and join forces in a kind of Bohemian milieu, from which vantage-point they could then challenge the entire class-system, and create a new alternative, self-sufficient, open-ended, system. It clearly didn't work, but the idea is now ripe for revival, and should help to provide a natural home for Outsider-Writers among others, who may not spearhead the movement, but could very capably bring up the rear with their aesthetic ammunition! It should come as no surprise however, that many Outsider-Writers prefer, like Emerson, to stay away from conferences! But the less 'conference-like' conferences, or counter-cultural gatherings, can be, the better.

Experiment might have a polemical application in the above-sense, but it can still also be indulged and pursued purely for its own sake. And so I'm turning full circle again on the foundational axis of the four base-modes of writing. Fiction, as I've already indicated, has to explode its way through the moribund conventions of contemporary narration to reveal new fields of endeavour. But what of the other three? Non-Fiction, on the face of it, is incompatible with Fiction. But in my view, there is simply no way of separating it neatly from Fiction. All Non-Fiction is in the final analysis Fiction, as one can never totally distinguish fact from invented, and also imagined, truth, any more than one can from value-judgement. Even the most rigorously quasi-objective historical and scientific description and analysis rests fundamentally upon interpretation and viewpoint and to a degree a subjective understanding of the world and reality. And Fiction is a process of creative elaboration from the same initial premisses, that moves towards the far end of the spectrum that begins with observation and ends with fabrication. 'We make our own Truths!' Vico, the Italian Renaissance Philosopher, once excitedly proclaimed. And Kierkegaard was echoing him, and might well have had him in mind, when he more famously declared that 'Truth is Subjectivity.' Although he was also of course taking a swipe at Hegel's Objective Idealism. But it is the crucial plank in the philosophical platform underpinning the whole enterprise of human thought and culture. For however attuned we might be to Eliot's tiresome and academically safe 'objective correlate', we are still at root Solipsistic creatures spun from the Cloud of Unknowing. And in the final analysis, we are still that—for all that! 'Solipsism is irrefutable, yet incoherent.' So said the bread-and-cheese consuming deck-chair thinker—or 'Witters', as J. L. Austin called him. Most philosophers fix on the word 'incoherent' in that remark, whereas I fix on the word 'irrefutable'.

This suggests Solipsism is the true source of all we are, feel, think and do, in relation to our own selves, others, and, not least, the external world. It is the one inescapable brute fact of our Being, which like the speculative claims of metaphysics, we cannot articulate without talking some variety of nonsense. But then when have we not talked nonsense throughout history? The entire struggle of humanity to enlighten itself has involved one long—not to say never-ending—battle with all the varieties of nonsense! And whether or not any beliefs, and systems of belief, are nonsensical is in itself a matter that is always, or very often, up for grabs. And I hereby maintain that the origins of the Self are both indivisible and indefinable, ultimately. Our autonomy as individuals, and our authorship of our own Being and the story of creation, is given and maybe guaranteed by these unfathomable and imponderable constituents. So, as science and history are our own inventions, they use descriptive and explanatory tools to tell stories about the world and the universe, just as mythology and literature tell stories, even though the criteria by which we evaluate them do differ. And this must be the foundation for claiming as I do, that fiction and non-fiction can and should be combined in writing, because in essence they're inseparable approaches to creative understanding. An experimental fiction that not only draws upon, but also incorporates, elements of non-fiction into its story, which may not even be a story as such, or in any conventional way, is thereby a perfectly legitimate exercise in corralling all the faculties to create a singular, yet multi-faceted and potentially all-embracing, piece of work. The possibilities of science fiction and fantasy and historical fiction are such that facts can be effectively distorted for sound fictional ends, whilst non-facts can be inserted into factual texts for philosophical ends.

All the permutations of the above are pretty well limitless, promising the development of many new kinds of writing in the future, where all the old rules and conventions have been broken down and swept away, and quite different conceptions of the whole relationship between meaning and truth abound. Sometimes semantic meaning will predominate, but at other times not. Sometimes it will matter whether something is in some palpable sense true, and at other times not. Fragments of fiction will interweave with tracts and treatises and all manner of exposition. Scholarly studies and pioneering breakthroughs in research and problem-solving will form palimpsests with mythical symbols, literary metaphors, and Monadic philosophical conceits. The dividing-lines between all the academic specialisms will disappear, as porous floods of anarchic human thought fill the gaps in the official records of our understandings, to reclaim the whole territory of cultural production for the Holistic Outsiders swimming against the currents and creating their own currents in the process. This may seem like an unholy chaos drowning the corpus of ordered knowledge, but will in fact amount to the revitalizing of our modes of cognition, democratizing intellect and learning in the best senses, and more truly reflecting and articulating the chaos permeating the very nature of things and all our ideas concerning this. Coherence is pretty hard to achieve, though it can start to coalesce fleetingly in the final stages of projects, and as such illuminate our self-driven obsession with imposing order on chaos and thereby giving meaning to our experience. But this may still limit the possibilities of projects unnecessarily, even though it remains an option that enables us to derive numerous lessons from our experiments. All projects begin and end in chaos. If there is only one law of writing, and of Life, then this is it. Coherence is often a fortuitous gift, rather than a pre-meditated form. And sometimes, perhaps more often than not, it's a tainted chalice. So let subjectivity and objectivity collide and collude forever.

One of the other directions we are led in is of course Meta-Fiction. This is a long-established theoretical practice in writing, taking many forms. It has encountered much hostility, stemming in the main from incomprehension, and the strong suspicion that it must be the preserve of pretentious pseuds, trying to impress readers with abstruse cleverness and obscurantist jargon. There's some truth in this charge, but it's certainly not the whole truth, for there has to be scope for fiction which literally contemplates itself while it develops a self-referential critical reflex, which is central to meta-fiction.

Meta-narrative and meta-textuality undermine the dominant assumption of traditional fiction that it should follow a definite sequence or progression, and possess a complete internal logic of its own that drives it on to its own inexorable conclusion. For just as narratives can fracture and fragment, so they can operate at different levels that contradict or interrogate each other in ways that split them or challenge their integrity. They can multiply and mutate and never reach a neat conclusion. They can grapple with the very nature and limits of serial story-telling—subverting its forms totally. And then they become something else themselves, something very elusive and slippery and uncategorizable, yet absorbingly fascinating and compelling, on the imaginative and intellectual planes. *Tristram Shandy*, by Lawrence Sterne, was a very early example of this, anticipating Joyce's *Ulysses* in a sense, by focussing at least as much on the rambling thought-processes of the main protagonist, interspersed with authorial digressions and animadversions, as on the crazily chaotic patterns of what still purports to be the story-line after a fashion. But the startling and relentless cross-fertilizing, and fusing of the voices of the author, narrator and characters, in all their bewildering profusion, threatens to make each strand indistinguishable or inseparable from every other strand. This was revolutionary in its day and the ramifications of such an experiment have been pursued by others right up to the present—Robbe-Grillet being one of its most famous exponents. And yet its possibilities are as inexhaustible as meta-language itself.

Outsider-Writers are in my view temperamentally or even constitutionally drawn to Meta-Fiction by virtue of being self-detached or decoupled from themselves and others—viewing the world from at least one remove. They are therefore, naturally inclined to initiate and follow all the tributaries of their own thought, as they attempt to tie them into a single stream of consciousness running through their projects. And sometimes they will fail to bend the tributaries to the will as it were of an overarching motif, and will pursue them whither they will, getting lost in the interminable intestines of their interior labyrinths, even as they struggle to get a reflective grip on the inveterate creative untidiness of their minds. And so they are launched into the minefields of Meta-Fiction willy-nilly, and must find some comprehensive way of negotiating their passage through them, and coming out at the other end with hopefully some slight control still of their mental disarray! The problem then becomes how to bring the accumulating layers of Meta-Fiction back to the ground of production so to speak, turning the full circle of a project, even if it can only end at a circumferential juncture that is forever revisitable. This may be beyond the powers of many writers undertaking such vertiginously heady labours. Or it might in the very nature of the project be strictly impossible without distortion or over-simplification, like the old geometrical conundra of squaring the circle or creating a perpetual motion machine! And so the writer could be in danger of getting infinitely lost in his head, like Cantor with his Alephs, and may never return to base as such. Instances of this are exceptionally rare. Although Pessoa with his Heteronyms, and Gadda with his interrogation of the I, will involve me in true tests of sane endurance in my attempts at analysis in later chapters!

And finally, what are we to make of Anti-Fiction? This I must confess is a personal favourite of mine, as I've always been instinctively drawn—for as long as I can recall—to the great Smashers of Fiction, and by extrapolation the world, the great haters and Contrarians and intransigently bloody-minded dissenters and destroyers, the mighty awkward squad, the bad boys—and girls!—the fearless purveyors of all the extremes and the dark stuff, the rule-breakers and the ball-busters! For these writers, Fiction is emphatically not a fetish to be suckled like a drooping nipple, some reified and commodified object of sentimental attachment and adulation; but a transitory form of expression to be fashioned like a tool at first, and then smelted into a weapon, that can be abandoned when its satirical killing work has been done. There is no good reason why anybody should still write novels in the twenty-first century, from the standpoint of Anti-Fiction, as they should have died with Dickens. They were in fact killed by Joyce, but no-one—or hardly anyone—noticed! For Joyce is as little understood today by the majority of writers as Einstein is by the majority of physicists. And he was only one of a number of twentieth century writers who tried in their very different ways to create a new Language, and thereby to revolutionize writing. But where the Anti-Fiction writers differed from all these writers was in their overriding aim to destroy fiction altogether, and emphatically not to create or re-create some replacement for the fiction that exists. Anti-Fiction writers, or simply Anti-Writers, want to put an end to fiction and writing in its entirety—dissolving or else resolving it into something else, that which lies beyond it, the sphere of emancipated practices that the Situationists envisioned and sketched out for others to come along and develop. Anti-Writers break writing down into its ultimate constituents, or as far towards them as possible, and then allow those constituents to assemble or disassemble themselves for their own inscrutable ends. Writing comes to write itself in other words, automatically, and yet in discrete bits, atoms and nuclei, that just might display or evolve their own intelligence and pursue purposes that may elude our comprehension. This is the end-point of the degree zero school of writing that Barthes *et al* essayed, carrying the Deconstructionist project beyond the critique of narrative and the author, to language, thought, action and Being entire.

Anti-Writing aims to write writing itself into extinction, even if it remains impossible to conceive of the after-life of language, so to speak. Although Anti-Writers are generally so maniacally, not to say diabolically driven by their insanely arrogant Supremacist desire to destroy everything, and then to embrace nothingness, that they almost constantly imagine that this goal is closer to being achieved than it actually is—or ever proves to be. But in the process, the most gifted of them take truly Preternatural strides in that direction. And if they don't die on the page as it were, they often contrive to sign off in mid-flight, or in free-fall, or in Abysmic disintegration. And they tend to remain ruthlessly wedded to their own annihilation through a medium of language that is turned inside out into something other than itself ultimately. This is doubtless the purest project a writer can undertake, as only a writer's writer *par excellence* would dream of doing so, for they would be doomed to total mass incomprehension, and excommunication! But it requires therefore, such a special, if not unique, degree and kind of Phenomenological perseverance in thus navigating, if not excavating, the Numinous, that perhaps only the severest Outsider-Writer would ever be equipped for this task. One could not picture any Insider-Writer being so masochistically magnanimous, as to saddle themselves forever with such an unforgivingly singular burden. Few if any of them would even wish to contemplate leading the life-style of a true Anti-Writer, let alone tackling the overwhelming enormity of dismantling the structures providing them with all their cosily conformist tropes, nostrums, genres and formats.

Glimpses of a Future...

Examples of Anti-Writers are numerous, if rather obscure. My favourites are: Lautréamont, Lorrain, Corbiere, Cendrars, Jarry, Céline, Jabès, and Stewart Home. I'll be saying more about them in volume 2. Although suffice to say here, they were, and are in Home's case, all varieties of Outsiders, profoundly and jaggedly at odds with not only the literary culture, but also the whole world(s) they inhabited. They were all revolutionaries, blazing their own almost inimitable trails, in Ethers so headily heightened and toxically rarefied, that few others even spotted them, let alone shared in the same atmosphere. And yet they remained unshakably fixated on the destruction of all that had preceded them and the creation of new worlds that were so radically different, they could barely even be acknowledged to exist in any of the traditions to which these writers were so vehemently hostile. And so a conspiracy of silence has formed in the stale and crusty upper echelons of the literary mainstream establishment, against all these lethally dangerous marginalized invaders of the centralized citadels of so-called high culture, to protect fashionably moribund and meretricious writers from swift fates delivered at the hands of masterful literary assassins. A cynic might say it was ever thus. But if so, it is in many ways a far worse stasis than ever before, thanks to the increasing technological corporatization of commercial fiction, which brooks no interference nor contradiction, within the Globalized market-place. All opposition to the present dominant trends and tastes in general popular fiction is squeezed out of circulation and banished well beyond the margins into the oblivious hinterlands of the outermost wilderness. And it is there that Outsider/Anti-Writers can and should commence their counter-attacks and assaults upon the complacently embedded forces arraigned against them. At least they can't be dictated to in the wilderness or easily policed. And if they have to live off self-conjured Manna from a false Heaven, while they launch their dedicated, unpaid for campaigns, so be it. But there is nothing like the desperate edge of starved dispossession to give writers the authentic anger needed to wage a war for autonomy.

In conclusion, the future for Outsider-Writers—and studies in this field—is looking paradoxically very enticing at a time when more and more serious creators and thinkers are being driven from the folds of both pseudo-elitist and pseudo-popular culture into the embattled forums where all Outsiders instinctively congregate. Just as the economic, political and social mess of the contemporary world is pushing people towards the radical alternatives to State-Capitalism once again, so the paralysis of the literary and cultural mainstream establishment is pushing people towards the whole variety of Outsider-stances and stratagems. The writing that can result, alongside the outpourings in other art-forms, should mine the treasure-houses and fault-lines alike in the human understanding, to plant exploding bombs of Spirit beneath the wreckage in the wastelands of the old Materialist dispensation. My own envisioned glimpse of all this insurrectionary stirring, amounts to only one strand in the entire Thebaid of strands weaved by each and every individual, minded to make a contribution to this subject—which is so vast and continually growing it may be one of the largest subjects there is. And so it is of necessity a collective effort, and this book of mine was never intended to be the definitive work nor a compendium of cases. I can attempt objectivity in analysis. But I prize subjectivity of inspiration. Readers may borrow and steal what they will from this partial offering, to fashion companion-studies of their own, that diverge from mine as much as they wish. There may yet be an ultimate unity, but diversity matters more for now.

☸

Chapter Four

A Brief Miscellany of More Obscure, Mainly Female, Outsider-Writers.

In this chapter, I want to draw up a list of some relatively little known and read writers, giving very short accounts of each one of them, before I shift my attention to the real heavyweights, for each one of whom I will devote a whole chapter. All these writers may have certain things in common, but they need not do so, except by virtue of the fact that they are all of interest to me! And there can be little doubt too that they all belong somewhere or other, on the complete spectrum of Outsider-Writers. And there are also a few women on the list, who have so far been conspicuous by their absence from this book; not from chauvinism on my part, but because it is probably true to say that there are far fewer of them in the overall ranks of Outsider-Writers than men, although I'm not precisely sure why that should be. But there are certainly some women. And they cut remarkably singular figures indeed. In the past, it could be argued that women were the outsiders of the world—or 'the niggers of the world', as Yoko Ono once said in an isolated flash of intelligence!—because of the arbitrarily and indeed preposterously cruel ways in which their social, economic, political, cultural and intellectual status was systematically demoted by patriarchy. And this has to be the main reason why up until the nineteenth century there were so few women who attained prominence in public life and education. And if they ever did manage to achieve something of real importance, they would either receive only posthumous recognition, or else have to struggle and fight for acceptance in their own lifetimes, like Mary Wollstonecraft, one of the bravest of them all. A lot of them pursued their talent, whatever it may be, in secrecy, and just resigned themselves to the fact that they would never be able to do so publicly—or even in some cases, with the knowledge of their husbands, who would prevent them from doing it on the grounds that women should never cultivate their minds as this may estrange them from domesticity! It seems quite incredible today that this attitude can ever have held sway.

The historic subjection and general maltreatment of women by men and by Patriarchal traditions and institutions, has been tantamount to arguably the worst crime against humanity ever perpetrated. The notion that women did not have minds is just so *prima facie* absurd as to be barbarically grotesque and obscene! I can even recall Enoch Powell—that notable liberal!—stating once that in his undergraduate days at Cambridge, the University Dons—all of them men to a man, and there were scarcely any female undergraduates—held the view that 'women did not exist.' And this was in the 1930s! I had to do a double-take at this juncture, whilst trying to determine whether this great admirer of the Negro was being serious or ironic. And I could only infer from the characteristically prophetic Gravitas of his tone and demeanour that he was in fact being entirely serious! Although whether he himself had approved of the said sentiment was quite impossible to divine from the famously impassive inscrutability of his expression. Certainly his old tutor, A. E. Housman, would have clung to this ludicrous nostrum with all the peevish ferocity his lifelong security of tenure allowed! And I'm sure one can trace the phenomenon all the way back at least to Plato, with his homo-erotic educational agenda, which has underscored if not undermined so much of Western Education since—although ironically, for all that Plato preferred his own kind, he did favour education for women as well. But when you consider the quite exceptionally brilliant contributions to both the arts and the sciences that so many gifted women have made since the extension of education to women was so begrudgingly conceded less than a century ago—at any rate in this country, which boasted the finest education system in the world—it not only blows this execrable conceit right out of the water, but also makes one wonder just how many women of talent or genius have been lost to us throughout history by virtue of it. And it is of course, in precisely this shadowy domain that so many female Outsiders quietly strove to make their mark felt in their chosen fields—if only for posterity. And they were not Outsiders from choice, nor temperament necessarily, but largely, if not entirely, from circumstance. And only a tiny number are known to us.

I suppose Sappho might have been one of the first female Outsider-Writers, certainly in Europe, and it is primarily for her lesbianism that she is famous, even though she was a very fine poet, period—and not just a lesbian poet *per se*. Although homosexuality has certainly been one recurring feature of Outsiderdom, even after the continuous, collective 'coming out' parade since the decriminalization of what the Marquess of Queensbury—no queen he!—once spelt as Somdomites! In the days when these merry fellows could simply be tossed, after being caught *in flagrante*, on well-oiled bundles of faggots—no further pun intended!—and set alight by compassionate emissaries of the Inquisition, they all had rather good cause not to put their best feet forward too ostentatiously in public places, but instead to congregate inconspicuously in the soft pink under-shades of the cruising posterior regions of the planet! But apart from Michelangelo, and possibly Shakespeare, and I suppose Horace Walpole, there were hardly any known homosexual writers—Outsiders, or otherwise—between Sappho and Plato, at one unstoppered end of the spectrum, and our dear old friend Oscar, at the other end. So the more obscure ones were so obscure, as to be pretty well totally unknown. And so they remain today, as far as I can ascertain. And what about that Leonardo?! I can picture the straight-batting geezer down the boozer trumpeting at once: 'Well, the jury's still out on that one'. For his boy amanuensis may have been just that and no more. The evidence is still wanting. Though since Oscar it's been open sesame—with figures as diverse as Jean Genet and Jean Cocteau, Colette and Gertrude Stein, who were all celebrities in spite of their marked Outsider-tendencies, especially Genet. And now we have 'Queer Studies' on top of 'Gender Studies', examining the contemporary gay novel. Though it's hard to see where one may slot someone like Peter Ackroyd in with the likes of Armistead Maupin or Gore Vidal—as one could easily read almost any of Ackroyd's novels without ever guessing at his sexuality at all, which is in no small measure irrelevant to the Gothic or occult themes of his work. His Outsider-status is maybe not so camouflaged, even though he has managed quite admirably to occupy an eminent position in the Mainstream as well.

But most of the women Outsider-Writers of the last few centuries have been straight: from Aphra Behn, Mary Wollstonecraft, Emily Dickinson, Dorothy Richardson, Anna Kavan, Jean Rhys, Sylvia Plath, to Christine Brooke Rose; this last still very much alive in her eighties yet exiled in Paris, and still woefully unacknowledged in Britain—which is hardly surprising, given the utterly uncompromising, meta-narrative complexity of her work, which involves the kind of experimental writing that the bovine sub-intellectual cadres in the UK always distrust: 'Continental.' Although Rose herself is as English as the proverbial rose! She is occasionally lumped together with B. S. Johnson. But she herself rather resists the comparison, having once described him as 'talking a good *avant-garde* novel, but never actually writing one.' Oxford-educated, she has long preferred the company of French theorists like Kristeva and Irigaray, and doubtless brings a quiet English authority, Gravitas and clarity to bear upon the wilder and more convoluted Hermeneutical effusions of her Gallic companions. Her books have beguilingly unpopular-izable titles, such as *Xorandor*, *Verbivore*, *Textermination*, and the wonderful collection, *Out, Such, Between, Thru.* In what exact sense she is an Outsider-Writer is not at all easy to define. She certainly isn't outlandish—being an academic or scholar of some distinction, producing critical studies of Ezra Pound for instance, as well as being the almost unique standard-bearer of English-Continental meta-fiction over more than half a century. She's been married more than once, worked at Bletchley during the war, and has been attached to universities ever since. So she is in a very demonstrable way, a sort of high-minded cross-breed of insider and outsider, highly respected in her own circles, and yet practically invisible outside them. Her work is more abstrusely measured than strangely obscure. And yet there is I think undeniably some essence of the alien eye and spirit distilled in the multiple perspectives and reveries of her anti-authorial constructions and conceits, that renders her a truly dispassionate type of Outsider-Writer.

The others on my list—with the exceptions of Dorothy Richardson, who was a quite scandalously neglected figure, and Anna Kavan, the despairing heroin-addict—are better known; and the exegesis and criticism of their work is well-trodden territory, which I would probably be best not to try to add to, save to say that they can all be regarded in their respective veins as female Outsiders battling against either the demons of male-dominated societies in Behn's and Wollstonecraft's cases, or the demons of inner disintegration in Dickinson's, Rhys's and Plath's cases. Behn envisioned a sort of liberated Utopia in works like *Oroonoko*, drawing on fantastic reserves of poetical imagination that were deemed only to belong in the incommunicable depths of a woman's dreams, a region private to her and her maker, and not fit for public consumption. As for Wollstonecraft, she felt more than a century later that she could turn her seeming isolation into a real rebellion that could and would effect change. She in a sense died for her cause, albeit in childbirth rather than on the barricades. But though she altered little directly in her lifetime through her work and activity, the noble tragedy of her shortish life inspired other women after her to follow her example and go further still in extending the debate in The Vindication of the Rights of Women. They thereby laid the foundations for the acknowledgement of women as representing and embodying one half of humanity, that like the dark side of the moon, could yet be exposed to the sunlight of Reason and Emancipation. But it still took well over another century before women's Outsider status was significantly and substantially shifted by the final provision of certain fundamental liberties and rights. And yet all the great Victorian female campaigners owed their efforts to the original, brave inspiration of Wollstonecraft, who was very like an Enlightenment cross between Germaine Greer and Boadicea! And yet in many parts of the world aside from America and Europe, women still suffered like chattels, and indeed in some parts still do today! Few of them may be able to tell their story, but they all have a story to tell.

Dickinson would be one of the most enigmatic and fascinating of female Outsiders in history, if our perception of her hadn't been so permanently moulded by innumerable layers of exegesis and interpretation of her work and her life—which of course has been nothing less than inevitable since her discovery. The almost pristine purity of her anguished remoteness from others, and the depthlessly subtle complexities of her self-torments, are in some measure lost to us behind all the filtering prisms of scholarship that have been set up to penetrate her mind and soul. The Belle of Amherst, with her precious and beautiful pain of sensibilities, spent much of her life indoors—albeit in spacious comfort and well-nourished satiety bordering on luxury in her southern mansion!—refining her education and musing rarefiedly, yet precisely, on all the fleeting nuances of her inner predicament, so remote from human otherness that its sudden appearance in her room would have shattered her Being into a myriad fragments—like the Phenomenological counterpart to a Porcelain statue. The poetry was a stream of consciousness fashioned into a testament, a vast tribute to a life lived in a strange Stoicism of the Spirit, which toyed often with Epicurean flights of fancy that never found their home in the pleasures of the flesh. We cherish her legacy, as she provided us with a litmus-test of reclusive thrival. And however truncated and Existentially stripped her life was, her interior outpourings were as richly profound as any recorded in the Annals of Literature. She anticipated the likes of Rhys and Plath and Kavan by a century. And having negotiated the same abysmal tightropes of the psyche as them, she retained almost miraculously a calm steadiness of nerve, if not serenity of outlook, that the other three proved quite incapable in the end of either attaining or else maintaining. In fact, she so easily could have succumbed to the hallucinatory madness of Charlotte Perkins Gilman, who for years was confined to her bedroom by her family, and entered into a sustained, de-realizing, ego-splitting and -annihilating, visionary fantasy-world, hidden in the multi-dimensional layers of the flowery yellow wall-paper all around her, from which she extruded the title and contents of a masterpiece. Yet Dickinson possessed a far steelier sternness of stuff in her slight frame.

Jean Rhys is best known for *The Wide Sargasso Sea*, a truly inspired novel that may have stemmed from an Outsider's sensitivities of vision, but which earned her nevertheless an unquestionable place in the Canon of insider-literature. She could not though contend with the demands that this high esteem put upon her, and retreated into a cut-off, secretive world of her own, ravaged by alcohol and mental illness, alternating in her moods between enervating gloom and murderous revulsion. She would spend an entire fortnight, consumed with thoughts of killing people. Yet she was a frail, birdlike woman, meek and nervy and reedy-voiced, who would not—and indeed could not—have harmed a soul in real life. Instead, she carried on producing books, not so much for a living—though like everybody else, she had to make a living—as for sheer life. As such, she could not *not* have written, it being the life-blood that she spilled on the page—or the spirit-blood in which she wrote—the ultimate writer's writer, perilously precarious beyond the pale of popular judgement. Racked with malignant shyness, it was a total impossibility for her to maintain a prolonged contact with any other human being, let alone an intimate relationship with a friend or lover, although there were disastrous, failed attempts at the latter in her early life. So she was an Outsider in several senses: a woman, someone who grew up in the Caribbean, a lonely and troubled soul, and a writer popularly known for just one book which is still not very widely read to this day. Her other books were connoisseurs' confections that barely kept the wolf from the door. But with the loyal support of an appreciative editor like Diana Athill, she was able to hold her fragile grip on the crag at one remote corner of the literary map. And subsequent biographies of her and critical studies of her work by Alexis Lykiard *et al* have held her name up in the rare ethers of the Firmament, pitched above the grey clouds of oblivion. She did not perhaps choose to be an Outsider-Writer, in a deliberately self-cultivated fashion, but had the predicament thrust upon her by bad circumstance and an inveterately difficult nature over which she had little or no control, but which manifested in some very striking work as well as suicidal-genocidal mood-swings.

Sylvia Plath needs no introduction here. But she cannot be ignored in a study of this sort, as she brought a vein of violence to her poetry that ultimately claimed her own life. Although a precocious Ivy League product, who married the pin-up of English poetry and combined a successful academic and writing career with a model housewife lifestyle for some years, there was the rawest of wounds lying open beneath the surface of her psyche, from which the pared, visceral nuggets of her Stanzas shot onto the page—dripping and spilling her essence like arterial black blood, draining and finally rushing from her brain. The clues to her demise sat like fingerprints in amongst the honed torrents of words, pointing with Runic cunning towards her inexorable, auto-fixated, assignation with the gas-oven. And mention of Runes is apposite here, for both she and Ted Hughes were adept in the black arts, and shortly before her death she was summoning Ouija curses to direct against the other woman in Hughes's life. And this may have backfired on her, albeit her deeper suicidal compulsion provided the more powerful trigger in her last deed. The exact details of this dark cloud of occlusion enveloping the final stages of her life have not been easy to piece together, or make clear sense of—whatever credence one attaches to the notion of accursedness. But there is enough evidence of her, or their, dabblings and delvings in these regions, to lend at the very least a degree of plausibility to the notion that some very destructive forces were incited at one level or another, that were sufficient to precipitate her onto the downward, spiralling path to her doom. However, she was by all accounts uncannily calm in the manner in which she plotted it, betraying no hint of her desperation or intention to others who saw her in her last days, not least her children, before clinically disposing of herself, whilst still in her prime and at the peak of her poetic powers. She was indeed a great poet, cutting across both the sentimentalised Romanticism and the laboured proto-Feminism of her female contemporaries like a swift blade of brilliance. Yet that blade was snuffed out, and only her voice echoes still in the dislocated words she left behind. She was an Outsider, who in the end refused to be an Insider, her glittering prizes of no account in the torture-cell of her soul.

Dorothy Richardson—'the genius they forgot'—was an altogether more sanguine figure, born in humble poverty in England in the late Victorian period, and living her long life in near-total obscurity, writing her own experimental fiction instead of Popular or Realist novels. She's even been credited with founding the 'Stream of Consciousness' Modernist movement in writing, ahead of Joyce and Woolf, albeit she herself did not care for this term, preferring 'Fountain of Consciousness', or better still, 'Interior Monologue'. Woolf felt indebted to her, but was unable to use her influence to help her promote her work. And so she remained unknown to the general Reading Public, even if certain *cognoscenti* in the Bloomsbury Circle and other *milieux* rated her very highly. But she eked a living Stoically, as a tutor and contributor to literary periodicals, possibly being content with her anonymity and creative freedom, which at any rate saved her from the potentially damaging scrutiny and razzmatazz that would have come with publicity. And the main fruit of her quiet, inconspicuous, patient, and unpaid labour, was the *Pilgrimage* Series of books—not unlike Henry Williamson's *Chronicles of Ancient Sunlight*, or Anthony Powell's *Dance to the Music of Time*, only not nearly as well-known or as widely circulated. It became a sort of secret treasure-trove for other writers in the know, who were more than happy to keep it a secret amongst themselves—away from the vulgar, prying eyes of the ignorant *hoi polloi*, greedy for potboilers! Not that it would have made very much difference if it had flooded the bookshops of Britain. For just as water finds its own level, so does the literary taste of readers. And the majority of people would have taken one glance at Richardson's books, and then put them down! They had no stories, plots, stock characters or dramatic incidents in them; rather masses of impressions drawn from life and imagination and impinging on the mind of the main protagonist, who figured in all the books like an enigmatic and no doubt auto-biographical centre, around which everyone else revolved. If her achievements were not quite of the same order of magnitude as Joyce's and Woolf's, they were still very considerable nonetheless, and all the more remarkable for having been pursued in her spare time, in relative isolation, over a period of more than half a century. And though her books were published in the main, their ripples only spread way below the surface of generic fiction.

Anna Kavan was of a more troubled breed altogether, a penurious, pathological, drug-damaged, nerve-shredded Pariah, who would never have taken her place in the commercial market if it had been thrust upon her, which it never would have been in a million years! Her work is almost unbearably bleak and dark, disturbed and deranged. And yet she did not spend her entire life subsisting in a dark hole, never daring to venture out into the light for fear of disintegrating like a mummy or transmogrifying into a soul-eating succubus. She married twice, bore children, travelled widely, held down jobs, and pursued active pastimes, including bizarrely, breeding bulldogs! And yet this voracious consumer of life had a black inner shadow that periodically blotted out the fierce sun of her days, plunging her into such deep moods of gloom and doom, that paradoxically, these released Lethean streams of literary creation that fortified her and prevented her from succumbing to a final gravitational crunch of self-destruction. Though, as already mentioned, she was a heroin addict, her addiction did not in fact kill her in the end, since she managed it for many years, like Coleridge with his opium—as if defying it to kill her, and extracting from it the bitter satisfactions of an impervious she-devil. She both wrote and painted, dealing with the extremes of experience and existence in a manner that would have unsettled Kafka even—with whom she has been justly compared. Today, she would be about as far removed from the Celebrity Culture as could be imagined, and her masterpiece, Ice, could well serve as a murderous, monstrous rebuke to the bland vanity and shallow indifference of our times—yet few people would read it, only the converted for sure, and everybody else would be spared the punitive lesson of a forced confrontation with their own emptiness! She even adopted her *nom de plume* from a character in one of her books, which I can't recall any other author doing off the top of my head; and very pointedly—like Lautréamont—left no memoirs or diaries behind after her death. She wanted to fictionalize herself and her life, in other words—having retreated from Reality into a world of madness and despair that she magicked into prose with the power to change the inner world and life of anybody who could be bothered to read her work. As such, she was a driven Recorder, and a tragic yet triumphant Muse.

I could of course add to the above list of female Outsider-Writers, and am indeed strongly tempted to do so in the case of a writer like Ann Quin, who has only very recently come to my attention. She wrote in the 1960s, principally a novel called *Berg*, set in a fictionalised Brighton, concerning a man who intends to murder his father, who walked out on him and his mother when he was a child. Although she was working class, she was not directly influenced by the kitchen-sink dramatists and the Angry Young Men—or Women!—but more by earlier English authors like Patrick Hamilton and Graham Greene, in respect of their fascination for the seedy squalor and sordidness of seaside resort-towns, run-down tenements, Pubs, Bars, Brothels, and back-street intrigues, etc. But she also lent this a more experimental, *avant-garde*, continental treatment in the manner of the *Nouveau Roman*, and even a Beat element reminiscent of Burroughs. Her style was dense and difficult, whilst at the same time being exhilarating and luxuriant: pared down yet radiant. As such, her voice was quite unique in the English Fiction of the time, and for a brief period she was well-regarded, if never exactly popular. But she was never able to make an adequate living from her writing, and drifted into obscurity. Then one day she went swimming out to sea from Brighton Beach, and never returned—echoing the words of Stevie Smith, 'not waving but drowning' perhaps? Though we shall never know whether she intended to commit suicide or else drowned accidentally. But the tragic symbolism of her end was in a quite real and terrible way foreshadowed in the very bleak and dispirited atmospheres or essences distilled into the abandoned sceneries in her books. And it's quite hard to see what would have saved an author like Quin, given the general direction in which fiction and popular culture were moving during the 1970s. Even if her books had sold better, she would never have felt spiritually at home in the increasingly Corporatized world of modern commercial publishing—never mind the celebrity-culture that Andy Warhol had first anatomised and drawn public attention to. She may have won scholarships, but as with ideas for Emerson, they didn't butter any bread! And yet the vocation of writing—if not the avocation—was in her life's blood, there being little else that she would or could have done.

I have also been alerted recently to Jane Gaskell—an author who is still alive, but is rumoured to have vanished years ago with some strange religious cult. Certainly no new books have materialized since. But previously she attained a degree of success as a cult-author, even writing a highly acclaimed book called *Strange Evil* when she was a girl aged only fourteen. After that she shifted into a Sci-Fi/Fantasy sub-genre or cross-genre all her own, and therefore became more and more estranged from the Mainstream, even though she wrote books like *The Serpent*, which were well rated. But at some critical point, in a mood of defeat and yearning, she turned her back on conventional society, embracing alternative religion, to be quickly forgotten except by a small coterie of enthusiasts—including Storm Constantine and China Mieville—who have striven to keep her name alive. She may not have considered herself to be an Outsider once, but she certainly is now—whether she wishes to be or not—and her work was always sufficiently odd in itself to make it more than likely that she would end up becoming one sooner or later. And there is nothing pejorative in this account, as some would have it, for being an Outsider has quite enough positive connotations to outweigh the negative ones, as I think I have shown already. But some may regard a retreat into a commune as a monumental cop-out for an Outsider-Writer. Yet if it is true that Gaskell has done this, we simply don't know how autonomous or otherwise she is within the group. Maybe the group encourages her in a continuing productive independence from the outside world, and her writings are only circulated amongst other members of the group rather than in the wider public domain. Or else she may just write for herself, always the most difficult pursuit of all—even though it is first and foremost what all writers do. But to do it in a purely Solipsistic vein is the acid-test of a writer's sanity and strength, persevering against the overwhelming odds of pure pointlessness. But perhaps, like Robert Walser in his Asylum, she has not gone where she has—and it's no Asylum necessarily!—in order to write. And so she does not write, but seeks rather a Way of Being that negates the necessity of writing.

There is one more woman-writer, who may or may not baulk at the attribution of the term Outsider to her and her work—and I met someone once involved with Outsider-Artists, who so despised the term he dismissed it as 'shit', patronizing, judgemental, and offensive; though he couldn't give me an alternative term, and obviously wasn't very familiar with the more favourable, literary-philosophical position I was arguing from—but who I would single out as the spikiest example I know of a contemporary heiress to the traditions of Sade and Crowley. If that does not make her an Outsider-Writer, *vis-a-vis* the corporate-commercial, mainstream literary establishment in this or any other country, I really don't know what would! But I suspect she may angrily and violently insist on calling herself an Insider, within the very particular traditions that she adheres to. Her name is Lucy Swan, and to the best of my knowledge she's only had one book published, *The Adventures of Little Lou*, by Savoy Books. These publishers were notorious in Britain for *The Lord Horror* Trilogy, by David Britton, who certainly insists on calling himself an Insider within the sort of Horror tradition that he has almost single-handedly carried to the farthest limits of degradation. He is in fact the last writer in Britain to have been jailed for writing a book, and has stated in the past that all writers setting out to smash—not push, smash!—the boundaries of fiction, should be prepared to go to jail for their work. This has to count in my view as an ultimate litmus-test of the convinced courage of a true Outsider-Writer, even if in a truly free society any writer could be as offensive as is possible, and only suffer verbal or written rebukes for being so. And no other publisher besides Savoy Books would ever have touched Britton's work with a burning Trident, never mind a barge- pole! And I have to say that Lucy Swan—whose book was published very much as a companion-piece to the *Lord Horror* Trilogy—proves herself to be the female foil to Britton. Kathy Acker and Poppy Z. Brite don't even come close to her, and who else is there among recent and contemporary female authors? Her anti-heroine—with the profoundly deceptive, innocuous-sounding moniker, Little Lou—is the most savage, grotesque, female sadist created in women's fiction for a very long time. Delight in torture, all sorts of depravity and eternal damnation are fused with occult symbolism, philosophical meditations and literary digressions. Lou is no Proto-Feminist, but an out-and-out monstress with no shame. She is less trans-gendered than a self-created mutant. She is so beyond the pale, she cultivates supra-human powers to ensure her survival and thrival, in an alternative reality conjured from her imaginings. There is no moral in the tale, only a self-justifying, endless indulgence in Hell's pleasures.

Swan is quite unique, in refusing her own publicity. Apart from the publicity on the Savoy Books website, one trawls Google in vain for any other posting by and about her. She wants to be an un-person in Cyberspace, as well as mainstream culture. She clearly doesn't care what happens to her as a writer, just so long as she can continue to inhabit her own chosen space, which is so far removed it's even beyond the outer-most fringes of the new Counter-Culture. Who knows whether or not she still writes, or wrote at all before Savoy Books discovered her, promoting her one known book—known that is, to scarcely more than a handful of Savoyard feasters! There is though just one published photograph of her—which is by far and away, the most obscenely defiant photograph of an author on a book-cover that I've ever seen. A thin and bony Punk-woman with blond hair, dressed in a sleeveless Lord Horror T-shirt and a Nazi helmet, and sporting tattoos, stares out of a void into a void, the middle stump on her right hand raised stiffly in a gesture of extreme *Contra Mundum* dismissal! *Fuck Off And Die!* was the charmingly beguiling Title of another of Savoy's world-beatingly commercial books, and Ms. Swan embodies the said Title in her person to a perfection of imperfection! Suffice to say, the likes of Random House and Harper Collins have not exactly been tripping over themselves to sign her up! One might well fear for their skin, not to mention their immortal souls, if they ever dared do so! Though the legions of 'pretty young faces'—mainly female—adorning the covers of so much of the meretricious trash routinely published nowadays, who ooze oleaginous poise in their pop-saccharine profiles, like aspiring, if talentless, flibbertigibbets who may be relied upon never to poop the party, would in my view benefit enormously from the application of a good dollop of Ms. Swan's triumphantly outlandish make-over! That of course is as likely a prospect as the imminent return of discriminative sense in the corporate assessment of true quality or merit in contemporary literary fiction! Those who milk the literary market for all it, or they—same difference!—are worth, will be the last to exhort the heresy that the market can in fact be bucked. But until the old Thatcherite commandment is u-turned, the rot shall never be stopped.

To swing the positive discrimination pendulum back a little towards male Outsider-Writers, I ought finally to mention just a few more obscure names to finalize a miscellany that can spark off further and more detailed researches at a future date. Iain Sinclair has recently been drawing attention to a mysterious Jewish writer from the East End of London, Henry Cohen, *aka* Roland Camberton, who died young in his early forties, and is only known to have written two books, *Scamp* and *Rain on the Pavements*. *Scamp*, which explored the old Boho Soho world, actually won Cohen the Somerset Maugham Award in the 1950s, beating Kingsley Amis's *Lucky Jim*, amazingly! So he had the literary world at his feet at this early stage of his life. But his next book, although equally picaresque, exploring the Jewish world in Hackney, was less successful. And after that, Cohen completely vanished off the Radar. Only occasionally he would resurface in parts of London, and have enigmatic exchanges with other little-known writers at the time such as Bernard Kops, or else with more notorious figures such as William Burroughs. But the Mainstream circles he totally avoided, for reasons that most probably had far more to do with contempt than anything else. But inevitably, he paid the price for his seemingly deliberate distancing from the world of commercial writing: poverty, near-total oblivion, and premature death. Sinclair considered him an early exponent of 'psycho-geographical' writing and taxonomy, given his fondness for drawing up lists of things and features in the predominantly urban environment in which he spent most if not all of his life, that criss-crossed the boundaries between fiction and non-fiction. He was also a crucial witness to the final days of the old Hasidic Jewish community in East London, that writers like Zangwill and Rosenberg before him had belonged to and chronicled in their own work. So he's a very significant figure to resurrect from his 're-forgotten' status. And for Sinclair, he was an 'outsider among outsiders'. So he deserves to be mentioned here, even if I'm not in a position to devote a whole chapter to him.

Across the Channel in France—'a nation of outsiders', according to a literary pal of mine—there are more unco-optable crazies than one can shake a stick at! And if they were based in the UK, they would be so shunned by the cultural establishment that even the remotest wilderness of old Albion would harbour no hiding-places for them! Just imagine how Michel Houellebecq's work would be received in the UK! He would be considered far more beyond the pale here than someone like Will Self for example, who might have started out as an *enfant terrible* of sorts, but has since slowly morphed into a tolerated lampooner, a licensed jester and establishment-pet. And as such, he's spread himself so thin with all his media and journalistic commitments, he could be at risk of becoming blanded out, and losing the untameable bile of his neo-Swiftian stylistic pyrotechnics. Although he still gives good value when he appears on Television, looking like a slightly mad moose, languidly intoning his satirical critiques from a totally unmuzzleable vantage-point! And Sinclair's recent influence on his work seems to have pointed him in new and interesting directions. Whether Self may be considered an Outsider-Writer, and if so in what way exactly, are somewhat moot points, but many of his sympathies probably tend towards such writers. And in so far as he does overlap with Sinclair's orbiting 'satellites', then he will have found himself ineluctably drawn out onto a liminal limb of psychotic pre-occupations and psycho-geographical phantasmagorias that chew up the five or six toes he has in the mainstream camp. The writer who didn't venture far enough into the gory, demoniacal psychosis of *My Idea of Fun*, may yet end up making a noble sacrifice of himself to the literature of landscape—if not the landscape of literature. As for Sinclair's satellites, I won't presume to encroach on territory that the Master himself has mapped out so exhaustively and inimitably in a long series of books for those of us possessed of the courageous curiosity required to enter it! Although my favourite Sinclair satellite probably has to be Gavin Jones, the forgotten artist, who at one time lived in an underground bunker in Bow, with two coffins for company, whilst painting minotaurs *et al* on the walls, his hands emaciated with battery acid, and 'his eyes as mad as Manson's', as Sinclair put it. His descent into underworlds unknown to Modern Man began with an Exhibition in St.

Anne's Church, in Limehouse, many moons ago, with well-known figures such as Melvyn Bragg and Peter Ackroyd turning up to find the mad genius had locked the doors, and was refusing to let them in! I wonder what's become of this splendidly deracinated Magus. Perhaps he's mutated into a minotaur and the second coffin's for an intrepid Theseus! Whatever state he's in, the likes of Damien Hirst should steer well clear of him.

And yet in France, where Houellebecq is a notorious, but hugely successful, iconic figure, a household name no less, there are lots of other writers that are considered far more dangerous, deranged and diabolical, who even the generally open-minded French literary culture and mainstream—receptive as it is to so much experimental writing, unlike its British counterpart—can never bring itself to accommodate. One such writer is Antoine Volodine, who is almost certainly quite unknown to the vast majority of the British reading-public. Like Pessoa before him, he employs various Hetero-nyms and has written about twenty books in his sixty years, dealing with unmentionable subjects of all kinds from a variety of non-judgemental viewpoints. He looks and sounds relatively sane and normal on 'You Tube', where he can be seen in an interview—in French of course—analyzing his work. But his writing is anything but sane and normal! Although to the best of my knowledge, only two of his books have been translated into English so far. And my French is just not good enough to do such a writer full justice trying to read him in the original. But it seems he deals in Extremes of all kinds, exploring ultimate scenarios in which humanity is pushed beyond itself into states of metamorphosis. And in *Minor Angels*, which I've read online, he portrays a post-Apocalyptic scene in which surviving humans mutate into monsters. The structure of the book is very fragmentary, with some chapters that are only a page or two long, bearing the most tenuous relationship to the preceding and succeeding chapters. Multiple themes are essayed, twisted and dropped, with a dizzying dance of method. Characters come and go like gold dust on a tide. Amidst the appalling degradation, where humans, animals, birds, plants, weeds and detritus of all kinds are routinely cannibalized for purposes of survival, and even grotesque pleasure, there are some characters—or more accurately, figures—who seek to save themselves and others from total extinction, if not from abomination. And so in one scene a bunch of gnarled old crones, reminiscent of the witches in *Macbeth*, take an embryo formed from abandoned rags and lint and perform magical rites to resurrect it into an Avenger, who will create or recreate an enduring self-reliant colony on all that remains of the planet. But in the event he restores Capitalism! And so he has to be executed—fattened up for the cannibalistic kill! All of the figures obsess in their mad, conflicting ways, about how to exist in a savagely traduced terrain, about how to commune with others or else consume them, and about how to transform a seemingly immutable post-human condition. It's hard to say what message for humanity such writing has, other than that cannibalism is a metaphor for what we're doing to ourselves as a species already. But I suspect Volodine doesn't really care if readers take this message away with them as a warning, or simply relish the ultra-decadent aesthetics of gross carnage and diabolism, that he himself seems to relish indulging in the most excoriating detail. If all his other works are as hideously provocative as this one, whatever the subject, then he must be an Outsider-Writer so devastatingly amoral that merely to read his work at all is to lock the Gates of Hell behind one.

A Brief Miscellany...

I could of course hunt down other names, then add them to the list. But the razor of parsimony must shave the limit. This field is so vast it expands the more one delves into it. And I aim to produce here more of a weighty pebble than a fatty doorstopper. And I think I've extracted enough illustrious corpses from the enmired repository of oddballs via the quiddities of the written word, to at least whet readers' appetites for their own researches into these darkly distinguished quarters—as well as for the real critical meat of the book, which I'll now address. For in the next chapter, I'll aim to lay bare the Outsider-Soul of a giant of twentieth century literature: J. C. Powys.

Chapter Five:

The Evolution of the Ichthyosaurus-Ego into the Cosmic Celt

John Cowper Powys was a quite extraordinary paragon of the mind, spirit and body: a Bard, poet, novelist, philosopher, mystic, magician, visionary, nature-worshipper, Pan-luster, and sadistic fantasist—all rolled into one! He was truly a 'one-off' in the world of English Letters, though the poet and artist David Jones came close to him in developing a similarly strange, arcane, and erudite Holistic vision of Life, which encompassed likewise, Pagan Mysticism, Neo-Platonist Christianity, Bardic Druidism, Manicheanism, and Modernism. But Powys articulated his vision in a series of massive fictional and philosophical works on a scale that Jones never accomplished, and may have lacked the energy if not the intellect to do so, even if he had not been so afflicted by manic depression. Powys was no stranger to afflictions of his own of course, but had such colossal reserves of energy, passion and dedication that he was able to overcome them in a highly sustained outpouring of creativity throughout the ninety two years of his life. The enormity of his achievements within the context of twentieth century literature were perhaps only equalled by Proust, with *In Search of Lost Time*, Robert Musil, with *The Man Without Qualities*, and Thomas Mann, with *The Magic Mountain* and other works. Hermann Hesse stood some comparison too, with *The Glass Bead Game* and other works—and I daresay Joyce, with *Ulysses*. So also D. H. Lawrence, come to think of it. And other names can be suggested too. But

Kafka and Faulkner, who are often lumped together with Proust and Joyce, although doubtless equally gifted writers in their respective veins, did not produce anything as mightily long and dense as Powys did—for what it's worth, and I have often thought that quantity does not necessarily equate to quality in fiction, and ideally no work of fiction should be longer than two hundred pages! Borges went even further—writing once that Kafka's novels would be amongst the greatest masterpieces ever written if they were only ten pages long! But Powys was no mere windbag, churning out door-stoppers for the *Guinness Book of Records*. His works were big—in every sense.

And although he isn't strictly speaking an obscure figure, it's still true that he hasn't ever struck the sorts of chords with a wide and popular readership that a writer such as Lawrence has. And yet he's received far too much critical acclaim not to be considered a truly Canonical figure. However, there can be little doubt also that he was a genuine outsider-writer—quite irrespective of his reputation or the lack of it. For me, he was an Outsider of the Driven-Visionary Type, an autonomous Autodidact—even though he was educated at Sherborne and Cambridge—who would have somehow contrived to create his own imaginative universe, even if he had been literally bound up in Hamlet's nutshell. The sources of his imagination lay in the lush wilds of uncivilizable nature, and the lonely voices of prophesy and poetry that speak and chant to us in the profoundest and most enduring registers of Being. Powys's use of language was exceedingly rich and dense, difficult and demanding. But the rewards it pays to those who persevere with it are immense. And it was above all a language for Everyman, and emphatically not for some academic or literary clique—much in the way that the great scriptures and old epics were. He refused to dilute his vision and voice, to render them accessible and popular—as is the fashion nowadays with so much commercial fiction. Yet he would have felt that he had failed in much of his purpose as a writer if some tramp in a ditch didn't engage with the wonders of his works as much as an aesthete in his ivory-tower or a scholar in his den, or anyone else for that matter. Though it may be hard to imagine your average merchant-banker wading through *Porius* from cover to cover—'Is this sad loser on pills or something?! Christ, he goes on a bit!' Though Powys may have felt just a little bit vindicated—if not flattered, or impressed—if such a person were even to toy with tackling such a tome, however incomprehensible he found it! It is after all never entirely a lost cause to try to rescue a philistine from his philistinism.

Powys had a very Welsh name, but was more of an Englishman in fact—even if he was as untypical an Englishman as one could ever hope to find. He was even once referred to as 'the degenerate Englishman', after he came out in defense of Joyce's *Ulysses*, when it was withdrawn from circulation in the UK. And his influences of course were in the main emphatically un-English: Rousseau, Casanova, Nietzsche, and Jung. Though curiously, he retained a fondness for Pepys of all people. Maybe because the latter was a self-professed rake, and Powys clearly regarded himself as such, even though he found full penetrative sex deeply distasteful, and preferred to fondle women instead, or else masturbate alone. And it seems his sexual fantasies also smacked of fetishism—the pun here saying it all! He was certainly striking in physical appearance, almost Olympian. But the fact that he was also wracked with complexes, not to say perversions, lent an incongruously pained expression to his otherwise classically handsome face. He may have striven to be a human Pan, but he spent far more of his total energies sublimating his carnal and other impulses in a sort of mental consummation of landscape, spirituality and ideas, whether within himself, or through the medium of his fictional characters. And he carried this displacement of lusts from his life into his work, to an utterly obsessional pitch. Even his intellect, as well as his intuition and imagination, was ultimately subjugated to this overwhelming passionate outpouring of energies and engagement with all that was other to him, especially nature and organic life-forms of all kinds. And I shall argue in this chapter that he was in this fundamental regard very similar to Stewart, a comparison that to the best of my knowledge has not been made before—though it is, I believe, a fruitful and instructive one. As for his books, since his output was so prolific, not only in literature but in criticism, biography, autobiography, occult studies, cultural meditations, and philosophy, I shall have to restrict myself to just a few for lengthy examination: *In Defense of Sensuality*, *Wolf Solent*, and *Porius*. These works encapsulated the highest and the best of his creativity and thought to my mind, but I'll make passing references to some of his other works as well.

The Biographical details of Powys's life are very well-documented. So I won't be paying much attention to them, except where I think they throw some quirky light on the nature of his work. His lifelong fascination with the Occult is certainly one area that interests me. And he did finally overcome his fear of meeting the 'Great Beast' himself, and the two Magi sparked one another off in almost uncharted Ethers! He also earned his living for a time doing lecture-tours in America, which went down surprisingly well considering that he broke with all academic conventions, thundering away like some latter-day Prospero-Colossus on any subject that entered his head from the most outrageously and intransigently unorthodox standpoints. It's also an interesting coincidence that Stewart earned his own living for a while doing precisely the same thing, with at least equally prophetic overtones no doubt! Although I know of no evidence that Powys was aware of Stewart, or ever read any of his works. But if he had done so, he would assuredly have been struck by the tremendous affinity of Spirit radiating off the pages! Both men were great walkers too, and impassioned lovers of nature and animals. They developed very similar methods of absorbing and discharging the energies of life-forms all about them, which governed their relationships, their sexual activity, and their writings. They were unstoppable talkers in company, overpowering self-styled prophets in their own singular voices, repudiating all orthodoxies. And though Stewart never wrote novels, he did write poetry, and always wrote prose in much the same vein of charismatically subjective intensity as Powys. If I believed in Reincarnation, I should say they were Avatars of one another—or Doubles of the same Archetype. Yet Powys developed his own individual variant on Stewart's Philosophy almost certainly without actually knowing, consciously, that he was doing so! Although this happens often enough in history for it not to be too baffling a coincidence in many instances. Goethe's *Elective Affinities* might operate at the level of Jung's Collective Unconscious, thereby perpetuating underlying streams of thought in a variable continuum. Maybe their one difference of opinion would have occurred over the interpretation of Pagan/ Animistic/Occult forces in nature and life, albeit Stewart had a pretty mysterious-seeming insight into cosmic energies, even if he dismissed all the terminologies of religion, mythology, mysticism and magic.

Powys however strove to see beyond God and the Devil and angels and demons, opening up realms of cosmic mysteries, suspended between the phenomenal and the noumenal, for which mankind had no names or descriptions handed down by scriptures and epics. Like Blake and Lovecraft, he was seeking to create his own 'mythos', which although steeped in all manner of traditions and influences, was also unique and distinctive and as far as possible elevated above all that had gone before. If as Voltaire said, 'There is nothing new under the sun', Powys vouched that eternal recurrence was still infinitely diverse within an ever-elusive unity. In other words, it was always possible, and of course desirable, to say the same old things in new and different ways. And for Powys, there were many things above the sun, even if the sun was the source of everything or just about everything on Earth. Though Heaven, like Hell, was a complex delusion, the image of an afterlife that purported to console or compensate us all for its felt absence in this life. Those of us who saw deeply enough into the richest treasures of this life, in this world, had no need of a Heaven or an afterlife at all, because we already saw into the endless dimensions of all that there is, where our own times touch eternity and thereby grant us a kind of immortality, in which every world interpenetrates every other world. This of course, is a key idea in theoretical physics nowadays: Entanglement. So although Powys was not strictly speaking a scientist, arguably he was in a broad philosophical sense anticipating the more thorough-going examination of this idea and other related ideas in many of his writings. And if he still retained a belief in, or a fascination for, Pagan, or more specifically Celtic, myths, this was because he felt they must have rested on a touchstone of Truth. And at the same time they could serve as very powerful and useful instruments or vehicles of a great self-emancipation and transformation, freed from the self-imprisoning dogmas of organized religions. In the realm of value and meaning, such anthropomorphic projections could give more purpose and significance to people's lives and destinies ultimately, than any other arbitrary or authoritarian belief-systems. And as such, they could complement scientific endeavours.

I first 'discovered' Powys as a teenager, when I came across *In Defense of Sensuality* in a Hampstead Bookstore. And being struck by the unearthly image of the man on the cover, and the defiantly out-of-step, visionary tenor of his language as I skimmed through the book's contents, I decided to snap it up at once. And to this day, it still stands out as one of the most remarkable, mind-expanding texts I ever read during my formative years. And yet it could not have been further removed from the kind of book I was supposed to be immersing myself in as a philosophy student; and its arguments jarred greatly with the arguments I was otherwise grappling with in my studies of thinkers like Kant, Russell and Wittgenstein. In fact, it would not be very difficult for a Rationalist logician to pick so many holes in Powys's central arguments in this book as to leave them in utterly irreparable shreds! And yet ineluctably it drew, not to say sucked, me back into the dreamier, inchoate, Protean depths of my own searching soul that had been nurtured originally more by literature, poetry and music than by hard, abstract philosophy, which I felt I was rather forcing myself to try to master—if only to prove that I had a great analytical mind as well as a great creative imagination and visionary intuitive power! The book reminded me more powerfully than most I read in those days, that Metaphysics was the core-domain of Philosophy, and indeed the true source of all things. And yet I had been learning that Metaphysics was nonsense, and that all philosophical enquiry was either purely deductive as in Logic, or else potentially at least a branch of Science. Anything else was akin to Hume's 'sophistry and illusion', to be consigned to the flames! And that applied not only to all pre-twentieth century Metaphysics, but also to twentieth century Existentialism and Phenomenology, and to all the 'New Age' currents of thinking about Mysticism and consciousness-raising, etc. Marxism was of course taken more seriously after a fashion, as was Psychoanalysis and Feminism. But there was a kind of intellectual fascism abroad, stemming from Logical Positivism and Linguistic/Conceptual Analysis, which in certain novel forms purported to be applicable to every branch of philosophy. I am glad that this is not still the consensus-paradigm in contemporary analytical philosophy, and that Metaphysics appears to have made some sort of a return since then. It might be impossible to provide geometrically rigorous proofs of metaphysical theories, but that does not mean that they don't at the very least strike at something so profound that it may ultimately be unknowable to us. And as such we cannot in truth simply dismiss it as meaningless. We should conjure with it in the innermost recesses of our Being. And this is where Powys comes in.

He started the book with a kind of Cartesian injunction to readers to accept the old 'I am I' principle as the solid foundation of Being and consciousness upon which he could then proceed to erect a labyrinthine superstructure of thoughts. He invited us to strip away everything that was extraneous within and without us—like Peer Gynt peeling off all the layers of an onion, to find nothing there in the end. But unlike Peer Gynt, Powys insisted there was something there in the end, a bedrock of the Self and Self-Consciousness which he later on called 'The Ichthyosaurus Ego'. I was so stirred by this expression, that I considered setting up a Philosophical Society comprising human ichthyosaurians militating against all the still-trendy murderers of metaphysics! But I soon talked myself out of this lunacy. And yet the slimy sensuousness of this terminology was so suggestive it persuaded me that philosophy could be still done in a serious and substantive way, without being aridly abstruse or thinly aetherial. But trying to convince any academic philosophers that such terminology may have currency and cogency in philosophical discussion would have proved just as arduous as bashing one's head against a mountain wall! Yet it was very much in keeping with the more ancient ways of doing the subject, in which it was totally fused with poetry and myth. Heraclitus and Plotinus would have recognized a kindred-spirit in Powys, I'm certain. And one may think that Socrates would have done so too. But Powys found the latter's ratiocinative habit of mind or mode of enquiry tiresome, preferring the aphoristic style and quasi-musical rhythms of meditation practised by the Pre-Socratics. And this earlier tradition has not died out since, not only because there have always been scholars investigating it, but also and above all because there have always been writers and thinkers drawing and drinking from its well-springs right up to the present day.

The Ichthyosaurus-Ego was an essentially lonely, non-gregarious, entity, from which all of human feeling, thought and wisdom emerged, however cultivated or re-directed by society, education and culture. It was each and every person's inner outsider, so to say. And Powys makes a declaration of war early on in the book, 'upon certain gregarious elements in our modern life, and upon certain gregariously human traditions among us, such as seem to me to be slowly assassinating all calm ecstatic happiness, the only kind of happiness that really is worthy of organisms with the long history and the large hopes of ours.' And he goes on to oppose in an organic, dialectical fashion the twin-urges of loneliness and love, saying each are of equal importance for our happiness and evolution, but everything which mediates between them, or just about everything, is to be resisted, especially the herd-instinct of Humanity—where he is clearly echoing Nietzsche. However, he parted company with Nietzsche, and Blake as well, in stressing that Good and Evil could never be equated nor superseded. They were built into the very fabric of the universe—or multiverse, a word which Michael Moorcock is often credited with having coined a few decades later!—and good was associated with kindness, and evil with cruelty—a starkly simple formula, but one which he was committed to, because cruel thoughts and actions would eventually create a Hell on earth, while kind thoughts and actions would create a Heaven on earth, which for all wise and sane human beings had to be preferable. The chain of Good and Evil—like all the other Dualistic chains, Self and Other, Mind and Matter, etc.—did not lead to an Infinite Regress, but rather to 'The First Cause', a famous philosophical expression used by various thinkers from St. Anselm onwards. He clearly treated this postulate as a 'given', which would have got him into trouble with numerous contemporaries, from Russell to Sartre, had he ever crossed swords with them. But he was untroubled by the notion of the Infinite Regress and the Transfinite Series, viewing the evolution of the Cosmos as a gradual development from a single source, which we could take for granted without needing to know what it was precisely. And there was no image or concept we could entertain about

The First Cause that would ever measure up to it or truly represent its entire progeny in the emergent worlds.

Already it is clear that Powys's method was to issue an unfolding sequence of startling statements, which rather than test to destruction in the manner of his sworn enemies the mathematicians, logicians and scientists, he would sink like plumbs into the echo-chambers of consciousness, rolling them around his Reptilian brain like pressed tobacco in a pipe, and withholding judgement on what he could not know with certainty to be either true or false. But the hypotheses that resonated with him the most were the most compelling and the most likely to be true. So he chose in the end to take them as 'givens', and to then impress them on others, with a remarkable, luminous, rhetorical power. He went on to develop not only a metaphysic which resembled a kind of poetical phenomenology, but also an ethic, in which some pretty stern standards are set, governing not only our conduct but also our fundamental attitudes and outlook in relation to all that belonged to 'the pure Not-Self', i.e. all that was external to 'the pure Self' of the pared down, Solipsistic, Ichthyosaurus-Ego. And it is in this third domain between Subjectivity and Objectivity, that his strengths and his weaknesses as a thinker and Seer can be found. He appeared to assume that once an Individual had sunk down into the deepest strata and sub-strata of his own true Self, that in some mysterious way all the dimensions opened up to him thereby would guarantee his self-sufficiency as a Being in the world. And this is where I have to part company with him, because if all of us went around the place the whole time steeped in and trumpeting our inner Ichthyosauruses, wonderful as it may be, the world as we know it would quite simply collapse—and ourselves along with it! The reason Powys—and his fictional characters—was able to get away with this for most if not all of the time, lay in the exceptionally eccentric circumstances and conditions of his life. He succeeded in living in the outside world pretty much as he did inside his head, partly because he was very lucky never to experience serious poverty, and partly because he was surrounded by people—not least his long-suffering wife—who tolerated his exasperating egoism *sans limit*, since they adored and revered the man for his undoubted talent and largesse. But how many of the rest of us can live like this, however much we may wish to? This is a question he did not adequately address in the book, because it would have taken him outside his main philosophical province into political, social and economic provinces, which he considered beneath him.

However, if I've struck a critical note above, that in no way detracts from my astonishment at the tremendous riches he unearthed in this protracted journey through his own brain, as it were. Even if one has to be in a sense privileged, to be and to live like Powys, and his characters, in the real world—which did not even exist in his eyes!—one is still glad that there are people in the world like him, who venture inside the luscious vegetable-swamps of the Visionary Imagination, if only to throw up treasures that others can marvel at. He never suffered as many other visionaries did, because he was blessed with luck and a gift or capacity for solitary happiness, which he believed ought to be within everyone's grasp, and then all of the problems of the world would eventually be solved. Though this may be a sound and solid foundation for our relationships with each other and Society, I don't however agree that it is enough by itself to solve any of the major or fundamental problems of the world—some of which he alluded to in the book, like poverty, exploitative labour, cruelty, suffering, disease, mal-education, popular culture, dependence on machines, and the pursuit of money and material things for their own sake. Solutions to all these problems require systemic collective efforts, synthesizing ideas and practices in an organized and efficient manner. But he rejected Pragmatism—in the philosophy of William James, for example—out of hand, seeing it as a betrayal of Idealism. And his Idealism was of a bottom-up rather than a top-down variety, more Spinozistic perhaps than Platonic or Berkelian or Hegelian. Like Stewart, he believed animation was at the very surd root of things—informing and guiding the whole of Evolution into the plethora of advanced life-forms, among which Man was the last manifestation. And what marked out human consciousness from other kinds was not just its self-reflexity, but also and above all its individual separateness from the collectivity or group-mind. The entire thrust of his philosophy arguably stands or falls on this one principle. And I incline to the view that it falls. But like a magnificent tower built so high it defied Gravity, it revealed hitherto unseen Vistas to all those who scaled it, before it tottered like Beckford's Abbey, and crashed down.

If Powys had been a species unto himself, then the tower of his thought may not have come crashing down. However, as an undeniable member of Homo Sapiens, his almighty autochthonous Atomism, splendid as it was, could not in the end hold out against the sweeping tides of cosmic chaos or the nucleic bonds of collective humanity. He was trying to be the Canute of a super-consciousness, and may have succeeded in the uninterrupted privacy of his communion with himself, his work, nature, animals, a few like-minded souls and even the primal source of all things. But beyond all of that, where the forces of the Not-Self intruded upon his privacy, he would inevitably have fought a long, slow, and in the end losing, battle. I don't just mean by this that he fell into decay and then died—like everybody else. I mean that even the greatest Outsiders, of whom he was I think one, cannot ultimately triumph against or over the Collectivity. They can fight it for all their worth, and shore all their energies up against their ruins, achieving a greater degree of autonomy than anybody else no doubt. But there are still limits to just how far they can go, in challenging human connectedness at its very core, which lies at the heart of the Antinomian Project to be sure, but the iron chains of nomic necessity cannot be broken asunder by the Anarchs of the Ego. And yet this need not be a cause for despair, as the strength in solidarity that fellow-outsiders can forge may stand a far better chance of re-assembling the collectivity, along the lines that people like Powys would have loved to have seen or achieved. But one cannot just commune with one's Doubles. One has to deal with the Devils, which involves taking on the world and being gregarious as well as solitary. Yet for Powys this struggle was not only beyond him, but misconceived. He genuinely believed that the key to the resolution of all conflicts, and the creation of a harmonious social order for mankind in the world, lay in the radical freedom and the inner power of the Individual alone.

So this is the measure of the man, which one is obliged to gage, as the book unfolds. And I can feel a profound sympathy for, and empathy with, his Alchemical philosophy of a race of saintly Beings pulling their own strings of destiny in a multiplicity of Monadic spaces—and Leibniz's Monadology is often referenced by Powys, so it was clearly a major influence on him. And the landscapes of language he opened up in exploring all the possibilities of manipulating the Self—from the 'sub-human' to the 'super-human'; and by sub-human he did not mean defective, but instinctual and intuitive—have to be read in places to be believed. On every page—and there are almost three hundred in all—there are passages of such felicitous beauty combining with magnetic potency, that one doesn't just feel, but truly knows, that one is in the presence, and the grip, of a Seer-like figure, who could be speaking out of an Abysm of antiquity. He did of course suspect that he was a Saturnian, and not an earthling, and reading his work one does at times wonder about his humanness. To take a passage at random, on Page 118:

> 'Where are now those voluptuous ecstasies of holy lassitude wherewith the great slippery-shouldered whale steers his course, spouting and floating, dreaming and diving, half-way round the world—feelings that in your place and in your measure you ought to share, O protean human soul? Where are now those dumb, blind, sub-human intimations, drumming dimly their cosmogonic responses to the pulse-murmurs of the terrestrial globe, such as pre-historic lichen-covered rocks have known? Hast thou lost altogether, O too-humanised and mob-bound soul, hast thou lost altogether and vulgarly purged off for ever the last royal vestige of our deep planet's consciousness of itself?'

What human being, since Coleridge in his *Biographia Literaria* maybe, had written English quite like this?! And he was writing this in the 1920s, and continued writing like it until his death in the 1960s. Not only is the poetic prose unearthly, but he reveals his capacity in a very Stewart-like manner, for communing with different life-forms, plus a detailed knowledge of the flora and fauna which teemed in, and literally peopled, his novels. I could quote dozens of passages like this, which are enough to drive the most determined decadent diabolist into the embrace of an exuberant sublimity!

Of course, I can well understand some readers simply dismissing Powys's style and voice as a preposterously archaic affectation, a risibly diarrhoeic effusion of purple pomposity. But in my view they would be quite wrong, because if one can persevere with this sort of writing, one will soon notice a number of elements that render it anything but devoid of substance. The attention to detail, the sustained force of argument, the descriptive range, the versatility of expression, and the muscularity of mind, all combine to enhance and elevate the symphonic progression of the writing into a truly majestic rhythm. I appreciate that few readers nowadays have the staying-power to last the course with books like this, but that fault is more theirs' than Powys's. There is nothing thin in what he writes. Every sentence of his pulses with vigour, which makes reading him a strenuous ordeal, yet also a most exciting challenge. And in our Age, beholden to science and technology, what would people make of a passage like this on Page 147:

> 'In revolting, on behalf of the free-will of the individual soul, against the gregarious traditions of humanity, there is nothing so necessary to undermine and explode as the tyrannical assumptions of science. The machinery created by science is something that proceeds from the active curiosity of man and the active energy of man, concentrated into a nature-dominating herd. Individuals originate it; but the anonymous, gregarious Monster, the Human Swarm, quickly snatches it from their hands and turns it into the dead-

> alive routine of a mechanical system. Human life, dominated by science, becomes year by year more closely akin to an ant-heap or a wasp-nest. And the same evil power that transforms our spiritual freedom into a hideous commercial-industrial slavery, does its best to strike with paralysis and atrophy our faith in the power of the individual soul! The defeatism of economic determinism, the defeatism of material behaviourism, the defeatism of mathematical logic—all these play into the hands of our industrial system in the same devilish campaign to make "the star Wormwood" prevail, and to take the creative force out of the soul!'

The ravings of a lunatic?!

Well—yes and no. Not since Blake ranted against 'Satanic mills', had such a vitriolic diatribe against what many regarded as a necessary and desirable form of progress in conquering the vicissitudes of nature, been issued. And it is hard to see what relationship mathematical logic bears to the industrial system exactly, being a purely abstract discipline. But after the 1960s, the critiques of mechanization or robotization, drawing on earlier concepts like Alienation and Anomie, became more widespread and forceful. Powys was prophesying the post-modern death of the Individual in a sense—not to say the Outsider—which is far more acutely experienced now, than it was even in his day. So anyone who takes their individuality at all seriously ought to be able to identify with this sentiment at least, even if the language defeats them. A more pertinent criticism would be of Powys's elitist, if not fascist, contempt for the human masses who are victimized by the above-tendency and who he accuses of capitulating to, and even conniving, at it. And there is also a dig at the old Decadents in the Wormwood reference, Wormwood being the main ingredient of Absinthe, which was frequently drunk by the Decadents, inducing brain-crippling hallucinatory torments. But I know of no evidence of Powys's links with Eugenicists, or Mosleyite Black-shirts, or Nazis, since he was clearly if not an a-political thinker, then *a fortiori* a meta-political thinker. But a distinct whiff of the Nietzchean Superman or of Splenglerian hauteur breathes out of passages like this, which indicates that for all his grand generosity of spirit towards suffering wage-slaves, he could also be quite sweepingly sadistic in his attitude towards anyone that he deemed to be standing in the way of the triumph of the Great Ego. And yet his afore-mentioned impulse of love counter-acting or complementing loneliness suggests he also wanted to merge his Ego with that of another, or others in general, and such dualities should form the basis of society.

This love may be a carnal or a spiritual or an intellectual passion, shared with other humans, a concern for the plight of the less fortunate, a pitying care for other life-forms, or a delight in the abundance of nature. The Ego sinks down into its depths in order to flow out more responsively to what lies outside of it, seeking sensations as the means to happiness, which can either be enjoyed solitarily or else shared. A striking example of Powys's Love, or pure Janist compassion, is recounted in this passage on Page 44:

> 'I picked up a dead frog this morning. Withered it was to a veritable husk of hollow emptiness, like a snake's skin bleached by months of burning sun. I suppose many a bird had hopped against it, brushing it with wings or tail, many a butterfly settled above it, many a rabbit spurned it with unstartled, jerky indifference.

> Why should they care?.... The ichthyosaurus-ego in us, however, is touched by a more vivid consciousness of the pitiful contrasts of our terrestrial lot. To its old saurian sensibilities, the basic alternations of life and death are more crucially evident than to these rabbits and birds; and thus, to its dreaming mud-spawned mind, this feather-light, horn-coloured simulacrum in the form of a frog is something that pulls at him to pause and think. A natural instinct of self-preservation, qualified by a nervous shiver of sympathy that fades out, like a reflection of something limned in water as the sky darkens, protects the rebound of our egoism and the resilience of our life-zest when we encounter a sorry sight like this.'

Many of us would walk on by, possibly fearing contamination or even a curse, reasoning that it is too slight a stain on the surface of life to warrant much conscientious fuss. There are more important deeds in the moral scale than to give one dead frog a decent, dignified burial! And yet as Powys goes on to note, small pangs of guilt affect us whenever we witness such things and hurriedly go on our way. And how much worse it is when we don't go to the rescue of a living creature, or worst of all, a person. And where do we draw the line in our daily calibration of priorities in these situations? Powys demonstrated here that for all his anchored remoteness in the invisible recesses of his own Ego, he is at his most energized when he shows spontaneous concern for all else that lives and dies in the undeniably interconnected web of creation.

The theme of saintliness versus profanity runs through the book, but Powys's Pagan bent is clear when he writes on Page 63:

> 'It is a great mistake to think the condition of being a saint depends on any definite religious belief. It does not even depend on believing in God. It does not imply any rigid morality. The saint is always very lenient to every kind of sex-sensation. The condition of being a saint implies in the first place a passionate faith in the possibility of a certain kind of thrilling happiness. The saint is one who holds the view that compared with happiness nothing is of any importance at all. Compared with happiness, fame is nothing, ambition is nothing, work is nothing, progress is nothing. But this happiness which the saint sets about to evoke—first for others, then for himself—is not the same thing as excitement or pleasure. It is a calm, deep-flowing satisfaction, mounting up at intervals into tidal waves of quivering ecstasy.'

His source here is Aristotle's Eudaimonia—only with a touch of The Temptation of St. Anthony, if not Epicurus's hedonism! Happiness began with sensation, then built up through the power of will into a spiritualized frame of mind. He would have concurred with Baudelaire, when he said that 'the only thing was to be a saint, by one's own standards.' Though what he would have made of Nietzsche's statement, that 'Man does not need Happiness. Only an Englishman needs that.' I am not so sure. Nietzsche was taking a side-swipe at Mill's Utilitarian doctrine of the greatest happiness of the greatest number however, and Powys I suspect would have held little truck with this slide-rule calculus and portion-control approach to the mass-distribution of something so unquantifiable as Happiness. Pleasure and Happiness are distinguished as a state and a condition by many Philosophers. But for Powys they were on a spectrum or continuum, graduating from the sub-human to the super-human. And God was no name for the loftiest pinnacle of this Anthropic ascent.

But if the First Cause he kept returning to—and he believed the Future as well as the Past was already predicated by it—or sacred fount of his 'Philosophy In Spite Of' all that offended him about 'machine-civilization', could inspire in Man a new religion, then he writes on Page 176 that:

> 'It will be a religion that will help individual men and women to shake themselves free from the factious, shallow, vulgar, sneering humour of the commonplace world. It will be a religion of intense gravity and intense earnestness. It will be a religion that actually worships the sun, the moon, the earth, the sea, the wind, the seasons. It will be a religion that strips off the hot, feverish, gregarious, over-human garments of the other religions. It will be a religion that could be shared by the non-human consciousness of trees enjoying the rain, of crows sailing across the sky, of cattle grazing in the fields, of fishes poised motionless in the river, of vipers basking in the sun, of ancient cosmogonic rocks breathing the air and feeling the magic of moonlight. In my own symbolic words it will be a religion of the 'ichthyosaurus-ego.''

He goes on to say that:

> 'Sleep, with all its mystical intimations, will be the greatest of its sacraments. Indolent, idle, dreamy, care-free thoughts will be the incense of its casual breath.

> Leisure will be its cathedral-court, and sensuous sensation its high-altar! Its piety will be drawn from the organic atavisms of planetary life, its ritual from the long centuries of human experience. Its moral virtue will consist in just being 'kind' in the most simple of senses, and in this alone! The best-remembered, though not the best-loved, of all its many gods will be the ultimate First Cause; and the great daimon Chance will be its Holy Ghost.'

This reads like the Gospel according to the Arch-Heretic, and has some things in common with Crowleyanity, bar its aversion to cruelty. The language evokes Rabelais at his wildest, an undoubted influence, yet Powys's voice is so distinctive as to be virtually unique. Any Outsider feeling miserable with his lot would be uplifted by these words into a rapturous assault upon all that excommunicated him. The words truly do work upon the mind like magical spells and incantations. And Powys's self-initiation into the Occult powered his use of language in a creative re-invigoration of ancient rites. Hence the uncanny effect of exaltation his work has had on readers.

Powys's philosophy was defiantly and heroically anti-systematic, at a time when the subject was becoming rigorously formalized within abstract notations that bore little or no relation to the Gnomic mainsprings of wisdom among the Ancient Greeks and their forebears. Although the organic holistic unity of his thought was very hard-won through a thicket of cosmic complexities, he always valued simplicity above all else, the Alpha and Omega of the prime sensations of consciousness that permeated all of life and was by far and away our most precious and mysterious faculty. And it is still mysterious today, as it represents the final frontier in scientific understanding, which would cause Powys's spectre to chuckle—one in the eye for his old bug-bear! If consciousness is a given, as he insisted, or an inexplicable, and quite possibly miraculous epiphenomenon, then it is the seat of the human soul and mind. Yet it is not confined only to living creatures, but is spread among all other entities classified as inorganic, in Powys's mythic scheme of things. The fact that we can't seemingly commune with natural objects does not mean necessarily that all objects are therefore non-conscious. It may mean rather that we lack the cultivated mental facilities to establish conscious connections with them. The parallel with Stewart's thinking here is obvious. Science may not confirm the truth of the hypothesis, but there may still be ways of energizing the deepest currents of our consciousness, so as to facilitate at some level or other of Perceptual Being a reciprocal relation with everything in the Universe—a Symphony of Sensations, one might call it. And both Stewart and Powys lived on this self-same wavelength. Stewart's communion with cows for example, was echoed by Powys in his description of cows as 'the divinest creatures', and one could easily imagine him performing at the very least a Lawrentian Eurythmic dance before herds on his long, solitary walks through wild, Elysian countryside! Though nowadays of course we're all being warned to steer clear of cows, as they can be dangerous and there have been cases of people being killed by them. 'Elf 'n safety Jeremiads of this sort would have been greeted with a snort of derision by the likes of Stewart and Powys, boldly going where no weedy neurotics or hectoring maids would dare explore—like Prometheans of the Sacred Flame, bar the split infinitives! How the times they have a-changed!!

In a more serious vein, these two great Outsiders shared the fundamental position of viewing life through the lens and prism of its 'dual oppositions', including even the moral order of the universe. Although neither thought this stemmed from some transcendent realm behind the scenes of the visible world, but arose entirely from its own intrinsic nature, which placed them firmly within the framework of Phenomenology. I myself have struggled with 'the moral order', being more drawn to the Nietzschean notion of 'very free spirits' roaming in a world 'Beyond Good and Evil', than to the Kantian notion of a clockwork calculus governing our every deed, if not thought. In fact, Powys himself asked on Page 17: 'Does a maggot in an apple visualize the Categorical Imperative? Does the fluctuating, undulating anima mundi conceive of the pursuit of Truth? Can a minnow in a river-shallow lift itself up to the idea of Self-Sacrifice, or the somnambulistic psyche of the Moon dream of Heroism?' But this was by way of a Rhetorical pre-amble to introducing the idea of the will to pleasure in the higher animals, especially Man. So he wasn't refuting the Kantian imperative so much as placing it on a different foundation: our duty to pleasure, as opposed to pain; instead of some abstract, unattainable Virtue. Put like this, I can warm to the idea. And a wonderful passage on Page 18 encapsulated it:

> 'It must be something that is the natural life-movement in us, only a little more "willed" and deliberate than breathing itself. It must be something that attends the flicker of a fish's tail, the thrusting-forth of a snail's horn, the swish of an elephant's trunk, the stir of a wolf's penis, the hovering of a hawk's wings, the cow's chewing the cud, the snake's basking in the sun, the

> urge upwards of the bulb's shoot, the unclosing of the fern's frond, as well as the creative thrill of the poet, the amorous thrill of the lover, and every muscular and intellectual activity of which our human nature is capable. It must, in other words, be something whose expansive quality lends itself to indefinite refinement and infinite ascent. It must be something that accompanied the somnolent stretching and yawning of an ichthyosaurus in the primeval mud, and that will accompany the tremulous consciousness of the first human soul that finds an unanswerable proof of immortality.'

I've never come across a finer evocation of 'the Great Chain of Being' than this, the whole of Evolution being captured within it, as he hymns a powerfully persuasive Paean to the original cause of Goodness in all things.

Both Stewart and Powys were well aware of the evils of the social hierarchy of their day: monarchicalism and mercantile capitalism in Stewart's case, and industrial capitalism in Powys's. But neither man welcomed the more radical alternatives on offer: Jacobinism, and communism. Both men were intelligent moral anarchists as I see it, who certainly didn't take a proto-Thatcherite line on non-existent society, but did insist on nature, the individual, regional community, and non-dependence on government bureaucracy, machinery or technocracy, serving as guiding principles behind ideally organic, harmonious, small-scale, mutually co-operative societies, that they wished to see being formed, but which scarcely existed anywhere around them. And this is still very much the case today, if not more so, and the threats to such projects being seriously attempted, never mind succeeding, are far more massive and severe. Yet both men believed profoundly in relieving the burdens unjustly placed upon the masses, in terms of back-breaking labour, generational poverty, systematic limiting of life-chances and the horizons for personal development. But they did not believe that Revolutions would permanently relieve these burdens, if at all, since they were more likely to simply rotate tyrannical power-structures than remove them forever. The pursuit of fundamental change in society had to occur inside each and every Individual, and then work its way outwards to establish vectors of concerted force and solidarity, but not on the basis of grand programmes or anything of that nature. The only grand programme Stewart and Powys were interested in was the happiness and fulfilment of the Human Person, emphatically not the building of a corporate state in any shape or form. Politics was an expression of the Personal, not the other way round. Although Stewart was more alarmed by the power of the Monarchical State than Powys—and perhaps with good reason, since it was far more Absolutist in his day. And Powys was more inclined to accept a version of Benevolent Dictatorship than Stewart, but only because he couldn't see, or hadn't really investigated, better alternatives. However, they were united in their support for minimal governmental intervention in personal freedom and the conduct of human affairs in general.

In summary, I'll round off my account of *In Defense of Sensuality* with a few final quotes and comments. Powys often reiterates certain themes and ideas in the book. But such is the power and versatility of his language, that this doesn't really matter at all. In fact, if anything this has an enlarging and enriching effect—like repeating Mantras with subtle shifts of tone, pitch and signification. His contempt for logical and mathematical philosophy is one recurring example: 'thin, wire-drawn, pseudo-scientific hypotheses, as remote from our real feelings as they are remote from giving us any real reality beyond our crudest experience.' 'It is not the love of wisdom at all, it is the love of mathematical word-puzzles!' 'To philosophise is not to analyze, with masochistic, photographic humbleness, the miserable fragment of so-called 'reality' that happens to be around one at the moment.' 'I feel a power (in the only world that I have a sure and certain knowledge of and a constantly verifiable proof of, namely the world of my own sensations) of willing. Why should I let it atrophy within me because Mr. Russell or Mr. Whitehead or Dr. Watson says I am a fool to believe in it?' And so on Anon! Of course this doesn't really count as what an academic philosopher would call hard argument. But it is still a very singular and in my view unignorable rejoinder from the Outsider's Fringe to a creeping and later sweeping dogma of how philosophy should be done, which may be defensible on technically ingenious grounds. But it still does not answer the profound inner need for what Wittgenstein called 'the mystical', that Powys articulated here with great eloquence and force—unlike Wittgenstein, who famously refused to say anything about it at all, fearing a lapse into nonsense, even if he considered it to be the ultimate inexpressible truth of philosophy, transcending science and logic! Also the mention of Russell intrigued me, because Powys and Russell did in fact meet, only once I believe, not to discuss Philosophy—which would almost assuredly have run aground on the arid sands of the *Principia Mathematica*!—but the rather different subject of marriage, touching no doubt on sex and infidelity, on which both men were notable experts, and on which they were by all accounts in pretty substantial agreement. Although of the two, Russell was the more consummate Priappist!

Yet Powys's distance from orthodox religion and morality, as distinct from metaphysics, mysticism, and magic, is clear from his account of Christianity, on Pages 226 and 227:

> 'Of course, it might be argued that the reason why the Christs of this world are so sad is that they cannot forget. Ever and always they feel upon their lips the bitter taste of the hyssop-sponge. Ever and always they hear upon the air innumerable voices crying aloud, "My God, my God, why hast Thou forsaken me?"....For though we read that Jesus wept, we never once read that Jesus laughed.
>
> Certainly the fact that Jesus lacked all humour, except a certain sad, world-deep irony, is an argument very helpful to my contention—on behalf of the solemn ichthyosaurus-ego, brooding upon its secret mystic-sensuous raptures—that the facetious humour of the herd-animal man is an enemy to the deep cosmic happiness I am advocating. Just as the spiritual solemnity of Jesus has always seemed "foolishness" to the clever pagan comedians of the world, so the sensuous solemnity of the ichthyosaurus-ego seems ridiculous to the human-all-too-human worldlings of our day.'

One wonders what the holistic heretic in Powys would have made of Islamism?! Christ's last words have always struck me as both the most harrowing, and the most hollow, in mythical history. Did he finally know in that instant that he was just a man after all and no Son of God? Powys refused to shoulder

Christ's suffering, and supplanted it instead with his own mythopoeic celebration of an earthy, yet also spiritualized, Nietzschean Joyful Wisdom. The occult dimension was also central, and is one of the reasons his work has not been as widely received as it should have been, since many people are ignorant of the Occult and just assume it's an irrational superstition and a mere genre. And it certainly can be a mad and dangerous obsession with some people, but it's no less a part of the whole inheritance of human culture and civilization than religion or mythology. And it should be studied as such. For Powys, it was what might be called an *aide imaginaire*, a very profound and exact source of inspiration and engine of creativity. But this disturbed and alienated a lot of readers. And it also augmented his standing as a true outsider-writer. And he always returns to the corrupting influence of Society. On Page 263, he writes: 'Society is the most insidious growth, into which all the most corrupt poisons of the human peril distil their plague-pus. Here indeed we touch the crux of the whole matter. This book is written to reveal the fact that it is possible, by invading the social humanity in us from both ends at once, to squeeze it out almost completely!' And yet we also know that he valued sexual, personal and even social intimacy, and coming from a Bourgeois background was not blindly contemptuous of the Bourgeoisie just because they were Bourgeois! Although he was keenly aware of the cultural and experiential limits of the money-governed, materialistic, professional life-style of the Bourgeoisie, he also recognized that individually they could elevate themselves in quite other directions, as pre-eminently did he himself. And I don't think he despised the Human Family itself, but rather the dehumanising constraints that rigid social hierarchies imposed upon the Human Family. And yet as he could ask whether 'the moment has come for the birth of what Spengler would call a New Culture?' one has to conclude that he was not especially drawn to the Politics of the Left! Though if he had more than a whiff of the Wagnerian in him, I firmly believe this was innocent of any truly sinister fascistic, or racist, leanings. Though his specific views on Race are not really clear from my reading of *In Defense of Sensuality*, and there wasn't necessarily any good reason why he should have even addressed that issue. But to end on a resolutely positive note, my impression of this book more than 35 years after I first came across it, is no less admiring, not to say awe-struck. It truly is a Testament for all times and a Bible for unbelievers! And it's only just to leave the Man himself with the last word(s):

> 'Alone, alone, Alone! The grand secret of cosmic happiness lies in growing more and more deeply aware of this loneliness, whether it be the "rich" loneliness that embraces a mate and offspring, or the "poor" loneliness that hath none. It is only by this feeling of loneliness that we can escape the gregarious warmth of the crowd, that murderous enemy of all deep joy, and detach ourself from the fever of human ideals. It is only by this feeling of loneliness that we can annihilate the preposterous claims of a life of action, and return to the calm reservoirs of earth, air, water, and fire, from which, as our soul contemplates them, emerge those lovely essences, the constant enjoyment of which constitutes the only indestructible ecstasy of life.'

I can only add, Amen to that!

Moving on then to Powys's fiction, which according to Colin Wilson was where his philosophy found its truest expression, I'm sorry that space doesn't really allow me to do justice to *A Glastonbury Romance*, which was Powys's attempt to out-Tolstoy Tolstoy, with a far larger cast of characters even than *War and Peace*—some fifteen hundred in all, compared to five hundred—and offer up the most sublimely sweeping Panorama of the macrocosm of English Life, contained in the microcosm of a small community. And there were other very fine novels, like *Owen Glendower*, a sort of *Piers the Ploughman* for more modern times, with eternally stirring ancient echoes; a mystical epic no less. But the two novels I shall be considering are as great as any of Powys's, and far better than most. And the first is *Wolf Solent*, a true oddity and mighty tribute to the inveterate strangeness of the lonely English Soul or Spirit. It's a work which still remains somewhat off the Radar of recent and contemporary consciousness, as one might expect for reasons well-rehearsed. And yet for people like Colin Wilson—also intriguingly the other Wilson, A.N., a very under-acknowledged figure in English Letters, yet enormously erudite nevertheless—it is one of the great novels of the twentieth century. Even the third Wilson, the late one, Angus, admired it greatly along with several others, since it was in his library that Colin Wilson first discovered the works of Powys! And even more curiously, Chris Woodhead, the ex-Chief Inspector of Schools in the UK, a champion of Grammar Schools and Private Education at the complete expense of State-Education, cited *Wolf Solent* as one of the deepest, most enduring literary influences on his entire life—even if the School portrayed in the book wouldn't exactly have satisfied an OFSTED Inspector! Even if it scintillates in the shadows, it has the potential to be the sort of obscure

Classic that can continue waxing and waning in discriminating esteem if not wide popularity for a very long time, even forever. So it will not evaporate in its own dust.

The book starts with a memorable description of a train-journey undertaken by the eponymous hero, anti-hero, meta-hero, ultimate weirdo Outsider!—whichever you want to call him!—on route from London to a school in Dorset, where he is due to be employed as a literary secretary by the radically eccentric headmaster. And the prose veers from very detailed documentation of the surroundings to sudden startling depictions of the character's inner world. Wolf's appearance is strikingly odd, with a receding forehead and hooded eyes, and his manner is dreamily detached in unfathomable depths, as if he bears no relationship to his surroundings. He muses, meditates, and observes. He is locked inside his vast interior world, and feels himself to be a sort of greyly eminent magician: just like Powys himself, and this book is by far and away his most autobiographical one. At one stage, Wolf imagines himself as a giant racing alongside the train to show that a mythical beast could keep up with, if not outpace, a modern machine of the kind he loathes! All the familiar tropes and themes from Powys's non-fiction are aired from the outset, and a few passages stand out as arrestingly enigmatic intrusions into the narrative. Wolf reflects on:

> 'the appalling misery of so many of his fellow Londoners' at one point, and recalls 'the figure of a man he had seen on the steps outside Waterloo Station. The inert despair upon the face that this figure had turned towards him came between him now and a hillside covered with budding beeches. The face was repeated many times among those great curving masses

> of emerald-clear foliage. It was an English face; and it was also a Chinese face, a Russian face, an Indian face. It had the variableness of that Protean wine of the priestess Bacbuc. It was just the face of a man, of a mortal man, against whom Providence had grown as malignant as a mad dog. And the woe upon the face was of such a character that Wolf knew at once that no conceivable social readjustments or ameliorative revolutions could ever atone for it--could ever make up for the simple irremediable fact that it had been as it had been!'

This reminded me of Blake's London, when he passes people in the streets, whose faces 'show signs of distress, signs of woe.' And reading the passage, one knows one is embarking upon a very unusual, and indeed universal, literary journey—not just a train-ride! Moments earlier, Wolf had pondered another scene in which while teaching school-pupils about Queen Anne and Dean Swift, he suddenly 'danced his 'malice-dance'', in which 'some mental screen or lid or dam in his own mind completely collapsed and he found himself pouring forth a torrent of wild, indecent invectives upon every aspect of civilization.' Here we see that we are in the presence of a man who is at once cultivated and deranged, a luminary and a madman. Also, he fantasizes constantly about girls—another well-known Powys trope!—although he's already 34 and seems in one way resolutely middle aged. But he's still just like an adolescent boy in another way: 'He clasped his bony fingers tightly together. 'Some girl who'll let me make love to her…white as a peeled willow-wand… make love to her in the middle of a hazel wood…green moss…primroses…moschattel…whiteness…' He unclasped his fingers, and then clasped them again, this time with the left hand above the right hand...' This has a rustling, Pan-like urgency to it, which in an adolescent might just be an excess of passionate intensity. But in an older man there's an almost obsessive, psychotic fixation about it. So we know from the outset our friend is as Jung would say, 'festooned with complexes.' When he settles into the quaint and quirky old household, full of characters almost as odd if not odder than himself, the scene is set for prolonged bouts of soul-sinking in the Powysian manner, as well as refined observation and emergent conflict, especially with his employer, Mr. Urquhart, an unworldly scholar-recluse, whose appearance and whole demeanour strikes Wolf as 'Satanic'. He is 'an antagonist who embodied a depth of actual evil such as was a completely new experience in his life.' His formal speech, elaborate courtesy and absent-mindedness barely conceal the unhinged leer of a man who is inwardly consumed with the very darkest morbidities.

He meets a young poet there too, Jason Otter, who has marked peculiarities of his own, including fetish-worship in the Hindoo tradition of Mukalog, the God of rain. Wolf is also a fetish-worshipper, but more in the Pagan-Celtic tradition, and in the intensely secret world of his own making, which he masks and cuts off from others behind a screen of torturous civility and studied attentiveness to others, and which he worries constantly will be invaded or smothered by influences from the outside world. And this struggle intensifies as all the plots develop inside the time-warped mansion that seems almost sufficient unto itself, and no longer needing to be moored in Reality. It's like a hidden colony of Grotesques that Wolf has maybe not quite stumbled upon by chance, but been drawn to instead through subterranean channels of elective affinity. All sorts of sinister, yet oddly sublime, dramas are being acted out, often in a highly coded clandestine manner, but at other times in a wonderfully revelatory manner. Powys pushes at just about every Taboo there is, opening up all the possibilities of imaginative experience and only stopping just short of irredeemable amorality. His concept of morality is sly and profane and elastic. However, he still acknowledges a dual morality in the end, at the limits of Heretical experimentation. The Taboos in question involve just about everything from Satanism to sado-masochism, via incest and homosexuality, lust and possession. Only incest among these is still regarded as a Taboo nowadays. But in the early twentieth century, just about anything that frightened the human horses in the Dorsetshire countryside, or anywhere else for that matter, was very broadly considered to be a Taboo, or quasi-Taboo at any rate. And yet Taboos are perhaps made to be broken. Powys probably had incestuous feelings for his mother and an occasional attraction towards young girls even. But his impulses were generally controlled, and therefore in the overall scheme of things essentially harmless, not unlike the fantasies of Lewis Carroll or J. M. Barrie. And what he was maybe not always able to achieve in life, transmuting fantasies into reality, he could impute to some of his characters, who achieved consummated relief from Onanistic frustrations. Fantasy was a very powerful tool for Powys, but more often than not he would get lost in its imaginary pastures and swamps, instead of blasting his way onto the Uplands of bliss and triumph. But he could still achieve the latter enough for it to infect his prose with the phallic thrust and angelic release, of a truly orgiastic poetry and a near-numinous prophecy.

New characters come into the story, such as the macabre bookseller, Mr. Malakite, who has had a grand-daughter Olwen by his own daughter. The daughter can't bear to bring up the child, who is then brought up alone by her grandfather after his wife dies. She grows up to be both unworldly in a bookish way and seductive in a Siren-like fashion. Wolf also has an illegitimate sister, Mattie, which his father concealed from him all along. And Olwen's protective aunt, Christie, has weirdly compelling charms of her own, with her taste in mentally 'melting' philosophical concepts into 'atmospheres', which intrigues Wolf's intellect while tickling his fancy at the same time. She shares Wolf's 'inhuman' bent—not being able to 'bear the Bible', which ruins her relationship with Nature! There are also other women in Wolf's life, such as his father's old mistress, Selena Gault, and always shadowing him from afar, his mother. But his meeting with Gerda Torp augurs the profoundest twinning to come. Their chemistry alights at once with an overwhelming feverishness, and they soon go walking in the surrounding country near Ramsgard—Sherborne—where a chase ensues. She disappears for a while, then he hears what he takes to be the song of a blackbird, 'more full of spirits of air and of water than any sound upon earth,' and 'it seemed to hold, in the sphere of sound, what amber-paved pools surrounded by hart's-tongue ferns contain in the sphere of substance.' And then it dawns on him that Gerda is the blackbird. It is as if she has lifted her carapace of reserve only to blend with the nymphs of nature, and he views her in both a sexual and a mystical light at one and the same time, desiring to possess her physically yet fearing that she may fly away, as she has from other men. This whole scene or episode has a truly wonderful intensity, and almost iconic resonance for the Reader, exemplifying with the greatest penetration the age-old rite of passage in human life: the stirring of sexual passion and loving intimacy, and against the idyllic background of one of Albion's finest ancient terrains. And yet Wolf and Gerda do not even touch, let alone consummate their serpentine desires, which rustle through the grass in a state of anxiety as well as excitement. One passage summarizes its impact on our unlikely hero:

> 'That bird-like whistling! Never had he known such a thing was possible! It accounted as nothing else could do for her queer, unembarrassed silences. In fact, it was the expression of her silences—and not only of hers! It was, as he recalled its full effect upon him, the expression of just those mysterious silences in Nature which all his life had, so to speak, waited upon and worshipped. That strange whistling was the voice of those green pastures and those blackthorn-hedges, not as they were when human beings were conscious of them, but as they were in that indescribable hour just before dawn, when they awoke in the darkness to hear the faint, faint stirrings—upon the air—of the departing of the non-human powers of night!'

The whole scene is evocative, but this part is emblematic.

The next time they walk in the countryside their love is consummated, and Powys reveals an uncanny feel for the rhythms, moods and vagaries of mounting passion, like a force of nature now delicate then sweeping, the earth itself being the bedrock of sensuality as well as the backcloth:

> 'When, after the slow ebbing of what really was a very brief passage of time, but what seemed to Wolf something more than time and different from time, they stood together again outside the hut, there came over

> him a vague feeling. As if he had actually invaded and possessed something of the virginal aloofness of the now darkened fields. With his hand over Gerda's shoulder he drank up a great mystery from those cool, wide spaces. His fingers clutched the soft collar of the girl's cloak. He was conscious of her breathing—so steady, so gently, and yet so living—like the breath of a warm, soft animal in the velvet darkness. He was conscious of her personality as something quivering and quick, and yet as something solitary, unapproachable.'

This description or evocation rather, is the equal of anything in Lawrence's writings, or Hardy's—the two writers most comparable to Powys, in modern English Literature. It touches the pulse and vital quick of conjoining bodies and souls—and yet has a deep, dark, almost alien, disturbing vein running through it, suggestive of an Outsider's intelligence that is continually surveying its own physical alienation in the world. Later on, while Wolf meditates upon his intimacy with Gerda, resolving to marry her in a sort of Martin Buber-like 'I-Thou' union, he feels he is about 'to bring that secret 'mythology' of his into relation with the whole world.' This takes the form of 'a certain imaginary city which from his early childhood had appeared and disappeared on the margin of his mind. It was wont to appear in strange places, this city of his fancy…'. And he goes on to list some of the more unremarked-upon eyries of existence, including 'bleak coals of dead summer-grates...rusty railings of deserted burying-grounds…nameless litter of pavement-gutters…' etc. This reads like a plea for the forgotten, a Hymn to the Abandoned—an Outsider's Lament.

In another scene, Wolf has a striking thought about the

machine age and its impact upon human beings: 'He thought to himself how, in some future time, when these formidable scientific inventions would have changed the face of the earth, some wayward philosopher like himself would still perhaps watch through a window a human head reading by candlelight, and find such a sight touching beyond words.' This is a wonderfully singular thought, conveying the imponderably strange essence of the man, and of course Powys himself, who articulated such ideas at great length in *In Defense of Sensuality*—as we've seen. The same Janus-faced consciousness would also gaze upon Urquhart a few pages later with the starkly different thought:

> 'There was something in his wrinkled white face, at that moment, which suggested an outrush of incredible evil—of evil emerging, like some abominable vapour, from a level of consciousness not often revealed. Wolf was tolerant enough of the various forms of normal and abnormal sensuality; but what at that instant he got a glimpse of, beneath this man's gentlemanly mask, was something different from viciousness. It was as if some abysmal ooze from the slime of that which underlies all evil had been projected to the surface.'

Few writers could conjure such malign 'occult' forces as this, and in such classically refined poetic prose as well. We are here in the realm of Austin Osman Spare's 'Raised Elementals'. And Powys, with his scholarly and working knowledge of magic, was perhaps Spare's equal in this capacity. Writing indeed was for him a form of magical incantation, casting its spells upon the reader through the power of language fused with esoteric erudition. A very different kind of magic again arises between Wolf and Christie Malakite, his real soul-twin if not his paramour in the full sense, when in a deepening phase of their relationship he comes to feel that:

> 'this was the first feminine creature with whom he had ever been left alone.... The slender little figure before him, with those thin hands and those touchingly thin legs, drew into her personality, at that moment, every secret of girlhood that had ever troubled him. Coming to him like the fragrance of wood-mosses to a city-dweller, the consciousness that this dream-like figure was really alive and tangible seemed to melt his bones within him. Those mystic syllables, 'a girl', 'a young girl', had always remained at the back of his mind like a precious well-watered flower-bed, but a bed empty of any living growth. Nothing, he now knew, in his life with Gerda had stirred the earth of that mystic bed. But here, in the centre of that bed, was a living, breathing plant, making everything around it enchanted and transparent by the diffused loveliness of its presence.'

This is Platonic Love with an ineffably mystical, rarefiedly sickly, twist. And it is always noticeable how frequently the expression 'at that moment' occurs in the book, as if it's far less a plotted narrative than an eternally extenuated 'moment' in which all its episodic and epic development accumulates in one long, mighty, oceanic swell. His conflicting infatuations gradually drive him into crescendos of self immolation: 'Only one life, between two eternities of non-existence...and I am proposing deliberately to sacrifice in it the one thing that I really want!' Gerda?....Christie?....What are they? Two skeletons covered with flesh; one richly and flexibly covered ....One sparsely and meagrely covered! Two of them...that is all...just two of them!' He is here the prisoner of his lusts on one level, and yet also striving like a sorcerer to square the circle of his impossible loves! This phantasmagoric driving obsession feeds into his nocturnal reveries too. Lying in bed awake next to a sleeping Gerda, 'He became, in fact, a living human head, emerging from a monstrous agglomeration of all repulsiveness. And this gross mass was not only foul and excremental, it was in some mysterious way comic. He, the head of this unspeakable body, was the joke of the abyss, the smug charlatan-pig at which the devils shrieked with laughter.' His philosophy of will totters on the crashing foundations of his 'life-illusion', and yet still he can purge himself of his perverse self-torments, laying 'hold of his will as if it were a lightning-conductor,' and then '...there came flowing in upon him, out of those secret depths of which he was always more or less conscious, a greater flood of liberating peace than he had ever known before!'. Powys's own philosophy of happiness, based on sensuality and moral Manicheanism, always comes to Wolf's rescue in the end—even though he has to traverse worse Sloughs of Despond in the process than John Bunyan's Pilgrim ever encountered! And the idea of pilgrimage is relevant here, for Wolf's spiritual equilibrium is found on:

> 'Roads and Lanes! Lanes and Roads! What a part these tracks for the feet of men and beasts, dusty in summer, muddy in winter, had played in his mental consciousness! The thrill that this idea of roadways gave him was a proof to him that his mind was returning to its independent orbit, after its plunge into that maternal hypnosis. His spirit felt indeed deliciously

> free just then, and expanded its wings to its heart's content, like a great flapping rook.'

He'd just endured a terrible sobbing showdown with his mother over Gerda, and at long last feels released from the suffocating grip of this Oedipal ogress!

Wolf perceives everything in life—including minds and souls—as interpenetrating. And this perception grows stronger and in some ways more disturbing as the book progresses. He says at one point, when a girl has been 'a man's bedfellow, even for a few months, some peculiar link establishes itself which is as difficult to break as if one tore a grafted sapling from the branch of a tree. I suppose,' he continues on, 'that my love is really more important, in this blind, primordial way, to Gerda—just because we have slept together for three months—than it could ever be to Christie, though she lives inside my very soul. I suppose it's the old fatality of flesh to flesh, of blind matter, proving itself, after all, the strongest thing on earth.' This wilful susceptibility to deep-layered entanglements is, paradoxically, the binding counterpart to Wolf's ineffable loneliness. He is in one way a Hermit. But he can never be a contented Hermit, as he must also have a twin—or more than one twin. Ironically, the more isolated a person is, the more vulnerable they are to connectedness, even to the point of a malignant, yet irresistible, fixation upon The Other. And his constant sense of being 'unhuman' amongst humans lies at the heart of it. His entanglements stem also from his psycho-spiritual, and psycho-geographical, relationship with nature, and the cosmic mysteries it contains. These centre upon Glastonbury, the heart of the Arthurian Legends. And its significance pre-dates all recorded history, its well-known hill or Tor 'being a far older portion of the planet's surface than the plain beneath it. Even if its magnetism is purely chemical and free from anything that reverts to the old religions, it may very well exercise a definite effect upon human nerves!' And then he pictures followers of Arthur and Merlin letting 'their souls sink down and down, into motions of primal matter older than any gods…this power that already was spreading abroad its influence long before Saturn was born of Uranus…' These nameless forces are stranger by far than the Mithraic Cults brought by the Romans to Ancient Britain. And Wolf, like Powys himself, feels he is a conduit for their transmission from Time Immemorial to the Present. Powys adumbrates this theme in more detail and depth in *Porius*.

Christie's sexlessness is a frustrating obstacle for Wolf. Although by slow degrees they arrive at a total understanding of each other as being in a sense lovers without making love. Olwen's existence is the key it seems to 'the cold, hard, inert mirror' of Christie's mind, 'reflecting what was there, but not feeling anything.' Wolf does make advances towards her at one stage, but she repels him angrily. But at the root of his longing for her, in parallel with his possession of Gerda, is not only lust, but the terror of aloneness, manifesting in the visions he sees of his dead father's skull emanating thoughts and images which take up residence in his own brain. Also the face he saw on Waterloo Steps continues to haunt him, until he realizes finally what it signifies: 'the upgathered, incarnated look, turned towards life's engines, of every sentient thing, since the beginning of time, that those engines had crushed.' 'It was, in fact, the Life-Eye, looking out on what hurts it, that he now knew he had caught glimpses of, all the days of his existence, in a thousand shapes and forms. From air, earth, water had he intercepted the appeal of that little round living hole…that hole that went through the wall…straight into something else. Into what else? No one knew or would ever know. But into something else. It was upon this he was crying out now… upon that eye…upon that little round hole…upon that chink, that cranny, that slit, out of which life protested against its infamous enemy!' And soul-sinking has led him to this awareness, only to compel his escape from himself into arms of the Other. But the Other can be a man as well as a woman, when he sees that both Jason Otter and Urquhart are homosexual in inclination—which he is not, except as Sartre would say, 'through the power of words.' Jason's poems are thinly disguised homo-erotic paeans, and Wolf may be their object. Jason's strangeness knows no bounds, even by Wolf's standards, one of his peculiarities being to wear cabbage- and rhubarb-leaves under his hat. He has 'a look infinitely wistful and sorrowful, the sort of look that a disguised and persecuted god, lost among some savage race that knew him not nor could have comprehended him if it had known him, might have worn;' He is a slime-spirit taking suggestively human form. Wolf's nightmares do not abate once and for all. In an extraordinary moment,

> 'His Mother and Gerda had lost their separate identities. They had become the point of a prodding shaft of yellow light that was at the same time the point of Darnley's trim beard! This shaft was now pushing him towards another misery, which took the form of a taste in his mouth, a taste that he especially loathed, though he could only have defined it, even to himself, as the taste of salad and vinegar! But, whatever it was, this taste was Miss Gault. The shaft of yellow light that prodded him on had the power of thinning out and bleaching out his whole world, taking the moist sap

> quite away from it, leaving it like a piece of blown paper on an asphalt pavement. Between these two things—the blighting light and the corrosive taste—he felt an actual indrawn knot of impotence tying itself together within him, a knot that was composed of threads in his stomach, of threads in the pulses of his wrists, and of threads behind his eye-sockets! Everything in the world that was lovely and precious to him was being licked up by a mustard-coloured tongue, while a taste of constricting, devastating sourness began to parch his mouth.'

This preternatural-preterhuman passage puts me in mind of Baudelaire's 'correspondences', and Scriabin's synaesthesia, which according to some neurophysiologists may well be the underlying mechanism of the human brain, rather than a distorting abnormality. Only in Wolf it is like a painfully contrived synaesthesia, mirroring exquisitely the permutations of sublime torments. There seems to be almost no limit to Powys's powers of description and evocation in these utterly diabolical, yet immensely delicate, spheres of imaginative delving. Wolf's mind 'hovers like a hungry cormorant over the heaving waters of his troubled senses,' while his soul is 'Like a slippery-scaled fish…' Only 'the mystical hill of Glastonbury', 'like the phallus of an unknown god', can offer him succour at times. He often attracts curious and suspicious attention from strangers too, which is intensified 'in certain particular eye-encounters, to a malignant hostility. He came to the conclusion that this occurred only when his own mind was especially harassed. It must be, he decided, the same psychic instinct that makes a flock of fowls attack the one that happens to be hurt or sick. Mentally, at such times, he was hurt—he was actually bleeding invisible blood—and it might easily be that this wounded 'aura' excited some mysterious irritation in those who caught it.' This is a highly astute analysis of the phenomenon of self-inflicted stigma in the eyes of others, or people-phobia becoming a malignant psychosis. Wolf is an extreme example.

All along his work with Urquhart has troubled him, concerning as it does the vilest eschatological probings into the secret habits of the local population—a far cry from the sort of respectable antiquarian researches he'd anticipated. And yet after a lapse from his amanuensis-duties, he decides to resume. Wolf's reasons for this have not just to do with money and the dullness of his job teaching History at the School. He wants instead to overcome his gnawing fear:

> 'It was an abominable book! A peculiar tremulousness took possession of the pit of his stomach, and a mist swam before his eyes. The atrocious attraction of a single page that he had encountered drew him towards a region of unspeakable images. Through an iridescent vapour, with the blood rushing to his head, he followed those images....All those drops of deadly night- shade which...had distilled themselves into his nerves...began to seethe and ferment again in his secretest veins.'

He is steeling himself here to face down the ultimate horror. And yet Powys gives barely a hint of the detail of the book, relying instead on intoxicatingly portentous allusions, which are nonetheless highly effective in themselves. And Wolf's own Dorset Odyssey induces a Protean Phantasmagoria: 'I've got a sort of underlife,' he thought, 'full of morbid hieroglyphics. Something must have died down there, and the blowflies are laying their eggs in it.' What other writer would ever come up with a sentence like this?! And Powys does it again and again, as if off the top of his head, until it almost ceases to surprise. While Urquhart produces his Doomsday Book of Dorsetshire deviations with Wolf's assistance, Wolf is also busy with his 'Doomsday Survey of all the trivial and repulsive objects he had ever passed by.' This includes, fantastically: '...the amber-coloured drop of rheum in the eye of a one-eyed doorkeeper of a house of ill-fame in Soho...the left arm of a china doll thrown on an ash-can under the west door of Ely Cathedral....The hair-clippings of an unknown head, wrapped in a French comic paper and dropped in the public urinal at Eastbourne...' etc. What a wonderfully weird conceit!

If occasionally the book sags under the cumulative weight of minor plot-twists and dialogic exchanges among its large cast of characters—who are not all equally compelling—it more than makes up for this with the inexhaustible quirks of digression, and the relentless build-up of the Wagnerian *Götterdämmerung* in Wolf's soul, and the major satellites in his orbit threatening to cast him into the Abyss. This Biblical Dark Night of the Soul steadily acquires a true chthonic dimension, that is relieved only occasionally by the remote and sporadic, Celestial Light of Love. Meanwhile, Wolf's love for Christie deepens, as do his intellectual and emotional confidences in her. But his attempt to break down their physical divide still fails, and he returns to Gerda as if only for consolation in his despair. He takes refuge in his work, turning Urquhart's sleazy survey into a true Swiftian satire—like Faust getting his own back on Mephistopheles. Christie is impressed, bemoaning the fact that so many of her favourite authors, including Austen and Eliot, couldn't write like some of their forebears, before the Victorian dispensation of genteel Bourgeois morality corrupted and suppressed their free, sardonic spirits. This is a fascinating insight, and one that applies just as much to contemporary fiction, in which a depressingly conventional new morality—or cluster of moralities—which has arisen partly at least in response to the permissive experimental extremes of the 1960s and '70s, has come to dominate so much of what gets written nowadays. Oscar Wilde would feel quite out of place in a world which could not begin to comprehend his meaning when he declaimed that only mental defectives concerned themselves with morality. As for Marx's laughter, it would echo without feed-back within a hollow void around his mighty head. And Nietzsche's splendid immoralist fulminations would always fall on the deafest ears stopping up the dumbest brains. For all that Powys was a moral dualist, he granted his main protagonists a free rein of testing the limits of morality to destruction, and the license of tasting the most dangerous fruits in the gardens of our own natures and the cosmic swamps beyond. He was not so far removed from Sade in this respect, even while he did condemn cruelty as such. But he was acutely aware of the sadism in himself, and of the attraction of playing with the possibilities or permutations of exercising power over others as well as oneself. And exploring them in fiction in a sense morally exculpated him from capitulating to such tendencies in real life, granting him the excuse of being a psychological and philosophical plumber in the murkier, yet entirely real, recesses of the creative imagination.

Although I've only touched on a few of the scenes here, there is definitely a kind of symphonic progression in the whole movement of this work, which demands a highly sustained attentiveness from the reader. But this is nevertheless immensely rewarding, if one has the staying-power to reach the end. Wolf has a likeable sort of detached eccentricity, yet also a willing penchant to unsettle with his alienness or unhumanity, which he feels to be both a Solipsistic blessing and a social curse. He's a highly engaging, yet utterly unfathomable, Type of Outsider—very like his creator. His relationships with women are based on lust vying with adoration and fascination, while his relationships with men are based on competition vying with courtesy, often of a rather strained sort. Almost every type of passion is explored, from physical desire and emotional bonding to Platonic communion with women, from bonhomie and close friendship to soul-destroying entanglements with men. And yet it is partly money which threatens to destroy the foundations of love and friendship—as it so often does—when he is offered a sizeable sum of money for his invaluable assistance to Urquhart, in monumentally doing the dirty in every sense on Dorsetshire's fine upright folks! Money and material possessions have never in themselves meant anything much to Wolf, apart from guaranteeing his survival with a bare modicum of comfort, dignity and autonomy in an alien and hostile society, that has always left him cold with perplexity. Only nature, like-minded souls, sex and love, deep and strange learning, and the mystery behind all things—the ever-elusive 'First Cause'—have ever meant anything to him. Indeed, they mean everything to him. His overwhelming urge to break Urquhart's intense hypnotic hold over him acts as a kind of mental break on his automatic loyalty to the great love of his life. So the battle for Wolf's soul, which he himself has been waging both internally and externally all his life, is now focussed on the Dialectical triangle as one might call it, of his two most crucial relationships: with his near-Heavenly amour, and his reptile-like evil employer. Jason Otter is also a spiritual enemy he realizes, in some ways more dangerous than Urquhart, as he is younger and less decrepit. And it is Jason's face he sees before him as he tries to destroy Urquhart's cheque—but to no avail, as Urquhart picks up the crumpled token, flattens it out and hands it back to Wolf, who is too inwardly conflicted to refuse it, and so simply pockets it all over again!

The rest of the book now begins to gather pace, galloping towards a coda-like conclusion. Wolf thinks he has triumphed over his predecessor, Redfern, who fell foul of Urquhart's Saurian spell, and vanished from his employ in mysterious circumstances. However, he still lurches from one crisis of uncertainty to another, even as the path of his personal evolution throughout the book retains an upward gradient overall. Fully in spite of the sudden drops into the morass, he can often quite quickly, sometimes very quickly, elevate himself back into an ether of his own divining:

> 'The warmth of the day was phenomenal. A light, vaporous mist, balmy and fragrant, as though millions of primrose-buds had opened beneath it and millions of jonquils had poured their sweetness into it, hung over the lintels of the houses and floated in and out of the doorways. Filmy white clouds, so feathery that they faded into the air at their outer edges, swept northwards over the roofs of the town; while the liquid blue of the sky, visible in fluctuating pools and estuaries between those fleecy vapours, seemed to obliterate everything that was hard and opaque from the whole terrestrial globe. So flowing and diffused was the heaven above, that it seemed to spill and brim over, making the pavements underfoot appear like clouds too, and the

> patches of grass in that or this little garden like interstices of another, a second sky, whose receding depths were green instead of blue!'

This reads like an oasis of numinous perception, surrounded by a desert of arid torpors and dusty abominations, in the non-human sphere alone. In the human sphere, Wolf is like one of T. E. Hulme's tall poppies, tossed hither and thither, and miraculously landing upright in a bed of ugly, if occasionally exotic, weeds. And he identifies so much with place, that he can say 'I am Poll's Camp. I am Lovelace Park. I am the Gwent Lanes. I am Nevilton Hill. I am Melbury Bub. I am Blackmore Vale and High Stoy. It is over me that Gerda and Lob are now walking down there by the Lunt.' This psycho-geographical immersion is a last refuge for Outsiders, the solid ground in which their invisible spirits can find connexion and ultimately be laid to rest.

Gerda's affairs with Weevil, and another man called Carfax, still trouble Wolf even if he is loathe to capitulate to anything as base as jealousy. But his longing for Gerda's loyal love is the last attachment he can treasure, after he jettisons the accursed Mukalog fetish and even his precious mythology: 'Dorsetshire had done for it!' London cannot pull him any longer. Christie is like an aetherial vapour in the grey mists of his consciousness. Only the cheque remains material, and he resolves to cash it at last, to keep Gerda in his life--if not always in his bed! She is comforted by this, but with the loss of his mythology he wonders how he can face the world, given that he can no longer escape it 'into a deep, green, lovely world where thoughts unfolded themselves like large, beautiful leaves growing out of fathoms of blue-green water!' He has come increasingly to hate his job, and his future security could only be guaranteed by his mother, which is a source of ambivalent agony to him. Urquhart can't influence him now though, with his 'secret of evil.'. 'And with the heart of life killed, what did it matter what happened to anyone?' He seems on the verge of breakdown consequent upon breakthrough, and yet it is still impossible to predict on what note exactly the book will finally end. Wolf feels he has lost his friend Darnley Otter, when Darnley marries. He has a suicidal fugue by his Omphalos, Lenty Pond, seeing it as more terrible than eternity and nothingness put together. His life stretches out before him, mapped by an alien Self that has cancelled out his inner Self. He is schizophrenic beyond all standard classification, an Avatar severed from his own Host. And yet somehow he goes on, 'Banquo's Ghost' or a Beckettian tramp, returning to a dead life and a living death rolled into one. And 'The Cause of all Life and of all Death' is 'an enormous shell-fish placidly breathing in and out on the floor of a sea-like infinity.' His private thoughts and mental imagery become 'mystical vignettes in the margin of an occult biography,', and his 'philosophy of the ideal road' seen as 'arranged under a certain light,' is 'all lost now…' as the old Wolf 'was stone dead.'.

But life always resurrects in the midst of seemingly terminal gloom. Thus Wolf's influence lives on in the pages of Urquhart's published book. Olwen is well looked after, and he comes to an accord of sorts with Jason Otter. After all, '…evil was no more than a thin-drifting, poisonous rain, that seeped through into everything….But it was just a slimy rain. It had no spiritual depths.' He has Darnley Otter as a firm friend to see him through any future travails. The sinister Mr. Malakite dies at last, the sight of his corpse both terrifying and transporting him, producing 'a new phenomenon in the world….It was as if the thing he had known in his experience of Mr. Malakite had completely vanished; and from somewhere else had arisen this frozen simulacrum.' It also confirms him in his love for Christie, even if it must remain Platonic. She cries on seeing her father, carrying him 'into an imaginary landscape' reminiscent of a Gainsborough painting, only with a river instead of a road, flowing with Christie's tears. He at last 'seized her fragile figure in the most self-effacing embrace he had ever bestowed on anyone since he was born.' And a reckoning of sorts is then achieved with the old lecher, Carfax, to whom he sees Gerda whistling while sitting on his knee, and he takes it in his philosophical stride, knowing Carfax will soon be gone from their lives for good. Wolf even manages to see Jesus Christ in 'the man of the Waterloo steps.'! Even if he can still curse God or the First Cause thus: 'Let the worm in your mouth be the tongue shot out at Him! Let the look in your eyes of that Waterloo-steps man be his eternal peace!' he knew that 'Christie did belong to him, as she had never belonged, and never would belong, to anyone else.' And his father's skull could no more 'cast a conscious eye upon him…' He is resigned to chaos, and thinking his way out of the 'contamination' of clay. 'Walking is my cure,' he thought, 'As long as I can walk I can get my soul into shape! It must have been an instinct of self-preservation that has always driven me to walk!' And 'He began to feel as if the perversity of Mr. Urquhart, the incest of Mr. Malakite, the lechery of Bob Weevil, the morbidity of Jason, were all of such slight importance, compared with the differences between being alive and dead, that he had made a fool of himself in making much of them.' He is in sum able to feel that 'an actual portion of his mind was outside the whole astronomical spectacle!' Even if his mythology has died, and God is not in his Heaven and all is not right with the world, and he has not solved what Gurdjieff once called 'the material question', life still has a charm, a point, and a purpose of a kind. Gerda will always be there for him—a shared vessel, yet never severed from his side. He has no need to end life, even as it carries on as before. He shall always 'endure or escape.' This is his Mantra. He has his Significant Others. And then, he has Himself. And in the end, he is roundedly content to say: 'Well, I shall have a cup of tea.' This is the solution to all of Life's problems—as they know all too well in soap-operas!

Wolf-Solent is like a companion-text for me, even if some aspects of the story drag, and there are occasional lapses into bucolic whimsy. But the wilderness-whispers in Wolf's ears and soul emanate from sources blowing likewise through Ibsen's Brand, Hesse's Steppenwolf, Wagner's Parsifal, Nietzsche's Zarathustra, Hardy's Jude the Obscure, Lawrence's striving Doubles, and Dostoyevsky's anything but idiotic Idiot. He is Powys the eternal Outsider, musing and wrestling in words his Creator bleeds. In *Porius* by contrast, we have an ancient *Middlemarch*-like epic Panorama of an age and a people and a society. It is so vast, that if T. S. Eliot had no words for Wyndham Lewis's *The Apes of God*, then he would have had no thoughts even for *Porius*—had he read it! It is like the ultimate shadowy cult-book. And I know of nobody who has ever managed to finish it—and plenty who have not even dared to start it! It is well-nigh impossible to summarize, and constitutes one of the most complete microcosmic reflections or portraits of the human macrocosm ever conceived, in literary, mythological, and philosophical terms. The cosmic vision has a Celtic foundation though, rooted in the Welsh Bardic and magical traditions, in which Powys was well-versed and adept. And the landscape of Wales filters through into the poetic prose and the prophetic tale of the book, not only grounding it, but also granting it its main thesis: that all comes from the earth and then returns to the earth—indeed we are the earth. Violence, war, and conflict arise from it, but then so do mystery, love, and honour. Wales would serve as the microcosm of the macrocosm, except that it is so vast in Powys's imagination as to represent and embody a macrocosm in itself. They say the Devil is in the detail. But in *Porius*, something even greater than both God and the Devil is in both the detail and the very essence of the book. It is the ultimately nameless source of all things—our old Powysian friend, the First Cause—which is beyond human classification and comprehension. And this source was for Powys, most strongly and intensely felt and intuited in the landscape he knew best, which he took in a sense to be his/the world and cosmos entire. And there is undoubtedly something very special, if not unique, about the mythopoetic/psycho-geographical stirrings and propensities of the Welsh landscape—twinned with its language, and its cultural/spiritual traditions—making it a true and worthy candidate for the title: 'Universal Particular' or 'Orbital Omphalos.' Though of course, some people may say the same about lots of other places—Jerusalem being an obvious example. But it's hard to imagine somewhere like Slough commanding quite the same degree of mystical-spiritual reverence! So there may well be something in the idea of special sites serving as repositories of deep energies and sacred-profane mysteries—even if this can only result from a powerful, and sustained, interaction between those sites and various forces, human or otherwise. Something of those forces remains behind at those sites, rendering them powerful 'magnetic' attractors in perpetuity.

Whatever the scientific explanation, if there is or can be one, historically these sites have been places that have been repeatedly fought over, as well as treasured for far more elevated, civilizing, purposes. And Powys's northern kingdom of Wales in the fifth century A.D. is a veritable battleground of conflicting forces, which strive after a privileged possession of the 'Holy Grail' of Landscape, the true home of the 'Old Ones', as Lovecraft would say. Porius is a warrior-king entrusted with power in the region by the Romans, just so long as he protects their outpost from insurrectionary uprisings among the indigenous and neighbouring Pagan-Celtic-Druidic population and vows to oppose the Mithraic religion that has spread among them. While Porius is similarly hostile towards this alien cult, he also feels trapped by the colonial deals and compromises that are so mandatory under the 'Pax Romana'. However, being a Romanized Celt, he feels obliged to remain loyal to this oath. In the process though, he finds himself fighting a protracted war for the Ancient Spirit of Albion as well as for his tribe and territory against the Saxons, who invade the old Roman outposts to free the implacable natives. So we have a Wagnerian Theatre of emblematic players, on a particular stage at a particular time, which in Powys's vision goes proxy for the whole world at all times. There is something present and eternal, in this mythicized *tableau vivant* of the past. Powys reckoned King Arthur must have lived during this period, even though there's obviously no clear or conclusive historical evidence for the claim. But some such figure, or figures, could well have made it so difficult for the Romans to keep control of their outposts, that their withdrawal from the colony became finally unavoidable. Where Boadicea failed, an Arthur or a Porius may well have succeeded. And there is no evidence either to contradict this. Thus, the classic Dark Age morass of history is extremely fertile for such mythological fabrications. And so *Porius* has more than enough verisimilitude to work as a timeless Allegory. It is a warrior-epic, a family-saga, a people's Panorama, and a visionary Template, all rolled into one. And Powys could do exhaustive justice to all of his themes.

In the Tolstoyan panoply of characters are Merlin, the magician, Taliesin, the Bard of the Isles of Britain, Arthur, Galahad, Morfydd—and a host of ancient, 'civil list' Royals, along with forest-folk, Druids, hermits, Gog and Magog, and Giants. Also the 'Three Aunties' preside as pedestalized bearers of ancestral founts of wisdom. Characters are not just drawn from antiquarian scholastic sources, like Tacitus and Geoffrey of Monmouth, but also more modern poetical sources, such as Tennyson. And as for the *Mabinogion*, this was not strictly speaking an historical source at all; but rather a fabulous, Herodotus-style mythical compendium of ancient Celtic lore. So the dividing-lines between fact, fiction and fantasy are continually blurred, and deliberately so—as indeed they were in his autobiography, which he wrote more as an imaginative chronicle of his inner world than a mere factual documentary about his life. History is something that men—and the Gods!—make for themselves. It is not a linear, objective trajectory of events, occurring independently of men's wills. And therefore, there is always scope for our subjective designs in the unfolding of historical narratives. And the kind of truth that is revealed in these designs is more philosophically illuminating than the far duller, more literal, taxonomically correct kind of truth, that conventional historians, biographers, autobiographers, and documentarists, etc. are generally concerned with. This is not to say that writers should necessarily always make a point of playing fast and loose with known facts; which Powys scrupulously avoids doing, by drawing on creditable sources in many cases. But it is to say that where the facts are not definitely known, the imagination is free to create them for higher purposes; and that even where they are definitely known, there are no edicts that could legitimately stop a writer from twisting them into far more telling, or interesting, or even more fantastical, versions, to test the elasticity of historical truth. And Powys excels at this most demanding and difficult form of writing. He's the supreme outsider-writer, inhabiting a Panopticon from which he re-imagines reality and presents it as the Utopian outcome of a Dystopian war. The whole story is packed into just one week at the very end of 499 A.D. which is comparable to Joyce's *Ulysses*, a work that Powys held in very high regard, doing as it did much the same thing for Irish culture, only on the basis of Homeric legend.

In view of the book's sheer length and detail, I shall only focus on a few episodes in it, which exemplify the truly Holistic visionary outlook and alienated genius of its author. We get an astounding insight into how Porius's mind works quite early, when he is contemplating the Pelagian Heresy, which denied Original Sin and emphasized 'the essential goodness of man's nature; and consequent upon this of the primal part played by the human will in the historic march of fate.' Porius clearly feels drawn to this doctrine, even though he agonizes over his Christian duty as a leader of men. His companion, Rhun, has been voicing what Porius himself muses on in silence:

> 'And thus the monotonous rain of these dangerous words, falling from Rhun's uncommitted lips, wrought upon him like the immersion of sun-dried seaweed in a rock pool by a high-water tide. His thoughts renewed themselves, expanded their cramped tendrils, glowed

> richly coral-red in their ancient sun-spawned freshness; while a spiritual bubble of interior excitement, drawn from the pool of his nethermost being that had been gathering in his soul all that day, floated off into the twilight.'

The poetic invention is uncanny, as is the palpable parallelism of thought and matter, a recurring theme in Powys's work. Also of course, he imputes utterly modern words to an ancient, as he does throughout the book. Strictly speaking, this could be an unwarranted license on his part. And yet it still works—and not just in terms of a broad verisimilitude, but also in terms of Powys's central philosophical conceit to the effect that past, present and future are one, and therefore the thoughts of an ancient can be linked through the Great Chain of Being to the thoughts of a modern, and indeed his own thoughts. It has been said that the characters in *Porius* were like the members of Powys's own family. But they relate to each other as paradigmatic specimens of the entire human race, in Powys's eyes. And whilst a fifth century counterpart to Porius may not have thought or spoken exactly like a twentieth century writer, his intellect could still have been constituted of the same Spinozistic stuff. So he could therefore have grasped the same essential fundamentals of human philosophical enquiry.

Later on, Powys coins an extraordinary word to denote the way in which Porius's—and that of some other characters'—mind works: 'cavoseniargizing'. No such word would, or could, have been coined by Porius himself. But never mind—Powys's ingenious, neologistical faculty rings true in precisely what it evokes, a Wolf Solent-like sinking down into the soul and the soily sources of things, as much a carnal as a mystical mode of consciousness, which he describes as 'a particular and peculiar form of Lotus-eating.' So there is a sense of deep, indulgent, even decadent, enjoyment in the way of feeling and Being of Porius and his contemporaries, of supping from the soup of sensations, all the way down into the very core of Creation itself. And this whole form of life is at least as important to them—if not more so—as the conduct of affairs, the preparedness for war and the living out of life among others in all manner of activities within the community. Fifth century Britons were closer to nature and more steeped in myth than their modern counterparts, having a more numinous sense of their souls or spirits, as both inwardly detached and cosmically connected. So they served as the perfect subjects for Powys's master-work—never mind how remote they were from his times. The narrative tributaries and sub-plots are bewildering—as are many of the characters and their criss-crossing obsessions. But the enduring, evanescent themes running through the Labyrinth of the book as a whole help to hold it together in its heady ether, while the incidents and growing suspense keep it simultaneously well-grounded. Powys even uses the Homeric and Ovidian device of metamorphosis, which may involve taking liberties from a strict Evolutionary perspective. But it helps him to address larger issues and open up the possibilities or the permutations of Allegorical fiction, exploring the conceit of the supra-human and its close cousin the sub-human or monstrous. We are on the cusp of the sacred and the profane, the sublime and the ridiculous—our minds and wills straining at the leash of the possible and the impossible, defying the dictates of our Evolutionary predicament however vainly to attain the miraculous. Scientists have subsequently usurped this imperative. But in Porius's time it is magicians, mystics and prophets who hold the upper hand in the awe-struck esteem of humanity.

Merlin has a shape-shifting, mutant aspect, befitting the Celtic shaman that he was. Although Powys unmasks the physical basis of this:

> 'Myrddin Wylt might put on a sheep's-wool jacket and hide his beard. He might trim his hair and tie ribbons in his boots. He might mount like a prince a well-appointed war horse or ride bare-back like a mad devil behind the horns of a stag. He might clothe himself in uncured skins like a savage or comb his beard like the King of Assyria; nothing could conceal the jet-black sheen of his glossy Africa-thick hair, nothing could conceal the green-black enormity of his cavernous eyes; nothing could disguise the apelike lowness of his primeval forehead or alter the subhuman manner in which his skull bulged out so monstrously behind his immense ears.'.

Merlin proves to be a pivotal figure in the story, as Arthur believes his supposed magical powers can protect the kingdom from the Saxon invaders, and uses him as a sort of supernatural scarecrow to frighten the foreign horses! In the end however, it is only Porius's martial prowess that saves the precious magical mascot from bloody martyrdom. But Merlin can cast spells upon the minds of the forest-folk and steer the seasons with his rites, in the eyes of Arthur and his Court. He can heal the sick, and commune with the spirits of living things and the Dead. So he must be revered—and protected—at all cost. Arthur himself is deemed an Emperor as distinct from a mere King, and has all the noble Tennysonian attributes and more besides. He embodies the essence of ancient Celtic culture and civilization, in terms of integrity, dignity, prowess, and the singularity of place and the by-product of place, which is carnal, passionate and spiritual all at once, but not in a monotheistic religious sense, Christian or otherwise. The distinctiveness of the Pagan-Celtic-Druidic belief- and value-system is proudly affirmed as a way of life and Being that is separate from others. And yet it strives to be at peace with them—even though war and conflict is a near-constant threat or reality. The Dialectics of light and shade are more alive with terror and sublimity in the wild old woods of Wales during Powys's beloved Dark Ages than they are today, being rooted in the echelons of earth and ether alike, in spite of the technological primitiveness.

Another fantastical female creature is Nineue, Merlin's love, who fascinates Porius also, but in a quite different way from Morfydd—and there are echoes here of Wolf Solent's dual infatuation—who, 'when his arms were round her, he was always aware of a whole little girlish figure from top to toe, aware of her feet, of her arms, her legs, her hips, her knees, her calves, her neck, her chin, and her forehead. As a rule too he was aware of her spine and, below her round childish breasts, of her ribs.' 'But with Nineue it was as if he were pressing against himself something boneless, ribless, formless; something that was a yielding image of femininity in the abstract, the resilient, lithe, magnetic, slippery Platonic idea of all the evasive allurements in the world that are the objects of impersonal desire.' Woman is not only the source of all succour in the image of the Other beheld in the gaze of the lonely soul of Man, but also the Object of the deepest mystification, and possibly falsification. Though the Object of Woman is so multi-faceted as to be ultimately indefinable, save perhaps as the paradoxical touchstone of true subjectivity. For men, women are the greatest distraction from the business of life--and the most indispensable rock on which the business of life can be conducted! Martial mystics and Sylph-like women flit in and out of the story like apparitions from beyond space and time, who then attach themselves to the locality. Merlin is transfixed by the Ouroboros, a worm-like snake that tries to swallow its own tail, a symbol of the creation-cycle in birth, life, death, and re-birth. He carries an emblem of it about with him, meditating on its meaning. The feminine principle underscores the masculine principle in all things, and God in his labour is more akin to Woman than to Man. The Christian Trinity never succeeded in dispelling the labour-pains of the living, who always experience a rupture within the eternal unity that is the wound of space-time, and the curse of Saturn or Cronos. There are many passages that convey and capture the mysterious essence of Merlin, the great Icon of mythical Albion, who might even have had some connection with Londinium, in the Pentonville Mound area, as well as south-west England, Avalon, and Wales. But Powys's following passage summarizes him as well as any:

> 'He was standing on the misty ridge at the end of the world between the precipices leading to the mouth of Tartarus and the cavernous entrance to Hades, listening to the dying away of the rumbling retreat and thundering execrations of the monsters who were destined to help his son destroy the Golden Age, when he found his eyes fixed on a vast smooth wall of jet-black rock against which the mist kept blowing in ice-cold gusts as it issued, driven by spiral volleys of wind that were incessantly whirling up, from the mouth of

> Tartarus. Half of these volleying winds were no sooner clear of the slippery precipices surrounding this abyss than they were caught by an irresistible indrawing suction, a suction that drew them, with a never-ceasing, low-murmuring roar, into the archway that led to Hades, from out of which, as they were sucked in, there arose a dark-throated gurgling noise, like the noise of a deeply buried weir....But the other half of these whirling eddies of ice-cold air struck against this huge wall of jet-black rock and visibly raced along its surface, for their contact with it precipitated a kind of icy film, which, as it moved beneath their impulse, created all manner of fantastic scrawls and curlicues and hieroglyphs, all of them to be dissolved as soon as they appeared, but only to be re-formed again in endless and infinite succession.'

Here we have Powys echoing Ovid and Dante, with a descent into Hell, or a journey to the centre of the earth from the forests of Wales. It is as if Merlin holds the spirit and the fate of Albion in his hands, and must steer them through Odyssean trials to save them in the end. Tartarus was of course where Titans were sent by Zeus for daring to challenge his supremacy, the lowest circle of Hell, where they suffered the very worst ordeals imaginable—like Prometheus and Sisyphus. Few writers besides Powys had the dark depths of imaginative power to create prose-poetic visions of this kind in twentieth century literature. *Porius* is like the *Paradise Lost* of Celtic Ancient Britain, and Merlin is its chief magical regainer. And the trials continue, in the horrors of the Styx and the temptations of the Abyss. But Merlin has the imponderable strength to withstand every such onslaught.

John Cowper Powys

Powys's physical descriptions have a peerless quality, as in his account of Arthur, which goes on for the best part of a page, two parts of which I'll quote here:

> 'His head was of the strangest shape; so strange indeed that it would have come near to deformity had not the attention been distracted from it by the extraordinary expressiveness of his face. And not only was his head abnormally long; it was covered by closely cropped thick brown hair, hair that naturally formed itself into small tight nut brown curls. He had extremely thick dark eyebrows pointing upwards towards the centre of the forehead, not downwards, as is more usual, towards the bridge of the nose....His eyes were the most remarkable thing about him. They were of a deep umber, a brown so dark and rich and yet so luminous that they made his hair look like the brown of dead leaves. There was not a trace of gold in either the brown of his hair or the brown of his eyes. He had a hooked nose of a dominant size and of a distinctly Roman cast, but what wasn't Roman about him was his mouth.'

Nothing in Mallory or Tennyson quite matches this. We have here an uncannily detailed invocation of an Archetype, a human deity. A great, if probably Apocryphal, figure is brought to vivid life by the magical power of the word. And the book as a whole is literally littered with such descriptions, which however imaginary, and even far-fetched, conjure dreamlike sequences of images that burn themselves into readers' brains forever. The outsider-writer, detached from common humanity, is able to summon this petrifying potency of expression, which acquaints the unimaginative or the less imaginative with the alien. The great Welsh Bard Taliesin figures also, as well evoked in physical description as poetic recitation:

> 'Taliesin was small in stature but very muscular and wiry. He wore his hair cropped unusually close to his skull, and he not only scraped all the hair from his face but as far as he was able to do so from every other portion of his body. In addition to projecting his soul from its physical envelope, he seemed to use all the power of his imagination to project the whole of his small, slight, fibrous, and sinewy identity into the particular inanimate or elemental substance whose existence he was at that moment anxious to share....But the most curious thing about Cynan ap Clydno's unusual king of the kitchen was that he had no relations or friends. He seemed to have no sex either. He resembled not so much an hermaphroditic idol come to conscious life with the vivid intensity of both its sexes as an elemental creature entirely devoid of all sex instincts and of both the sex organs....Thus he was enabled to compose a species of poetry whose peculiarity was that it was not only absolutely "a-sexual", or devoid of sex, but devoid of all the emotions connected with religion and piety where sex enters.'

For Merlin—and Powys no doubt—Taliesin 'was an undying child', and his poetry was so 'primeval, so artless, so unadorned...that it left upon the mind a curious feeling of paradisic obscurity,' resulting from his 'almost babyish abandonment to pure unadulterated sensation.' And as such it was not mystical in a transcendental sense, but experiential in what we would call a phenomenological sense now. He had an almost unique faculty of totally immersing himself in all that was other to him, whilst by-passing sexual attachment. He was a pure magician of the word, who had no beliefs as such, but sourced the metric rhythms of his verse in spirited, prismic relation to the whole world. He was an epicene of nature, or of supernature, a rare evolutionary plant or flower unsullied by human imperfections. He was the poet that Powys himself wanted to be, but was not, as prose remained his medium, however poetically charged and freighted. I shall not quote the entire poem on pages 377-379, but just the first sentence to give readers a soupcon of his scintillating empathy with Essence: ‘With the roots of a thousand worlds dangling beneath me, with the mouths of a thousand worlds sucking the nipples of Nothingness round me, I’ve fled from the Mothers to ride on the life winds that whirl round Annwfyn!’ It reads like an Entelechy of breath, and anticipates the rangy forms of Whitman and Ginsberg nearer our own time. All outsider-writers find an ultimate home inside the numinous nests of such wildly out-flowing language. The soul of Morfydd even in a sense mutates and transmigrates under the influence of Taliesin’s verse:

> ‘The wandering brambles, when the horses of the sun burst through the forest, turn triads into quincunxes or threes into fives?’ ‘She began to feel with everything she looked at as if she were made of a material more porous than ordinary flesh. They had, for instance, all three of them, to step across a little rivulet, in which the water, though it was only a couple of feet wide, was churned up, by reason of a series of minute waterfalls, into constant bubbles of restless foam; and instead of crossing this little stream…she paused and turned and

> stared down in fascinated wonder while a particular sequence of tiny bubbles met and lost themselves in a larger one till it came to resemble a subhuman and at the same time superhuman eye!'

This she realizes is 'the eye of matter itself' through which everything passes like a kaleidoscopic stream, in which all modalities of Being interpenetrate and coalesce. This indeed is the multi-dimensional domain of the Book itself. Morfydd however is not as pure as Taliesin, for she lusts after her husband-to-be's friend, Rhun, again echoing the love-triangle in *Wolf Solent* and perhaps in Powys's own life. But Taliesin towers above them all.

Powys applies the term 'Aboriginals' to the old Celtic forest-folk of wild Wales, suggesting some ethnic bond of ancient anthropological groups across the planet, and portrays a truly uncanny world of deciduous, fungal primordiality, admixed with magic, war, love, and all manner of greater than human or natural passions. Giants and metamorphs and mythic beast-men wander the woods under the spell of evil Elixirs, like Hesiod's 'Men of the Third Race'. Only Merlin, resembling a 'corpse-god' or 'Head of Hades', can commune with these phantasmagoric throwbacks to the peace of primitive communism and the Dawn of Atlantis. He blesses the spaces they might otherwise inadvertently curse with their presence and passage, not to mention the tribe he is sworn to protect. The Lands of King Brutus and Lud, Gog and Magog, are painted with such a phenomenally sustained richness of detail, imagery and incident, that it reads as if it had been written in, or before, the time in which it is set--rather than over fifteen hundred years later! Porius marries Morfydd, and duly deflowers her. Although she is really in love with Rhun, whilst knowing that she can manipulate her 'good-natured Hercules' as she pleases. And so she intends to lead a free life, enjoying the best of her betrothed and adulterous worlds. Porius though savours his conquest in blissful ignorance of her duplicity, feeling 'he could let his mind wander over the whole cosmos of his consciousness while a delicious drowsiness invaded his satisfied senses.' But he dreams also of greater conquests of his own, of the Aboriginal women or Amazons of the Welsh forests, the Cewri. He later beholds one of these giantesses with her father, and is so struck by her majestic magnificence he is totally frozen with awe:

> 'He became conscious of his mind as a living entity, using his body but distinct from his body. His mind felt as if it had suddenly become a new creature, strung up in itself, flexible and porous in itself, compact and resilient from centre to circumference, and able, as it had never been able before, to choose between opposite possibilities of action, and taking hold of its lumbering brother-in-arms to use that simple companion for purposes that must seem to it both fantastic and obscure.'

His whole conception of man's union with woman is torn up by the roots and utterly revolutionized, and by a creature that may be a monstrous phantom. Then he follows her, and after an intense groping succeeds in raping her in a Leda and the Swan fashion. She is the opposite of passive however, and drains him of his strength. It is like sex with a Demoness who also has the sweet charms of a Siren. Powys is fantasizing here about his own Pan-like, yet clearly unfulfilled, lusts. But she is later brutally killed for having succumbed to violation with a mere man.

Porius's trials continue, listening to the Fisher King's chant, and witnessing the performance of rites at the Old Stone. Merlin's powers seem formidable, though they stem as much from ceremony as from some singular inner gift. Taliesin on the other hand, seems to be automatically spiritually in touch with the elements of nature, and through them the mysteries of supernature. Even Merlin is bewildered by his facility. A conflict exists between poetry and prophecy, and history is its dialectical outcome. Yet history occurs on many different planes, inner as well as outer. Do we make history ourselves, or does history make us? Are there more powerful forces than any of us which shape our destinies? Powys explores this dilemma and paradox as deeply as any writer I know of. And he ultimately comes down on the side of the solitary soul with its solipsistic sovereignty. Yet its struggles in the worldly domain threaten to rob it of its sovereignty at every juncture, whether through its interaction with human hierarchical forces, or else more mysterious cosmic forces. But an irreducibly complex illusion of free self-determination has in the end to be held on to, or otherwise we sacrifice what is most essential and precious in us. The Henog—or chronicler and storyteller for the tribe—challenges Porius's sense of self-sovereignty, as he seems to concoct tales with more spell-binding potency than Herodotus himself, the father of lies. Porius feels at times he is little more than a character in the Henog's fictions. So he strives to resist his influence, yet finds it immensely difficult to do so. Though many of the characters are highly literate, versed in Plato, Pythagoras, Pelagius, etc. the oral tradition still remains dominant. And as with Biblical history, it is inherently unreliable or at any rate questionable. Though the central importance of myth—especially creation- or origin-myth—in ancient tribal societies, is so great it is virtually impossible to challenge it. It serves as the social cement as well as the spiritual, intellectual, and imaginative sustenance of whole peoples. And in this cultural atmosphere, miracles of possession and regeneration seem to occur, which may well defy reason, yet strike undeniable chords of significance.

There is blood and guts in *Porius* too, for those who want it; as when the Saxons rearrange the corpses of their victims by displacing the severed heads of each on different bodies, even deliberately mixing up male and female corpses in this exceedingly gruesome manner. Porius avenges the victims by deploying one of the corpses as a weapon, clubbing the Saxons and their leader to the ground! Powys would give any Horror and Fantasy writer today a very good run for their money in scenes like this. Only there is a total absence of hi-tech, and in its place a preternatural and preterhuman savagery that compels as it invites disbelief. Perhaps the Chapman Brothers would switch their attention from Goya to Powys, should they ever get wind of this—which might be good news for Goya's shade, though maybe not such good news for Powys's!! But the mental recesses of savagery in the characters exceeds the physical. Porius reacts in anger to Medrawd, Arthur's nephew, who has raped his mother, thus:

> '...Porius really did feel with something akin to a dark, savage, devilish relief, as though he were permitting the terrible privilege of beholding from his watchtower above the gate not only the stubble-coloured mist he had seen wavering down from the Cader, but an unfathomable black flood of some unknown element, an element as different from water as it was different

> from fire and as different from fire as it was different from air, an element that was as free from blood as it was free from tears; an all-obliterating, all-annihilating will to perish, a will that every conceivable condition under which this universe could reappear should perish, that ultimate will, in fact, that all that is, was, or could be, should be swallowed up in irretrievable nothingness!'

Such reserves of wrath were scarcely even summoned by the Devils of Dostoyevsky! It is so outside the normal range of human passions as to emanate from a source truly other than human. Wolf Solent's 'malice-dances' spring to mind here, and no doubt Powys too was susceptible to similarly volcanic eruptions of rage. And further on, Porius 'found himself wondering, and not for the first time, whether he oughtn't to be horrified by his inhumanity and regard himself as some sort of monster.' His mind was very far removed from the Platonic 'mind of God'.

Porius fears the kiss of Drom, a Being reputed to be able to purify life and raise the Dead. He is too inured to the Manichean lure of sin, and cannot countenance an eternity of Heavenly bliss. And yet Taliesin still inspires him with his clairvoyant verses. And I can't resist one more quote:

> 'Greatest of all the enchantments of Annwn is the full moon, for the full moon changes everything. It lifts up the low and brings down the high. It steals their fluidity from the waves of the sea and their solidity from the peaks of the mountains. It makes murder a sound far off and birth a wailing upon the air. It makes yesterday's love seem like laughter in another life and yesterday's

> hate like an owl hooting over the rooftops of a city of ghosts. It turns death into the crying of kings' daughters forgotten in frozen forests; and it turns the battles of old races into the sinking of deserted cities lost in the sand.'

Taliesin drinks the nectar of the Numinous, and must be a chief source of Powys's own ethereal yet earthy eloquence. Events gather pace with the death of the Three Aunties, resonating through Edeyrnion like the Death of God in a later Age. And Porius comes to inhabit many worlds at once, like an eidetiker who only has to envision a scene or influence for it become actual for him, be it sexual, magical, martial or mythical. And Morfydd sets out to become an early Feminist—if not the world's first!—using her wiles, and her mesmerizing powers, to ensnare both men and women in her traps and designs. Her only loyalty is to herself, though she appears to be loyal to all, especially Porius. She even summons a Chimaera, a half-woman or Echidna, whose shadow becomes palpable like a living entity. She becomes aware of her sorcerous supremacy: 'There isn't a man in the world who doesn't cling to some woman—though she may be a dead woman—but all men are children to women—every one of them! And every woman, yes, even the most virginal of maids, at the bottom of her heart is a mother to the whole world, and, like Nature, absolutely alone!' Powys intuited that Woman is the ultimate Outsider. Some women realize this and tap it as a source of power in apparently subordinate roles, whilst men go about their worldly business imagining that all the power is theirs and theirs alone. And this is Porius's 'life-illusion'.

However, their infidelity is forever underscored by their deep and prolonged soul-twinned intimacy. Sex is ultimately 'comical' for them, and they both strive for a 'supersexual' union, not only with each other, but with whoever can help them to achieve it. They share 'a mutual mania for a shameless and outrageous analysis of all their feelings, however scandalous'. This is redolent of the Roman Decadence, anticipating the modernist permissiveness of free and open relationships! But their essentially Manichean morality still extends to dark magic and carnal brutality too. Porius witnesses further terrible ritual atrocities and inexplicable happenings in the primeval forest of the earth and the imagination. The scenes are so phantasmagoric, he is witnessing tricks with time and space. The Saxons though, under their leader Colgrim, are pushing forward all the time. The hope for the tribe rests on its leading men. Merlin sets about proving his powers by conjuring a girl from an owl trapped under his cloak, while in a shared trance with his witch-woman, Nineue, the 'Whore from the beginning of the world!' The writing takes off into unearthly echelons of transcendent terror and awe, beggaring belief yet binding attention:

> 'The creature was beyond all words beautiful, in that wild-tossed torchlight under that far-flung moonlight. Her form hadn't only taken into itself the spring-time blossoms of its first engendering; it had taken unto itself all the moss-deep unfoldings and unsheathings of the loneliest places, all the fibrous disentanglings of velvety filaments from the undersides of silvery-veined boughs, all the tangled growths that hide the secret processes of new life between the dark retreats of marsh waters and the still darker retreats of ancient forests.'

The magical creation of an unhuman creature is one of the ultimate driven dreams of desire in an embattled Outsider striving for a reciprocal confirmation of their Being in a mystical or spiritual, affine Other.

The book climaxes in fantastical paradoxes and dilemmas partly on a philosophical plane, and partly on a dramatic plane, ending with a curious serene coda. The wise men and elders argue the toss over the Greeks and the Jews, Mithras and Pelagius, the Roman cults, the early Gnostic sects, and the divine light of the Christ himself, agreeing to disagree over the knottiest aporias of Dialectical discourse: The First Cause and the Infinite Regress, the One and the Many, etc. And yet the Dark Age Heresies finally exert a more magnetic pull on their minds than the more ethically sober doctrines of the Ancients. The crisis of succession and leadership cannot be resolved, as the men want warriors or Celtic philosopher-kings, whilst the women want angels of perpetual peace. Cosmic secrets are inherently 'incomprehensible,' beyond 'mystery' even. Only the perspective of 'Eternity… swallows up…this contemptible, this miserable, this wretchedly human thing, Time!' Space alone is the ultimate reality, the 'Apotheosis', and even the 'I' is situated in it somewhere or other. The future is unknowable, but the will may yet influence fate or fortune. All that is left to men or women in exercising their powers is to 'enjoy to the end'. The exercise of power over mankind is an empty riddle in the end, as nobody can reign over the solitary soul of anybody else. And yet hierarchy is still built into the very fabric of human association. This is a dilemma that persists to this day, even though societies are far larger and more complex. Powys insinuates modern thinking into ancient perplexities, and leaves the most burning questions—and quests—tantalizingly, yet compellingly unresolved. After exhausting his rhetoric and logic with Rhun and the other seers and sages, it falls to Porius to follow Merlin on his final climb to the hill-top apex of all authority; and like the young Arthur before him pulling Excalibur from the rock, to lift one of the four mighty stones that had been forever unturned, as the supreme Talismanic shrine to divine communion. In the process, he resists Nineue's undying sorcery, and in freeing the stone beholds Merlin prostrate before him, a spiritually traduced figure, awaiting the true seal of destiny delivered by a worthy successor:

> 'Balanced as he was above this motionless figure in the form of a man, from beneath which rose a phosphorescent gleam of inconceivable decomposition, Porius, as he swung his thunderbolt, had the feeling that he was suspended above the whole rondure of the earth, and that worlds upon worlds of every sort surrounded him, and that he, the child of Time, was absolutely alone with this physical mirage, this primordial abyss, this necessary illusion, this holy nothing, that is called Space.'

Porius is so overwhelmed by the spectacle of the great father-magician reduced to animalistic gibbering, partly perhaps under the influence of the flown Nineue, that he inadvertently drops the stone, which lands on Merlin's head. Incredibly, it doesn't kill him. But immediately below him in a terrible ravine, eagles begin to stir like the Promethean liver-peckers of legend. But these 'friends of tyrants' are bizarrely pacified by a potion that Merlin both drinks and pours into the seething pit beneath him. It is left ambiguous whether he dies or survives, as he sinks into 'the most delicious ocean of dreams he had ever known.' He speaks in tongues as if in immortal Limbo, as Porius himself swallows 'the Saturnian

Nepenthe' and reality and vision become blessedly fused. Resolving to return to Morfydd, if not the tribal throne, he summarizes his unfathomable predicament thus:

> "There's nothing I can do....But just accept this crazy loneliness in this unbounded chaos, and hope for the best among all the other crazy lonely selves! And why not? Such a chance-ruled chaos of souls, none of them without some fellow-feeling, some kindliness, at least to their offspring, at least to their friends, is a better thing than a world of blind authority, a world ruled by one Caesar, or one God, or one—"

And so this maddeningly far-fetched, yet extraordinarily triumphant work reaches its apogee in a trans-human morass that portends still a positive human future. It is without doubt one of the most remarkable, and towering, works of fiction ever written. But at times, it is both truly exasperating and utterly exhausting. The detail is overwhelming, and the scenes, especially those involving minor characters, are clogging and cloying to the point of tedium. But when Powys elevates the thought and action of the main protagonists to higher planes, or else pulls them down to the Tartarean depths, the writing catches fire and exhilarates in a manner that is well-nigh incomparable—peerless indeed. Porius is a Bible for an unnameable religion, testing the mettle of faithlessness in the furnace-core of agnostic despair.

In conclusion, I have to say that Powys is a writer I would rather read in exquisitely small doses, elliptically condensed to an unquantifiable essence. Not favouring narrative fictions myself, I would happily do without all the epic, panoramic sweeps and the nit-picking episodic threads in the ever-stretching Thebaids of his novels. But the man himself was a veritable Phenomenon, infinitely deserving his pre-eminent place, alongside Mann and Musil, etc. in the Pantheon of great twentieth century Literature. And yet the over-riding fact or truth about Powys for me, was of course his enduring Outsider-status and defiant separateness from the mass and the mess of mankind—and the insufferable prison of society. However, for all that he was an indefatigable Solipsist, he still strove to connect with others at their very best, and spoke in his inimitable, intransigent voice to anybody with the perseverance and the perspicacity to follow him whither he led, not as a disciple but rather as a diviner in their own right. And his works are labyrinthine wells at which the true diviners among us can forever drink at their exalted leisure.

In the next chapter, I shall be examining the work, and a little bit of the life, of another equally astounding literary-philosophical Giant of outsider-writing: Fernando Pessoa, who was in many ways startlingly different from Powys. But this proves yet again the astonishing diversity of types in this field.

Recommended reading:

Wolf Solent. Penguin, 1964.
Porius. Duckworth, 2007.
In Defence of Sensuality. Village Press, 1974.

Chapter Six

Fernando Pessoa: Hidden in the Heteronyms, the Man who Never Was

I recall with searing clarity my first discovery of Fernando Pessoa years ago, and the cataclysmic sense I had while I stood rooted to the spot devouring the pages of *The Book of Disquiet* in a quiet bookshop, that I had just discovered: Myself. If this sounds unconscionably arrogant, I can elucidate. The work unfolding before me resembled the contents of a recurring dream I had in which I was wandering all alone, through some vast, magnificent, unearthly Hall—a little like The Hall of Eblis in Beckford's *Vathek*—filled with priceless objects and decorated in gold, ruby and turquoise colours. And in the middle of it, on the dazzling marble floor, stood a gold Lectern, towards which I gravitated. When I arrived in front of it, a quite extraordinary illuminated manuscript lay on it, opened at a particular page. And then I looked closely at it, hoping to divine its contents. And it was of course written in a language that at first sight appeared not only foreign to me, but also non-human. And yet, within moments I was reading it with full comprehension, and in the manner of lucid dreams was becoming conscious of myself in my unconscious state. But then of course, after an indeterminate and indeterminable elapse of dream-time, the inevitable happened, and I woke up! And needless to say, to my unutterably acute frustration, I could not remember a word of what I was absolutely convinced I had understood automatically on the other side of the dreaming-divide. And I've occasionally had this dream since with slight variations, and have thought long and hard about how one might consciously mine one's unconscious mind, to retrieve information one might already in a sense 'know', without ever having actually learnt it in a waking state. But for the life of me I cannot do this, and I know of no reliable case of anyone else doing it either. Yet I have a hunch that dream-life might provide us with a source of instant enlightenment on a whole range of subjects, that one may struggle to master in any other frame of mind: mathematics, e.g. as well as languages.

However, although I was obviously reading *The Book of Disquiet* in English translation—rather in than some exotically extra-terrestrial, Enochian-style tongue!—the contents of Pessoa's *Book* were still remarkably reminiscent of the dream-manuscript, in that luminescently suggestive, vague sense one so often has of the qualia of a dream-state, even if the pertinent and precise details are forgotten. And the *Book* is sufficiently fantastical on its own merits to deserve such a comparison—as if I had actually anticipated my discovery of it in reality later on, in a premonitory or precognitive fashion. But above all I sensed a very powerful affinity with the man behind this extraordinary fictive creation, dissolving away into discrete miasmas of gestation the more one endeavoured to pinpoint his presence. He was in fact an absence, and an absence to himself as much as to the Reader, and also a tortuously contrived absence. He clearly did not know who—or what—he was, or whether he even existed, such was the intense fragility of his conscious grip on the fleeting solidity of the suppositional Self, as it fluctuated through its flashes of Identity. Nothing was fixed in Being and consciousness. So as the Self moved through itself, it left the impalpable yet indelible sense of having come and gone without ever actually having been. I reckon we all experience this ineffable transience within ourselves. Yet I sensed that Pessoa experienced this to a degree of extremity, that was psychologically disorientating to the point of existential disintegration. He himself was like what he once termed 'the Hetaeras of the Abyss'—evanescing in an insubstantial light whilst they clawed endlessly at the imaginary scaffolding of the Dark. And in an exceedingly strange way I got the impression that he had almost enjoyed this predicament, even as he endured its torments like a Tartarean Titan. It was as if he felt he had been sentenced by cosmic agencies beyond his control or awareness even to suffer the worst imaginable spiritual evisceration, and to be its supreme witness or Recorder, a privilege of pain that he had to turn to his satanically stoical advantage! And his prize for doing this was his master-work—an inherently unfinishable, labyrinthine compendium of diamantine fragments.

The Book of Disquiet will comprise the main subject of my study here, in addition to the odd minor digression and biographical detail, since it does represent, not to say embody, the man himself in all his mesmerizing, and unfathomable, prolixity. Like Lautreamont, Proust, Cendrars and Powys, Pessoa did not really believe in biography as a main source of revealing or illuminating truths about authors. It was only a dull and unsophisticated method of recording the base outlines of literal truth, as distinct from the depthless and roofless realms of greater imaginative truth, that captured the essence of Beings more fully engaged with, and immersed in, irreality than reality. I have already written about Pessoa before, having an article on him published in *Wormwood Magazine*, Number 2. So I shall attempt to present some fresh material here. And the man himself, however deliberately elusive, still compels fascination, if only for this very reason. The bare facts of his life might not have been all that significant in themselves. But the whole manner in which he was oriented, or rather not oriented, in life and the real world, holds profound significance for, and relevance to, the very notion of his having been an utterly confirmed outsider-writer. The man may have been a 'multiplicity', as he insisted. But he was also in one sense at least, himself, in and through each of the manifestations of multiplicity. At any rate, this is the perhaps philosophically contentious or as yet unfounded assumption that I wish to make here. Pessoa didn't actually cease being Pessoa when he was being any of the Heteronyms that he adopted or impersonated or wrote under, but was having experiences that were more or less detached from these Personae, however deep-sourced they were in his psyche and his imagination. And in this way, the unities in his work can perhaps best be teased out. For it all emanated from him in the final analysis, even if he wasn't completely *sui generis* as he may have wished to be, or even have appeared to be, but was instead the sum-total of his influences—as indeed we all are in the end.

I've said before that he was stranger even than Kafka, and I believe it still. The latter suffered from a pathological fear amounting to malignant shyness. Pessoa suffered from the same pathology, only to an even greater degree. Both of them were insomniac nocturnalists, requiring only a few hours sleep each night—like Margaret Thatcher as well; though I would be hard-pressed to think of anything else they had in common!—producing their best work in the early hours of the morning. But of the two, Pessoa was even more determinedly and resolutely alone—and loveless. Kafka at least had a sort of long-distance love affair with a woman—the subject of his *Letters to Milena*—even if he could not bring himself to meet her again in the flesh. He was also attractive to women according to some accounts, and could be friendly and sociable on occasion. Pessoa by contrast, swiftly and cruelly terminated the one relationship he began with a woman, Ophelia Queiroz, almost as if he were masochistically punishing himself for having given himself the one opportunity to consummate love—as well as sadistically punishing the woman after she had already developed feelings for him. And he was very distant and aloof, with the few literary friends he had. And as for strangers, though he could be elaborately courteous at times, setting great store by good manners and formal rectitude, he could also be very cutting with them if he thought they were trying to ingratiate themselves with him, however innocuously. Kafka most probably did not die a virgin, whereas Pessoa most probably did. Not that I wish to judge or condemn Pessoa for this, and I don't want to suggest that his writings were simply a vast Freudian sublimation of his frustrated and unrequited sexual urges. In fact, they were far more complex and extraordinary than that—as if he had somehow conquered the sex urge and love instinct, and the religious impulse, and turned himself into a sort of icy Olympian monster or gleefully sardonic Diabolist freak. If he didn't want to be a Christian, it seems he didn't want to be a human either!

It has been suggested by some people that Pessoa was really homosexual. This may have been the case. But there is of course no real evidence one way or the other, precisely because of his insistent secrecy. He had a close friendship with the poet Sa Carneiro, who committed suicide in Paris. But there is certainly no evidence that Carneiro was gay, and there were no third party witnesses to anything other than an apparently heterosexual liaison in public places. So we can only speculate. And my own hunch is he was probably a very rarefied example of an a-sexual person in real life, whilst being a pan-sexual figment of his own imagination in the privacy of his fictional world! Otherwise, I frankly couldn't care less. What especially fascinates me about Pessoa is his almost unique, unclassifiable, preternatural, savagely aestheticized, phantasmagorically heathen, morbidly psycho-spiritualized, sheer and utter trans-human weirdness!! Many people who know about him and his work are put off both, by their perception of his terrifying negativity. But I find this a truly compelling challenge, if only because his language is so spell-bindingly magnificent that one literally forgets one is caught up in an intractably binding vision of Hell. There is truly no hope in *The Book of Disquiet*. Yet this fact is rendered quite exquisitely exhilarating in the whole manner in which Pessoa weaves his outrageously antinomian conceits into the Thebaid of the work. It's as if he were standing on the edge of the Abyss, saying: 'Ah! Home at last! And may my readers taste of your viscerally aetherial delights for as long an eternity as I!' Before examining the text, I will just add that Pessoa did in fact have an encounter, and indeed a long correspondence, with the Great Thelemic tat-queen himself, the mighty monster with the three reverse-charge digits—old Aleister Crowley no less! It's mind-bogglingly difficult to imagine this mountainously larger-than-life, obscenely extroverted, ultra-mesmerizing mountebank sharing an Ontological space with the fibrillatingly fastidious, eye-eviscerating shy, Tyro of self-torturing torments! But it is true, and the fat Beast even bowed to Pessoa's superior Astrological acumen for what that's worth—and actually enlisted his help in faking his suicide at the Mouth of Hell near Cascais; where I myself enjoyed a wonderful fish supper around seventy five years later! Pessoa reported having seen Crowley's ghost—indeed he had, in all-too-living form!—whereupon the charlatan-conjuror duly re-appeared with a Twainian twinkle, a short time afterwards in Germany!

Fernando Pessoa

The first thing to say about *The Book of Disquiet* is, that it both was and was not written by Pessoa. He had at least some seventy two Heteronyms, and the one who wrote the vast bulk of his masterpiece was Bernardo Soares, who he regarded as being the most similar to himself, or a 'mutilated' version of himself. He was an assistant bookkeeper, with an exquisitely bored, superciliously refined, moodily resigned aura about him, endlessly musing and meditating the hours of his life away, to keep reality at bay, and merely fill the useless void between birth and death. He cannot be a man of action, but a superior dreamer only, who writes purely in order to lend the illusion of significant attainment to an otherwise inveterately and incurably senseless existence. So Pessoa pours all of his nightmarish, yet superbly polished, broodings into the vessel of this alter ego—which is purportedly separate from him, yet undeniably his own creation, and arguably a thoroughly central and crucial facet of his Being. Indeed, I may be alone, or certainly sticking my neck out among Pessoa purists, in refusing to be too spell-bound or downright blinded by the plethora of his Heteronyms, for I'm convinced that a part of Pessoa the man was in each one of his Heteronyms. And the man as a whole was still in some sense, a continuous work in progress throughout every imaginative incarnation of the plurality of his personae. Whilst I don't obviously take the view that his Heteronymic habit was a mere Freudian defence-mechanism, nor a symptom of multiple personality syndrome or schizophrenia; there was clearly a profoundly escapist fixation that took root in him, albeit it became an intensely self-disciplined and masterfully composed artistic recasting of his Self and his life into an ultimately and necessarily fractured unity. But enough of the man himself surfaces and re-surfaces throughout his work, as in his life, for it to be possible to extract his essence as it were, and say that here and there it is he speaking as well as, or even instead of, or underpinning or over-shadowing, Heteronyms X, Y, or Z. This goes against the grain of his own thinking, and the entire corpus of modernism and post-modernism, not to mention the scholarly consensus about the man, his life and his work. But so be it.

To make out the above case, I could first take a swift detour around philosophy—which Pessoa himself studied at University—from Hume and Kant, to Freud and Chomsky *et al*, to reach the near-certain conclusion that if the Self does not exist or inhere in the immaterial domains of our Being, then it does in the material domains, i.e. the brain and the body. So it does possess an integrity and therefore an identity which remains substantive throughout the accidents, in Aristotelian terms. There is a continuity to the Self in other words, which need not depend upon the Transcendental Ego that I've already discussed, nor even the Unconscious Mind. It could be grounded in the inter-connectivity of the brain-parts and events, along with the bio-chemical constituents of the body. This may be a sufficient criterion. And it's hard to see how we would hold or hang together at all, if this were not in some sense true, even if we cannot as yet fully define or comprehend it. So I offer it as a plausibly demonstrated working assumption or principle governing my ensuing discussion. There is then further evidence of Pessoa's own distress over his own enigmatic opacity, as when he admitted in desperation to friends that he 'did not know who he was.' This was not a proud affirmation of his mysterious multiplicity, but the closest thing to a *cri de coeur* that he ever uttered. He regarded his endless, self-driven complication and elaboration of himself as an affliction, and even a curse in his life and relationships; although in the Solipsistic privacy of his home and head, he could treat this Mephistophelian mass of misanthropic misery as a curious, almost joyful, creative blessing. Furthermore, his increased reliance on alcohol to blot out the agony of his isolation and truly Dantean burden, which killed him in the end, as he developed Hepatitis, suggests quite categorically that he was not remotely happy with his unhappiness! I say that he did wish and strive with every fibre of his sand-bogged Being to be who and what he was simply and transparently, if only for one perspicuous and conspicuous moment. But he felt as if this had never once happened to him. And this makes the whole aetiology of his Heteronyms all the more strange and dark and Heterotrophically destructive. He was surely erecting a wall of mirrors between himself and others or the world, and even between himself and himself, in the dizzying maze of self-multiplying, controlled madness that he engaged in from a very young age. This must have involved at least some element of the afore-mentioned Nietzschean Artifice of Self-Preservation, which doesn't so much serve to protect weakness, as to nurture steel in the soul, and talent or genius even. It is more akin to ring-fencing treasure than hiding from slights. Also, he wanted to cultivate a weapon, or an entire arsenal, to deploy in articulating his contempt for much of human civilization, in the firm belief that he was in truth superior to it. His Heteronyms were thus ways of confusing or perplexing the enemy as much they were ways of camouflaging himself. Above all, they were ways of understanding the true nature of the Self, by means of an interior distanciation or Ontological playing with masks, to objectify material which should otherwise remain imperceptible. So in the final analysis, they were devices enabling him to integrate rather than disintegrate himself, as if often supposed. But the pain and suffering of existence still proved too much for him eventually. So the whole architectonic carapace of his created Self slowly collapsed in on itself before he could either impose a coherent structure on his work or experience a moment of happy fulfilment in his life that he could then prolong indefinitely. That did forever elude him. And yet the fragmented residues of his work remain all the more richly, and rawly, authentic for never having been tied up neatly like a detective story. His Outsider-Archetype shines jaggedly through the mess of his manuscripts, like some unspeakable Ozymandian ruin of the immemorial personality that he had. And like Blake, he was able to commune with the spirits of historical personages, even if he did—unlike Blake—profess an amused scepticism concerning their provenance. But the power and depth of his Heteronyms undoubtedly stemmed from his determined pursuit of Occult or Hermetic Arts, including a kind of clairvoyance or mentopathy which enabled him with great clarity and vividness to mentally inhabit the personae of his Heteronyms, with their detailed biographies and characteristics, etc. He even worked out their Horoscopes, which he famously did for himself as well.

This then provides me with a foundation and a framework for analysing the man as he manifests in his masterwork, which starts very like a diary, but swiftly segues into something much larger: a disquisition on life's barely visible discontents. Pessoa is writing as Soares, and yet he is still Pessoa as he writes. His hand-held pen etches the words on each page, as he quietly agonizes at his desk in a stilled chaos of inner creation. This one must never forget, as the indescribable work unfolds. It is neither a novel nor a memoir. It is a fiction that also negates itself as it unearths its layers of construction in pursuit of foundations which turn out only to be other layers, and so on *ad infinitum*. Soares claims to be writing confessions of a sort, or a 'factless autobiography', which is a private record that nobody else can corroborate—nor even the narrator and author, who are trapped in the transitoriness of happening and the unreliability of memory. So what might appear to be a description may only be an imagining or a speculation, that swells up and then subsides. Life is truly like this for all of us, with external events appearing to mirror internal impressions. Soares gives us fleeting details of his work, his boss Vasques, his traipses around Lisbon and occasional trips elsewhere, his eating-places, his accommodation, his solitary life and absence of ambition, interspersed with arresting and startling digressions on the general meaninglessness of everything. On Page 20, he suddenly states out of the blue: 'We never know self-realization. We are two abysses—a well staring at the sky.' Then in the next passage he compares the dread routine of living with crocheting! This is typical of the seemingly non-sequential structure of the *Book*, with slow depth-charges sending out shock-waves that collide and criss-cross below the surface. It is divided up into Tropes of varying lengths, and often with no obvious connection to the preceding and succeeding Tropes—a little like propositions in Wittgenstein, only it's supposed to be some kind of reverie! But at times, the philosophical resonances are at least as deep as anything in Wittgenstein—albeit less rigorously formalized, in terms of notation and strict deductive logic.

But the reservoirs of images, thoughts and vagaries crowding the pages have uncanny, fathomless depths that fill the unspoken spaces of a Wittgensteinian mysticism. And streams of consciousness run through the Book too, though they are patterned in quite different ways compared with the writings of Joyce, Woolf or Richardson, who were writing novels, however experimental and subversive for their time. Pessoa was writing a kind of anti-fiction, in which the fictional motif is continuously turned upon its head in a relentless spin of self-scrutiny. Nothing quite like this had been attempted before, and precious little since. Edmund Jabès perhaps comes closest to Pessoa among twentieth century European writers, and I suppose Carlo Emilio Gadda also. The poetic impulses submerged in the *Book* threaten to spill out and flow in wonderfully smooth and sustained passages. But they are constantly interrupted by jagged contra flows of intellectual denial, and a reflex morbidity, which dam up the sources of inspiration at almost every juncture. So an extraordinary inner dialectical tug of war develops throughout the innumerable scenes and reflections that issue forth one after another from the protean morass of nigritude that lies at the heart of both the narrator and the author, who are at times two and at other times one I insist on saying. There are, above all else, two doctrines—that Pessoa, and/or Soares, would doubtless disavow as doctrines, with characteristic ambiguous perversity!—that inform and illuminate the jumbled accretion of entries which make up this unique testament. And they are firstly Sensationism, and secondly Intersectionism. The first states that everything is ultimately composed of sensations, including our bodies and the material world, which makes it a variant of Idealism. And for Pessoa, it allowed him to indulge the notion repeatedly that nothing is truly substantial or impermeable, thus giving him a strange kind of succour in his abiding, overwhelming sense of himself as a vacuity and a nullity. If everything and everybody else is likewise, then he could feel a little less lonely in his peculiarly potent form of Existential Angst. Whether it is true or not is of course another matter. But like Wittgenstein's Solipsism, it may be impossible to refute on metaphysical or scientific grounds. And quantum physics may well have come charging to its rescue after a fashion.

As for Intersectionism, that states that the distinction between Subject and Object is bogus, and that the Subject can through its intersection with the Object in ideal space, interrogate and take possession of it, as an inert thing-ness which it can re-construe and re-create as an extended field or domain of experience. This became in Pessoa's mental hands a curtain of starry night with which to enwrap the world in his own vision. It was his way of retaliating against the world in subjective triumph for being so cast out from it—and within it—from his earliest memories onwards. His was a vengeful escapism, in pursuit of a dreaming victory. Retreating from reality into his ideational and sensational ivory-tower, he fortified his Self within impregnable walls of words, or halls of Heteronyms, re-casting the world in the putty of his phantasies and sloughing it off like a serpent's skin. Of course he could only do this by virtue of being financially quite comfortably off, which he was—partly from inheritance, but mainly from his job as a commercial translator, which paid well, and he could more or less work his own hours. So he was to that extent cocooned from economic hardship and social dependency, and was able to live as a man of leisure cultivating his awkward aesthetic by looking askance at the world around him, and removing himself from it at every opportunity. Whilst he claimed to be anti-Salazar, he really was a kind of fantastical Fascist in the realms of artifice, gazing down upon the Parnassian pigs from the heady peak of his own oracular Olympus through the refracted lens of an imaginary monocle. Though he did also feel tenderness as well as contempt towards these specimens. And for all his quietistic sinisterness, he can still elicit empathy in those who feel compulsively fascinated by his Thaumaturgical impenetrability. But there was in fact a touch of D'Annunzio in him, though a rebarbatively shy D'Annunzio, who would have been temperamentally and probably constitutionally incapable of the rakish antics of the flamboyant Italian poet, but still hankered after a comparable Palace of Art if only his somewhat lesser means could have bought and furnished it for him. As it was, he made do with a modest apartment and lived simply so he could embrace his passion for books and *objets d'art* as far as space permitted.

Pessoa's great conceit that he did not exist was in part an Abysmal terror, but also a self-staged vanishing act—behind which he could secrete the ubiquitous venom of his seventy odd fellow-conspirators. There was a French philosopher—whose name escapes me, though it began with an M as I recall, and may well have been a Pessoa-inspired Heteronym for all I know—who claimed in a series of peerlessly unintelligible books that he did not exist, and extrapolated the permutations of his non-existence in his writings. And to maintain the illusion, he ensured that he was never once seen in public, and so never gave an interview. Legions of far-sighted Acolytes hunted the hemispheres for a sighting of him—in vain. And to this day I do not know what's become of him. Maybe he has died, or he truly never existed, and somebody else, or a committee perhaps, kept the illusion of his paradoxically existent non-existence alive. Only in France—eh?! But Pessoa to some extent got there first. Though he was in the spectrally privileged position of never needing to go literally into hiding, for nobody knew who he was anyway—in his lifetime. So he could go around Lisbon being the living ghost of his unacknowledged Genius—enacting his fantasy of himself, without anybody ever noticing! And of course he did exist, fully in spite of his multiplicities, which might have divided or split him up, but only to form a total unity from the resulting threads of singularity dangling in the void. We may not be able to grasp our essential selves. But this is not to say that they aren't there inside us, as the organizing principles of our enduring personalities. I might be aware of widely differing facets of myself at times t1....tn. But I'm also aware of the broad familiar continuity in my sense of being who or what I am, which more or less inheres throughout the history of my inner mental life. The fact that I cannot substantiate this in a definitive way, doesn't mean that there isn't a plausible Phenomenological grounding to this sense, like the Ontological pasture in which I have my life. And I do not believe Pessoa was fundamentally any different, even though he clearly imagined that he was. But his mood of indifference to the very notion of Identity was not tantamount to any proof of its non-existence.

What started as a psychological subterfuge became a full-blown super-structure of the Self, a Hubristic multiplier of frigidly controlled madness. Pessoa's choice of loveless solitude might well have given him the freedom and the scope to immerse himself in his egotistical—not to say mythomaniacal—researches and writings. But it slowly and ineluctably drove him to such degrees of despair that his Heteronymic artifice could not shield him from the intense and unrelenting misery. He had taken up his own Cross of the Anti-Christ, and drawn out the agony of his self-mutilation in exquisite, unending sentences, the blood of the spirit transmuted into the gold of language. But the price that he paid for this was more than he bargained for, and in the end more than he could bear. He was one of the most exotic outsider-writers in history, but also one of the most masochistic sufferers too. He could not rid himself of this terrible propensity, and could only take refuge in achingly beautiful writings or else the bitterest irony and most supercilious sardonicism. Even if he'd jettisoned his only chance of love from stern self-regard, I think it may also be true to say that he suffered insuperable fright on the cusp of a sudden escalation in passion and intimacy. He had never experienced this before, and did not know how to respond to it. It was totally beyond him, and he must have flailed in panic and then backed off abruptly. However much he treasured his subsequent independence, I think he must have deeply regretted missing out on an experience and commitment that for many of us is not only life-enhancing, but self-defining. And he might have felt guilt over the pain he caused his only love, who was probably shattered by his rejection. This is only conjecture on my part, but goes deeper I think than his Heteronymic veneer into the raw, if unexposed, heart and soul of the man himself. And there may even be textual evidence for this, in his uncharacteristic tendency to address an unnamed person as 'my love' in the *Book*. Who this is, we don't know. But my hunch is that it could be his mourned-for paramour. Pessoa is definitely speaking through Soares here, even though he has to hide the fact as he does so. He could of course, be addressing himself! It's very unlikely he's addressing a notional Reader. But I think he was addressing the object of a rare affection, and assuming it wasn't Sa Carneiro, it can only have been Ophelia Queiroz. This might well be the Pessoan equivalent of identifying Shakespeare's Dark Lady of the Sonnets, although that was much more likely to have been a man than a woman—contrary to Rowse's assertion!

Returning to the *Book*, on Page 62, Fernando Soares—or is it Bernardo Pessoa?!—says with stark simplicity: 'Blessed are those who entrust their lives to no one.' An admirable sentiment we may well say, although for the narrator/author it is almost literally a matter of life and death, of wrenching a split Self free from the clutches of others. And he goes on to say: 'I'm physically nauseated by commonplace humanity, which is the only kind there is. And sometimes I wilfully aggravate the nausea, like someone who induces vomiting to be relieved of the urge to vomit.' One can empathize with the sentiment here, even if it may be grotesquely exaggerated. I'm reminded of a Situationist I once knew, who'd carry a piece of bacon-rind around with him in his pocket, so if he passed anybody in the street that he found instantly contemptible, he could dangle it down his throat and throw up all over them!! But this contempt shades over into psychotic arrogance in some persons—a Diabolistic decadent *hauteur*, that risks plopping from the profane sublime to the guttural ridiculous. The attitude reeks of fearful inadequacy, and an over-compensatory sense of superiority accompanying it. Pessoa may have been justified to some extent, but most inferior imitators are simply riddled with meretricious spite. Pessoa lived on a knife-edge of vertiginous refinement and people-phobia, that could have tipped him into rabid insanity on the streets, or else catatonic confinement in the lofty Asylum of his little kingdom. He retained just enough icy self-control to opt always for the latter. On Page 82, he twists the tourniquet of his disdain a further notch: '...Christianity was but the prophetic degeneration of a debased Neo-Platonism....' This led via the Judaic legacy to the decline of the Great Classical Greek and Roman Ideals, which had reigned supreme before the corruption of Monotheism set in.

Platonic Metaphysics vies with abject Aesthetics, compounded of alien strangeness and human pathology—a fascinating fuckhead, if ever there was one! It's a little too facile to say that Pessoa is consumed with Marxian false consciousness—though he is assuredly festooned with Jungian complexes!—just as it is to say that he's fleeing from the common connotations of his name, Pessoa meaning Person in Portuguese! But he is like a cripplingly inverted peacock of preciosity—very like Proust indeed—who at times exasperates even as he intoxicates with an unearthly incense. However, he is acutely aware of this dichotomy in himself—or even more complicatedly in his Heteronyms—as he is of every shade of every nuance and every disquieting dissonance. And I can well understand the utter desperation of one man confronted by the spectacle of a Hell-bound civilization wholly beyond his control. I feel this myself, every day of the week in relation to the contemporary world, which poor old Pessoa and his ilk wouldn't survive in—or rather choose to stay alive in—for five minutes! One could be profoundly ambivalent about being totally alienated from society—or not, as the case may be—but there are all too many aspects of society that in so far as they appear to be as wretchedly immutable as the Firmament, propel anybody possessed of a full complement of brain cells, not to mention classical cultivation, into the ambiguously welcoming arms of the most astrally remote aethers and aeons of alienation! If Revolution is impossible, then space-travel—both outer and inner—is the next best option. The main reason revolutions fail is because they are far too Utopian, which suggests that the theory and practice are doomed to misalignment, and the formulaic march of Dialectics will always falter in the messy regions where random conditions, human nature and behaviour, and historical designs meet. And Pessoa's inability, and indeed refusal, to marry the life of dreaming with the life of action mirrors this deep fault-line running through human existence. We are necessarily incomplete, and have to accept this fundamental fact and flaw—if it is a flaw—in the essential nature of our Being. Some people would rebel against this limit, but its consolation lies in the life of the mind itself, which ultimately eclipses material pursuits, and could point the way to the transformation of the Self or Selves, if not to the transformation of the world or reality. And we must be content with this.

But Pessoa still gives this fatalistic wisdom a peculiarly perverse twist, as on Page 85, where he asserts that the mandatory outlook of the Higher Man is to engage in useless activity. Only a pursuit of the inconsequential can yield anything of value. In other words, give up on real life and the world, and retreat into the inner world of dreams, art and philosophy, where everything is so much richer and more varied than in the mundane realm. But remember also that one still has routines to follow, in procuring a livelihood and in the general business of survival. One must negotiate reality as best one can in the knowledge that one cannot truly change it, but can save enough of oneself for one's own invisible life to make this worthwhile. There is here a note of Stoical pessimism or resignation tempered by a form of passive resistance, tantamount to a secret defiance of a pre-ordained scheme of things. This would never satisfy a radical idealist, but it may be the last refuge for individuals striving to protect their autonomy in a world that constantly militates against it. And on Page 94, he adds: 'The truly wise man…..can keep external events from changing him…..' He develops strategies to fortify himself against the incursions of reality, by picturing even worse states in his mind, akin to the Nietzschean 'artifice of self-preservation'. These realities are inner not outer realities, the palpabilities of the imagination and intellect combined. And yet *in extremis*, his armoury removes him from outer reality so much it's as if he becomes a purely ethereal entity, as on Page 97: '…like hovering smoke, with the same moment of twilight forever paining the curves of the hills…..' His use of dots, reminiscent of Céline, along with dashes and parentheses, accentuates his imagistic technique, conveying fleeting states of mind like quantum packets of energy disconnected in voids. And the referent 'you' recurs, as if he's conducting a long distance love affair through the power of words alone. And yet he wishes to banish it into a smoky spirit of nothingness. Like a Gnostic, he tries to discard his body and all that connects him to materiality. But he knows he cannot. On Page 99, we have his aesthetics of abdication: 'I cultivate hatred of action like a greenhouse flower. I dissent from life and am proud of it.' And this goes hand in hand with the aesthetics of artificiality, where like Huysmans' Des Esseintes, he affects a wilful and decidedly superior attitude towards manifestly less refined Others—and quite often he confidently assumes and asserts that this is so. However, he is also aware of the absurdity of this pose, and probably even its effeteness too. But he can still see no more valuable path to follow in life. And yet an Anarch lurks within, as on Page 109: 'I refuse to submit to the state or to men.' As long as he refuses to act, the state can't control him. I can almost hear the bombs going off in his psyche whilst this passage unfolds. As an alien agent he feels no sense of obligation to society, like a Wildean Immoralist, a Powysian Solipsist, a Tolstoyan Free Radical, and above all a true outsider-writer. To give things up is to be free and powerful, not a prisoner of desires. All he has to do is stay put and delve into his Selves. Travelling is for inferior Realists of the mundane. On Page 119, he notes his ideal: 'The sensibility of Mallarme in the style of Vieira, to dream like Verlaine in the body of Horace; to be Homer in the moonlight.' Here we have all the contrarieties of Apollo and Dionysus in one synthesis: Classicism, Romanticism, Epic, Symbolism, Mysticism, and Modernism. His project of the Poet-Synthesis involves bringing together all of these movements, and more besides, into a felt and intellectual unity. This amounts to a Holism of the Individual.

On Page 124-125, he remarks on the appalling desuetude that he feels, which he cannot get rid of by means of any action. He discounts suicide yet cannot wait for natural death. He longs rather for an *a priori* negation of the possibility of his ever having existed, insinuating the Indian doctrine of Nirvana, which he doesn't refer to by name, but clearly means, thinking it confused. And yet he claims an original insight into 'the sinister absurdity of this incurable sensation.' I myself once called this sensation 'Neance', signifying the active power of negation at the heart of Being. Only writing can, ironically, alleviate the desolation—not living. And he takes further comfort on Page 132, from the thought that the gap between a 'superior man' and a 'common man' is greater than that between the latter and an 'ape.' This is an unashamedly elitist, if not somewhat fascistic, attitude. But anyone who's seen a bunch of inebriated rowdies in the streets on a Friday night will have some idea of what he means here—though if anything it's a bit harsh on apes, who can solve symbolic puzzles and show no signs of developing drink-dependency! But on Page 137, he gives a wonderful description of writing itself, which makes me forget and forgive his occasional right-wing outbursts. Being lost in this act without joy is 'like a puddle left on the beach by the high tide, its stranded water never returning to the ocean but merely sinking into the sand.' I too have felt this sentiment very intensely, albeit I have expressed it in different words. And I cannot picture anybody but the most loftily remote and angelically gifted outsider-writers sharing in it at its very source. On Page 141, he describes what I take to be his Muse in classic terms: 'For a man who has ravished Proserpina like Dis........................... how can the love of an earthly woman be anything but a dream?' He may well have been attempting magically to see Ophelia Queiroz as Proserpina, and she didn't measure up. I once 'saw' Astarte Syriaca alive in Rossetti's painting. Nerval drove himself mad doing this, and Pessoa probably came quite close as well. But Goddesses belong in Myth and Art, and one should not deify real women if one wants real loves. Pessoa however dreamt ideal loves in parallel paradises of his own.

The darkness in the *Book* deepens. On Page 149, he mentions his fear of post-mortem consciousness—in a buried as opposed to a cremated condition—'as if gross horror and non-existence could coincide there, as if my coffin could entrap the eternal breathing of a bodily soul.................' He is nodding to Poe and Lovecraft and Frederick Rolfe here, and their tales of terminal confinement. And who else among us possessed of imagination has not envisioned this Sarcophagus-scenario, like a black inversion of Hamlet's kingdom 'of infinite space bound up in a nutshell'? Writing for Pessoa is a spell that consoles him and yet curses him also. The Book of his life, or non-life, consisted of merely fragments, which he could not piece together into a whole. And yet what fragments they are! And so much finer than the neat confection he had in mind for them, had he lived. Reading them at length can be oppressive, but never less than startling. And yet he was so convinced of his own worthlessness, he could never believe that he had even begun to write the Book—the Ideal Book—that he purported to write. Every sentence died like dust in the very act of composition. Is this simply a disease from which he could have been cured, or some deep underlying sense of Ontological futility denied to most other people, which he nevertheless contended with in a unique Sisyphean manner, and lit up with the rarest Solipsistic joy? On Page 150, he confesses his solitary habit of compulsive writing, 'under an ironic sorcerer's spell,' where he can only live what he thinks, inspiring his illusions. Each sensation negates the next, in an unconcluding, self-decimating Dialectic, creating a jumbled up fleet of perplexities. And thus the *Book* goes on. And so He goes on too—whoever He is. And if He didn't know, then we certainly won't. He was the unnamed and unnameable outsider-writer—whose name, just for the record, was 'Person'! That might be a good enough reason in itself, for him to have hidden in Heteronyms!! Yet the life-blood he spilled over many years agonizingly generating each fragment of the *Book* from his gut and his sensorium, and who knows what else, was real—as real as anything else emerging in his imponderable shadow of a passage on this planet. And so really one ought to spend a comparable time reading the *Book*. But I am spending just a month researching and living with it, condensing my Exegesis into one chapter that must stand as a sufficient testament in a Domino-set of similar studies. (And due to copyright restrictions, I'm bound to truncate my quotations to such a thin exigency that readers must fill in the missing dots for themselves by consulting the text.)

Jumping ahead as I must—diving through the interstices of a labyrinthine argument—further gems of surgical self-scrutiny are thrown up from the wallowing welter of his *Weltanschauungen*. On Page 161, he writes in a reverie of self-scrutiny whilst his soul is retching: 'All things .... have the colour of my boredom.' His severance from the world is so nearly complete, yet in being so wilfully detached from his own Race is he being unconscionably arrogant or blindly delusional? Or is his stock of imagery and ideas so inexhaustibly detached from the world, that he no longer needed it to live in except as an occasional refuse-station for his body? His sense of Self was so jagged and fibrillated, that his illusion of his own identity may not even have been satisfied in the absence of a world to which he was gravitationally and bodily attached. Although his virtually impregnable fortress of inner Being was so *sui generis* that he tested this assumption truly to destruction. He inhabited the holes of history, as if they were the holiest places in or outside Christendom. Still the nectar of nothingness pours out of him like the juice of shipwrecked jewels, on Page 164, as he longs to be 'spiritualized into Night, absolutized into Darkness'. Oddly, he delighted in taking imaginary refuge in Dickens's *The Pickwick Papers*, claiming on Page 171, he had 'wept genuine tears over that novel,' wishing he could spiritually transport himself into its pages forever. If anything was genuine in Pessoa's world—in the sense of being beyond or beneath a necessary artifice, as he saw it—then it must have been tears. Actors can fake tears, but he was a Creator. Des Esseintes read Dickens also, and felt he knew England so well in his imagination that he didn't need to travel there in real Space. But very like Pessoa, he could travel there in imaginary Time. Tears though were more alien to Des Esseintes. Pessoa grieved for the dead with a rare authenticity defying his insistent inauthenticity, as on Page 173, lines 14-16, where he describes himself as being reduced to the most abject state of all. I think we can safely assume it wasn't just his Heteronym speaking here: 'A chasm opens up in my soul and a cold breeze of the hour of God blows across my pallid face.' How many writers would sweat blood for a sentence like this? Pessoa sweated blood constantly, yet not only for his sentences.

Needless to say, Autumn is Pessoa's season, and on Page 179, there's a sickly stream of imagery distilling his mood, in which he describes how he will feel his soul 'like a whistle of stark anxiety, a pure and shrill howl, useless in the world's darkness,' This image could well have served as his Epitaph, or his mourning Mantra perhaps. But so could many others. His whole burden of Being is encapsulated in this one endlessly ramifying ellipsis. On the subject of morality, Pessoa differed subtly from Nietzsche and Wilde. He had no wish to do evil, since the world contained quite enough evil as it was. But he had no wish to do good either, for he profoundly resented the external imposition of virtue, which could not be taught as Socrates said. He was 'inoffensiveness incarnate.' But he felt 'nothing in the heart.' This indifference may seem almost worse than downright viciousness to some people. But sincerity nauseated him, and he had never loved anyone. He was glad that he had no family left. He refused to be obliged to anyone by feeling. All he wanted was to covet what he saw. What he felt was his personal business alone, and he professes on Page 184, that his morality was 'just an abstract centre of impersonal sensations, a fallen sentient mirror reflecting the world's diversity.' He neither knew nor cared if this made him happy. He is nothing. This granite impassivity was only one mask he wore, but it occasionally became his face. And maybe in his pathologically peculiar world he was at these times more contented—if not happy—than he was at other times, when his paranoical depression and probably virginal loneliness drove him to the obliterative comforts of the bottle. And he was arguably right in suggesting that if morality has any foundation at all, it lies in our Ontology first and foremost. If it doesn't spring directly from this egoistic nexus, then it is nothing but a false abstraction that is doctrinally enforced upon us.

Pessoa's meditations on himself and his selves grow more complex still when he remarks on how he cannot recognize himself in some of his past writings—as if they were the work of another. He cannot understand the facility he once had, or seemed to have, but which he believes he no longer has. This fact does not square with his subsequent development as a writer, and he interrogates his purely presumptive Self again on Page 187, over whether 'in the Platonism of sensations there might not be another, less vertical anamnesis.....' He agonizes in the infinite interstices of his identity. Becoming conscious of what one was once unconscious of in any time, might be an example—in some instances at least—of Platonic Remembrance. Or it may, in the case of extraordinary writing such as Pessoa's, be a sudden angular awareness of a conduit of Genius, that once flowed automatically but which has since dammed up—or appears to have done so. It is a bit like adults forgetting baby-talk! But the philosophic perplexity over Identity dazzles here, like a kaleidoscopic consciousness turning its scatter-gun illuminations upon itself. And the images now grow ultra-fantastical, as he licks and milks the black bile of his psycho-poetic wounds, as on Page 189, where he laments his chronic incapacity to seek and find his own Self 'like a feudal lord of swamps at twilight, solitary prince of a city of empty tombs.' The language flows like ichor. He is now vertiginously intoxicated, fractured and terrorized by his own unstoppable inner poetical and philosophical searchlight, which burns as its beam brightens. And yet this is not quite halfway through his masterwork. So how much more supra-human can his writing become? Only the breaths taken between his Tropes keep him going.

Interestingly, Pessoa preferred prose to poetry. He wrote poetry, but poetic prose which at times segued into prose-poetry was clearly the infinitely elastic form in which he was most at home, and could say just about everything he wanted to in voices, and with visions, which were his alone. He sees all the rhythmic laws that bind poetry as being akin to those of music. But in prose, we are freer in expression and can also think. The two forms are curiously non-commutative also: prose is enhanced by poetry, but poetry is flattened by prose. Yet there is no subject that prose cannot touch upon and elevate, ranging from the most simple expressions to the most complex speculations and analyses. Poetry by contrast was 'for children, to prepare them for prose,' he says on Page 198—a view that few writers today would endorse. But I think I would, because prose can accommodate philosophy as well as poetry, and indeed anything else, and contains many more options for articulation syntactically and semantically than poetry. It has a 'sinuous choreography' and 'Immortality depends on the grammarians.' Although elsewhere Pessoa champions the wilful breaking of grammatical rules, so as to free up the linguistic suppleness of writers and thinkers trying to express ideas that would be deemed literally unthinkable within conventional verbal constraints.

Yet however great his mastery of super-grammatical poetic prose, he knew he could never be satisfied with anything he wrote—not only because it could not be perfect, but also because once it was written, then what it expressed would be gone from him forever. Life and Art could never be reconciled. And it was wise to accept this dichotomy, whilst also choosing between them. One could not choose both, nor choose neither. 'I'm the bridge between what I don't have and what I don't want.' he says on Page 201—a broken bridge. From the point of view of Dialectics, this is False Consciousness, a conflicted Limbo. But Pessoa felt no sympathy for this mode of thought, and represented a very powerful counter-example to the revolutionary thinkers who claimed to embody the synthesis of life and art, reality and ideality, theory and practice, etc. He was a shameless Aristocrat of the Soul, who had no interest in modern Democratic movements, resenting and resisting all attempts to define or pre-define individuals such as He within any kind of collectivistic social and political framework. I don't know if I can agree with this, for his politics are too detached and reactionary for my liking. Though on a purely subjective level, my felt affinity for him remains unshaken. He stood all alone, in the most unspoken depths.

His unwillingness, and inability, to love stemmed from a kind of weariness of sentiment—of not wanting to be bothered to bother about anybody else's feelings, especially if they were covetous of him or compelling him to respond in kind. He felt burdened, assaulted, and nauseated by the loves of others. Quoting Chateaubriand on how he tired of loving, he realized that he'd suffered in this way all his life, and had only felt humiliation, not anything reciprocal. It is hard to follow him here, as he saw others as shells recalled or imagined, not Beings experienced and engaged with through shared feelings. Again, I can't decide if this was purely a kind of malignancy, or a very heightened, rarefied, sensibility, and sensitivity to the Self, which took priority over all else. But it marked him out as an extraordinarily strange human Outsider, almost a literal alien in the whole orientation of his sympathies. This certainly would explain his total lack of ambition and aspiration in the world; the only important thing for him to be an aesthete by his own standards in an utterly Hermetic domain, not unlike Baudelaire seeking to be 'a Saint by his own standards.' But in the real world, he still needed security. So an ordinary job had to be obtained and kept—ensuring survival and self-management—beyond which his life and pursuits were nobody else's concern. He paid a terrible price for this—a profound Faustian Pact with his own monad—yet clearly achieved contentment of some sort. And the *horror vacui* of his inner predicament, which he wanted all of us to feel and share in reading his Book, is extenuated on Page 208, where he populates the hideous of his own mind: 'a sinister well full of murky echoes and inhabited by abhorrent creatures .... the snot of subjectivity.' On Page 209, he lists the phantoms that pester him one by one, although space permits me only one instance: 'They're Oriental dragons from the abyss, with their red tongues hanging outside of logic and their eyes deadly staring at my lifeless life that doesn't stare back.' This is in the same territory as Spare's 'Elementals', Nerval's terrors, and Redon's nightmare heads.

Pessoa's delvings in the Occult seeded phantoms in his brain at least as frightful as Goya's monsters bred from sleeping Reason. And yet with astonishing, icy calm, he declares on Page 210, that 'a retired major' would be the best of all earthly options, and regrets he could not be that and nothing else forever. I can't agree with this of course—finding it quite impossible to equate such an exotic freak as Pessoa with the Disgusted of Tunbridge Wells! But I can well see that for him this was the gravest matter of restoring equilibrium to his soul. Classicism is a restorative for him too, unlike Romanticism, which he viewed as a quite shallow, sentimental over-excitation of the passions. It also encouraged a popularization of sentiment, partly through its links with Revolutionism, which he thought responsible for the decline of Aristocratic influence. Yet again, I have to part company with him here, even if I acknowledge that the Cult of Genius opened a Pandora's Box of multitudinous follies. Though he also steeped himself in Alchemy, Astrology, the Cabbala, Rosicrucianism, the Knights Templar, etc. seeking super-sensible powers and the divination of great mysteries, which only perplexed and troubled him more than before, opening up realms of mystical correspondences that taxed his febrile Reason beyond its limits. Although he clung to a belief in God being the soul of everything, which permitted him to still view the world as intelligently, if not benignly, ordered; albeit in ways that required to be taken on trust, because they surpassed comprehension. And yet he was more a Pagan than a Christian, or believer in organized Religion. God is somewhere in the unknowable recesses of the human soul, where we are all strangers to one another, and even to ourselves. This is why relationships, not least marriages, cannot truly succeed. Only by not looking too deeply into each others' hearts can couples bear to live together, with the shared illusion of their intimacy reaching all the way down to the very darkest core of their Being.

Pessoa's scepticism about the Occult was based less on the unprovability of its claims, than on the often ungrammatical way in which they're expressed by its so-called Master-practitioners. They are like rarefied poets who refuse to write like anyone else. But they still require to show that they are elevated above the standard rather than failing to reach it. How remarkably down-to-earth he can be sometimes! I wonder if he was taking a side-swipe at Ezra Pound here. The two men would have got on pretty well however in a political sense! Also they valued pretension over authenticity, both as a higher aesthetic form of truthfulness, and an artifice of self-preservation. He confesses that all his efforts to love have been a pretense, to himself as well as to others—chiefly, the poor Ophelia Queiroz, his only real prospect of love. The roots of feeling, ambition and aspiration lie precisely in pretension. Yet this has a bad press, because it is generally associated with very obvious charlatans and poseurs and bad actors. But in the best sense, it partakes of everything of value and significance that we attempt to achieve. But not even the depths of pretension can help him when he sees in a flash that he is a literal-cum-figurative nonentity. He writes agonizingly on Page 228: 'My soul is a black whirlpool, a vast vertigo circling a void, the racing of an infinite ocean around a hole in nothing.' And it isn't so much his human-faced demons, but the whole of Hell resonating with laughter inside him: 'it's the croaking madness of the dead universe, the spinning cadaver of physical space……' If the infinitesimally large and the infinitesimally small do meet, as physicists are now striving to show, then it may well be in some dimensional cross-over between the human brain and the universe entire. Pessoa was plumbing the psycho-physical recesses or vortical echelons like an astral voyager through his own brain. There, amidst the tedium constantly enveloping and permeating his inner life, he felt he was trapped in 'the fiendish reflection of an elfin demon's sorceries,'—Page 229—bewitched by nothingness, cursed by the underside of a shifting self-image.

His phantasmagorical thoughts persist like an infinitely coiled film-reel fed into his consciousness, and ours, from a parallel place. There is too much to quote, and yet just about every Trope strikes off some fresh facet of the indestructible diamond of his brilliance. He praises decadence as a source of intellectual vigour and condemns might as a source of philistine stupor, offering a coded riposte to Nietzsche. Human ideals are sweepingly dismissed in an incredible image on Page

236: 'leaves dragged along by the train of a royal robe stolen by beggars.' He pictures a Borgesian Labyrinth of interconnected dreams and fictions, in which every person in real life is transposed into imaginary, yet truer, versions of themselves. He runs through a whole gamut of literary influences: Homer, Shakespeare, Milton, Goethe, Heine, concluding that none of them have written an absolute masterpiece, because only God could do this! Drama and Epic were flawed forms. Lyric poetry was superior. And yet his own works are superior still! In the second paragraph on Page 249, he sounds like a syphilitic madman. One pictures Pessoa's retired major saying at this juncture: 'The poor fellow appears to have taken leave of his senses.' But perhaps not. And if the voluminous magnificence of *The Book of Disquiet* is anything to judge by—which it most certainly is—then indeed not! It is a unique masterpiece. But it isn't written by God, nor by the Devil. And Pessoa would have us believe it isn't written by him either. But it's actually written by all of the vocalizing entities crowding in upon him, and slowly squeezing him out of the framework into God knows what indescribable regions. '*Reductio ad absurdum* is one of my favourite drinks.' he says on Page 252, as if the bottomless oceans of torpor within him amount to little more than a conjuror's ironic game, which in a sense is true. And because he is empty, he can see into everybody else's souls behind their external facades, as an invisibly porous mental eye floating about like Gogol's 'Nose'. He lives vicariously in others, clairvoyantly feeling and thinking their experiences so as to create or re-create their personae for his own absurd amusement. He pictures himself surveying the whole of human existence. He lives as a stalker of souls.

Fernando Pessoa

Pessoa's Heteronyms may have been in part composites of people he knew and saw around him in Lisbon, as well as stylistic inventions of his own. Because he grew so addicted to never being himself, but to being others or being in others, he cultivated alarming, quasi-magical, methods of vampirizing off others, and stealing from them what was valuable to him after sloughing off what wasn't valuable, as on Pages 259- 260: 'I live their dreams …. I ubiquitize myself in them …… and am, a multitude of selves'. He spreads himself out across the spectrum of humanity, fusing projection and introjection, like a nest-flown swarm of knowing serpents. Our imaginary friend at two removes, the major, might say of him here: 'He appears not to have anything better to do with his time than watch the world go round.' Well—as Chateaubriand observed: 'There is nothing more noble than the contemplation of the world.'! But more seriously, Pessoa, in his supreme sweeping arrogance, both loved the banality around him as an anchor in his alienation, and hated it as a vulgar, inertial drag on his almost limitless imagination. In spurning society he affirmed his own superiority, or his belief in it, and yet maybe overlooked the fact that many other people of superior abilities saw their calling in life as fulfilling themselves in society, and in so doing changing it fundamentally, or as fundamentally as possible. And yet ever the Outsider, he could not—or would not—contemplate a role in society that was in any way commensurate with his exceptional, albeit almost impossibly idiosyncratic and unpittable capabilities. Effort is vulgar, effortlessness a gift of articulation. The genie of his startling apophthegms effervesces and spills indefatigably. So would he have admired Stewart's cows—I wonder—for appearing somehow to know this truth, in the subconscious syrup of their vegetative nervous systems? Or would he scoff at this delinquent suggestion of mine? If the latter, his own Book involved some effort alright—and reading it is certainly an effort, though a lugubriously exhilarating one—even if he didn't write it, as his Heteronym compiled random doodles over time. But my hunch is, like Des Esseintes, Pessoa was not wholly averse to the idea of being a criminal, albeit a social and a purely spiritually decadent and secretly diabolistic sort of criminal. This was another of his fascinating contradictions—or paradoxes—given his equally apparent respect for Nietzschean hierarchies of rank, like our major.

Being so frequently isolated from human contact, and withdrawn into a hypersensitive eidetic sensorium—a Solipsorium?—human speech afflicts him as if he were 'exiled among spiders'. And yet the innocent, if ignorant, unconsciousness of mass humanity endears him to them, fully in spite of his intermittent disgust and alarm: And so on Page 265, he can write with apparent ingenuousness: 'That's why ….I love them all. My dear vegetables!' The agonizing ambivalences of the man are well revealed here, and with a twist of empathy one can fully understand his dismay. Although we're not really supposed to publicly express such sentiments nowadays, in this preposterously PC world that we're all living in. Were Pessoa alive now, he would be swiftly driven beyond his customary despair into the meadows of suicide I reckon. On Page 266, he says it's a matter of the greatest pride for him not 'to know the name of his country's chief of state, or whether he lives under a monarchy or a republic.' Baudelaire wrote in a similar vein in *Intimate Journals*, and Flaubert also in *Bouvard et Pecuchet*. And if such ignorance is truly bliss, I'd feel ecstatic to be quite oblivious of Tweedledumb and Tweedledeep in the coalition-catastrophe, and the marshmallow-minded parasites pedestalized on the regal dung-heap! But I'd be suspected of early onset Alzheimer's in my sixth decade, if I pretended to such ignorance! Pessoa could get away with it in his day. On Page 269, he confesses he's only ever been 'a bodiless gaze, whose only soul was a slight breeze that passed and saw.' This is not just Mythical Thought, but Phenomenological Thought as well, which Pessoa described as Bohemian in essence. But he considered himself a non-gregarious Bohemian, which is contradictory, and a spiritual Bohemian, which is likewise. As an erstwhile habitué of the Bohemian café-society *demi monde*—which Pessoa was too—I can vouch for the rootless transience of the whole scene, based as it was on chance encounter and non-commitment, even to friendship. The point was to blaze across the sky like a comet and then fizzle out, as Coleridge said of Byron. One was notionally anti-establishment, and indeed anti-everything, including achievement. Only idleness, exuberance and excess, and occasional melancholia, were positive virtues in Bohemian counter-cultures. Pessoa retreated from this scene—and I've sat near to his statue, outside a café in the Chiado district of Lisbon, which he would once have frequented, absorbing into my sensorium the most unearthly atmospheric airs imbuing that space; sipping my imaginary Absinthe, whilst my paramour stared patiently into a middle distance beyond—into his estranged aesthetic eyries. I turned my back on it to indulge in the criminal and rather anti-bohemian effort of my subsequent, and no doubt ultimately futile, life's work! I still value the licentiousness of bohemianism. But perhaps unlike Pessoa, I should align it with both productivity, including of course poetic productivity, and a much sharper, contemporary, vein of counter-blasting Radicalism.

On Page 273, he says: 'Action is a disease of thought, a cancer of the imagination.' Here is the Aesthete's Credo *par excellence* written on a Tablet of sand! And yet by a Religious analogy, God becomes Jesus, and then Jesus becomes Man, but with a profoundly diabolical twist for Pessoa. In the realm of myth it has a definite resonance—yet God never existed. And Jesus was merely an imaginary, sado-masochistic, megalomaniacal chippie! And not being quite so Solipsistically screwed up as Pessoa—though I do have my moments—I still think action defines us in ways that he was too terrified to confront, fully in spite of his loftily fastidious distaste. 'The vegetable academy of silences…' What an image! I am reduced now to just quoting at riveted random, as I plough on through this miraculous monstrosity of a Book, adding my own impishly perverse commentary, my analytical coherence and critical faculties having been brutally ground down into the dust of delirium. On Pages 276 -78, Pessoa refers often to his 'Love', as though it were the Reader. Could my Dark Lady theory be mistaken? Maybe it was just good old boring A. N. Other! No—I'm not giving up on it quite so fast. After all, Pessoa was one of the most elusively fickle writers who ever lived. So why must such expressions always have an impersonal referent as he switches from one universe of discourse to another in one sentence, never mind one page? But I'll let the conundrum lie—for now. The sum-totality of his loves may be both infinite and null. The ground is slipping beneath his feet here, unless Ophelia had become truly opaque to him. Or is this too Pessoan even for Pessoa? Perhaps I really must let it lie—for good. And lying obsesses him too. He echoed Nietzsche, knowingly or unknowingly—'Error is a species of Truth.' 'I write this book to lie to myself, to be unfaithful to my theory.' In his dream it is perfection. But in the act of writing it becomes imperfect. And so out of perversity and his love of absurdity, he writes it!

On Page 279, Pessoa states unequivocally for once that he cannot be a materialist, as he cannot begin to see how the ever-elusive knotty tangle of his Ego, or I, relates to the tangible machinery of his brain and body. He describes a headache which recurs as causing him to feel angry with the universe outside himself. And this stems in his view from what he rather weirdly terms 'the social relationship' between the 'pure spirit' and the 'body's spirit'. Few academic philosophers today would concur with any of this. But having been under Pessoa's phenomenal spell for some time now, I have the impression that he could in some privileged sense really know the truth of what he's saying here. He feels like dying because of the headache, but is most annoyed because the discomfort has robbed him of the eloquence to evoke 'an entire metaphysics of woe and misery' derived from which he concludes is caused by a cruel force in his own subjective or personal universe which delights with duplicity in his suffering. 'To feel is a pain in the neck.' a stranger tells him on Page 281. I had a French girlfriend years ago, who got somebody to correct a crick in her neck, which she felt was giving her an incurable headache. The relief was such that she said at once: 'Whenevair I 'ave a pain in the neck, I will think of yoo!' Gallic good faith vied with English irony! Pessoa might have laughed behind his inner smile. A strange American I knew, once told me he felt the conflict between Good and Evil at the back of his neck. A solitary MDMA experimenter and immersed in Einstein at 17, he said he had read only one novel in his life: Anthony Trollope's *The Warden*. Some choice! Nausea is the key here. When feeling is dammed up, it may coalesce around the thinking centre—

'Nothing is bad, but thinking makes it so.'—and cause a philosophical headache sometimes resulting in relief in charming *double entendres*!! And of course Keats famously wished for a life of feelings rather than thoughts. The sight of the world causes him pain in both real and imaginary registers. On Page 285, he unrelents, saying he doesn't believe in landscape, in opposition to the Swiss philosopher Amiel's saying that 'the landscape is a state of emotion,' which Pessoa astutely reversed. Yet Pessoa is considered a precursor of psycho-geography in some circles, in view of his descriptions of Lisbon, which became like a state of his mind or a character in his head. But of course, his inner world came first—as always—and the landscape was little more than a backcloth which distracted him, and provoked a range of sentiments, most of them unwanted. But occasionally a view, like a sunset over the city, would curiously console him.

In a remarkable reverie on Page 286, he stops me dead in my eye-bulging tracks: 'I sphinxly discern myself.' What an incredible sentence! He is as so often describing his poor, wretched little, unpinpointable soul hidden inside an imaginary manor-house, where he watches it slither in 'a nameless, mortuary horror.' This is Gnostic Gothic carried into its final grave. On Page 288, he praises sterile women, saying that should he ever be seduced into marriage no issue may result! To abort conception if not birth in Pessoa's resolutely unregenerate scheme of things is the demographic duty of all superior spawn of Plato's seed, being 'lofty, perverse and absurd.' He is like a counter-factual child-murderer here, Gilles de Rais in Imaginary Time!! Cyril Connolly's famous precept that 'The pram in the corridor is the enemy of Promise' couldn't have had a more fervent follower than Pessoa-- though the old porn-stashing miserabilist drought of Hull declared himself a fan. He meditates on the nature of Time, possibly abreast of Einstein's Space-Time manifold, wondering if it really exists or whether there are different Times that multiply in our consciousness of different, and not necessarily synchronous, events. He compares Time itself with a person. As for Art, its function is to lift us out of the mundane, as for Baudelaire. His sudden, ceaseless, short epigrams never fail to startle. Love is a mistake, because it presumes on our possession of the unpossessable: our sensations, souls, bodies, each other. But although I'm in awe of his stoical resistance to this most fundamental human passion, I cannot really follow him here. True love should not in fact be based on possession, but on sharing. Yet I think he's right in saying that we can never fully know one another, not even those we purport to love the most. But for me this is no reason to abandon love, but all the more reason to pursue it as deeply as possible, even if we can't unite with each other totally. Some great artists need to be solitary to create, but not all of them do. So there is no inviolable Law governing this life choice. Yet the poetry in Pessoa's soul still counterpoints his eschewing of Love, suggesting a yearning in him for something that transcends him altogether. On Pages 301-302, some of the most beautiful sentences in the entire *Book* appear: 'The tilted urn of twilight pours on us an oil in which the hours, like rose petals, separately float.' e.g. And he asserts that Decadence is his Destiny—the Credo of an unbeliever.

Only Pessoa could say this, on Page 305: 'I play with my sensations like a bored princess with her large, viciously agile cats.' To do this, he had to be literally a God over his own mind. (Baudelaire's Dandy, who allowed nothing 'accidental' in his appearance, was the outer manifestation of this inner prestidigitation.) He imagined a man and a woman in a *tableau vivant* engaging in a disarming dialogue, which in fact only revealed deeper layers of artifice in their purportedly authentic natures. Nobody could ever be wholly authentic. This anticipated the *mauvais foi* doctrine of Sartre. Only Absurdity is worthy of praise: 'Let's absurdify life, from east to west.' on Page 309. Nothing is definite or classifiable or graspable. He dreams reality as if reality were dreaming him. Not distinguishing between nostalgia and prophesy, he slips in and out of gluey autumnal moods. His imagination had life even if reality didn't, and his daily job didn't interfere with his inner invention. When he didn't write, he ceased to exist, and became someone else. He didn't think, and so he didn't exist. Thinking is a philosophic privilege of Being. Only tedium is its constant cloud. And tedium is not simply boredom—or the feeling that life is empty and meaningless, or that everything has shrunk into a small vacuum. It is the feeling that even infinity and eternity can only ever be enervating for the soul, or 'an imponderable body of anguish and desolation...and everything is an incurable sickness.' on Page 317. Manic depression segues here into a condition that I would call Transcendental torpor. And few writers I know of were quite so terribly afflicted by it. Our old friend, the major, would say: 'He should pull himself together now! A cold bath and a bit of square-bashing never fails to lick the old Black Dog, what, what?!'

But martial rigours were no more appropriate than trendy therapies in dispelling the sudden, unearthly, atmospheric visitations of Lisbon, which weren't foggy or smoky, but 'a torpid haze' in which every object cast an obscurely luminous silhouette—Page 318. This freak mutation of the light—which I reckon I have seen from the Pena Palace at Sintra, one of the most scintillatingly sinister sites on earth—

mirrored the turmoil in Pessoa's spirit, with an electrifying nullification of feeling, a chaotic frisson of fibrillation. And he yearns for any avenues of escape from the evisceratingly enervating dolour of 'this bluish, forlorn indefiniteness of everything!' He remembers, or in his dilated vision recalls imagining, a walk in a forest with An Other, who is of course mysterious—a soul-twin, a lover, a friend, a Double, or a visitation. Yet they were apart as much as together, communing silently from within the separate spaces of their Selves. The forest extends the further they walk, enveloping them like the dark, primeval source of life, and the symbol of itself. Lost in its Labyrinths, everything surrounding them is shadowily incorporeal and yet presumed to exist in a noumenal realm of leaves, air, darkness and light, along with their bodies. This Autumn of all Autumns forever misted, is like a mirage that never occurred. The supernally spell-binding poetical passage, which I've had to paraphrase for Copyright, may partly have been a Paean to his lost Dark Lady, yet also maybe his only inward Cathartic recourse in the blackest slicks of despair.

His resignation to Decadence on Page 321, in 'those sad glimmers of artificial eccentricity that incarnate an anxious and artful soul in unusual words', and his attempt to provide a quasi-mathematical schema for his aestheticized feelings, were vital means of restoring a semblance of order to chaos and conjuring the comedic from the tragic. If Soares was mainly tragic, Pessoa was much more capable of being comedic—even if that did him little good, in the end. In a Creator of Indifferences, he could endeavour to remain outwardly calm in the storms of his inner seas and insouciantly ignore what other people thought about matters of little or no import, this carapace providing a sufficient recompense for his fathomless and incurable intellectual inertia. The question of how many men lived differently from animals to some extent reassured him, for he knew the answer was: a tiny minority of them, and He was pre-eminently among their number! The Tropes shoot forth from the most sublimely scattered sources. On Page 326, He addresses himself to a prince, declaring his former passion for him as a princess, 'with another kind of love,' the recollection of which makes him mourn. Is Pessoa being homosexual through the power of words here, as Sartre once put it? Or is he eavesdropping on the imagined memories of a stray self? Both perhaps. But then he offers up a prayer to some unnamed female Goddess on Page 327: 'lady of Obscure Designs, Mother of Endearments and of Blessings…' as a plea for oblivion. There is a spiritually valedictory omen here, as his inner loftiness is subtended by outer landscapes and skies. And rain. He states his Heteronymic Credo on Page 328, echoing and refining the Whitmanesque doctrine of multitudes: 'In the vast colony of our being there are many species of people who think and feel in different ways.' He then refers to Borges's desk, something in his possession, as if he had met the celebrated Jorge Luis. Pessoa did in fact correspond with Borges, but this was presumably a fictionalised reference. And it was of course in keeping with the strict Sensationist, rather than Rationalist, statement he was making, insinuating imaginary liaisons.

On Page 329, he confides that his consciousness of Lisbon is inseparable from his self-consciousness, and it's ambiguous which has primacy over the other. He was pouring himself from the well of loneliness into the saucer of land-scape. And in its reflections nothing he thought could ever be propitious for him, believing that he was 'born, spiritually speaking, on a short winter day. Night fell early on my being.'—Page 330. He wasn't an Idealist, for he knew that all Utopian dreams were dead in the water—and he despised Socialists, altruists and humanitarians. I can sympathize with him there, although not so much because they want to change the world—and mankind—but because in doing so, they imprison their philosophies in frigid dogmas and then assume an authoritarian attitude. Pessoa wanted to live in his own cathedral, consisting purely of sensations. The Situationists by contrast, wanted everybody to live in their own cathedrals, consisting of self-produced materials. 'To be reincarnated in a stone or a speck of dust' is what every fibre of his Being craved, on Page 333. Pessoa wanted to be akin to a dead Situationist! And he wanted to be a dead Decadent too! Each fleeting Self had a different desire, and thus a different destiny. He quoted Heine's saying about our blowing our noses after great tragedies, with approval. Just think of all the mortality statistics today in foreign wars, and how desensitized we are, and have to be, since none of us could bear Life if we were really aware of it, like Eliot's Reality. He rejected Hegel's Absolute, on the grounds that ontological contradictions cannot be resolved by sleight-of-hand syntheses, the triadic tiddlywinks of Dialectics. And yet he only believed this on one afternoon! What would he have made of Dirac's anti-matter, I wonder? It counter-balances matter almost exactly, pouring into space from nowhere.

As with Nerval's bombardments in the brain, he responded like a chaotic electron to all stimuli. A street-singer once enraptured him with Fado music—Fado being the national folk-music of Portugal, dating from the 18th century, when widows of men killed in battles would stare out to sea from shores, intoning their misery in the most hauntingly beautiful, unscripted, chants. And the untranslatable word

Saudade is commonly used to describe or evoke the spirit of this chanting, being a kind of soulful yearning for the unattainable, rather than mere sentimental nostalgia. And I myself have heard it, most poignantly sung by a little bird-like woman on a street-corner, who demanded no money but entranced me and my companion with the most exquisitely melancholic emanations from an admittedly untutored voice I have ever heard. And Pessoa must have heard similar chanting in his day—singing in a state of 'stupor', 'ecstasy', and with 'rapt intensity', on Page 337—that soothed even Pessoa in his sadness, and nourished his dreams. Yet obviously Fado singers who performed in public were policed in Pessoa's day, as the singer in question was arrested—no doubt it was seen as soliciting under Fascism! But we saw no arrests ten years ago—to us it resounded everywhere, like some great spontaneous Song of Portugal on the airwaves of the nocturnal Ether. He took a swipe at café society on Page 339, the arena of squalid souls whose fantasy was to be 'a hit in Paris.' How well I knew this scene he excoriated with such precisely targeted venom! But in my case it was the bum-bohemian *demi-monde* of Hampstead, already noted—full of exotic pseuds, sinister émigrés, criminals, vagabonds, desperadoes, lost souls, Satanists, perverts, vagrant visionaries, suspiring poets and artists, pauper-radicals, mad mystics, Messianists and minstrels! It was a left-over from a headier milieu clinically anatomized by Pessoa. His cultivated indifference oddly inured him against pessimism. Because he didn't fundamentally care about others and the world, he didn't complain about life's horrors, just the dread sterility of his own existence. What aggrieved him the most was the unconquerable divide between the contented idiocy of others and his own jaundiced burdens: 'And this book is a lament. Once written, it will replace *Alone* as the saddest book in Portugal.'—Page 341. How prophetically true this was, and yet how little appreciated still. And yet in his crippling sadness there resides an unexhausted oneiric succour, as he secretes himself into a muted mythic realm: 'Let us sculpt in hopeless silence all our dreams of speaking...' he writes on Page 343. This passage is the diseased dirge of the most wilfully self-estranged, morbid aesthete, savouring the quintessential scraps of sublimity that get filtered through the prism of a poisoned consciousness with the most exquisite angst of all. And yet weirdly, he wasn't entirely unhappy in this state, because happiness could not exist without knowledge. And people who lived unconsciously like most human animals, could only be happy without the knowledge that they were happy, which was useless to him. So he salvaged some respite from his self-estimated superiority. Yet he hated reading ironically, because as he read, he'd find himself intruding upon, and infiltrating, other authors' minds and voices. Before long he would be writing their works himself, albeit in his head, and not on the page. This may be more Soares than Pessoa speaking here, as Pessoa was highly disciplined in his reading habits—if only to hold onto his fragile sanity, even more than to extract what little pleasure he could from life. I also am certainly aware of this mental tendency whilst reading, as though by Solipsistic stealth I am driven to subvert whatever I read and thereby recast it in my own idiom. I am even doing it with Pessoa himself now—and Heaven knows, that is not an easy thing to do!! But for my own sanity's sake, I am having to cling on to a quivering rudder of Reason and wit as I navigate the perilous phantasmagoria of Pessoa's inner world.

On Page 348, the Hierophant voyages out from his room—into the halls of Death: He pictures the River Ganges in lieu of his street. 'All eras exist in this cramped room.' I myself have used this ubiquitous/omnipresent conceit in my own writings. Everything coalesces inside one mental space. Baudelaire spoke of the Abyss outside his window in *Intimate Journals*, a palpable entity in the real domains of the imagination. Pessoa envisioned the world likewise in his compressed Panopticon, where he'd ponder at night, losing himself in 'The blond light of the golden moon.' This was like a sort of astral projection through the power of words: On Page 350, he looks into the skies above, where 'floats a tiny white cloud left behind by the universe.'—a whiff of Himself? On Page 351, he sails closer to his sexuality: 'Women are a good source of dreams. Don't ever touch them.' Proof positive of his virginity? Or only proof presumptive? Crude cynics may consider him to be stuck up the arse of his own artifice! Especially when he says on the next page: 'Let's internalise the aristocrat.' And all it implied and entailed. But I've lived with his *Book* for weeks now, and he's far too multi-faceted to dismiss in such a vulgarly ungenerous manner. On Page 353, he even employs the term 'outsider', admitting that he been viewed as such by others throughout his life. This is music to my Thematic ears, as it was as much Pessoa speaking as his Heteronym here. He speaks of having been an orphan starved of and craving love. Such was his yearning, it could not be satisfied. Pessoa lost his father whilst a child, and was of course an only child. Like Baudelaire—and Wilde for that matter—he felt compelled to destroy what he loved. Or whatever he felt drawn to, including a person, could never truly reciprocate. And so he withdrew sternly into himself, to deny himself the repeated pain of that fixation, whilst also sentencing himself to a life of increasingly painful privation, to become like an alien inside his own Being. Though at the same time he forever strove to live, in the fullest, richest consciousness of his sensations, lucid dreams, and imaginings. But life blotted them out. He was consumed with night-thoughts at least as much as day-dreams, living as he did with a restless, if often creative, insomnia. Alone at night in the silence, 'an anonymous lamp flourishes behind a window…' he writes on Pages 362, and the light given off by the lamp is a lunar substitute. If the lamp serves no practical purpose, it is still chthonically enchanting for all that, as if his existence depended upon it, like a source of life-giving light that threw the surrounding and all-enveloping darkness into sharp relief. Lamplight jaundiced the night, sustaining him nonetheless. But he was never more acutely reminded of his emptiness in the still, quiet deathliness of the early hours, annihilating all pulse of life: 'in-betweenness, a gap between me and myself, something forgotten by some god or other….'—Page 363. Pessoa often wrote of 'in-betweenness', a notion that preoccupied Spare as well—to do with the vortices, lacunae and interstices in all existing phenomena, which opened both his and Pessoa's eyes to what they took to be magical, or certainly mysterious elements, aspects and even dimensions of reality; that were possibly also analogous to, if not strictly congruent with, 'Quantum effects'. Pessoa had a long friendship with Crowley, who may have mentioned Spare to him, and he might have familiarized himself with his work—an interesting conjecture, but I can pursue it no further here. Pessoa continued to be haunted by the worthless failure of his fragmented writings, producing a dull sensation of repetition: 'I agonize in tattered silks.' he writes on Page 363. This sense of worthlessness is reminiscent of one of his closest cousins in psycho-spiritual strangeness, Kafka, when he described his writings as 'scribblings' that must be burnt on his death.

Well—better this gold-flecked ordure from the darkest depths of the soul, than the mountainous heaps of cleansed and polished matter, bearing the twin-seals of canonical and popular approval, is all I can say in response to this!

Pessoa felt he had bottomless, cataclysmic depths within him, and yet he always remained outwardly unruffled, if in a brittle way—Page 364, Section 443. There was a fiendish, tortuous, schizoid tug of war constantly going on inside the man himself—boiling with magnanimous furies, whilst frozen with meek restraints! He took refuge in the precept of Omar Khayyam: 'Drink! Drink!' What started as an Epicurian mannerism became a Dionysian addiction however, in which a rational acceptance of the irrationality of the world gave way to a demonic drive to self-destruction. His search for the consolations of secret wisdom, Sufi or of other sorts, ended in the perplexity of a great magician who said he'd seen and touched Isis but didn't know if she existed. Is he referring to Aleister Crowley here, who famously saw Isis Unveiled in a magical ritual, and was reduced to a gibbering idiot? If so, the vision was doubtless self-induced, and may well have revealed Crowley's unresolved fears of women more than any ancient mysteries. Pessoa's perplexities and perturbations were even more pertinent. His everyday consciousness sinks into a sump of churning degradation—Page 369, lines 5-6. And of all the elements, rain mirrored his madness the most, like a voiceless black curtain clouding the air. And of course escaping by travelling is no therapy for him, as he sees no contrast between the sameness and the difference of passing scenery. Des Esseintes, his fictional Double, scarcely made this point better! Although I of course beg to differ, as even though travel only broadens the minds of those with minds to broaden—or appropriately attuned minds—one may sometimes be so thrown out of oneself by the sight of a far-off land or whatnot, as to be able to create fresh facets of oneself in the writing of oneself as oneself, or as landscape, or as both. Although Pessoa felt abandoned by the astral intelligence of a guardian spirit, who accompanied him on childhood journeys. And his subsequent disenchantment with the world could never be re-enchanted in adult experience. In daylight, when free, he'd sit at a café table watching people pass by like a visionary vampire, feeding and being fed, attaining clarity in a Rimbaudian derangement of the senses, as he flies out on the astral plane in a supine state, like a great bird of prey. He had no more ambition than to remain in that position, with its vantage-point, in the knowledge that nothing matters or makes sense, and life is a bad dream that only the imagination can turn to good. Reading newspapers only depressed him further, as they routinely paraded the horrors resulting from the futile aim of improving humanity. I would say that Humanity may be unimprovable, or imperfectible. But life itself, or its general conditions, can and arguably should, be ameliorated.

Pessoa was only himself when disguised. And for him, the condition of his soul was more troubled by his being clothed, in forever mismatching suits, than by any material misfortune and tragedy! He couldn't see anything or anyone as having an actual tangible reality. Instead, they provoked awe-filled visions of cosmic secrets—as with Nerval, a close cousin in spectral suffering, who he was undoubtedly familiar with, though he made no mention of him anywhere. He refused to accept the notion that anyone could think of themselves as his Master, or that any prophet or guru had died for him or could command his reverence or enlighten him in any way. He upheld here the true outsider's Rubric, *sui generis* to the end. He wanted no convictions, since finding new beliefs meant losing cherished lies. Life was only worth cherishing for its illusions. In a rare state of peace, he felt he could look upon the world as Christ did when Satan tempted him, and not be tempted, because temptations in the form of material things were null and void. On Page 382, he invokes a heroic figure steering between the Scylla and Charybdis of Order and Chaos, Darkness and Light, where men create their guardians. He hints at a Lovecraftian Mythos of 'The Old Ones' here. Although he can no more have known of Lovecraft than of Kafka. Unlike Poe's Egaeus in *Berenice*, he was never rich enough to live out or enact his dreams. Though his high window looked out on infinity, only the sunsets compensated for the warehouses. Outwardly, he was a Bourgeois. Inwardly, he was a Poet—but inveterately and inevitably manqué. He hated seeing his face in a mirror, as the reflection cancelled out the eye of the soul. He had no vanity, just a horror of the real. Yet he could only suffer from an inability to suffer, the petrified acceptance that he could only feel sorrow—for others especially—if he manufactured it. He contrasted himself with the fictional Peter Schlemihl, as he had sold his substance, not shadow, to the Devil. Writing loses its appeal. Speaking involves showing others too much respect. He compares Oscar Wilde to fish in this regard, irresistibly hoisting himself with his own petard. He diagnoses Wilde's disease with skewering accuracy. God was an indefinite Being without attributes, the absolute noun. Only conceived in this way, could God be reconciled with his Creation, and still be believed in. Otherwise, there were only the transient Gods of the gaps, who could never rescue Pessoa from the trap of Himself. Yet Lisbon by moonlight could cause him to forget himself, in an unreal phantasmagoria of unearthly projections and introjections—a lunar landscape of human alienness. But he knew one day he would no longer walk this city's streets, being the Being that he was inhabiting his own fictitious Firmament. Other people might wonder vaguely what had become of him, and then simply forget him like an unfelt, unmissed absence. And he lived this future annihilation in every moment of his present consciousness, ticking away the pulse of life that stops with death.

The *Book* really ended here, but was supplemented with an Anthology, and all manner of addenda, notes, letters, fragments, after-thoughts, etc. which I cannot quote from, so will have to just refer the Reader to the Text. It is very difficult to separate the man from his Heteronyms here, and the inner Outcast in him was lying down with the beggars as much as rising up among the Greats. There was contradiction and conflict there. But they were two equally undeniable facets of Himself. His greatest gift was for Effective Dreaming as he puts it, and he included a kind of Manual of maxims for the Magician's Initiate or Sorcerer's Apprentice. One thing he was adamant about was that artificial stimulants like opium, alcohol—and even masturbation—would not aid the true dreamer. One had to cultivate the art of dreaming for oneself, and in certain specific ways, in which one would eventually come to live one's life fully, as if in a parallel universe or reality. Enclosing oneself in one's own hermetically sealed world was his most precious, yet dangerous, advice, following in the wake of the 1890s Decadent aesthetes and Diabolists. Ultimately, dreaming may even supplant reality as well as subvert it. But whether this is sustainable in the material universe is a question that Pessoa could not satisfactorily answer, to my mind. But then who else has answered this question? In fact, he acknowledged the suffering it would bring, but reckoned the art it would import into the world and the succour it gave to individuals—especially supremely gifted ones—would more than compensate for the pain of the clash with dud mundanity. And also, dreams could replace the Self, pulverizing the personality. Yet it was essential not to direct dreams, but to open oneself up to their potentialities, and in so doing allow them to reveal new phenomena. But would this help me to remember my manuscript-dream?!

The beauty of dreaming was that it required no effort, unlike Reason and Love. But there was a certain discipline involved in the art of dreaming as such. The trick for Pessoa, was to expend energy only in the desire for what a dream may reveal, and then allow the unconscious mind to unfold it without conscious interference, beyond ratiocination. It's rather like the idea of God setting the initial conditions for the creation of the universe, and then taking a back seat to allow it to unfold as it will, with the capacity to surprise him in what would otherwise be an eternal state of boring predictability. In this way, one can subtly engineer one's dreams without disruptively interfering with them. And Pessoa claimed that he had mastered this technique. Although books also helped him, their scenarios and contents feeding into the pastures and textures and themes of his dreams. And amusingly, in view of the fact that I've just ploughed through his *Book*, he advised that one shouldn't ever read a book from start to finish without deviation. I wish I had taken his advice! In fact, I've always loved books that one can read backwards, and zig-zag through, and dip into on any page like a pebble dropping into a pond, and then divine their essence in a passage. And this wonderfully fragmentary Book is of course one of the finest examples of precisely this kind of Book, because it isn't a narrative fiction, structured with a beginning, a middle and an end. It's a crazy kaleidoscope of a creation—not even strictly cyclical, but amorphously non-linear, and throwing up its secrets in practically every sentence. And yet I still felt I had to read it from cover to cover to write this account. In dreaming, sensation must first become physical; then mental; then creative. This three-stage process gave Pessoa dream-fluency, so that he could carry on dreaming effortlessly when tired, and his mind could continuously create its fictions with a will or whim of its own, and in all of the different voices and registers of his Heteronymic personae. Ultimately, we sieve our selves through all these multiplicities. And so we might then dethrone God and become Him. This beats Freudian wish-fulfilment any day or night of the week! Dreaming for Pessoa, was a truly Promethean triumph.

In 'Declaration of Difference', Pessoa distanced himself from hierarchies of virtue, sympathizing with both anarchists and occultists of the left-hand path, acknowledging the attraction of Satan and Mercury, astral larvae and the evil geniuses who glory in divine discontent and strive for their own impossible perpetuation. But as he only wanted to be emptied of himself, the only valid reason to be an occultist was for the sake of a greater magnitude beyond morality rather than for mundane ethics. The ceremonial secrecy and Hierophantic obscurantism of the Occult either amused him or left him indifferent, for he had no desire to act upon himself in a way that would elevate him through the degrees of a false initiation. His Diabolism was of the Olympian Nihilist variety, redolent of the highest cynical intelligence. And a clue to his sexuality lies perhaps in his declaration that that he lacked the guts to be homosexual, even though his inertia rendered him effete. He is even tempted by transgendering, whilst knowing perfectly well that he wasn't born biologically female. But the paradox holds a visceral fascination for him. His sexuality was like a multi-faceted figment of his own imagining. He was a-sexual in one imaginary/tive incarnation, and Pan-sexual in another—and so on *ad infinitum*! But he insisted on his weakness more than his meanness, his love of badness and deviating intently being a vicarious feminine characteristic, as it were. And any Occult laws were an affront to his own failings in self-direction. Crowley may have had some difficulty grasping the serpentine suppleness of this anti-doctrine! His melodramatic Mantra, 'Do what thou wilt shall be the whole of the Law!' might have evinced a timidly angular retort from the goggled, neurasthenic, porcupine-quilled, recluse, hunched before him, along the lines of: 'To Hell with all Laws!' There follows several rather imperial imaginative fairy-tale like fantasias on such themes as estrangement and possession, which elaborate almost chivalrously on already treated subjects, so I don't need to refer to them here.

But in 'Lucid Diary', Pessoa made some of the most revealing remarks about Him-Self, through the burning lenses of his multiple Selves or his Not-Self: Paraphrasing as I must, he compares his whole existence on the planet to a theatrical performance in the lap of the Gods, which gets aborted before it's even kick-started. He acknowledges his friendlessness, wistfully averring that his acquaintances only felt for him in the abstract, but would feel inconvenienced by having to attend his funeral in bad weather, should he meet some appalling demise! He cannot attain to a state of lofty calm, in which his aloneness becomes peaceful without anxiety. He notes that he can never receive the world's sympathy, because the intense pain of his spiritual plight is too unobvious, too camouflaged even; and physically he has no deformity; and he is at no disadvantage in his circumstances. So he falls endlessly through an invisible hole in the fabric of human compassion. He sees that it requires immense bravery to accept his human degradation, and then to adjust to his plight without complaint, yet in a quietly resilient way, squeezing virtue out of a stigmatic vice. He knows that he is totally unloveable in the eyes of anyone whose discernment he could value, and so any stray affection he receives from baser specimens is worthless. He then peers into the abysses of separation between all conscious Beings, and is reminded of Christ's penultimate words on the Cross, the most harrowing in all Scripture. But he cannot utter Christ's final words of despairing hope. That is beyond him. All these thoughts and the sublime articulation he fashioned, are as movingly bathetic as any I have ever read, distilling into a quintessence the blights of his pains, thwarted passions, fierce fastidiousness, limitless linguistic gifts, and imaginative ingenuities.

His favourite dream however, concerned our old friend, the major! He would picture himself as this nameless Heteronym, seated in a post-prandial, vegetative slumber, surrounded by others with whom he has no connection. And Pessoa is oddly reassured by the comatose simplicity of this figure, as though to have been born like him would have been an ignorant bliss of the greatest bovine magnitude. All the cuts of his razor-sharp consciousness would have been mercifully spared him. But he had no interest in this creation's past. He just existed eternally in one space, in a hotel emblematic of provincial stupor, where he feels the vaguest stirrings towards his fellow-vegetables and his environs, but never gives them expression, either outwardly or inwardly. The major was Pessoa's only comical relaxation fantasy, in which he could sink almost painlessly into the mentality of a harmless old senescent fish, burbling platitudes and feeling himself occasionally superior to the lower-grade geriatric coelacanths in his midst: 'I say, Fernando! How about a glass of port to settle your disquiet?' This impish imputation of mine contrasts strongly with the great chthonic conjuror's ensuing maxim, in which he embraces the alienation of his calling, and then endorses supremely the belief that his written works should remain unread, if in the possession of those who can treasure them as repositories of unknown contents. And then there is the peerless poetry of 'Milky Way', that I cannot for the life of me paraphrase or précis, his genius being too great even for mine! But in honour of the above-precept—and in dishonour of copyright!—I leave it to readers to search out. The science of sensations was his aim, erecting an architectonic of the awkward, that would militate against the tyrannies of precision. How he would have adored Chaos-Theory, had he lived. And yet he insisted that he had managed to achieve an absolute objectivity in his dreaming perceptions of reality, to the point where, e.g. an external and an internal sunset became indistinguishable and inseparable. He could even delete objects through active dreaming negations, to reveal their true essence more clearly in absence. He pictured the souls of others detached from their bodies, and coalescing in his mind! The apparent existence of material objects convinced him of the world's unreality. In the subtle intensity of his sensations they were just minute adjuncts, that could be reduced to impalpable, phantasmal constituents that drew him into immeasurable, illimitable, infinitesimal, and irrefutable, worlds within worlds—that went on unfolding forever, in a continuously dreamt present moment.

In 'Our Lady of Silence', he addressed a visionary woman who could have been a woman of his acquaintance—Ophelia Queiroz maybe—a goddess, the Madonna, or any Being of his invention, that shadowed and traversed the entire terrain of his inner life, his visions, his ideals, his fears, his possibilities. And for me the absolute stand-out passage in the entire Book is included in this section, which I quoted at length towards the end of my *Wormwood* essay, but cannot quote here. All I can say is that it takes the form of a prayer which turns all prayer on its head, negating any prospect of salvation or redemption or any positive grace. And yet it is expressed with such sustained power and beauty, it supersedes the language of scripture to rescue an old classical voice in a new modernist ferment. It can be found on Pages 439-440. And he goes on in a similar vein through several Tropes, a dream-language floating into print with a mesmerizing concision, crystallizing all of his dread sicknesses of the soul, and his most humanly touching aspirations towards the Ideal. The woman has no reality, and is not even a woman—or not just a woman, but an amalgam of all his othernesses, towards which he feels disgust, awe, terror, and reverence.

In 'Peristyle', he made an unbearably poignant proffering of his *Book* to the Reader: It could not be further removed in spirit from the callow, shallow posturings of ego-obsessed celebrities today, turning the cheapest tricks of desperate self-promotion in a shameless parade of crapulous cultures. It has a harrowing humility that knows the true worth of all our most evanescent efforts, and casts the saddest spell of yearning for lost communion and a place in the Pantheon of Phantasmagoria. A more incredible dedication I have never read. And it confirms me in my view that Pessoa was one of the purest angelic—and impurest diabolical!—voices of alienation amongst all the outsider-writers I have ever studied. To paraphrase myself: If Christ could touch a leper, should we not read Pessoa? And the answer to that is a world-deafening Yes! And on it still goes, if only for a few more pages that I cannot put aside! In 'Random Diary', he simply states how shunned he is by the material world and all that lives in it. And yet this only serves to fuel the fire of his animus. His image of himself as a grotesque deformed goblin in the eyes of humanity is magnified to excruciating degrees: It goes beyond mere paranoia into the most rarefied realms of massacre and martyrdom, yet stripped of all religious and moral connotations. Clearly his visceral fear of others verged on a crumbling evisceration of ego, existence and essence here. But however genuinely strange he was to others, there is no denying that the incomprehension of unimaginative people is a veritable curse for the hyper-sensitive and the nervously disturbed, and the pathologically afflicted, as Pessoa undoubtedly was. So he wasn't simply projecting and introjecting his own peculiar people-phobias. He was seeing profoundly and acutely into the rancidly empty souls of the rodents and robots of mass-humanity, who could only react to him with hostile prejudice.

In 'Self-Examination', he listed the saving graces of his most cherished influences: Heraclitus, Ecclesiastes and Job ring truest of all. In Pascal, Vigny, Amiel, Verlaine and the Symbolists, he found the most intimate echoes of himself. Yet he despaired of originality, feeling doomed to imitation, except in that which he had dredged from the Darkness, his sole source of Light. Only he didn't feel responsible for this, as though he were a mere conduit for something else that was ineffably mysterious. And his favourite writers, like his Heteronyms, tended to bore him after a while, such was his own feverishly relentless self-insinuation, and they seemed most precious to him in his waking and sleeping dreams, when he could reconfigure them in fantasy. Towards the very end he declared that he didn't write for public acclaim, or for the sake of his art, or to change the world, but to perfect his own mastery over his inner life and all its unending fabrications.

And there is an almost masochistic melancholia in his relationship with his own soul, in which he courts it oneirically and eidetically like a slave to his own anima, as an unbearable twilight descends over a cosmos of colour. He showed here the least trace of vanity in subordination to his Self, twinned with the most ardent inner striving after an unrealisable conceit. And in 'The Visual Lover', he emphasized, or pleaded maybe, that he didn't suffer from psychic onanism or erotomania, but a special mode of coveting what he saw, particularly inside himself, as uncorrupted as possible by degraded external objects and images. And then finally, he disappeared off the pages—onto other, unpublished pages, of course—in 'A Voyage Never Made', which is a fitting Epitaph for *The Book of Disquiet*, or 'The Book that was never written by the man who never was'. But the voyage in question could not have been further removed from the shamelessly plugged rites of passage of the candyfloss-celebrity authors of today. His journey traversed timeless realms beyond chronicling, that were no less immaterially extant for eluding all signification. Although he still imaged a ship on which he made his Baudelairean Voyage of Being as unnameable, a Titanic of Transcendence, ploughing its pathways to all the dreamt places of the Earth, and on into the waterless aeons of the Ether, leaving the most tantalizing imprints on memory, and never of course reaching a final destination. I would certainly like to share in his belief that his Voyage did go on, even after he passed away, on the high sea air-waves of the Great Chain of Being itself, which may yet bring all of life and death into a unity through its eternal cycle.

In conclusion, it's quite impossible to summarize such a vast, sprawling, contingently and necessarily inconclusive masterpiece as *The Book of Disquiet*. It wasn't all that Pessoa wrote of course—the trunk he left behind him after his death contained more than 27,000 separate pieces of writing, albeit some were very short fragments—but little of the rest has been published, or even fully annotated, never mind translated. And though his life was quirkily fascinating, it resists biography just as he resisted conventional autobiography. If ever a writer was secreted into his work, it was him. And the best of him—also the worst in merely human terms—was contained in what has been rendered in English in the most accomplished manner to date by Richard Zenith. So I had nothing better to work with, to illuminate the nature of the man as well as assess his enormous contribution to literature, psychology, and philosophy. Although I examined his Heteronymic artifices in the abstract, I refused to get too bogged down in the exasperating minutiae of all the different Personae—which for all that they displayed the man in his infinitely elaborate complexity, also concealed certain elusive truths which I believe could be ascertained in a more direct way; even if that contradicts Pessoa himself as well as most scholars. In addition to Bernardo Soares, there was Ricardo Reis, the austere Classicist, who Pessoa sought to emulate, but felt uncomfortable with in his Modernist perplexities. And then there was Alberto Caeiro, the simple nature-poet, who Pessoa sometimes envied, though could never have been. There was Alvaro de Campos, an engineer who wrote Whitman-like verses and lived liked a Decadent, which Pessoa was too shy to do in real life. Though it was in Campos's name that he told Ophelia Queiroz to 'flush down the toilet' any hopes she had of a romantic relationship, which showed fear as well as cruelty and indifference, on Pessoa's part. And then there was Vicente Guedes, another assistant bookseller like Soares, who played a minor part in writing bits of *The Book of Disquiet*. And there were numerous others, in whose personae Pessoa would write and even live at different stages of his life—partly to distance himself from himself, and partly to explore himself more fully, playing games of identity; ultimately perhaps at his own expense, whilst contriving to keep the world at bay. He even had English Heteronyms—since he spoke and wrote fluently in English—one of whom, a poet called Alexander Search, wrote a story entitled 'A Very Original Dinner', in which the diners ate human flesh without realizing it! He even had a Heteronymic brother called Charles, who worked as a translator, like Pessoa.

One could work out a fascinating Mathematical map of the maze of interrelationships between all the various Heteronyms he adopted, but that wasn't my main concern in this chapter. I wanted to try and tease out the recurring motifs in the constant interchange of mental motions between Pessoa the man and author on the one hand, and Pessoa the mask-shuffling Harlequin of his own *danse macabre* on the other, the success of which readers will have to judge for themselves. My sympathies or empathies with Pessoa shifted almost as mercurially as his moods, and the split shards of his segueing selves, as if I were in my own dialectical dialogue with him, rising and sinking to epitomes and nadirs, as tourniquets of tension tightened around the crescendos of symbiotic creativity! I was in a competition of sentences with him, usually with the feeling that I was coming off second best! I was broadly in agreement with the main tenets of his philosophy, as I don't believe we know enough yet about the nature of consciousness and the human mind, or for that matter the mysterious moving ways of a putative Supreme Being, to be absolutely certain of the truth of a materialist framework of reality. Even if we understood everything about the brain, the cosmos and the quantum world—which we don't!—we could still ask: and where is the invisible spirit? Where has it flown? This might be philosophical nonsense, but then again it strikes at the very roots of metaphysical perplexity—for which our old friend, the bread-and-cheese eating deck-chair thinker, retained a lifelong, although somewhat stringently silenced, reverence. And for all we know, matter itself might just be an illusion, albeit one that militates against our most instinctual sense of reality, pace old Sam Johnson's celebrated stone-kicking rebuke to bonkers, or maybe not so bonkers, Bishop Berkeley's, treasured 'Idea in the Mind of God' conceits. Pessoa on the other hand, was a kind of wilfully warped inner Idealist, driven by the most terrible, traumatic compulsions, to absent himself as utterly as possible within the wondrous wastes of his depthless visions; like a giant snake of Sensationism, sloughing off the skins of its material body as useless encumbrances.

As for Pessoa's aesthetic stance *vis-à-vis* the outside world, that may have flown in the face of noble Marxian correctitude—and Wilde, as a Socialist, experienced much the same difficulties—but I have no ideological intolerance of this subjective suprematism; since it is the mark of the Solipsistic Individual in Powys's sense too, and of course the true outsider-writer, the main preoccupation of this Book. And if there is any validity in the old Marxian Collectivist Project—and I believe there still may be—then it has to take fully into account the arguably unself-limited freedom, even the license, of individuals to live and to be, in the largest possible sense. In a word, it has to take into account the Pessoas of this world. And Pessoa was no arch-capitalist. He despised the Bourgeoisie! But he also despised Revolutionaries, which is where I rather part company with him. His politics I can't altogether share, with his somewhat mystical admiration for monarchy and aristocracy and Nietzschean hierarchies of rank.

Yet he was no curl-moustachioed Blimpish reactionary, but an incredibly complex individual stranded in a world with which he felt no affinity. I have to say I found myself seizing up with the most savagely sardonic mirth over his contemptuous, supercilious portraits of inferior specimens of humanity! But at the same time, the old Radical Democratic reflex kicked in violently, with Lautréamont's adage that 'Poetry shall be made by everyone.' That would have been Anathema for Pessoa, as he was absolutely convinced of the inviolable distinction between superior men like himself, and—well, the rest of the herd! And one has to acknowledge the sheer force of this position with as open and receptive, albeit critically flexed, a mind as possible. Pessoa was not exactly likeable—although there are profoundly unlikeable people, who are in a sense likeable for this very reason, not least outsider-writers!—and was far too severe ever to court anybody's affections. Although cruelty to children moved him to cataclysms of anger and grief, no doubt reminding him of his own bleakly loveless childhood; as though like Baudelaire, he felt himself to be born evil, with 'a destiny eternally solitary'. Nietzsche could write: 'Goest thou to Woman? Forget not thy whip!' And yet he once broke down when he saw a horse being senselessly beaten. The monstrous deformations of the Abyss never entirely rob a man of the residual vestiges of his humanity.

Even Pessoa's mutilated psycho-pathology and spiritual wretchedness I could get the measure of, as it is no part of my brief here to be in any way normatively judgemental in such matters. I might differ from him on the matter of loving others, and engaging with the real world, but I share his antipathy to the destructive possessiveness of many relationships, and the banality and futility and incurable inertia of so many aspects of life, which deplete any sense of felt urgency one may have about the just necessity and desirability of social change. Pessoa was an example of Julie Kristeva's 'Abject' Persons, who are neither subjects among subjects, nor objects among objects; but totally separated off in paradoxical spaces of their own—alive yet dead, other to all including themselves; problematical aliens. Yet she didn't go near Pessoa—and may not even have heard of him!—preferring the likes of Céline instead. And Pessoa would have tested even her powers of abstract theoretical ingenuity to, and possibly beyond the limit; for he twisted his own abjectness into a vengeful art-form after a fashion, not caring about his terribleness except where it prevented him from freely indulging in his own at times exquisitely metaphysical massacrings of the Self and the World. And needless to add, he was about as far removed from the Arena of Wilson's Positive Consciousness—remember that?!—as could be. And yet he provided the most rigorously austere, Negativist counterweight imaginable for anybody who wants to subject Wilson's doctrine to the ultimate test of truth and endurance. If one can plough through the Negativist nightmares of Pessoa's Slough of Despond, and not only survive it, but come out of it stronger in the Nietzschean sense, then one will truly have earned the right to the Creed of Positiveness. There will be absolutely nothing of saccharineness in that! And this in the end is the great virtue of Pessoa's almost unique Testament, along with, of course—the Language, the Language, the almighty Language!

In the next chapter, I shan't be making life much easier for myself! For I shall be considering the work of that other perhaps equally strange and certainly colossal figure, the Italian writer, Carlo Emilio Gadda. However, as a scientist he was an insider and far better known in his lifetime than Pessoa. But as a writer he was as much of an Outsider as Pessoa, and of the entrenched and wrathful variety, if not a contender for the Title of Emperor among the mighty weirdos of Literature!

Recommended reading:

The Book of Disquiet. Penguin, 2002 (Trans. Richard Zenith).

Adam Daly: Fernando Pessoa. *Wormwood.* Number 2.

Chapter Seven

Gadda The Untranslatable: The Forbidden Genius Scowling in Society's Shade

Carlo Emilio Gadda was if anything like an even fiercer version of Pessoa, and equally preoccupied with the knottiest conundra of Identity, the Self, or the 'I', as he simply and starkly put it. But instead of concocting a plethora of Heteronyms, Gadda agonized furiously and relentlessly, over what he was convinced was the irreducibly complex, illusory referent of the expression 'I'—and so by extrapolation, the illusory nature of the Self. And as he squirmed and thrashed about in this vertiginous void of the phantasmal Ego, he refused to be seduced into using the 'I-word' so to speak, in anything he wrote, said, or even thought! He strove to extirpate it utterly from his consciousness. But the non-referent of the Non-Identity that he struggled in, with, and through, remained strictly unnominated, and unnominatable to coin an expression. So all he was left with in the labyrinth of his own vacuity, was the deathless stream of descriptive terms and phrases, that never amounted to anything truly explanatory or definitive in the disciplined maelstroms of his creative, imaginative, and analytical thought. And out of this Protean nexus of raging confabulations issued a body of work that is almost uniquely extraordinary—rebarbative, impenetrable, intransigent, repugnant, and brilliantly bloody-minded! His novels sickened all but a few of the Italian Intelligentsia, never mind the general reading-public. But above all, they perplexed people with their philosophic dimension. And he was of course hailing from a mathematical, scientific, and engineering background, as well as a philosophical, classical, Hermetic and Modernist one, synthesized into a Heuristic unity. Ferociously learned, he employed his erudition as a jugular- slicing weapon aimed at the idiot-populus that he so despised, in both fiction and non-fiction, which he thought of as being inescapably intertwined.

I have already written one essay on Gadda, which was published in *Abraxas Unbound*, in 2007, which I refer the Reader to, as I shall be aiming not to reiterate much of what I said there, but as far as possible to break new ground—which is needless to say an exceedingly difficult thing to achieve with Gadda. This is partly because of the pseudo-academic industry of Gadda Studies that has enveloped his work in the Terminological tosh of 'Continental Theory' at its wilfully blinding, and unconscionably blinded, worst. Also, it is immensely hard to clearly and fully understand Gadda's work in English, let alone see beyond its range of nuances and allusions and philosophic parameters, when not for nothing has he been called 'Gadda the Untranslatable'. Of course, there is always a limit on how exactly we can understand foreign texts translated into our own languages, pace Quine's famous 'Indeterminacy of Translation' thesis, which made it clear that there is no perfect model of translation between any two languages that would not involve the mediation of a third language. And that would lead to a further language—and so on *ad infinitum*. And so we are all trapped in some measure at least within the broad perspectival framework of our own language, which will invariably colour our understanding of other languages, however well the texts in those languages are translated into ours. Gadda's work therefore is not a special case or exception to the rule. But it is an enormously challenging task for a translator—comparable to James Joyce, albeit stylistically Gadda was quite different from Joyce, but perhaps equally demanding. And there is little question that he strove to make his work as incomprehensible to the general reading public as he could—as if that were the distinguishing mark and virtue of a superior, not to say a supreme, Outsider. He didn't want the Reader to get on familiar terms with him, but rather to be endlessly guessing at what his true meaning was—if indeed it admitted only of one interpretation, or for that matter, any interpretation whatsoever!

Partly he went down the Pessoan path of writing dense meditations, especially The Milanese Meditations, which I shall be mainly concentrating on here. But unlike Pessoa, he also wrote novels, albeit novels that were so difficult and experimental in content that all but a few found them indigestibly unreadable. As for formal experimentation, that didn't concern him so much, as form was very much determined or dictated by content in his understanding. Though structurally speaking, his narratives and meta-narratives were still fiendishly complex and ingenious, with all the plots and sub-plots—such as they were!—constantly underscored, or else undermined, by Leibnitzian and other leitmotifs. In Gadda there was somethingly inveterately, and monstrously, perverse, as if he could only ever take pleasure in, and derive satisfaction from, warping every *Weltanschauung* known to Man! Hence his love of Leibnitz's Monadology, which endorsed the most radical metaphysics of Solipsistic speculation. Being 'windowless', the Monads were both impenetrable and inescapable at one and the same time! We were trapped inside them, whilst protected from the stealthy probing and divination of others. So we were free to mentate in our own ultimately inconstruable subjectivity. Language is meaningless and communication impossible, when you carry this thesis or construct to its inconcludable conclusion. We just go through the illusory motions of trying to understand one another and to advance our knowledge of the universe, when in the first and last analysis, all we are doing is arbitrarily and artificially configuring, and reconfiguring, the elaborations of thought, which stand in an unknowable relation to whatever it is we are purportedly thinking about. And no amount of exact science, or pure deductive logic, or irrefutable mathematical formulae, can help us here in the end. We're in the lap of the Hydra-headed Gods of chimaerical consciousness! The Infinitesimal Calculus might generate or build a quantum computer at the end of the cosmos. But the stuff of this miasma we call consciousness, or soul, shall remain as unquantifiable and incomputable as the most whimsical wisps! And this indefinable, if not indescribable, region was where Gadda was always heading, if not coming from, with a genocidally abstruse vengeance—fully in spite of his absorption in the civilized ordering of the classical humanities.

Gadda was the most savage kind of Encyclopaedist aesthete imaginable, even if like Pessoa, he was deeply troubled in his personal life, had difficult relations with his family, never married, had only a few friends, and always lived alone, in a state of profound ambivalence towards his fellow-countrymen. He wasn't likeable, and even amongst other leading writers like Lampedusa, Pavese, and Calvino, was still something of a self-tormenting Pariah repelling the intimacy of equals. But he was financially more comfortably off than Pessoa, earning a lot of money from his early engineering contracts, and then succeeding in selling his novels on the strength of his profile, even if there was a backlash later on amongst the general reading public. There were some similarities between him and Gabriele D'Annunzio, the

Decadent Fascist Poet, whose house near Lake Garda is today a Temple-Shrine to a cult of Wagnerian mythomaniacal perversity. But D'Annunzio was both a more confident, extrovert figure than Gadda, and a great womaniser, which Gadda could never have been. Though however fine a poet, and novelist, D'Annunzio was, he was a lightweight by comparison—a shallow self-publicist, the tin-pot Mussolini of Italian Letters. Gadda was a scintillating satirist and a profound philosopher, using fiction as a medium and device for laying bare the entire Architectonic of his sustained Philippics against the world, by which he thrust his Metaphysics and Poetics from the darkness of the soul into the light of a transfigured truth and reality. This Herculean project not unnaturally tottered at every juncture. But he still managed to produce a pretty formidable body of work, aided by a fairly long life, in which he progressed from science and mathematics through literature and classics to philosophy and the *corpus hermeticum*. He wasn't the kind of writer who thought in terms of churning out a series of narrative fictions, for a particular readership, just to earn a living. Rather he was waging a constant war with himself—and the world—to generate kinds of fiction that had never been seen before. And to a considerable extent, I think he succeeded.

Gadda lived under the shadow of Manzoni, the writer he regarded as Italy's greatest—having been born in the same year Manzoni died, 1893, and then dying in the same month, May, one day before Manzoni, the 21st, 80 years later! He felt driven to emulate if not excel Manzoni, and in the end thought he'd failed to do so, creating only the shadow of his substance if not the substance of his shadow, in his own work. In his dotage he had people read him passages from Manzoni's *The Betrothed* over and over again, as if to torture himself with his own failings. And yet, in his combination of Classicist and Modernist techniques—Macaroni writing, as Italian scholars call it—it could be said that at his best he superseded Manzoni, and was more like a synthesis of Rabelais, Joyce and Celine, all rolled into one, and more besides. Cendrars was a similar figure too, who I'll be commenting on later. The erudite energy of his writing exploded like a star onto the page, shooting ripples of rage and eddies of exuberance along almost infinitely ramifying tributaries, which may or may not have returned eventually to the great rushing rivers of his central themes and conceits. His chaos was disciplined, but in such an exhilarating, giddying fashion, that the material was constantly threatening to overspill its boundaries in crashing tsunamis of transcendence. For me, the quintessential spirit of his writing manifested in the long, digressive diatribes and obscenely comic satirical evocations of people and scenes and incidents which he found absurd; and yet he felt an obsessive compulsion to describe them in the most excoriating detail, piling facet upon facet like Helion upon Ossa; dredging the depths of his great learning to mythologize mankind in its most debased state, thereby emphasizing the exalted state of pariahs who were also paragons. And the beauty of this is that, as if with Pessoa, one can literally dip into his works at any juncture, and not simply sample their flavour, but absorb something of their totality, as if it were injected into its every part like blood in a body.

Although he employed narrative and plot as skeletal frames upon which to hang the spreading corpus of his creations, they were more mere devices than integral elements, as he clearly didn't view either life or fiction in terms of such narrowly boxed formulations. People were hustled and bustled through their existences in his view, like suppressed

Supernovae, unable to burst out of the straitjackets of their life-stories, save in the stealthy subversive twists applied by highly creative minds, plundering them as dud raw material to ignite the treasure-troves of their fictions. Autobiographical incidents were both embellished—or fantasticized—and degraded, to reveal them either in a more dramatically exacting manner, or else in the harshest light of truth. Otherwise, he would dissect the world around him, with clinical precision and scathing irony. Fiction was a means to express the trickiest truths, that belied the clichéd and the official. It could toy with the 'facts' as it pleased, substituting an angular subjectivity for a bland objectivity. He could then be both icily dispassionate and fiercely passionate at one and the same time: an Outsider feeling quirkily privileged in his disgusted detachment, and an almighty scourge of society holding up a deadly cracked mirror to mankind. The only concessions he made to popular nostrums were to write a novel in the form of a detective story, and another in the form of a family-saga. However, these formats were deceptive, in that they provided him with very elastic frameworks within which he could insinuate the most unpopular constructions and conceptions he could devise. He was always working towards philosophic purifications of the inveterately messy human predicament, which he knew were so riddled with contradiction and paradox as to be unattainable in any event. Language was the main vehicle of his self-transportation beyond the vacuity and futility of his characters, leading him into atmospheres so finely suspended above their discourse as to defy all Dialectics. No conflicts could ultimately be resolved, just delicately balanced in the articulation of aporias that resisted any final synthesis. And so nothing could be concluded either, not least the works themselves, in which he aired the antipathies of feeling, and the antinomies of thought, to the fullest limits of his capacities.

All of the above lent itself strongly to the treatment of Continental Theorists, with their talk of Totalizability, etc. obfuscating what they purported to make clear in all their post-structuralist, post-deconstructionist analyses—complete with jugged jargon, or twot-terminology! I said before in the essay I refer my readers to, that Gadda should have been at best bewildered, and at worst outraged, by the pseudo-academic colonization of the 'studies' done in his name. And I can think of no good reason to alter my view of this now. Although of course, he's very far from being the only 'victim' of this whole trend, which has swept across Post-Modern Western Thought for well over half a century. Not that I'm averse to experimental methods or modes of theorizing—on the contrary. But there's a depressing uniformity of what I call 'bubble-think' in the discourses and writings of so many officious academics and scholars—in these and related fields—that rarely if ever gets critically exposed by anyone, except Outsiders like me perhaps! It's like coming across a tribe—and a very entrenched tribe!—who all talk a variety of nonsense. But because they have been talking nonsense for longer than anyone recalls, none of them know they are talking nonsense; and moreover, they all believe or imagine that they can understand each other perfectly, and that only uneducated people outside the tribe are unable to do so! The moment anybody tries to point out that they're all talking nonsense, they pounce on them and dismiss them as ignorant and backward. But all one is wanting to do is to get back to talking some variety of sense—just for a change!—and with a renewed emphasis on independence of thought, which is always lost where individuals are sucked into dominant schools of thought of any kind within academic institutions. This isn't to say that consensus is always invalid. Not at all. But individuals should always be free to make of any consensus what they will, and should not be pressured or herded into swallowing the idiolects and mindsets of pecking-order cliques—especially in fields as contentious as literary theory and cultural studies.

My own concern is with a sort of classical clarity of thought and expression, combined with a preternatural penchant for imaginative, speculative daring. Foucault was one of very few continental theorists who in a sense shared my outlook, in books like *Madness and Civilization*; although he was capable on occasion of writing utter gobbledegook in a similar vein to sausage-machine-Saussure, risible, derisory Derrida, and last-but-not-least Lacan(t)! But he did in the end remain his own man refusing to adhere to any school of thought, be it Marxism, Psychoanalysis, Existentialism, Phenomenology, Feminism, Structuralism, and all the piss-pot-posts showering from them. And above all, he developed in no small measure a distinctive, and coherent, style. And if it's still true that *'Le style c'est l'homme'*, then it was never more true than of Gadda, as Foucault would have swiftly spotted—had he read Gadda, which as far as I know he didn't. But since Gadda was in Foucault's heyday still little known outside Italy, that's not surprising. Yet a man who could work himself up into a frenzied masturbatory orgy, whilst he watched and heard *les evenements* unfold in Paris, in May, 1968, from a safe vantage-point in North Africa, must surely have something to be said for him! Gadda on the other hand would have had a more Pessoan view of revolutions. But for Foucault, outsiders and outcasts of all kinds could find some meeting-point in spontaneous, dispossessed revolts—even dyspeptic Dandies of noble Reaction like Gadda! And Gadda certainly shared Foucault's hatred for all institutions founded upon arbitrary violence, that are historically legitimated by bunches of self-appointed crooks as indisputably necessary social hierarchies. Gadda was like one of Foucault's madmen—albeit intensely cultivated, and in a wilderness rather than an Asylum—who see into the entrails of the political-legal machinery of a ruthlessly driven ideological State from an incorruptible, outside vantage-point, a marginalized Panopticon counterposed to the centralized Panopticon of corporate power and authority, on the cusp of subversion. Only Gadda's weapon was the violence of language rather than the body.

Italy, and by extrapolation the world, were similar in Gadda's fictionalized or fantasticized version of them in his novel, *Acquainted with Grief*—Maradagal was the name he gave to this supposedly real, yet palpably allegorical society, where veneer, sentiment and mass-hysteria held sway, in lieu of anything that remotely resembled a desirable state-of-affairs, never mind a Utopia—to Foucault's Asylum, elaborated from Bentham's Panopticon, and reproducing the power-relations found in Civilization, in a magnified and brutally oppressive form. And this vast, veritable prison going phonily proxy for some advanced social order is mirrored in its most mutilated condition in families, where the rivalries between parents and siblings develop stage-by-stage into syndromes that dictate en masse the conflicts with which communities are riven. Gadda's own family history was more Oedipal, since he lost his father young, and then his brother in the First World War. After that, his relationship with his mother became one of emotional dependency combined with growing hatred. She had no sympathy for his literary aspirations, and insisted on his training to become an engineer instead—a proper job, as we might say now!—which he certainly had the ability to do, and do well, but not the inclination, as he saw engineers as little more than glorified mechanics. And being imbued with the Classicist bias in favour of high culture over base science, he was internally conflicted over this maternal pressure for much of his life; even though he was actually highly successful in both his careers. But his solitary bent and his anguished belligerence belied this success; and the female characters in his novels were in the main different versions of his mother, and the male characters different versions of himself. He even had a Register of five different modalities—a bit similar to Pessoa's Heteronyms, except he never thought of these as Personae with names and life-histories, etc. but more as cognitive syles that he adopted in different contexts. And occasionally, they would cross-fertilize in his works. There was the mathematical-logical-scientific modality; the philosophic-poetic-Romanticist modality; the Classicist modality; the decadent aesthete modality; and the simple, intuitive, creative modality. So there was an overlap here with Pessoa—who he might have known about in later life, as he outlived Pessoa by nearly forty years—but Gadda applied his methodology in a different way.

He was also far more strongly committed to giving the real world its head over the ideal world(s), in all its bewildering variegation and intractable ghastliness, than Pessoa ever was, even though both men lived in ivory-towers to all intents and purposes. But whereas Pessoa sought to eclipse the real world in an eidetic imposition, Gadda sought to confront it head on, deploying a magnificent array of verbal and intellectual tools, to expose it in its utmost hideousness. And this was where his Modernism went even further than Pessoa's, dismissing as he did the rarefied, de-realized phantasies of the Symbolists, whose long shadows had cast their spells upon Pessoa's morbidly retreating sensibility and imagination. But this tendency still went deeply against the grain for Gadda, for his psycho-socio-pathology was really just as marked in its way as Pessoa's. He was well-known for his savage temper, as Pessoa was for his quietly cutting put-downs, and may even have suffered from having been an Adolf Hitler look-alike! Not that the comparison went in truth any deeper than mere appearance, because he wrote a lengthy denunciation of Fascism—distancing himself from the idiocies of the Futurists, and the Treitschkeian-Rosenbergian degradations of Nietzsche that ideologically paved the way for the growth of Nazism. Though no more a man of the Left than Pessoa was, he was violently anti-Bourgeois and -Aristocracy, believing only in a kind of open sesame for genius-*auteurs* like himself! His prose seemed Baroque and grotesque to many, but he repudiated this, saying that the world exhibited these traits, not he. Yet he mirrored these traits in his work, with a sardonic twist in its thaumaturgical tail. And the language he used to convey the kaleidoscopic mess of everything was in some senses akin to Joyce, though with an arguably greater rhythmic swell, drawing on a highly arcane vocabulary, but with a more coherent Semantic force. Joyce read better as a syntactical dissector of language, where the semantics are constantly lost amidst the welter of mutilated idioms and neological concoctions. Gadda however, swept the Reader along on gathering tides of multiple currents, rising up and falling down and rising up again without end, like the world itself.

His fiction was really a vehicle for the promulgation of his philosophy, for he saw no fundamental contradiction between the two activities. They may have been conflictual, but they could also be complementary. Not that he imposed an arid schema, abstracting pure form from impure content. This was the very antithesis of his whole approach to writing and the world, since his philosophy was founded upon the particularities of content, serving as the raw materials for a general picture of reality. And so the detail in his fiction was immensely rich, as well as raw, spilling onto every page in a dazzling, multi-faceted profusion of seemingly disconnected, yet fundamentally connected, features, expressions, incidents and apercus, that summarized in very open-ended ways the totalities of events, characters and forms of life, comprising a microcosm of the world. But his philosophy is the fitting starting-point for any study of Gadda, and as *The Milanese Meditations* has not been translated into English—as it took the form of a dissertation—I have had to rely on a commentary instead, a study of Céline, Gadda and Beckett, by Norma Bouchard, published in 2000. This was in part an exercise in 'bubble-think'—but a superior one for what that's worth—which enabled me to extract a helpful framework for the articulation of my own resolutely heterodox thinking. And for an academic document, *The MM* was wildly unconventional, if unignorably brilliant. Gadda was harking back to the good old days of the scholarly seers, from the Pre-Socratics, and Socrates himself, all the way on to Nietzsche, who was arguably the last of the great anti-systematic, anti-academic, philosophers; and a truly great writer amongst philosophers too. And of course it's very much in this arrogant Antinomian vein that I myself am writing this book. So *The MM*, in all its untranslatable glory, chimes with me in my dim unitalianate comprehension!

Gadda's intention was to mount a thorough-going critique of a whole range of prevailing orthodoxies in western thought: 'I will dissolve the heroes and their arms...their Daedalus-like arms' he declaimed, before proceeding—and in the 1920's at that—to systematically demolish the famous

Kantian *a priori.* He insisted that this innate category or fundamental principle could never be in any meaningful way derived or deduced from any other Nomic law, let alone from experience or observation; and that everything in existence is *a posteriori*, contingently given, or else constructed by us, in every 'mutable', 'historical', and 'contextual' framework of reality. The same sweeping *tabula rasa* treatment was applied by Gadda to other moribund, architectonic pillars of philosophy, such as 'The Absolute', which whether in a Hegelian or any other sense was a total metaphysical fiction, unsupported not only by empirical evidence, but by the new Relativistic Cosmological model pioneered by Einstein also. Nothing was not 'relational', as such. Likewise, the tired medieval nostrum of 'stable, self-identical substance', and unitary identity, had to be swept away. Thus the Indeterminacy of the Subject and the Object—and the Multiplicity of the Self—needed to be affirmed as governing conditions of existence. Even human well-being and happiness were often misconstrued as 'static', rather than dynamic, conditions. For Gadda, they were as fluid as the oceans. The human Self was 'a compound of relations never perennially unified.' The condition of change in space and time crucially affected such an apparently detached, immaterial substance or essence, which in truth was an artificial conceptual construct like anything else, including cause and effect. Therefore Objects everywhere were complicated with each other—like 'gnocco', a type of pasta, which is sticky, gelatinous, and porous. This was a startlingly perspicacious if simple analogy, using an image to denote a complex idea that anticipated the Quantum Theory of Entanglement, that has since been developed into a mathematical model.

Gadda also anticipated Guattari's and Deleuze's concept of the Rhizome, with his adumbration of a Holistic symbiotic system of evolving, multi-causal, non-hierarchical, agencies and influences, operating on things, persons, and events, wherever and whenever they are and occur. He may have had a far more elitist bent than they did. But he still recognized that nobody could be detached from the totality of human life so much that they ceased altogether to be dependent on and engaged with it, as emergent creatures in the chaos of all creation. And thus the boundaries between Outsiders and the rest were forever submerged in the post-primordial soup of society—their delineations shifting along endlessly re-defined vectors of determinism and self-determination. His critique of what militated against the fuller emancipation of naturally superior minds, wherever they may manifest, amounted to a 'Rabelaisian meal' of the philosophers, and their philosophies—portending a more constructive line of argument! What we now think of as Heuristic Methodology, or Hermeneutics, respecting the complexity, and also the immanence, of 'Substance', and all that partakes of it, had to replace—which it has since done—the rigidly fixed 'identity-thinking' of the pre-modern metaphysical schools of thought. This methodology promoted the new principle of 'the greatest number of relations and the amplification of the "n+1"', allowing for a bridge to cross the old divide between the finite and the infinite. And each amplification here, was a 'pause' in the developing picture of reality, or a 'station' of knowledge in a limitless process of elaboration. As such, there was no final destination for the process, nor over-arching, all-encompassing, system; which prompts the thought in me—with the benefit of decades of hindsight—that this inherently open-ended philosophical habit of mind, may not square with what physicists nowadays call The Theory of Everything. But it seems that this theory has stubbed its TOE, if the pun may be forgiven, on the fact that new problems arise out of every solution. And it is in any case a misnomer, since it only purports to describe mathematically the general laws and properties of things. And how would it account for consciousness, thought, or artificial intelligence? The Devil continues to foil the best-laid plans, etc.

Gadda's new 'Monadology' as he conceived it, also reversed Leibnitz's weird stricture regarding so-called 'windowless monads', endorsing instead systems of relations between things that were 'provisional and removable'. Ideas such as entropy, a-symmetry, and synchronous a-causality, were hinted at by Gadda in a range of ingenious examples, some of them strikingly simple yet not at all obvious: Light-sources became weaker as their rays moved from the centre to the periphery; open bookshelves could have outer-right and left side volumes leaning diagonally, upsetting a closed system of forces; a Polygon could have one side left open, confounding standard Topology; etc. These and other clever anomalies suggested later developments in fields as varied as Maths, Physics, Geometry, Philosophy, Psychology, Critical Theory and Cultural Studies. And they had implications for Literature or Fiction also, conceived as a creative act with all-embracing, labyrinthine ramifications, which we humans have uniquely turned into our own art-forms—and anti-art-forms too!—and treated as a base on which to launch ourselves beyond ourselves, into what I term the meta-human realms. And Gadda understood these realms well, in my view. Though he saw himself as unmoored in a sea of space-time, rather than as a God gazing upon his fellow-humans from a secure Olympian Summit: 'I leave from the unstable bridge of my boat to observe: and I am not the celestial being who has descended from the absolute... But I am a compound of relations, a tangle in reality's web.' His was a 'convoluted philosophy', comprising a self-limiting, self-correcting, 'epistemic model' from which our ethics, aesthetics, and even politics, could be derived. The age-old dualistic concepts of Good and Evil, e.g. were not for him 'a corpus of fixed, static attributes, but are categories relative to contextual interpretation.' Good occurred only 'when no relations and convergences have been excluded, when no selection and reduction have been imposed on life.' And conversely, Evil occurred when there was a 'decomposition of life's relations, with the rigidity of simplicity and finality of non-life.' Powys would have concurred with these even more elaborate definitions than he himself had ever ventured.

Aesthetically, Gadda took Kant's and Burke's theory of the 'Sublime', combined them with Schopenhauer's theory of 'will-lessness' in the imaginative transformation of reality, and developed his own concept of artists and writers, etc. willing themselves to 'feel' their creative passage or pathway in 'the baroque meandering of the world.' This was a rhetorical practice diametrically opposed to Cartesian or Structuralist axes of 'opposition and closure'. Gadda went on to champion Vico's idea of heroic metaphors in his work, The New Science, reviving the spirit if not the forms of the Italian Renaissance-style of neo-classicism. Vico was one of the first philsophers—living in an era that has often been viewed as philosophically barren and bereft—to divine the vital importance of the Subject, in apprehending Truth: 'We make our own truths!' he declaimed, like Archimedes jumping out of his bath and streaking down the street shouting Eureka! upon discovering the Law of Displacement. The echoes and resonances of this declamation were still felt by Gadda a few centuries later, even if for him the Subject was an infinitely complex multiple entity that had no unitary definition. But it was still a central problematic that dogged and haunted him like a noumenal shadow forever hovering out of his phenomenal reach, phantasmal yet somehow palpable. And this unlocatable nexus was the true source of the great myths of mankind that powered the works of the creative imagination, and should always be unreligiously revered as such. Gadda opposed this conception or mythos to Saussure's model of Structural Linguistics, with its cod-Newtonian clockwork machinery governing 'apprentice telegraphers in a train station'! Extensional or Analogical thought had to replace pure abstraction or non-particular generalization. And then the whole world would open up to mankind and reveal its inner riches as it never had before. Philosophy, maths and science could thereby cross-fertilize with the classics, humanities, art, mythology and the occult, in ways barely even envisaged by the pre-Enlightenment natural philosophers. Gadda envisaged, or envisioned rather, a new Renaissance.

Gadda had points of contact with all the avant-garde movements of his time, from the Imagists, Futurists, Dadaists, Surrealists, and Abstract Expressionists, to the Eisenstein Film School—which Lionel Britton was a member of for a while—and Vertov's Kino-Eye Collage technique, in which no photographed scene, character and incident takes precedent over any other; but the whole Kaleidoscopic mass of events crowds the unfolding picture equally and simultaneously in each successive frame, thereby totally de-thematizing—if my momentary slippage into bubble-think may be pardoned!—the subject-matter, and presenting a series of real time chaotic snap-shots, where the significant and the insignificant are mutually and perpetually up for grabs as it were, in the Kino-Eye of the viewers, as well as the director. But Gadda also distanced himself to some extent from all these influences, and others, determinedly resolving to push his own Anarch-agenda as far out as he possibly could—synthesizing the seemingly unsynthesizable, in startlingly different ways from his contemporaries. Classicism and Modernism were the two main intersecting nodes of his thought, from which a far more fruitful outpouring ensued than from the childish whittlings of Marinetti—whose wholesale destruction of syntax made Gadda shudder with dismay! However, it was not so much the fact of his linguistic nihilism that troubled Gadda, as the manner of it. The philosophical assault on the rigid hypostases of classical grammar was profoundly necessary, in Gadda's view—as indeed it was, in Pessoa's view—especially with regard to the referential deployment of the 'I', as already mentioned. But Marinetti issued forth an endless logorrhoeic spew of barbarisms that amounted to nothing of any real philosophical significance, or conceptual coherence. Language needed in a sense to be destroyed, but in an educated way, with a view to re-creating it as a more transparent tool of effective intelligence. Marinetti totally abnegated such an aim, descending wilfully into a mindless morass of mutilated meanings from which he could never extricate himself. Gadda drowned in the seas of language periodically, then rose to the surface again and again with fresh-minted treasure from the shipwreck of souls, its threads of dissolution spinning new connexions. The 'precedent of project to work, of meta-language to creation', was a sound Futurist precept. But the Fascist idolatry of gadgetry was drooling puerility.

Eisenstein's 'Dialectical montage' impressed Gadda greatly, with its dramatic development of the crises of contradiction and conflict, between Capital and Labour, empire and colony, class and class, etc. *The Battleship Potemkin* was a truly Marxist experiment, releasing the true anarchic force of the Kronstadt uprising, which though crushed in reality, displaced its energy of momentum elsewhere, on a cusp where nothing is realized but everything is still possible. The idea will not die, and later waves of revolt will break. Film could take on the mantle of Theatre, being far closer to contemporary reality as it was lived and more able to manipulate reality for the purpose of altering people's ways of perceiving it, and galvanizing them into changing it for their own ends. In Art, Gadda had a high regard for the under-appreciated Belgian, James Ensor, who enjoyed the rare accolade of having been banned from the infamous XX Group, one of the most wildly avant-garde art-movements in turn-of-the-century Europe. He was too strange, extreme, and idiosyncratic—even for them! Gadda spoke of Ensor's 'multiform vision' and 'thematic interchange' in his biblical, classical and medieval allegories, subverted by visceral and obscene Pagan elements, and more modern allegories like the 'Doctors' series, where Hypocratic clinicians became enwrapped in the almost Pollockian entrails of their patients, as if modern medicine had become a hideously out-of-control, surrealistic, regime of torture for science's sake! Ensor's grotesque visions—and Hermann Nitsch and Joe Coleman are his successors—burned themselves out by the time he was 40, and he devoted the rest of his career to bland still-lifes! The Belgians *et al* forgave him his previous excesses and he became an Establishment-Icon thereafter, in a supremely perverse twist of irony. For his talent had utterly deserted him, as if he'd succumbed to premature senility!

This fate did not befall Gadda. If anything, his life followed a reverse-trajectory: as an engineer, he was taken seriously by his peers when young; yet as a writer, he increasingly alienated his peers and the wider public when he got older, even if his books did continue to sell on the strength of his repute. He took note of the fate of Céline also, whose works he admired, who scandalized even his unshockable fellow-French with his anti-semitism and general depravity, and had to work as a Doctor—which he originally trained as—to make ends meet financially. His writings had a cultish following, but a very small one, and his posthumous reputation barely improved on his living one. The curious parallels with Gadda's life were not lost on the latter, even if he was not as racist as Céline—nor even as right-wing. But his severity and his superciliousness rendered him similarly unpopular—the most common manifestation of the curse of the outsider-writer! Yet he could parody himself—and in ways that were lost on many readers—not least in an early novel, *The Philosopher's Madonna*, which bore some slight resemblance to Huysmans' *A Rebours*, except it was much shorter, and didn't take its protagonist nearly as seriously. It was obviously quasi-autobiographical. Yet one senses Gadda was trying to distance himself from his former self or incarnation—sending himself up as a prelude to sloughing off one of his more clinging skins. The jaundiced or poisoned aesthete was the 'Type' that beset him the most in his youth, albeit largely self-cultivated with a contemptuous vengeance towards much of humanity. Yet Gadda insinuated that his protagonist's conceits were more than a little absurd. And though he prized his detachment like Des Esseintes, he was still incontrollably obsessed with others, or 'the Other', and in particular a woman, for whom he entertained a somewhat Nervalian fantasy of fixation. The novel ends melodramatically, and as always in Gadda's fiction, inconclusively, because it couldn't end, rather than because he couldn't finish it—as was the case with *That Awful Mess on The Via Merulana*.

This was a new conceit, which is now commonplace in post-modern fiction, and invites ridicule on the grounds of pretentiousness. But actually, if fiction is to capture and convey the rounded textural totalities of life, then it must of necessity have an element of incompleteness built into it, because life is not just a linear process, with a beginning, a middle, and an end—as I've already observed. And in Gadda's hands, fiction wasn't simply a naturalist or realist representation of reality and the world, which would be scarcely more than a documentary mode of writing. It was a whole array of methods of revealing the essence of life in its details, and of re-creating the world in images with which it is unfamiliar, but which illuminate it far more than mere Historical records. The disaffected salesman, Baronfo, resembled Gadda the engineer—a frustrated philosopher, who built up his Library to provide an escape from the crushing vulgarity of the outside world. But his downfall lay not only in this impossible retreat from reality, but also in his persistent obsession with Maria Ripamonti, the lone daughter of poor Aristocrats, who was confined like some fairy-tale princess in a castle. The year was 1922, when Musolini marched on Rome, and the forlorn heroine still mourned her long-lost lover in the first world war. The absurdity of a would-be ivory tower dweller seeking union with a reluctant Gothic prisoner, only to re-confine her in his own version of a castle, to ward off the misery of self-imposed privation and the inevitable incursions of the inescapable outside world, was brilliantly spear-headed and lampooned by Gadda, with the troubled sangfroid of his own scrutinized Self seeping through to the surface in places. The scenes were hilarious, more so than in his late, mature novels, which were so freighted with extraordinary verbal baggage and grim sardonicism, that they lacked the lightness of touch and fine honing of detail in this paradoxically more polished early fictional outing in 1931. The heroine dabbled in the Occult, and did long-distance battle with some witches to prevent them from laying curses on Doctors! Baronfo—Gadda too—shared this fascination with forces as yet unexplained by science, which only served to propel his impassioned voyage out into the ultra-monadic realms of soul-twinning.

The meat of the book was in the middle, where Gadda dissected by proxy a pathological superiority-complex that was his own. And yet he affected an almost amused, somewhat indifferent, dispassionate neutrality towards his own fictional alter ego or imaginary cast-off, that purported to be the voice of Reason, but was in truth more akin to the twisting serpent-tongue of the Great Deceiver! I should quote at some length here to substantiate this:

> 'horrible doubt that the soul might…be one with the nervous system … to drive away this phantom, he ended up spending … two thousand lire on baths, medical checks and pick-me-up syrups, and stuffed the house with a preposterous collection of bottles… boxes, flasks, pots and phials.'

He hoards these things, always unsure which is the most curative. Continuing in this vein, like some infinitely more neurasthenic version of Moliere's Alceste, working himself up to a tragi-comic climax:

> '... he ... reworked ... the apologium of Menenius Agrippa: ... the brain should not want everything for itself, but the intestines, and the liver with respective gallstones, and the legs and feet and lungs and backbone...have a right to...treatment. Which final point we heartily approve of.'

This is reminiscent of Des Esseintes' fear of demonic possession, and ill-heath brought on by isolation and confinement, to the point where he is forced to call in a doctor—who tells him he needs to get out more! But also note the casual authorial throwaway line in the last sentence, as if the character is a sort of tragic puppet being set up for a cruel denouement.

The sinister spoof has the ultra-rarefied hypochondriac dosing himself back into synthetic health, whereupon he dwells afresh on the highest purpose of his life: He had entertained the

> '...awful idea...he should get out of business....And dedicate his life to thinking...the 'spirit'...set himself...upon a path lined with thorns...the philosopher. The tendency to criticize...everything he...always had: then halfway through the job he would stick his pick in the indocile earth and leave the weeds ....Live and let live, he sneered.'

This is a well-trodden territory, but it isn't clear why the idea should be considered awful, except in the obvious sense that it may prove economically disastrous. But why should an aesthetically advanced Outsider NOT want to alienate himself further from all the repugnant realities around them? Gadda's sub-text here was that however superior any Outsider felt himself to be, he still had to run the gauntlet of the mess on his doorstep! Even though his fictive ego railed on against the crowning stupidities of contemporary life, he thought the:

> '...post-war world too sloppy, too vulgar, too overrun with cabarets and motorcycle salesmen, populated by too many mortar-boarded asses and Sunday-best peasants: and most illiterate ladies, filled with all kinds of food, lounging in the swaggering cars of bankrupt braggarts.'

Gadda's streams of diatribe are gathering invective momentum! But he put the break on at once, tripping up his own Tyro by dismissing it all as a 'neurasthenic fuss.' But then he was off again, in sly tandem:

> 'Everything was... a shadow... torture. The gramophone 'demolished his nerves'; the mandolin tore from him pent-up diatribes against 'Mediterranean Civilization'... the piano playing 'foxtrots' or barcarole... made him grit his teeth in a clamp...and dogs, when they start barking for the most futile reasons, he would... have paid them back by pouring nicely browned fried butter in their ears through a funnel... as for their owners, in their navels; while some of his fellow citizens' bad syntax and mispronunciation ... brought on black moods of vertigo and agoraphobia.... He got to hate Puccini, Leoncavallo, and Mascagni, whom Italy and the world ...hailed with glorious titles. He dreamed of ...crowning emperor of the Occident some deaf Lapp.'

This was clearly Gadda speaking here, working himself up into a fine rage, pin-pointing his pet-hates with exquisite savagery, and releasing the pent-up steam of years of semi-silenced suffering. And it doesn't stop there either. In fact, he's only just getting started, as elsewhere in his work, using narrative as a crazy device in which he can insert long, diabolical digressions at his whim; not for the sort of programmatic, propagandistic, didactic purposes that Brecht served so leadenly, but for the sake of a sparkling satire, that spread everywhere like an ongoing cosmic critique. Hatred was a refined drug that hooked him like a fiend, a very un-Kantian end in itself that he devoured with a Nietzschean relish.

While in the grip of this manic mood, Baronfo gave up his job and immersed himself in the almightiest trials of lost causes: 'he studied philosophy.'!!! (My exclamation marks.) But in the past, he had often lacked within himself 'the faith and strength to push ahead on this deserted path.' Religion wasn't the only barrier to demystification:

> 'What if it were a fabrication of the philosophers?' ….Baronfo asked himself about the world, terrified… while a fellow resident's gramophone, "from the grey heavens", demolished…the…castle of...comforts he had…built up by dint of protoiodide…the business he had liquidated; and others were sucking the breast.'

The Unnamed was like some Gothic Egregore, shadowing and doubling Gadda's protagonist. His life and mind were unravelling before him, and all this was the main cause of his misery and disgust with the world,

> 'not "Mediterranean civilization"; he was apathetic ...an ass...his life dissolving...a life without rhyme or reason...he thought of his revolver, where was it, ... was it loaded or empty;'.

Violence was beckoning: but murder or suicide? Perhaps both in succession—and then 'mourder' first, as a logical Irishman would say! Unless philosophy could save him from either or both. Yet:

> 'these crises of depersonalisation ...came on ... with one philosopher or another, when the brew was... grim or fearsome.'

If Nietzsche philosophized with a hammer, Gadda philosophized with a gun. Only he transferred his Martian temper to his protagonist, observing his turmoil with a clinical coldness. He pictures Baronfo going about his esoteric searches in:

> 'an old bouquin picked up in Paris ....Among others a certain Mr. Ishmael Digbens was brought in, and quoted with ...respect by the ... polished writer, who called him ..."l'illustre ecrivain anglois", and "Messire le chevalier de Chelmsford".'

This seems like an elaborately mischievous hoax on Gadda's part. But in fact there really was an Ishmael Digbens, and he did indeed hail from that most philosophically putrified place: Chelmsford! A radical eccentric—and a true Outsider amongst philosophers no less!—he had developed mad theories that especially appealed to Baronfo, and possibly to Gadda as well. The text in Baronfo's hands:

> 'smelt….. of ancient presses and inks, that scent... beloved of collectors and … himself. Baronet Digbens …appeared…skinny, wearing pumps; with dessicated …calves; two buckled shoes that looked like …frigates; a short jacket with a frond of lace, like a salad; a book in his hand; ... an enormous wig, as curled as could be, with a parting down the middle; and beneath this pergola…a long thin face; in which tiny eyes and a sharp acquiline nose made up the face…a quite uncommon specimen.'

Gadda is playing with Russian dolls inside Chinese boxes, as if inside each spectral influence another one appears, and so on *ad infinitum*.

Digbens' allure deepens. He had written eminent treatises in Natural Philosophy, in particular, on the subject of 'Pneumatology… the science of the soul.' In his writings on physiology and physics he arrived at no less than a dozen:

> 'proofs of the existence of God, against the "Lockeian" Burner, which he subdivided into three groups: four he called metaphysical, four physical, four mixed. These proofs operated like catapults against the castle of false syllogisms of this atheist Burner, who, being given to a most disorderly way of life, died shortly after in Paris.'

Aquinas famously offered five proofs, all of them nonsensical. Digbens' proofs were doubtless no less nonsensical, and yet possessed the undeniable Gnostic sparks of lunatic divinity! He claimed to have shown by rigorous proof that animals in general had no intelligence, though in some special cases they exhibited what he called 'a second-rate reason.' So Stewart's cows may not have qualified! But Darwin's monkeys might have done, if Evolution had been in the air! And in 'Physics,' he had argued against:

> 'Democritus, Epicurus, and Gassendi, that there exist atoms in a state of rest… ice, and frozen substances in general, were composed of such restful atoms.'

Instead of attempting to create an impossible perpetual motion machine, like other amiable crackpots, he beheld the cosmos, in part at least, as a perpetual stasis machine! If motion ceased, God died no doubt! But the big picture was in a steady state. He thought that:

> 'regions... exist in space devoid of matter…. The intervening space between the solar planetary system and the fixed stars … must be of this sort…the brains of spastics, of born idiots, and of those that died without being baptized, were a "plenum" …scarcely endowed with modal aptitude, so…it could …be compared with the void.'

This was a wonderful piece of blue sky thinking in the tug-of-war between natural philosophy, individual mysticism, and post-rational, Enlightenment science. We know now it's all bilge. Yet it's the sort of delightfully far-sighted bilge we should all treasure.

And then he came on to the Soul itself, which he regarded as a:

> 'being, or simple Substance…therefore a "plenum" …as it was a substance, and, though simple, capable …of differentiation, as long as it was prompted to action by the senses…here Samuel Beatty saw the catastrophic consequence of the most pernicious sensism, "*dont les amphibolies captieuses et les pitoyables paralogismes avaient pu egarer jusqu'a un philosophie de si bons sentiments, tel que Messire de Chelmsford.*"'

My French might be stuntedly schoolboyish, but methinks there are a few howlers here, and Gadda is secreting another layer of comic manipulation into an archaic dispute. But Digbens' Soul still manages to escape continental censure! 'The soul's differentiations could be benign or malignant. The first conducive to eternal health and salvation, the others…eternal chill.' Instead of burning in Hell, the damned would freeze in—Siberia perhaps? But the power of prayer could still come to the rescue, as an agency of the benign. And it was a distinguishing mark of the human among other things. He thought animals had no 'sense of duty' or 'shame', unlike men, in whom such complex attributes were inborn. There were 'exceptions' that might seem to 'link Adam's lineage to the most vulgar quadrupeds'. But these cases only occurred in a rare 'pneumatic imbalance between void and plenum,' and a 'prolonged neglect of the practice of piety.' A man became like a 'beast' under such conditions, and risked permanently damaging his 'health and salvation.' In this edict Digbens gives the game away, for those able to spot a Pneumaticist behind a Pietist! The Pneumatic Society was a classically bonkers, English Gallimaufry of charlatans, pseuds, madmen and fanatics—like precursors of the Mesmerists—who believed in bodily fluids, complementing the humours and the Ether. But whilst they found no real scientific evidence, a few charismatic Seers like Digbens were perhaps getting on to the trail of something more well-founded: namely, Psycho-Somatics.

Be that as it may, Gadda continued to have exquisite fun with Digbens through the eyes of Baronfo, and other commentators. When he learnt that a certain Sir William Cudoss had once while on horseback bumped into a statue of Napoleon III, with a man a woman at its base, and they 'had gone on finishing the work of nature without showing the slightest concern', Digbens had speculated that this obscene indifference:

> 'might depend…on lack of observance of the principle of authority…by which some peoples are led to neglect …the true foundations of Ethics and Pneumatics.'

I think another exclamation—mark is in place here! Coitus non-interruptus in wide open spaces could obviously lead to an embarrassingly wasteful spillage of pneumatic fluid, if not Adam's seed! Kant would have been impressed with Digbens' continent inconcupiscence, as one foundation for the meta-physics of morals! Having one's movements across a town-square monitored for purposes of watch-setting, was an altogether more estimable basis for the Categorical Imperative than the flagrant rhythms of naked fornicators blocking traffic on the Royal Highway! Though I suspect the old Marquis de Sade might have had other ideas! Baronfo drew from Digbens' Canute-like cosmogeny in an heroically futile attempt to stop the tides of the contemporary world crashing in upon the ravaged beach of his own brain. Other influences are taken up with the same backward-looking resolution of the stranded

Classicist or last Baroque Genius—like old syphilitic Schubert, especially in his String Trios. Though this siege-conceit inevitably floundered in the end, as the whole tragi-comedy of the failed aesthete's existence devolved upon something as corny as whether or not he got the girl! Yet there was something truly Wagnerian in the melodrama that ensued, which lent an undeniable mythic dimension to an otherwise meaningless and unillustrious life—however inwardly seething with aspiration and ambition, and festooned with unpromotable gifts, he was. And this was definitely Gadda's predicament, even if his irony protected him from suffering to some degree; and he did achieve, as I have said already, quite considerable worldly success.

If Gadda descended slightly more to earth in his later novels, at any rate in terms of plot—such as it was—his language became even more craftily convoluted and densely layered in a phantasmagoric palimpsest, packed with the most recondite references and allusions whilst exploding with a venomous ire in every direction. I have selected some different quotations from his two main novels—*Acquainted with Grief*, and *That Awful Mess on the Via Merulana*—to the ones I cited in my aforementioned *Abraxas* essay, which I shall cite here, partly to show the way in which his language bloomed over time, and partly to put down concrete markers for the abstruse philosophical contentions that drove him slowly to his death. He was perhaps a little more sociable during his long life than Pessoa, but even more irascible at times, and very much an Outsider in spite of his insider-status in Italy. And he should rather have remained alienated on principle, than been gregarious from sentiment, given no better choice, which was indeed the case to his perception. And not being a doctrinaire Marxist, he was not all that troubled by a failure to resolve

Dialectical contradictions and conflicts in society. He was much more concerned with true cultural emancipation for those individuals possessed of the mind to benefit from it. If the end-result was a hierarchical society, then so be it. But this end-result was nowhere in sight, and he knew it would never be attained in his lifetime, if ever. So he was embattled, if not exactly embittered, to the end. His familial traumas stayed with him to some extent, even if he developed stratagems for contending with them and easing his liaisons with non-familial persons he encountered, and in some instances befriended. But he never lost his sense of being a man on a mission—albeit a pretty hopeless mission!—not only to perfect himself, but to elevate others, or those who could and would be elevated. And it was first and foremost an intellectual process of education and refinement. Such was the only valid basis for the wild freedoms of a forgotten Enlightenment.

The story—or meta-story—of *That Awful Mess on the Via Merulana*, revolved around a detective's increasingly irresoluble, and ultimately absurd, difficulties in solving a horrible murder of a woman he was infatuated with whilst also being a friend of her husband. This complex fact should automatically disqualify any detective in real life from investigating a case, especially a murder—given their 'emotional involvement', in the crassly clinical jargon employed! But of course no-one but Ingravallo, the detective, knows about his infatuation with the victim, which he keeps secret, thereby opening up a monumental can of morbid worms, which Gadda then milks for all his eschatological worth. The victim is known to befriend street-orphans, and it's thought that one of these orphans out of a deep resentment at being saved, kills her. But there is also a witch, Zamira, who is rumoured to kidnap street-orphans for abominable experiments; and one of her little monsters might have performed the hideous deed. In the end, the murder remains unsolved, and Gadda appears almost indifferent to this failed denouement; given that he explores so many other tributaries and dimensions, that the book almost ceases to be a detective-story—however thorough his portrayal of police-procedure; and his character-analyses or assassinations more like, of Ingravallo, a semi-autobiographical figure inevitably, and his colleagues—and becomes instead a satire on the grotesqueries of contemporary Italian society as a global microcosm; a headily indulged linguistic experiment; and a bewildering philosophical mystery. The impossibility of establishing causes of events—due to the irreducibly complex, multi-factorial background to every event, not least murder—consumes both Gadda, the author and narrator, and his alter-ego, who in the end is more like a metaphysical sleuth than a working detective. The irrealism of this becomes increasingly irrelevant and insignificant as the weight of critique, speculation and paradox built up to the point of literally pushing the ostensible plot aside. Gadda is clearly saying that this is exactly what life is like. It cannot be subjugated to a novelist's plot! Though the detective is still a telling Symbol of Man, in his relation to the whole world around him. We are all like detectives, trying in our varying capacities to piece together the jig-saw puzzle of a world so inexplicable, we cannot hope to fathom it in all its mesmerizing depth and variegation. Though most of us lead lives in which virtually no plots occur, and we have to make do with fictions to try to satisfy our innate cravings for imaginary excitements. So it is a profound Trope in that sense, rather than a familiar genre-prop. And Gadda is no genre-writer, but a writer of genius.

To give my readers some idea of the incredible distracting potency of Gadda's digressions—in which the dark heart of the man can be divined—I shall cite at length a few passages where a colleague of Ingravallo's, Pestalozzi, examines various objects, including jewels, at the scene of the crime, searching for little evidential clues to help him build up the killer's profile. Gadda portrays him as a typical porcine operative, yet uses the scene as the launching-pad for a survey of everything that swims into his ken:

> 'The objects froze, like little frightened animals, ladybirds who fold their wings, not to be seen, in the wretched lap of poverty; and instead, they were seen: they were seen as so many unmasked lies, recognized by the jeweller with the hooked nose, on the counter, after theft and recovery: of every most curious colour and every form: a little cross of some semiprecious dark-green stone, which the fingertips of the future sergeant could not stop savouring, turning over and over: a handsome, shining little green-black cylinder, for interpreting horoscopes by the shitty priests for Egypt more than Pythagoras drew ravings from the apothegm of the pentagon, standing towards the west to blather, to gaze at the tops of their baked pyramids: mysteriosophic candy, concealed in the ancient womb of the earth, seized from the earth's womb, one day geometrised to magic.'

I'll let the reader pause here for breath, if not for comment, which I'll supply shortly!

> 'A poor little egg between pale-blue and milk-white like a little gland of a dead pigeon, to be thrown in the refuse: and two earrings, with two big drops a sky-blue, isosceles triangles, rounded at the tops, dangling and weighted, with a marvellous felicity-facility, for the lobes of a boobified laughing girl dressed in blue; who in one of their almost transparent striations laughed enriched, as if by wisps of gold enclosed there, to freeze. And a heavy ring, a gold-bound cylinder which had circled the thumb of Ahenobarbus or the big toe of Heliogabalus, with a big caramel orange-green, then a moment later, lemon-colour: pierced by all the rays, slightly, of the equinoctial morning as the tender flesh of the martyr by his hundred and ninety arrows: perfused by pale-green lights, like the sea at dawn, to the brightness of flint: which made the two men dream at once, spellbound, of a mint syrup with soda in Piazza Garibaldi at noon. And a little ring of golden thread, with a red pomegranate seed that a chicken might peck: and a final bangle, a tiny bauble, like a little ball of methylene bluing to get the yellow out of the wash, held by a little gold cap and by a pimple: and through this, attachable, by a golden link-chain, to another and equally essential organ of adornment, whether to the swelling beauty of a breast, or even the male fold of a lapel or the paunched and gold-watched authority of the protector of this breast, administrator, moderator and, in the last analysis, husband, "and damn fool!" thought Pestalozzi, his teeth clenched.'

Another pause is in order here, to let readers briefly unscramble their brains!

'A garnet cross, dark red moments of domestic shade. Rings, brooches: unbelieved marvel. And the ruby and the emerald shone and lay in the trench of the little mouse-skin bed, fellow tenants of the moment with the verecond ambages of the pearl, on the worn and almost ragged tegument of that old woman's couch: amid the precious gleam and the twists or polygons of the gold objects that kindled the minds, after the pupils and the retinas. Pins and earrings were tangled in the little chains, or mixed up with one another, like twin cherries amid the twinned stems of their sisterly couples: the pendants, in the immediate cataract, had taken the rings with them. Ruby and Emerald took on a name and a body on the gray poverty of the cloth, or of the tatter, in the closed mute splendor innate in certain beings and signifying their rarity, their natural and intrinsic affinity: that mineralogical virtue which through false fanfares and winks is trumpeting so often, in trumpeting carnivals, by so many bits of bottle-bottoms, as, in said derrieres, the quality is totally lacking. The corundum, pleochroic crystals, revealed itself as such on the rat-gray of the ambience, come from Ceylon or from Burma, or from Siam, noble in its structural accepting—splendid green or splendid red, or night-blue, also—of the crystallographic suggestion of God: true sesquioxide A2O2 truly spaced in the ditrigonal scalenohedral modes of its class, premeditated by God: despite the value-work of the Gadfly. Gadfly di Revello who was to last in his chair for an hour, chief economist of the Turkey and cock-minister of his screwed non-finances…'

Space, or copyright, dictate that I must stop here! It's difficult to know quite what to compare such writing with. And of course, one doesn't have to compare it with anything, and perhaps ought not even to try. On its own terms, one can instantly see why Gadda has been called 'The Untranslatable'. And I for one haven't a clue how well or badly the above-passage, and any others in his works, *have* been translated. I can't explain all the references and allusions in this passage—nor could many Italian scholars, I suspect!—and some words sent me scurrying to the *Greater Oxford*—pleochroic, e.g.—where I found them luckily; but other words may have been ingeniously made up, whether by Gadda himself or the translator. As for the mesmerizing segueing of the content, with its learned disquisition on precious gems, evocations of classical myth, satiric spoofing of police-procedural, Hermetical asides, and scathing political caricatures, which threaten to turn the ostensible subject-matter of the plotted narrative upside down, this might upset genre-purists and stolid advocates of sequential logic. But it doesn't bother me in the slightest. In fact, I welcome it as a sweeping subversive force, carrying a fictional project—of whatever kind—up to and beyond its merely commonsensical limits. And the virtuosic stylistic display is as dazzling as the jewels that are being anatomised; so much so there seems to be a kind of elective affinity or progressive homology at work, in which the matter at hand is transcended in the potentialities of the idea of the Book as a whole in its unstoppably sprawling development. And this happens if not on every page, then on almost every other page—as if the novel were a depthless sounding-board for the author's mental regurgitation of the world he inhabited. His visceral disgust at the bovine crassness of his fellow-countrymen, if not fellow-humans, far from dwelling on inner vacuities, spilled out in great gobs of victorious vituperation, and flashes of intricate illumination of not only pieces of life, but entire prisms of life. And he could do this virtually in a single paragraph—never mind a few pages. He achieved an Archimedean leverage of language on the entire culture and civilization that he was inescapably a part of, whilst feeling himself to be incurably, antagonistically estranged from it. This is a Classic Outsider's quandary of an heroically defiant intellectual visionary neutralized by numbers.

The music of Gadda's language carries one along on torrential tides of exhilaration, even if one only comprehends parts of the whole. The fact that it may not succeed in communicating is neither here nor there in this respect, as it is the syntax rather than the semantics that is doing the transporting. And unlike in Joyce's work, it is a far less disjointed or diffuse music, even if it moves like a multi-legged monster across the page, pulling all its tributaries with it into a mighty magnetic sponge of creation, glistening with colour and shooting ink into its own futures. I haven't the space to quote more from the same source. Yet readers will find plenty of fizzling firecrackers of this sort if they investigate. But I shall cite a not dissimilar passage from Gadda's other novel, *Acquainted with Grief*, which is a kind of Allegory on the theme of Utopia ruined by Dystopia, and a warped family saga elevated to the plane of a corruscating satiric Panorama. Running through it all is the struggle of the main protagonist, Gonzalo—again clearly a semi-autobiographical figure—to free himself from the tyrannical clutches of The Matriarch—Gadda's mother!—a monstrous scourge of relative and community alike. Eventually, she is murdered in a brutal manner, her head bashed in like the victim in *That Awful Mess on the Via Merulana*. Only as it occurs near the end of the novel it is never investigated, but serves as a kind of bloody sacrificial emancipation from a sick society for the hapless Gonzalo—who spends the rest of the time raging against everybody and everything like a supra-rarefied Jimmy Porter, and muddling terribly through the traumatized mess of his life and relationships bequeathed to him by heredity and history. The following summarizes as well as any other the essential thrust of the story—which is like a kind of inverted Epic, devolving upon the nullity of the 'I' from the mad multiplicity of the 'Not-I'. One can argue that all of Gadda's works were in some sense unfinished, whether from necessity or failure; and this work was not only no exception to this doggedly perverse rule, but probably the most unfinished of the lot, because it opened up the deepest, gaping wound inside the churning void of his own heart, fatally diseased as it was by his antecedence.

> 'The son, standing, looked, without seeing, at the modest display, the scant steam it was exhaling: as his old mother still hunted for some fork, a plate, a pretext, in the side-board and the kitchen cupboard. She was again uneasy. Boys: with legs like two asparaguses. Idiots in their heads worse than if they were made of tubers, speechless of any sort of language: after twelve generations of Indian corn and of Indian poverty with dirt-green feet emerging from the bastard Ark of the generations, to try to stammer out some mean boast in the market-place: the crooked forum of Pastrafuzio! Come down, down, from the stinking cheeses of Monte Viejo to the more resounding failures of the Uguierre, silent and acephalous in Castilian, deaf to Latin, reprobates in Greek, inept in history, their brains below zero in geometry and in arithmetic, unsatisfactory in

> drawing, even in geography they were unsatisfactory! One had to waste one's breath for weeks, for years, to make them understand what a map of victorious Maradagal is! And how maps are made: and they still couldn't make it, poor darlings! And yet they came down like a kind of oil to their bannered launching, launched finally into nonsensedom with full honours and every sanction: keels tallowed with stupidity. The more witless they were, the happier and smoother the ways beneath their bottoms, down, down from the green croconsuelo of Monte Viejo to the swelling tide of the avenida, with their full complement of crock-crest. Some wrinkled old woman could always be found, in the old-women's shop, with six or even seven teeth left in her mouth, to break the propitiatory bottle over the prow of the illiterate...'

If readers' heads are reeling already, then they may even come off before long. So if you do continue reading, then it will be wholly at your own risk!

> '...Turks, pancake vendors, Circassians, guitar-playing beggars of Andalusia, Poles, Armenians, Mongols, Arab medicine-men in bowler hats, Senegalese big-lips with club feet, and also the Langobardoi of Cormanno, immigrating from Cormanno, to achieve, even in the new world, the record for foolishness and lack of imagination. And the agent of the perfume firm, of Greek lineage; and the other, the Jew, from the house of carpets. Who sold also...in his leisure hours, pictures, although second-hand, lots of rags for paper, and heretic furniture of the sixteenth century.... All had

> their life, their woman…they had allowed themselves to be launched; and they were in a position to be taken seriously—each in his field…even the man who operated the clay pigeons. Many in evening dress. Everybody believed,…that he was something serious. Members of the Maradagalo-Parapagalese Grand Orient, many adorned themselves as a further help, with frills, little beads of cornelian or of polished bone, assorted trimmings. The Free Masons of the Scottish Rite, on the occasion of their annual meeting, there, at the end of Saenz Pena…could be seen with something coming out of their jackets, swaying between their legs, a kind of tassel of sheep's wool; or else, across their checked shirts, more tassels, but a bit smaller, and ribbons, and green braid, and a two-coloured or orange frill. Some of them, moreover, on holidays or patriotic anniversaries of old England, appeared bedecked with buttons of exceptional shininess, or in eighteenth-century dress, with wig: two days later Fray Mocho published the glory and the magnesiac splendour of the horseshoe banquet, amid a downpour of cockades, ribbons, goblets, flowers, braid, Masonic turbans…'

If readers' heads are still in place, then by all means read on! If not, then you may, by the grace of Gadda, or power of phantom-consciousness, grow new heads!

> 'Where was her humiliated knowledge going, with the torn edges of memory in the wind, without cause now or end? Where were busy minds active about truth, with their rightful certainty, ulluminated by God? Black waiters, in the 'restaurants', wore tailcoats, though

> covered with stains: and the slab of starch, with false tie. Only the slab, of course: that is, without that, the most imposing of all pectoral dignities, ever becoming rooted in a totalitarian harmony, in the necessitant physiology of a shirt. Which was lacking entirely. The Lazies were affected by a tiny shudder, the moment they heard themselves honoured by the appellation of Madame by such obsequious tailcoats. 'A mixed chocolate-vanilla for Madame, very well, Madame!' It was, from nape to heel, like a thrashing of sweetness, 'the pure and hidden joy' of the hymn. And also in the men, for that matter, the secret itch of complacency: up, up, from the groin toward the meninges and the eyeballs: the illusion, almost, of a moment of marquisial power. All the strikes were forgotten, abruptly; the shouts of death, the barricades, the Communes, the threats of hanging from the lamp-posts, the purple at Pere-Lachaise; and the black and clotting rennet on the Goyesque abandon of the outstretched, the spent; and the uproar and the blockades and the wars and the massacres, of every quality and of every land;'

Whether headless or reborn in Gaddaland, readers must now feed themselves. Cutting off the flow so abruptly is very much in keeping with the driving, dream-like drift of the writing, which seems to spring from everywhere and nowhere like an ubiquitous flood of verbal ichor. And quoting it at such length gives readers the chance to immerse themselves in the bewildering galaxy of words rolling its course through scene after scene, subject after subject, and target after target. It reads like a mercurially deranged, if brilliantly disciplined, non-stop effusion of supra-Swiftian satire, which has no starting-point and no finishing-point either. It swells and subsides like a bloody ocean of language, that fills our unconscious, and then our conscious, minds forever. Gadda's ability to tap into his inexhaustible streams of invective, and sketch far-flung tone-paintings, is uncanny and maybe unique. His knowledge of arcane words in many tongues, and scholarly curiosities in both the arts and the sciences, and his searing analytical perspicacity, furnished his writing with its weighty, yet endlessly levitating, archival architecture. And yet all of his rabid prejudices, intensely snobbish conceits, and accursed animosities, well out sans inner or official censorship! His racism is plain to see—even anti-semitism—although it was not of the ideologically doctrinaire, programmatic variety. Rather it stemmed from a judgementally refined 'intellectual aristocrat's' outlook on the melting-pot of humanity, that rose to the surface in the era of European Fascism, but stopped well short of the barbaric fanaticism of Hitler and Mussolini. Gadda treated politicians with supreme contempt, reminiscent of Bertrand Russell's caricature of cabinet-ministers as being lower than pigs, and the wilder fulminations of right-wingers like Wyndham Lewis and Pound. But as I've said, he denounced Fascism publicly, which is more than either Pound or Lewis did. And his critique cut all ways, slicing through the shallow superiority of the dining-classes as much as the petty pomposity and jeering sycophancy of their servers. And Maradagal is of course a fantasy-land, like Liliput and Erewhon, and More's Utopia. But it had the most penetrating parallels with Fascist Italy, and many other countries, in that period. And so it could be read as a coded warning about the future of society, as well as an unsparing expose of the ills and idiocies of contemporary life. Though above all, it is an

Exemplar of the kind of moveable literary feast that would have left simple old Papa Hemingway agape with uncomprehending incredulity!

The violence in so much of Gadda's writing was no doubt therapeutic, in that he might well have been driven to violent acts himself if he hadn't had a literary outlet through which to release his ornately crafted barbs of savage disdain. Whether he would have posed any threat to women is hard to say, as there's little evidence that he ever overcame his tortuous mother-fixation in a full relationship with another woman; and appears to have had no desire to live in any other state but that of solitary bachelorhood—like Pessoa. But unlike Pessoa, there is more bitterness directed specifically at women in his writings. Women get murdered horrifically, or they tyrannize and torment men, or practise dark sorcery, or kidnap and abuse children, etc. The things that Gadda's female characters get smeared with are utterly hideous, and there was surely in Gadda a ferment of psycho-pathology underpinning this whole tendency in his work, if not his life and relationships. Inevitably, his sexual orientation has been called into question, mainly by the Continental Theorists! But as with Pessoa, a blank has had to be drawn in the absence of any real evidence, one way or the other. He might well have been a repressed homosexual. But equally he might have been a troubled a-sexual Onanist, who failed to fulfil his basically heterosexual urges! I really do not know—and in one sense at least, I do not really care. It's obvious that it does not affect the issue of how good or great a writer he was. And for me, it was significant that he managed to find a precarious balance in his life—between the Apocalyptic war that was constantly going on inside him, the catharsis of his writings and researches, and the few friendships that he did maintain. His famous angry outbursts were probably necessary releases of pent-up tensions that might otherwise have found more truly sinister and dangerous outlets. As for his never declaring his sexual orientation—whatever it was, and in Fascist Italy it may have been inadvisable!—that was not merely his business and nobody else's, but also and above all, irrelevant to the larger aims of his work, which transcended Gender-Politics altogether, even if he was intrigued by the mutations of Gender in some of his characters. But to think of him as a 'Gay writer', or a writer concerned with 'Trans-Gender issues', would be an insult to the sheer enormity of his pre-occupations. In my opinion, he was a Titanic figure, a true Olympian amongst the ill-assorted scribblers of his Time.

Gadda wrote a kind of sequel to the *Milanese Meditations* towards the end of his life, called *L'Ultima Rimeditazione*, which has certainly not been translated into English, and I have not been able to find a proper commentary on it. But I gather that he revisited the themes of his earlier work with a somewhat sad and sceptical resignation—wondering at the possible delusions of grandeur in his younger incarnation, and questioning the paradoxically dogmatic certainty of his sweepingly anti-dogmatic stance! How much this was due to the creeping senescence of old age—as he lived into his eighties—or to genuinely profound philosophical perplexities, I am not certain. But I hope one day this work will be translated along with its prequel. In my afore-mentioned *Abraxas* essay, I cited a short story by Gadda, called 'Ashes of Battles Past', which was my first experience of reading him. And though I shan't repeat myself here, I refer my readers to it as a useful entree into the astonishing world of this phenomenally difficult and demanding writer. But before drawing the concluding threads together, I should quote from one other piece of writing—and I don't know what else to call it, as it was not a short story or a fiction in any conventional sense, though it wasn't straightforward documentary either—in which he described at characteristic length, a fire on a street. And as always, the premiss of the piece became twisted and transfigured into an argument unencompassably greater—before the unconcludable conclusion is finally reached! But it offered one of the best quintessential summaries of the man as writer—and Outsider—I have come across; and served as a model of its kind for just about any high-flown, speculative, experimental writing, that delves into the darkest depths of every dimension of experience and imagination conceivable. As such, it is like the Paradigm of simplicity, generating complexity. The fire is an incident and a pretext, a symbol and a scourge. A world in miniature gets consumed in an unfolding catastrophe, a cosmic deluge laying waste to human flotsam and jetsam. Gadda seems to delight in the Baphometic cleansing of scum:

> 'amid the unending shouts, screams, tears, babies, and wails of anguish, and the thump and crash of valuables and bundles of goods thrown out of the windows hitting the ground ... the fire could do no less than let loose its own fearful sparks, so eagerly awaited! And twisting red tongues in sudden spurts darting here and there, with whorls of black smoke, pitchy and thick as if from some infernal roast, billowing out in puffs…or coiling itself up like an ashen python risen from the depths with sinister flashes of light; and blazing butterflies… all over a sky befouled with soot, adding to the terror of the dishevelled women … amid the screaming and crying of their thousand babies. They

> could already feel their heads, and their vainly waved hair, ablaze in a horrid, living torch.'

Is this fact or fiction, truth or fantasy? Does it matter? No--it doesn't! Although there is an almost numinous realism in the detailed descriptions, as well as a fantastical, phantasmagoric intensity in the evocation of an unfolding vision of Hell. Creative Writing students today would be exposed to much more than their empty heads could absorb from reading something like this: this is true Creative Writing, of a kind that is scarcely done at all nowadays. And it doesn't matter what the subject-matter is, and what angles the writer is addressing it from. What matters above all else, is the sheer overwhelming, spell-binding, quality of the writing itself—and the enormous amount of terrain it covers in a small space or a short time, its super-charged poetic prose crashing like a Tsunami over human heads! And on it goes, as it must:

> 'From the…nearby factories the sirens screamed to the sky roasting above: the cryptosymbolic network of electrical alarms perfected the desperate cries of anguish. Distant fire stations flung open their doors, batteries of fire trucks rushed forth, immediately intent on swiftly bringing every evil eruption of flames under control … suddenly the electrified warning signals stop them short at the intersections; and, instantaneously, the onset of the sirens overhead. Streetcars nailed to the track; horses held at the bit by their dismounted drivers…with the wagon pressing against their rumps, the corners of their blinded eyes showing white at the unknown terror.'

Already the Outsider's Eye is strongly apparent, in his morally ambiguous Olympian observations, sublimating mundane horror for a supra-mundane effect. Yet as Phenomenological writing, it works superbly. A man is trapped in a room of a house with a screaming baby, and a talking parrot that shrieks louder than the baby:

> '...she screamed in terror; while over there, beyond the other end of the table, the multi-coloured bird, with a beak like the nose of a duchess...called out to him from the street...though sometimes he was overcome by a kind of melancholy or lethargy without remedy ... but this time ... it was quite other ... there was...a certain smell of something burning which he had already noticed, not so strong yet as to be disturbing. But when he saw the orange petals of that sinister magic dart diagonally across the open window and enter directly into the room like so many blazing bats and begin to lick at the rips in the old upholstery and the yellow blinds' ashwood slats...then, he, too, suddenly began to screech from the bottom of his gullet whatever came to mind, all in a jumble, like a radio. And in his fright, he tried to escape towards the baby in quick bursts of flight, each time cut short after scarcely a foot and a half by the inexorable perfidy of the tiny chain that held him to his stand by one claw.'

There is a kind of sadism in this long-drawn out registering of a devastating anguish, that many writers would skate over in a sentence or two. But Gadda is honestly detecting a strain of comic human absurdity even in this most tragically appalling scenario, and is testing to destruction the unconscionable conceit that a baby and a parrot are sharing as Ontological equals almost in a common Existential threat.

> '... confronted by the swirl of smoldering banknotes which seemed to be issuing up from the mint of Beelzebub himself, his wit deserted him and he completely lost his bearings. It seemed as if he had gone crazy: "Hiva-i-Ita-ia!..." he began to squawk loud enough to rupture his gullet, flying wildly this way and that with the chain tied tight to his claw, in a flurry of feathers and an infernal shower of soot and charred paper, hoping to secure for himself a propitious fate, while the baby girl screamed...howling terror-stricken in her crying, and beating on the table top with the handle of her spoon.'

Both the baby and the parrot are saved, along with a gold watch. But it seems as if Gadda has slightly more sympathy for the parrot, seen as a refreshing oddity, with the unknowing facility to satirize the whole of Humanity. Like the philosopher-king counterpart to a vituperative human-hating parrot, Gadda goes on to anatomise the aftermath to the Holocaustic cataclysm:

> '... amid the self-sacrifice of those blessed fire-fighters ...amid cataracts of good drinking water pouring over the couches, piss-stained discoloured green, though this time menaced by a really ugly red, and over the sideboards and cupboards, custodians perhaps of a quarter pound of oozing gorgonzola, but already licked by tongues of fire as a python might lick a fawn in its coils; with spurting, hydrous needles, out of the swollen

> sodden serpents of hempen fire hose and long piercing javelins from the brass nozzles that ended in white plumes and clouds in the torrid August sky; and pieces of half-scorched insulators that fell and shattered to bits...and melted the telephone wires, detached from the red-hot brackets that had held them, fluttering about in the evening sky, with black airborne peninsulas of charred cardboard and montgolfiers of carbonized upholstery and smoldering wallpaper, and down below ... bends and coils and hoses rearing back as they spewed parabolic streams up from every part of the mired street, jagged pieces of shattered window glass immersed in a swamp of water and slime, enamelled iron chamberpots full of carrot-length turds, thrown from the windows, even now! slopping...against the leather uppers of the engineers, of the carabinieri, and of the firechiefs commanding the men; and the insolent and uninterrupted chick-chac...made by the old wooden sandals of the women as they went about gathering pieces of combs, or fragments of mirrors, and blessed images ... among the splash and spill of that catastrophic laundering.'

There is both a clinical detachment in the listing of the effects, and an almost vampiric all-consuming delight in the purging mayhem, as though it were a divinely diabolical gift of ravaged raw material for a writer possessed of a rabid craving for the most extreme visitations of violence upon his reluctantly shared species imaginable. Gadda was at his best in portraying devastation—whether in reality itself, or his own vision of a degraded reality ripe for the imaginative onslaught of his murderous metaphors. And there are hardly any writers around nowadays producing work in this vein, no doubt due to the all-contaminating influence of political correctness and lukewarm moralism. One by one, Gadda pin-points the impact of the disaster on individual victims, which I haven't the space to detail here. But Apocalyptic expressions like 'The finger of God was seen' proliferate.

Although Gadda is describing a truly terrible human ordeal, one gets the sense—at least from the inevitably imperfect translation—that he is barely moved by the human sentiments involved; but focusses instead on the hubris, vanity, and self- interest of the victims, thereby injecting a vein of sick humour into their plight. The grotesque absurdity of the situation impresses him far more than its actual bathos; which shows him in a cruelly dispassionate light, with the mentality of an alien Outsider, who would happily thrust much of Humanity into the flames of Judgement. Yet the writing does not suffer as a result, but has what I term a meta-human classical coldness of outlook that elevates into a sphere all its own. As the imagery builds up and intensifies along with the searing heat it describes, Gadda's writing reads like a gruesomely vivid painterly sketch very much in the style of Ensor, Schiele, Dix and Gross—a monstrously uncharitable, yet uncomfortably true, vision of his fellow-men and women, or fellow-Italians at least. Some of the people inevitably perish appallingly, while others are saved. Meanwhile Gadda's had his fear-feasting fun at dear old Hugh Manity's expense; and in showing ill-assorted specimens of the species exposed to the worst extremes of terror, torment, and devastation, extends a rare branch of Outsider Literature, unconcerned—or little concerned—with the sentimentalities of normal affairs or relations; but focussing on what happens to these creatures in life-defying moments of transformation. Are they simply extinguished? Or do they change in some extraordinary way? In truth they do neither, but slowly disintegrate in tragic-comic banality, as Gadda adds the finishing touches with a Rabelaisian relish. And it is Rabelais that he comes closest to here, that great and virtually forgotten Genius-Pariah of French Letters—in both senses of the expression!—who, after Villon and Boccachio *et al*, paved the way early on for writers like Sade, Lautréamont, Rimbaud, Jarry, Cendrars, Céline—and Gadda himself.

The account of the fire ends with a death in an ambulance, which then has to re-route from a hospital to a morgue, 'and all the way out to hell and gone.' It has the feel almost of a news-report on one level—although I don't know if it is or not, and as I've said it doesn't matter one way or the other—and yet it also reads like a journey through a burning Inferno viewed in the prism of a burning brain: Gadda's brain, aflame with savagery at the Strand of compassion. And he was drawn like a magnanimous moth to the igneous sparks of a fierce creation, wherever he saw them, clinical curiosity in a duet with classical cruelty. Though if compassion did not entirely elude him in the end, then mankind had to earn it by virtue of an unstinting resistance to ignorance, sentimentality, vulgarity, and bigotry. Wilful stupidity and shameless imposition he would treat only with the haughtiest contempt imaginable, and no waste of false Christian charity.

In addition to the above-works, he produced a very long list of short pieces of writing of this kind—as distinct from his novels and his lengthier philosophical works—which don't fall into any obvious category of fiction or non-fiction, but are like squibs, meditations, confessions and fantasias all rolled into one, where the man himself in all his diseased brilliance is most nakedly revealed. They all have bizarrely beguiling titles too, like 'A Kangaroo and Kant', a scathing critique of the old Puritan Prussian prude, who'd never have lied to save his best friend's life—nor even his own, poor fool! Nietzsche understood the subtle virtues of Untruth, when he called error 'a species of truth'; and Gadda developed this insight with astonishing ingenuity and perseverance in a Dialectic of fantastical artifice.

But in a more traditional, mainstream vein, he wrote a Journal documenting his experiences in the First World War, which early in his literary career won him a lot of admirers—even though they had no idea at that stage, of the directions he would later go in as a writer. As a Memoir, it was doubtless more reliable than Cendrars'. But in it he was clearly straining at the fictive leash, which he broke free from in his later work. And being so versatile helped to cement his stature as a canonical writer, which was entirely deserved and justified—even if he did remain defiantly on the outside of the literary, cultural, and political, establishments, and indeed any of the fashionable intellectual currents. For although he kept abreast of the latest developments in a very wide range of fields, like Gore Vidal and academics more lately, he refused either to join ranks with academics or show them respect; like a superbly angry Colossus among Renaissance Men, or as my title has it, The Forbidden Genius scowling in Society's Shade.

In the next volume, I shall be looking at the likes of, most notably: Edmond Jabès, Lionel Britton, Blaise Cendrars and, in the opening chapter, I'll be considering another, very different, kind of Outsider-Writer—namely, Robert Walser, who was far too shy and meek a figure ever to strike the sort of attitudes of a Gadda, or even a Pessoa. But for all his apparent simplicity and bucolic charm, he concealed, or half-concealed, both a strangeness and a rare talent, that invite serious comparison with Franz Kafka.

<u>Recommended reading</u>:

The Milanese Meditations.
The Philosopher's Madonna. Atlas Press, 2008 (Trans. Antony Melville)
Acquainted with Grief. Peter Owen, 1969 (Trans. William Weaver)
The Awful Mess on Via Merulana. Quartet, 1985 (Trans. William Weaver)
The Fire on Kepler Street. Translated by Arnold Hartley:
http://www.gadda.ed.ac.uk/Pages/resources/babelgadda/babeng/hartleykepler.php

Norma Bouchard: *Céline, Gadda, Beckett: experimental writings of the 1930s*. University Press of Florida, 2000.
Adam Daly: 'Gadda the Untranslatable'. *Abraxas Unbound* (Vol. 1), 2007, p. 7-23

Around the Outsider

A major publishing event by O Books marked Colin Wilson's 80th birthday in June 2011 - the tribute *Around the Outsider: Essays Presented to Colin Wilson on the Occasion of his 80th Birthday* was published on May 27 in the UK and in the US.

This landmark book of 345 pages, which collects 20 essays by academics, authors and other key commentators internationally, is edited by freelance writer Colin Stanley, Wilson's bibliographer and the managing editor of Paupers' Press who edits the series *Colin Wilson Studies* featuring extended essays on Wilson's work by scholars worldwide. Colin Stanley also provides the preface and two essays for *Around the Outsider*.

Contributors from the UK, USA, Australia and New Zealand have written on their favourite Wilson book, or one which has special significance for them. The outcome is a diverse and indispensable assessment of Wilson's writings on philosophy, psychology, literature, criminology, the occult and autobiography over more than 50 years, with critical appraisals of four of his most thought-provoking novels. Five of the contributors are musicians as well as writers.

The line-up includes three professors, Thomas Bertonneau (literature), Stephen Clark (philosophy) and Stanley Krippner (psychology), the author and critic Nicholas Tredell, the author and former editor of the literary magazine *Abraxas*, Paul Newman, the author Gary Lachman, a founding member of the rock group Blondie who was inducted into the Rock 'n' Roll Hall of Fame in 2006, and the author Steve Taylor, a lecturer and researcher in transpersonal psychology.

Other contributing authors include Simon Brighton, Antoni Diller, Chris Nelson, David Power and journalist Geoff Ward, who established and runs the Colin Wilson World website.

The novelist Laura Del Rivo, a contemporary of Wilson, contributes an appendix, as does writer and poet Vaughan Robertson, and author Terry Welbourn with a personal appreciation of Wilson and T C Lethbridge, the archaeologist and psychic investigator. Murray Ewing, of the David Lindsay website at violetapple.org.uk, Philip Coulthard of colinwilsononline.com, and George Poulos complete the list.

Colin Wilson Studies:

Books on the life and work of Colin Wilson written by experts and scholars worldwide

ISSN: 0959-180-X
Series Editor: Colin Stanley.

#1. **MOORHOUSE, John** and **NEWMAN, Paul:** *Colin Wilson, two essays: 'The English Existentialist' and 'Spiders and Outsiders' (including an interview with the author.)* £5.95. Paper. 50p. 0-946650-11-X.
#2. **STANLEY, Colin:** *'The Nature of Freedom' and other essays*. £5.95/ £16.95. Paper/Hardback. 33p. 0-946650-17-9 Paper/ 27-6. Hard.
#3. **TROWELL, Michael:** *Colin Wilson, the positive approach: a response to a critic*. £5.95/£16.95. Paper/Hard. 36p. 0-946650-25-X .Paper/ 26-8. Hard.
#4. **SMALLDON, Jeffrey:** *Human Nature Stained: Colin Wilson and the existential study of modem murder*. £5.95/£16.95. Paper/Hard. 38p. 0-946650-28-4. Paper/ 29-2 Hard.
#5. **DALGLEISH, Tim:** *The Guerilla Philosopher: Colin Wilson and Existentialism* £5.95. Paper. 40p. 0-946650-47-0.
#6. **LACHMAN, Gary:** *Two essays on Colin Wilson: World Rejection and Criminal Romantics & From Outsider to Post-Tragic Man.* £7.95. Paper. 64p. 0-946650-52-7
#7. **NEWMAN, Paul:** *Murder as an Antidote for Boredom: the novels of Laura Del Rivo, Colin Wilson and Bill Hopkins*. £8.95. Paper. 74p. 0-946650-57-8.
#8. **SHAND, John** and **LACHMAN, Gary:** *Colin Wilson as Philosopher and Faculty X, Consciousness and the Transcendence of Time.* £6.95. Paper. 35p. 0-946650-59-4.
#9. **DOSSOR, Howard:** *The Philosophy of Colin Wilson: Three Perspectives*. £6.95. Paper. 42p. 0-946650-58-6.
#10. **STANLEY, Colin:** *The Work of Colin Wilson: an annotated bibliography & guide. Supplement to 1995*. £15.95. Paper. 220p. 0-946650-69-1.
#11. **ROBERTSON, Vaughan:** *Wilson as Mystic*. £8.95. Paper. 83p. 0-946650-74-8.
#12. **GREENWELL, Tom:** *Chepstow Road: a literary comedy in two acts*. £9.95. Paper. xii, 120p. 0-946650-78-0.
#13. **STANLEY, Colin:** *Colin Wilson, the first fifty years: an existential bibliography, 1956-2005.* £24.95. Paper. 507p. 0-946650-89-6. SOLD OUT
#14. **WILSON, Colin:** *'The Death of God' and other plays.* £17.95. Paper. 476p. 9780946650934. Limited edition of 100 numbered copies.
#15. **STANLEY, Colin:** *Colin Wilson's* Outsider Cycle*: a guide for students*. £7.95. Paper. iv, 158p. 9780946650965.
#16. **WILSON, Colin:** *Existential Criticism: selected book reviews* [Edited by Colin Stanley] £14.95. Paper. iv, 283p. 9780946650989. Limited edition of 100 numbered copies.
#17. **STANLEY, Colin:** *The Colin Wilson Bibliography [1956-2010]*. £24.95. Paper. 576p., 9780946650644. Limited edition of 50 numbered copies.
#18. **DILLER, Antoni:** *Stuart Holroyd: Years of Anger and Beyond.* £7.95. Paper. 56p., 9780946650149.
#19. **CAMPION, Sidney R.** *The Sound Barrier: a study of the ideas of Colin Wilson*. £12.95. Paper. iv, 194p. 9780946650811. Limited edition of 100 numbered copies.
#20/1 **DALY, Adam**: *The Outsider-Writer, vol.1*. £16.95. Paper, xxxiii, 361p. 9780956866301
#20/2 **DALY, Adam**: *The Outsider-Writer, volume 2*. Price/date not set. 9780956866318

All quoted prices subject to alteration.

Paupers' Press, 37 Quayside Close, Nottingham NG2 3BP
United Kingdom
www.pauperspress.com